HOW THE EXPERTS HELP YOU PASS:

- **PROVEN TEACHING METHODOLOGY** Text based on thousands of hours of classroom experience — Global gets people certified. (150,000 professionals can't be wrong!)

- **MORE PRACTICE TESTS** More practice exam questions than any other study guide/CD-ROM—hundreds! Includes hyperlinks from questions to answers in electronic book.

- **AUTHORITATIVE INFORMATION** Developed and reviewed by master MCSE and MCT professionals.

- **EXAM WATCH** Warnings based on post-exam research identifying troublesome exam questions.

MCSE Windows NT 4.0 Certification Track — Candidates must pass 4 core and 2 elective exams	MCSE + Internet Windows NT 4.0 Certification Track — Candidates must pass 7 core and 2 elective exams	
CHOOSE 4 CORE & 2 ELECTIVE	**CHOOSE 7 CORE & 2 ELECTIVE**	**CERTIFICATION PRESS STUDY GUIDES**
CORE	CORE	MCSE Windows NT Server 4.0 Study Guide (Exam 70-67) 0-07-882491-5
CORE	CORE	MCSE Windows NT Server 4.0 in the Enterprise Study Guide (Exam 70-68) 0-07-882490-7
CORE	CORE	
CORE	CORE	MCSE Windows NT Workstation 4.0 Study Guide (Exam 70-73) 0-07-882492-3
CORE	CORE	MCSE Windows 98 Study Guide (Exam 70-98) 0-07-882532-6
CORE	CORE	MCSE Networking Essentials Study Guide (Exam 70-58) 0-07-882493-1
ELECTIVE	CORE	MCSE Microsoft TCP/IP on Windows NT 4.0 Study Guide (Exam 70-59) 0-07-882489-3
ELECTIVE	CORE	MCSE Internet Information Server 4.0 with Proxy Server 2.0 and Internet Explorer Administration Kit 1.1 Study Guide (Exams 70-87, 70-79, 70-88) 0-07-882560-1
ELECTIVE	CORE	MCSE Internet Information Server 4.0 with Proxy Server 2.0 and Internet Explorer Administration Kit 1.1 Study Guide (Exams 70-87, 70-79, 70-88) 0-07-882560-1
ELECTIVE	ELECTIVE	
ELECTIVE		
ELECTIVE	ELECTIVE	
ELECTIVE	ELECTIVE	
ELECTIVE	ELECTIVE	
ELECTIVE	ELECTIVE	MCSE SQL Server™ 7 Administration Study Guide (Exam 70-28) 0-07-211904-7
ELECTIVE	ELECTIVE	MCSE Exchange Server 5.5 Study Guide (Exam 70-81) 0-07-882488-5
ELECTIVE	ELECTIVE	MCSE Internet Information Server 4.0 with Proxy Server 2.0 and Internet Explorer Administration Kit 1.1 Study Guide (Exams 70-87, 70-79, 70-88) 0-07-882560-1

MCSE Windows 98
Study Guide

MCSE Windows 98

Study Guide

(Exam 70-98)

Syngress Media, Inc.

Osborne/McGraw-Hill

Berkeley New York St. Louis San Francisco Auckland Bogotá Hamburg London Madrid Mexico City
Milan Montreal New Delhi Panama City Paris São Paulo Singapore Sydney Tokyo Toronto

...w-Hill
2600 Tenth Street
Berkeley, California 94710
U.S.A.

For information on translations or book distributors outside the U.S.A.,
or to arrange bulk purchase discounts for sales promotions, premiums, or
fund-raisers, please contact Osborne/**McGraw-Hill** at the above address.

MCSE Windows 98 Study Guide (Exam 70-98)

Copyright © 1998 by The McGraw-Hill Companies. All rights reserved.
Printed in the United States of America. Except as permitted under the
Copyright Act of 1976, no part of this publication may be reproduced or
distributed in any form or by any means, or stored in a database or retrieval
system, without the prior written permission of the publisher, with the
exception that the program listings may be entered, stored, and executed in a
computer system, but they may not be reproduced for publication.

1234567890 DOC DOC 901987654321098

ISBN 0-07-882532-6

Publisher	**Copy Editor**	**Illustrators**
Brandon A. Nordin	Kathleen Faughnan	Lance Ravella
		Brian Wells
Editor-in-Chief	**Indexer**	
Scott Rogers	Jack Lewis	**Series Design**
		Roberta Steele
Acquisitions Editor	**Proofreader**	
Gareth Hancock	Stefany Otis	**Cover Design**
		Regan Honda
Project Editor	**Computer Designers**	
Madhu Prasher	Roberta Steele	**Editorial Management**
	Ann Sellers	Syngress Media, Inc.
Technical Editor	Michelle Galicia	
Michael Cross		

From Global Knowledge Network

At Global Knowledge Network we strive to support the multiplicity of learning styles required by our students to achieve success as technical professionals. In this series of books, it is our intention to offer the reader a valuable tool for successful completion of the MCSE Certification Exam.

As the world's largest IT training company, Global Knowledge Network is uniquely positioned to offer these books. The expertise gained each year from providing instructor-led training to hundreds of thousands of students worldwide has been captured in book form to enhance your learning experience. We hope that the quality of these books demonstrates our commitment to your lifelong learning success. Whether you choose to learn through the written word, computer-based training, Web delivery, or instructor-led training, Global Knowledge Network is committed to providing you the very best in each of those categories. For those of you who know Global Knowledge Network, or those of you who have just found us for the first time, our goal is to be your lifelong competency partner.

Thank you for the opportunity to serve you. We look forward to serving your needs again in the future.

Warmest regards,

Duncan Anderson
Chief Operating Officer, Global Knowledge Network

January 12, 1998

Dear Osborne/McGraw-Hill Customer:

Microsoft is pleased to inform you that Osborne/McGraw-Hill is a participant in the Microsoft® Independent Courseware Vendor (ICV) program. Microsoft ICVs design, develop, and market self-paced courseware, books, and other products that support Microsoft software and the Microsoft Certified Professional (MCP) program.

To be accepted into the Microsoft ICV program, an ICV must meet set criteria. In addition, Microsoft reviews and approves each ICV training product before permission is granted to use the Microsoft Certified Professional Approved Study Guide logo on that product. This logo assures the consumer that the product has passed the following Microsoft standards:

- The course contains accurate product information.
- The course includes labs and activities during which the student can apply knowledge and skills learned from the course.
- The course teaches skills that help prepare the student to take corresponding MCP exams.

Microsoft ICVs continually develop and release new MCP Approved Study Guides. To prepare for a particular Microsoft certification exam, a student may choose one or more single, self-paced training courses or a series of training courses.

You will be pleased with the quality and effectiveness of the MCP Approved Study Guides available from Osborne/McGraw-Hill.

Sincerely,

Becky Kirsininkas
ICV Program Manager
Microsoft Training & Certification

About Syngress Media

Syngress Media creates books and software for Information Technology professionals seeking skill enhancement and career advancement. Its products are designed to comply with vendor and industry standard course curricula, and are optimized for certification exam preparation. Visit the Syngress Web site at www.syngress.com.

Contributors

Melissa Craft is a consulting engineer for MicroAge in Phoenix, AZ. She has a bachelor's degree from the University of Michigan. After relocating to the Southwest, Melissa became increasingly involved with technology, and obtained several certifications: MCSE, CNE-3, CNE-4, CNE-GW, MCNE, and Citrix. Melissa Craft is a member of the IEEE, the Society of Women Engineers, and American MENSA, Ltd.

Chris Krakowski (MCSE) is a computer consultant with CIBER Network Services, Inc. Previously he has been a freelance computer consultant, and a Technology Partner with Strategic Business Management Co. He has been involved in the IS/IT industry for five years as a LAN administrator, network engineer, and trainer. Chris has a master's degree in Geography from Southern Illinois University at Carbondale and a bachelor's degree in History from the University of Illinois at Urbana-Champaign.

Dale Hackemeyer is an MCSE residing in Atlanta, Georgia. He has over seven years experience in the IT field, the last several of which have been spent working with various Windows NT networks. He is currently working for a large southeastern bank, implementing Microsoft DHCP, WINS, and DNS servers to support 20,000 desktops. When not shackled to a computer, he enjoys mountain biking and *Simpsons* reruns.

Stace Cunningham is a systems engineer with SDC Consulting in Biloxi, MS. SDC Consulting specializes in the design, engineering, and installation of networks. Stace received his MCSE in October 1996, and is also certified as an IBM Certified LAN Server Engineer, IBM Certified OS/2 Engineer, IBM Certified LAN Server Administrator, Microsoft Certified Product Specialist, IBM Certified LAN Server Instructor, and IBM Certified OS/2 Instructor.

Stace has participated as a Technical Contributor for the IIS 3.0 exam, SMS 1.2 exam, Proxy Server 1.0 exam, Exchange Server 5.0 exam, Exchange Server 5.5 exam, Proxy Server 2.0 exam, IIS 4.0 exam, IEAK exam, and the revised Windows 95 exam. He recently was an instrumental force in the design and engineering of a 1,700-node Windows NT network that is located in more than 20 buildings at Keesler Air Force Base in Mississippi. Among his current projects is assisting in the design and implementation of a 10,000-node Windows NT network, also located at Keesler Air Force Base.

His wife Martha and daughter Marissa are very supportive of the time he spends on the computers located throughout his house.

Brian Mayo is a Microsoft Certified System's Engineer (MCSE), Microsoft Certified Professional + Internet, (MCP + Internet) and a Compaq Accredited Systems Engineer (ASE). He comes from a deployment and support background, and currently works as a systems engineer for CompuCom out of their Indianapolis branch.

Ed Wilson is a senior networking specialist with Full Service Networking, a Microsoft Solution Partner, in Cincinnati, Ohio. A former naval officer, Ed has been working with computers for nearly 15 years in a variety of industrial and corporate settings. He teaches adult education computer classes at Maysville Community College on an assortment of Windows-related topics, including PowerPoint, Access, and Internet Explorer. He has his B.A. in Journalism from the University of Mississippi, and an A.S. in Electronics from Maysville Community College. Ed holds the Microsoft Certified Systems Engineer + Internet certification as well as the A + certification.

Trevor Glenn (MCT, MCSE + Internet) works as a project manager for NewData Strategies, a Microsoft Solution provider, and winner of the FastTech 50 for the fourth year in a row. NewData Strategies was also the recipient of a 1997 Microsoft Outstanding Performer/Partner Award, being honored for our track record as leading Windows NT and Exchange business solution providers. Trevor is also an Instructor at Southern Methodist University, a Microsoft ATEC, where he teaches the full MCSE curriculum. He dedicates his contributions to this book to his supportive family and friends, and especially to his wife Niecey, who puts up with his late-night studying and "playing" on the computer. He can be reached at tglenn@newdat.com.

Mark Larma is a senior systems engineer for MicroAge in Phoenix, AZ. He has an MCSE in both the 3.51 and 4.0 track, with an emphasis on messaging. He currently has certifications on Exchange, versions 4.0, 5.0, and 5.5. Mark taught himself to program in BASIC at the age of 11 and hasn't stopped using the technology since. Mark dedicates his writing to his patient family: his wife Mary Ann, daughters Alexis and Veronica, and newborn son Hunter.

From the Classroom

Robert Aschermann (MCP, MCT, MCSE + Internet) has been an IS professional for nearly ten years. During his career, he has worked in technical support, systems design, consulting, and training. Mr. Aschermann has been an MCSE for almost three years, and has passed fifteen Microsoft certification exams. Currently Rob works as a trainer and consultant for one of Microsoft's oldest and largest Authorized Technical Education Centers (ATEC), Empower Trainers & Consultants. He holds a degree in Management Systems from the University of Missouri at Rolla, as well as an M.B.A. from Baker University.

Technical Review

Michael Cross is an MCSE, MCP specialist: Internet, computer programmer, network support specialist, and an instructor at private colleges. He is the owner of KnightWare, a company that provides consulting, programming, network support, Web page design, computer training, and various other services. In his spare time, he has been a freelance writer for several years, in genres of fiction and non-fiction. He currently lives in London, Ontario, Canada.

ACKNOWLEDGMENTS

We would like to thank the following people:

- Richard Kristof of Global Knowledge Network for championing the series and providing us access to some great people and information. And to Patrick Von Schlag, Robin Yunker, David Mantica, Stacey Cannon, and Kevin Murray for all their cooperation.

- To all the incredibly hard-working folks at Osborne/McGraw-Hill: Brandon Nordin, Scott Rogers, and Gareth Hancock for their help in launching a great series and being solid team players. In addition, Madhu Prasher, Cynthia Douglas, Jody McKenzie, Steve Emry, Anne Ellingsen, and Bernadette Jurich for their help in fine-tuning the book.

- To Becky Kirsininkas and Karen Cronin at Microsoft Corporation for being patient and diligent in answering all our questions.

CONTENTS AT A GLANCE

CONTENTS

PREFACE

This book's primary objective is to help you prepare for and pass the required MCSE exam so you can begin to reap the career benefits of certification. We believe that the only way to do this is to help you increase your knowledge and build your skills. After completing this book, you should feel confident that you have thoroughly reviewed all of the objectives that Microsoft has established for the exam.

In This Book

This book is organized around the actual structure of the Microsoft exam administered at Sylvan Testing Centers. Most of the MCSE exams have six parts to them: Planning, Installation and Configuration, Managing Resources, Connectivity, Monitoring and Optimization, and Troubleshooting. Microsoft has let us know all the topics we need to cover for the exam. We've followed their list carefully, so you can be assured you're not missing anything.

In Every Chapter

We've created a set of chapter components that call your attention to important items, reinforce important points, and provide helpful exam-taking hints. Take a look at what you'll find in every chapter:

- Every chapter begins with the **Certification Objectives**—what you need to know in order to pass the section on the exam dealing with the chapter topic. The Certification Objective headings identify the objectives within the chapter, so you'll always know an objective when you see it!

- **Exam Watch** notes call attention to information about, and potential pitfalls in, the exam. These helpful hints are written by MCSEs who have taken the exams and received their certification—who better to tell you what to worry about? They know what you're about to go through!

<table>
<tr><td>EXERCISE</td><td>

■ **Certification Exercises** are interspersed throughout the chapters. These are step-by-step exercises that mirror vendor-recommended labs. They help you master skills that are likely to be an area of focus on the exam. Don't just read through the exercises; they are hands-on practice that you should be comfortable completing. Learning by doing is an effective way to increase your competency with a product.

</td></tr>
</table>

■ **From the Classroom** sidebars describe the issues that come up most often in the training classroom setting. These sidebars give you a valuable perspective into certification- and product-related topics. They point out common mistakes and address questions that have arisen from classroom discussions.

■ **Q & A** sections lay out problems and solutions in a quick-read format:

QUESTIONS AND ANSWERS

James must be available to troubleshoot the computers in any office in the four buildings of the company that he works for...	Implement a roaming profile for James so that he can access his desktop no matter what computer he is using. This is especially handy since his roaming profile can include the mapping to a network drive that holds his diagnostic tools.

■ The **Certification Summary** is a succinct review of the chapter and a re-statement of salient points regarding the exam.

■ The **Two-Minute Drill** at the end of every chapter is a checklist of the main points of the chapter. It can be used for last-minute review.

■ The **Self Test** offers questions similar to those found on the certification exams, including multiple choice, true/false questions, and fill-in-the-blank. The answers to these questions, as well as explanations of the answers, can be found in Appendix A. By taking the Self Test after completing each chapter, you'll reinforce what you've learned from that chapter, while becoming familiar with the structure of the exam questions.

Some Pointers

Once you've finished reading this book, set aside some time to do a thorough review. You might want to return to the book several times and make use of all the methods it offers for reviewing the material:

1. *Re-read all the Two-Minute Drills,* or have someone quiz you. You also can use the drills as a way to do a quick cram before the exam.

2. *Re-read all the Exam Watch notes.* Remember that these are written by MCSEs who have taken the exam and passed. They know what you should expect—and what you should be careful about.

3. *Review all the Q & A scenarios* for quick problem solving.

4. *Re-take the Self Tests.* Taking the tests right after you've read the chapter is a good idea, because it helps reinforce what you've just learned. However, it's an even better idea to go back later and do all the questions in the book in one sitting. Pretend you're taking the exam. (For this reason, you should mark your answers on a separate piece of paper when you go through the questions the first time.)

5. *Complete the exercises.* Did you do the exercises when you read through each chapter? If not, do them! These exercises are designed to cover exam topics, and there's no better way to get to know this material than by practicing.

6. *Check out the Web site.* Global Knowledge Network invites you to become an active member of the Access Global Web site. This site is an online mall and an information repository that you'll find invaluable. You can access many types of products to assist you in your preparation for the exams, and you'll be able to participate in forums, online discussions, and threaded discussions. No other book brings you unlimited access to such a resource. You'll find more information about this site in Appendix C.

MCSE Certification

Although you've obviously picked up this book to study for a specific exam, we'd like to spend some time covering what you need to complete in order to attain MCSE status. Because this information can be found on the Microsoft Web site, www.microsoft.com/train_cert, we've repeated only some of the more important information. You should review the train_cert site and check out Microsoft's information, along with their list of reasons to become an MCSE, including job advancement.

As you probably know, to attain MCSE status, you must pass a total of six exams—four requirements and two electives. One required exam is on networking basics, one on NT Server, one on NT Server in the Enterprise, and one on a client (either Windows NT Workstation or Windows 95 or 98). There are several electives from which to choose—and many of these electives also count toward Microsoft's new MCSE + Internet (MCSE + I) certification. Indeed, the most popular electives now include the Internet Information Server 4.0 exam, which counts toward both certifications. The following table lists the exam names, their corresponding course numbers, and whether they are required or elective. We're showing you the NT 4.0 track and not the NT 3.51 track (which is still offered).

Exam Number	Exam Name	Required or Elective
70-58	Networking Essentials	Required
70-98	Implementing and Supporting Microsoft Windows 98	Required
70-63	Implementing and Supporting Microsoft Windows 95	Required (either 70-63, 70-73, or 70-98)
70-67	Implementing and Supporting Microsoft Windows NT Server 4.0	Required
70-68	Implementing and Supporting Microsoft Windows NT Server 4.0 in the Enterprise	Required
70-73	Implementing and Supporting Microsoft Windows NT Workstation 4.0	Required (either 70-73 or 70-63)

Exam Number	Exam Name	Required or Elective
70-14	Supporting Microsoft System Management Server 1.2	Elective
70-59	Internetworking with Microsoft TCP/IP on Windows NT 4.0	Elective
70-81	Implementing and Supporting Microsoft Exchange Server 5.5	Elective
70-85	Implementing and Supporting Microsoft SNA Server 4.0	Elective
70-87	Implementing and Supporting Microsoft Internet Information Server 4.0	Elective for MCSE and Required for MCSE + I
70-88	Implementing and Supporting Microsoft Proxy Server 2.0	Elective
70-28	System Administration for Microsoft SQL Server 7	Elective
70-29	Implementing a Database Design on Microsoft SQL Server 7	Elective for MCSE and MCSD
70-79	Implementing and Supporting Microsoft Internet Explorer 4.0 by Using the Internet Explorer Administration Kit	Elective for MCSE and Required for MCSE + I

The CD-ROM Resource

This book comes with a CD-ROM full of supplementary material you can use while preparing for the MCSE exams. You'll find an electronic version of the book, where you can look up items easily and search on specific terms.

How to Take a Microsoft Certification Examination

by John C. Phillips, Vice President of Test Development, Self Test Software
(Self Test's PEP is the official Microsoft practice test)

Good News and Bad News

If you are new to Microsoft certification, we have some good news and some bad news. The good news, of course, is that Microsoft certification is one of the most valuable credentials you can earn. It sets you apart from the crowd, and marks you as a valuable asset to your employer. You will gain the respect of your peers, and Microsoft certification can have a wonderful effect on your income.

The bad news is that Microsoft certification tests are not easy. You may think you will read through some study material, memorize a few facts, and pass the Microsoft examinations. After all, these certification exams are just computer-based, multiple-choice tests, so they must be easy. If you believe this, you are wrong. Unlike many "multiple guess" tests you have been exposed to in school, the questions on Microsoft certification examinations go beyond simple factual knowledge.

The purpose of this introduction is to teach you how to take a Microsoft certification examination. To be successful, you need to know something about the purpose and structure of these tests. We will also look at the latest innovations in Microsoft testing. Using *simulations* and *adaptive testing*, Microsoft is enhancing both the validity and security of the certification process. These factors have some important effects on how you should prepare for an exam, as well as your approach to each question during the test.

We will begin by looking at the purpose, focus, and structure of Microsoft certification tests, and examine the effect these factors have on the kinds of questions you will face on your certification exams. We will define the structure of examination questions and investigate some common formats. Next, we will present a strategy for answering these questions. Finally, we will give some specific guidelines on what you should do on the day of your test.

Why Vendor Certification?

The Microsoft Certified Professional program, like the certification programs from Lotus, Novell, Oracle, and other software vendors, is maintained for the ultimate purpose of increasing the corporation's profits. A successful vendor certification program accomplishes this goal by helping to create a pool of experts in a company's software, and by "branding" these experts so that companies using the software can identify them.

We know that vendor certification has become increasingly popular in the last few years because it helps employers find qualified workers, and because it helps software vendors like Microsoft sell their products. But why vendor certification rather than a more traditional approach like a college degree in computer science? A college education is a broadening and enriching experience, but a degree in computer science does not prepare students for most jobs in the IT industry.

A common truism in our business states, "If you are out of the IT industry for three years and want to return, you have to start over." The problem, of course, is *timeliness;* if a first-year student learns about a specific computer program, it probably will no longer be in wide use when he or she graduates. Although some colleges are trying to integrate Microsoft certification into their curriculum, the problem is not really a flaw in higher education, but a characteristic of the IT industry. Computer software is changing so rapidly that a four-year college just can't keep up.

A marked characteristic of the Microsoft certification program is an emphasis on performing specific job tasks rather than merely gathering knowledge. It may come as a shock, but most potential employers do not care how much you know about the theory of operating systems, networking, or database design. As one IT manager put it, "I don't really care what my employees know about the theory of our network. We don't need someone to sit at a desk and think about it. We need people who can actually do something to make it work better."

You should not think that this attitude is some kind of anti-intellectual revolt against "book learning." Knowledge is a necessary prerequisite, but it is not enough. More than one company has hired a computer science graduate as a network administrator, only to learn that the new employee has no idea how to add users, assign permissions, or perform the other day-to-day tasks necessary to maintain a network. This brings us to the second major characteristic of Microsoft certification that affects the questions you must be prepared to answer. In addition to timeliness, Microsoft certification is also job task oriented.

The timeliness of Microsoft's certification program is obvious, and is inherent in the fact that you will be tested on current versions of software in wide use today. The job task orientation of Microsoft certification is almost as obvious, but testing real-world job skills using a computer-based test is not easy.

Computerized Testing

Considering the popularity of Microsoft certification, and the fact that certification candidates are spread around the world, the only practical way to administer tests for the certification program is through Sylvan Prometric testing centers. Sylvan Prometric provides proctored testing services for Microsoft, Oracle, Novell, Lotus, and the A+ computer technician certification. Although the IT industry accounts for much of Sylvan's revenue, the company provides services for a number of other businesses and organizations, such as FAA pre-flight pilot tests. In fact, most companies that need secure test delivery over a wide geographic area use the services of Sylvan Prometric. In addition to delivery, Sylvan Prometric also scores the tests and provides statistical feedback on the performance of each test question to the companies and organizations that use their services.

Typically, several hundred questions are developed for a new Microsoft certification examination. The questions are first reviewed by a number of subject matter experts for technical accuracy, and then are presented in a beta test. The beta test may last for several hours, due to the large number of questions. After a few weeks, Microsoft Certification uses the statistical feedback from Sylvan to check the performance of the beta questions.

Questions are discarded if most test takers get them right (too easy) or wrong (too difficult), and a number of other statistical measures are taken of each question. Although the scope of our discussion precludes a rigorous treatment of question analysis, you should be aware that Microsoft and other vendors spend a great deal of time and effort making sure their examination questions are valid. In addition to the obvious desire for quality, the fairness of a vendor's certification program must be legally defensible.

The questions that survive statistical analysis form the pool of questions for the final certification examination.

Test Structure

The kind of test we are most familiar with is known as a *form* test. For Microsoft certification, a form usually consists of 50–70 questions and takes 60–90 minutes to complete. If there are 240 questions in the final pool for an examination, then four forms can be created. Thus, candidates who retake the test probably will not see the same questions.

Other variations are possible. From the same pool of 240 questions, *five* forms can be created, each containing 40 unique questions (200 questions) and 20 questions selected at random from the remaining 40.

The questions in a Microsoft form test are equally weighted. This means they all count the same when the test is scored. An interesting and useful characteristic of a form test is that you can mark a question you have doubts about as you take the test. Assuming you have time left when you finish all the questions, you can return and spend more time on the questions you have marked as doubtful.

Microsoft may soon implement *adaptive* testing. To use this interactive technique, a form test is first created and administered to several thousand certification candidates. The statistics generated are used to assign a weight, or difficulty level, for each question. For example, the questions in a form might be divided into levels one through five, with level one questions being the easiest and level five the hardest.

When an adaptive test begins, the candidate is first given a level three question. If it is answered correctly, a question from the next higher level is presented, and an incorrect response results in a question from the next lower level. When 15–20 questions have been answered in this manner, the scoring algorithm is able to predict, with a high degree of statistical certainty, whether the candidate would pass or fail if all the questions in the form were answered. When the required degree of certainty is attained, the test ends and the candidate receives a pass/fail grade.

Adaptive testing has some definite advantages for everyone involved in the certification process. Adaptive tests allow Sylvan Prometric to deliver more tests with the same resources, as certification candidates often are in and out in 30 minutes or less. For Microsoft, adaptive testing means that fewer test questions are exposed to each candidate, and this can enhance the security, and therefore the validity, of certification tests.

One possible problem you may have with adaptive testing is that you are not allowed to mark and revisit questions. Since the adaptive algorithm is interactive, and all questions but the first are selected on the basis of your response to the previous question, it is not possible to skip a particular question or change an answer.

Question Types

Computerized test questions can be presented in a number of ways. Some of the possible formats are used on Microsoft certification examinations, and some are not.

True/False

We are all familiar with True/False questions, but because of the inherent 50 percent chance of guessing the correct answer, you will not see questions of this type on Microsoft certification exams.

Multiple Choice

The majority of Microsoft certification questions are in the multiple-choice format, with either a single correct answer or multiple correct answers. One interesting variation on multiple-choice questions with multiple correct answers is whether or not the candidate is told how many answers are correct.

> EXAMPLE:
> Which two files can be altered to configure the MS-DOS environment? (Choose two.)
> Or
> Which files can be altered to configure the MS-DOS environment? (Choose all that apply.)

You may see both variations on Microsoft certification examinations, but the trend seems to be toward the first type, where candidates are told explicitly how many answers are correct. Questions of the "choose all that apply" variety are more difficult, and can be merely confusing.

Graphical Questions

One or more graphical elements are sometimes used as exhibits to help present or clarify an exam question. These elements may take the form of a network diagram, pictures of networking components, or screen shots from the software on which you are being tested. It is often easier to present the concepts required for a complex performance-based scenario with a graphic than with words.

Test questions known as *hotspots* actually incorporate graphics as part of the answer. These questions ask the certification candidate to click on a location or graphical element to answer the question. As an example, you might be shown the diagram of a network and asked to click on an appropriate location for a router. The answer is correct if the candidate clicks within the hotspot that defines the correct location.

Free Response Questions

Another kind of question you sometimes see on Microsoft certification examinations requires a *free response* or type-in answer. An example of this type of question might present a TCP/IP network scenario and ask the candidate to calculate and enter the correct subnet mask in dotted decimal notation.

Knowledge-Based and Performance-Based Questions

Microsoft Certification develops a blueprint for each Microsoft certification examination with input from subject matter experts. This blueprint defines the content areas and objectives for each test, and each test question is created to test a specific objective. The basic information from the examination blueprint can be found on Microsoft's Web site in the Exam Prep Guide for each test.

Psychometricians (psychologists who specialize in designing and analyzing tests) categorize test questions as knowledge-based or performance-based. As the names imply, knowledge-based questions are designed to test knowledge, while performance-based questions are designed to test performance.

Some objectives demand a knowledge-based question. For example, objectives that use verbs like *list* and *identify* tend to test only what you know, not what you can do.

EXAMPLE:
Objective: Identify the MS-DOS configuration files.
Which two files can be altered to configure the MS-DOS environment? (Choose two.)

    A. COMMAND.COM

    B. AUTOEXEC.BAT

    C. IO.SYS

    D. CONFIG.SYS
Correct answers: B, D

Other objectives use action verbs like *install, configure,* and *troubleshoot* to define job tasks. These objectives can often be tested with either a knowledge-based question or a performance-based question.

EXAMPLE:

Objective: Configure an MS-DOS installation appropriately using the PATH statement in AUTOEXEC.BAT.

Knowledge-based question:

What is the correct syntax to set a path to the D:directory in AUTOEXEC.BAT?

   A. SET PATH EQUAL TO D:

   B. PATH D:

   C. SETPATH D:

   D. D:EQUALS PATH

   Correct answer: B

Performance-based question:

Your company uses several DOS accounting applications that access a group of common utility programs. What is the best strategy for configuring the computers in the accounting department so that the accounting applications will always be able to access the utility programs?

   A. Store all the utilities on a single floppy disk, and make a copy of the disk for each computer in the accounting department.

   B. Copy all the utilities to a directory on the C: drive of each computer in the accounting department, and add a PATH statement pointing to this directory in the AUTOEXEC.BAT files.

   C. Copy all the utilities to all application directories on each computer in the accounting department.

   D. Place all the utilities in the C:directory on each computer, because the C:directory is automatically included in the PATH statement when AUTOEXEC.BAT is executed.

   Correct answer: B

Even in this simple example, the superiority of the performance-based question is obvious. Whereas the knowledge-based question asks for a single fact, the performance-based question presents a real-life situation and requires that you make a decision based on this scenario. Thus, performance-based questions give more bang (validity) for the test author's buck (individual question).

Testing Job Performance

We have said that Microsoft certification focuses on timeliness and the ability to perform job tasks. We have also introduced the concept of performance-based questions, but even performance-based multiple-choice questions do not really measure performance. Another strategy is needed to test job skills.

Given unlimited resources, it is not difficult to test job skills. In an ideal world, Microsoft would fly MCP candidates to Redmond, place them in a controlled environment with a team of experts, and ask them to plan, install, maintain, and troubleshoot a Windows network. In a few days at most, the experts could reach a valid decision as to whether each candidate should or should not be granted MCSE status. Needless to say, this is not likely to happen.

Closer to reality, another way to test performance is by using the actual software, and creating a testing program to present tasks and automatically grade a candidate's performance when the tasks are completed. This *cooperative* approach would be practical in some testing situations, but the same test that is presented to MCP candidates in Boston must also be available in Bahrain and Botswana. Many Sylvan Prometric testing locations around the world cannot run 32-bit applications, much less provide the complex networked solutions required by cooperative testing applications.

The most workable solution for measuring performance in today's testing environment is a *simulation* program. When the program is launched during a test, the candidate sees a simulation of the actual software that looks, and behaves, just like the real thing. When the testing software presents a task, the simulation program is launched and the candidate performs the required task. The testing software then grades the candidate's performance on the required task and moves to the next question. In this way, a 16-bit simulation program can mimic the look and feel of 32-bit operating systems, a complicated network, or even the entire Internet.

Microsoft has introduced simulation questions on the certification examination for Internet Information Server 4.0. Simulation questions provide many advantages over other testing methodologies, and simulations are expected to become increasingly important in the Microsoft certification program. For example, studies have shown that there is a very high correlation between the ability to perform simulated tasks on a computer-based test and the ability to perform the actual job tasks. Thus, simulations enhance the validity of the certification process.

Another truly wonderful benefit of simulations is in the area of test security. It is just not possible to cheat on a simulation question. In fact, you will be told exactly what tasks you are expected to perform on the test. How can a certification candidate cheat? By learning to perform the tasks? What a concept!

Study Strategies

There are appropriate ways to study for the different types of questions you will see on a Microsoft certification examination.

Knowledge-Based Questions

Knowledge-based questions require that you memorize facts. There are hundreds of facts inherent in every content area of every Microsoft certification examination. There are several keys to memorizing facts:

- **Repetition** The more times your brain is exposed to a fact, the more likely you are to remember it.

- **Association** Connecting facts within a logical framework makes them easier to remember.

- **Motor Association** It is often easier to remember something if you write it down or perform some other physical act, like clicking on a practice test answer.

We have said that the emphasis of Microsoft certification is job performance, and that there are very few knowledge-based questions on

Microsoft certification exams. Why should you waste a lot of time learning filenames, IP address formulas, and other minutiae? Read on.

Performance-Based Questions

Most of the questions you will face on a Microsoft certification exam are performance-based scenario questions. We have discussed the superiority of these questions over simple knowledge-based questions, but you should remember that the job task orientation of Microsoft certification extends the knowledge you need to pass the exams; it does not replace this knowledge. Therefore, the first step in preparing for scenario questions is to absorb as many facts relating to the exam content areas as you can. In other words, go back to the previous section and follow the steps to prepare for an exam composed of knowledge-based questions.

The second step is to familiarize yourself with the format of the questions you are likely to see on the exam. You can do this by answering the questions in this study guide, by using Microsoft assessment tests, or by using practice tests. The day of your test is not the time to be surprised by the convoluted construction of Microsoft exam questions.

For example, one of Microsoft Certification's favorite formats of late takes the following form:

Scenario: You have a network with...
Primary Objective: You want to...
Secondary Objective: You also want to...
Proposed Solution: Do this...
What does the proposed solution accomplish?

    A. satisfies the primary and the secondary objective

    B. satisfies the primary but not the secondary objective

    C. satisfies the secondary but not the primary objective

    D. satisfies neither the primary nor the secondary objective

This kind of question, with some variation, is seen on many Microsoft Certification examinations.

At best, these performance-based scenario questions really do test certification candidates at a higher cognitive level than knowledge-based questions. At worst, these questions can test your reading comprehension and test-taking ability rather than your ability to use Microsoft products. Be sure to get in the habit of reading the question carefully to determine what is being asked.

The third step in preparing for Microsoft scenario questions is to adopt the following attitude: Multiple-choice questions aren't really performance-based. It is all a cruel lie. These scenario questions are just knowledge-based questions with a little story wrapped around them.

To answer a scenario question, you have to sift through the story to the underlying facts of the situation, and apply your knowledge to determine the correct answer. This may sound silly at first, but the process we go through in solving real-life problems is quite similar. The key concept is that every scenario question (and every real-life problem) has a fact at its center, and if we can identify that fact, we can answer the question.

Simulations

Simulation questions really do measure your ability to perform job tasks. You must be able to perform the specified tasks. There are two ways to prepare for simulation questions:

1. Get experience with the actual software. If you have the resources, this is a great way to prepare for simulation questions.

2. Use official Microsoft practice tests. Practice tests are available that provide practice with the same simulation engine used on Microsoft certification exams. This approach has the added advantage of grading your efforts.

Signing Up

Signing up to take a Microsoft certification examination is easy. Sylvan operators in each country can schedule tests at any testing center. There are, however, a few things you should know:

1. If you call Sylvan during a busy time period, get a cup of coffee first, because you may be in for a long wait. Sylvan does an

excellent job, but everyone in the world seems to want to sign up for a test on Monday morning.

2. You will need your social security number or some other unique identifier to sign up for a Sylvan test, so have it at hand.

3. Pay for your test by credit card if at all possible. This makes things easier, and you can even schedule tests for the same day you call, if space is available at your local testing center.

4. Know the number and title of the test you want to take before you call. This is not essential, and the Sylvan operators will help you if they can. Having this information in advance, however, speeds up the registration process.

Taking the Test

Teachers have always told you not to try to cram for examinations, because it does no good. Sometimes they lied. If you are faced with a knowledge-based test requiring only that you regurgitate facts, cramming can mean the difference between passing and failing. This is not the case, however, with Microsoft certification exams. If you don't know it the night before, don't bother to stay up and cram.

Instead, create a schedule and stick to it. Plan your study time carefully, and do not schedule your test until you think you are ready to succeed. Follow these guidelines on the day of your exam:

1. Get a good night's sleep. The scenario questions you will face on a Microsoft certification examination require a clear head.

2. Remember to take two forms of identification—at least one with a picture. A driver's license with your picture, and social security or credit cards are acceptable.

3. Leave home in time to arrive at your testing center a few minutes early. It is not a good idea to feel rushed as you begin your exam.

4. Do not spend too much time on any one question. If you are taking a form test, take your best guess and mark the question so you can

come back to it if you have time. You cannot mark and revisit questions on an adaptive test, so you must do your best on each question as you go.

5. If you do not know the answer to a question, try to eliminate the obviously wrong answers and guess from the rest. If you can eliminate two out of four options, you have a 50 percent chance of guessing the correct answer.

6. For scenario questions, follow the steps we outlined earlier. Read the question carefully and try to identify the facts at the center of the story.

Finally, I would advise anyone attempting to earn Microsoft MCSE certification to adopt a philosophical attitude. Even if you are the kind of person who never fails a test, you are likely to fail at least one Microsoft certification test somewhere along the way. Do not get discouraged. If Microsoft certification were easy to obtain, more people would have it, and it would not be so respected and so valuable to your future in the IT industry.

1

Planning the Windows 98 Installation

W hat is Windows 98? Well, to discover the answer to that question, we have to look at the history of disk operating systems by Microsoft.

First, there was DOS, a text-based disk operating system that allowed a person to run a single program at a time. People running DOS had to know a lot of commands and syntax in order to customize anything. Using batch files prevented massive frustration, but the end user still had to be pretty savvy to use the PC. DOS was originally created for IBM PCs and compatibles, and did not require much in the way of hardware. As graphical programs came into use, the need for a better operating system came about.

Next, Microsoft introduced an enhancement to DOS, called Windows. In the first few versions (1.x and 2.x), Windows was little more than a graphical menu system. In the next version (3.0), Windows (along with DOS) supported the Intel 386 processor, such that a user could execute two programs almost simultaneously and switch between them. Version 3.0 was followed fairly quickly by version 3.1, and then this functionality worked quite well. However, Windows was not an operating system. It ran on top of DOS. It did not inherently support networking, but because the ability to multitask was present, it became popular in the workplace as a productivity enhancement.

Microsoft released two products to enhance networking in Windows. One was Windows for Workgroups 3.1 (followed immediately by 3.11), and the other was Windows NT 3.1 (followed by 3.5 and then 3.51). Windows for Workgroups was an enhanced networking version of Windows 3.1. Windows NT, however, was a 32-bit operating system that did not require DOS at all, and was somewhat similar in concept to IBM's OS2. The problem with both of these Windows products was that the user interface never changed from the original Windows graphical menu system, and adding new hardware was difficult.

Microsoft Windows 95 was heralded as a great step forward in operating systems for Intel processors. First, it was not a menu system that worked on top of DOS. To install Windows 95, you didn't need any DOS at all. It still allowed for DOS applications, however, and could be configured to boot directly to a command prompt that was the same as a DOS system.

Windows 95 supported more hardware than Microsoft Windows NT, including legacy systems. Windows 95 made adding new hardware simple, and could run 32-bit applications, plus a slew of legacy DOS and Windows 3.1 applications. Moreover, Windows 95 had a remarkably easy-to-use Graphical User Interface (GUI) that was designed to manage documents. It was even called "document-centric."

Since Windows 95 was released, there have been two "updates" to it that could easily have been considered separate releases of the operating system. In 1996, there was a service pack released that updated many of the internal components of Windows 95 and several hotfixes, too. In 1997, there was an update of Windows 95-OSR2 that was only released to Original Equipment Manufacturers (OEMs) for distribution on already-installed PCs. In some ways, these updates could be considered "Windows 96" and "Windows 97," respectively.

Microsoft released Windows NT 4.0, in response to a need for the better GUI and higher security in organizations' networks. Even though NT 4 has the same GUI as Windows 95/98, it works in a completely different way. The differences between NT and Windows 98 will be examined later in this chapter.

What makes Microsoft Windows 98 an altogether different system from Windows 95 (rather than being another update), are the tremendous changes that have been made to the way the operating system works "behind-the-scenes." Plus, the addition of the Internet Explorer active desktop has evolved the GUI even further. (NOTE: If you use Windows 95 or NT 4.0 with Internet Explorer 4's active desktop, the GUI will work much the same as in Windows 98.)

CERTIFICATION OBJECTIVE 1.01

Windows 98 Features

Windows 98 inherited a lot from Windows 95. It is capable of running applications that were designed for Windows 95, plus most applications designed for DOS, Windows 3.1*x,* and Windows NT. Improvements have been made to the display, disk, modem, and monitor drivers. Internet capabilities are not simply an add-on; they are now optionally integrated into the GUI through Microsoft's Active Desktop. Boot times are faster, and security has been improved. To make maintenance easier, Windows 98 comes with a multitude of new wizards and system utilities.

Of particular interest to engineers and administrators:

- **Update Wizard**   Just like Internet Explorer 4's update method, Windows 98 can connect to a Web site in order to download and install the latest patches, drivers, and enhancements in a simple and easy step. See Figure 1-1 for the Update Wizard.

- **Maintenance Wizard**   This utility, shown in Figure 1-2, makes maintenance simple. Users can clean out shortcuts to non-existent programs from their Start menu, check for viruses, defragment the

FIGURE 1-1

Update Wizard

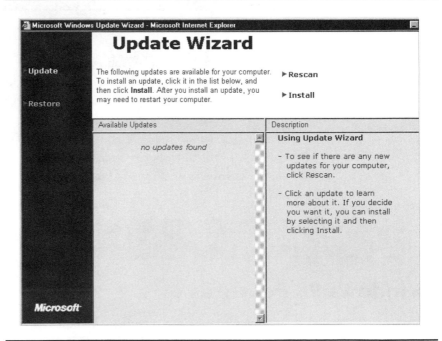

Maintenance Wizard

hard disk, and delete unnecessary files, in order to speed up the operating system or fix problems.

■ **System Information** This utility, shown in Figure 1-3, comes with a Tools menu packed with all sorts of tools that can: check system

System Information and
the Wizards

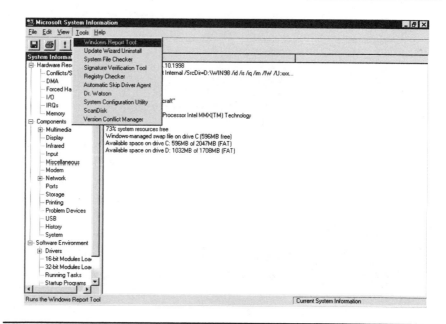

files (System File Checker) for corruption and restore originals; check the Registry (Registry Checker); make sense out of configuration files (System Configuration Utility); and otherwise monitor or maintain the PC.

The remaining new features fall into several different categories:

- Installation changes
- Disk and driver support
- GUI reconstruction
- Networking enhancements

Installation Changes

Microsoft redesigned the Windows 98 setup process. It is still comparable to the Windows 95 process in that it checks the hardware and space available, and then asks for basically the same information to be input: user information, computer name and networking information, and applet choices.

For enterprise networks, a file with preselected configuration options can be used to install multiple computers in an unattended mode. Windows 95 had a similar capability using a file with the default name of MSBATCH.INF. The upgrade to the MSBATCH.INF file includes an addition of a multiple-machine-name text file. This fixes the problem with the old MSBATCH.INF file where the machine name (the NetBIOS name of the computer, which must be unique on a Microsoft network) had to be changed for each machine—the MSBATCH.INF file had to be edited each time it was used. The new Windows Batch 98 program allows a MACHINE.TXT file with all the machine names in it to be integrated with a MSBATCH.INF file to create multiple unique batch setup files. Windows Batch 98 is a program provided in the Windows 98 Resource Kit that can gather all the information on an existing Windows 98 machine, and then automatically create an MSBATCH.INF file. The file can be created manually, also.

For a Windows 95 upgrade to Windows 98, the setup process has been shortened time-wise, with the assumption that the existing Windows 95 machine has the correct hardware drivers installed. This means that the initial full hardware detection is not required. Instead, information already in the Windows 95 operating system about the hardware is used to update drivers to Windows 98. Windows 98 setup does allow a full upgrade of Windows 3.1x to Windows 98, but still requires full hardware detection.

Disk and Driver Support

Windows 98 includes support for many new hardware devices. Since Windows 95 was introduced, new hardware devices and standards have been developed. To use the new hardware in Windows 95, the drivers that allow the Windows operating system to access the hardware had to be manually installed using manufacturer-supplied disks to allow access to the new hardware. But since Windows 98 includes these drivers in its source files, it will support these new hardware devices natively.

Monitors

Of all the improvements made to the Windows family of operating systems, the most spectacular has to be the support for multiple monitors. Here's how it works: If the PC has a Peripheral Component Interconnect (PCI) bus or Accelerated Graphics Port (AGP), and two or more (up to eight) PCI or AGP video adapters are installed, then two monitors can be used on that PC in order to increase the display area. An application can be maximized and take up one monitor, while the other is used for other applications. This works well for 32-bit Windows programs, but does not work as well with DOS and 16-bit programs, since they do not access hardware through the Windows 98 operating system the same way 32-bit programs do.

Disk Support

Windows 98 includes native FAT32 support. FAT32 was introduced in Windows 95/OSR2. FAT32 is a 32-bit upgrade to the FAT (File Allocation Table) file system that originally came from DOS. The benefits of FAT32 include optimal use of disk space and larger partition sizes than the maximum 2GB size allowed by FAT.

New Win32 Driver Model

Windows 98 comes with a new driver model that allows developers to create a single driver for a hardware device or bus that is usable by both Windows 98 and the upcoming Windows NT 5.0. This strategy allows an administrator to use a single driver in an environment that has both of those operating systems.

Backup

Backing up a Windows 98 PC does not require a third-party program anymore. Instead, Windows 98 includes a backup application (shown in Figure 1-4) that supports SCSI tape drives and other devices. This program

FIGURE 1-4

Backup applet

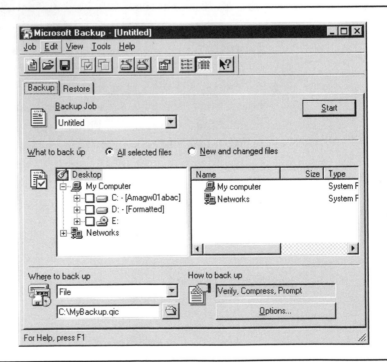

can even back up selected files to a single backup file on a local hard disk or network drive.

Drivers and Devices

Windows 98 supports all sorts of new hardware devices. While including more than a thousand new and upgraded drivers for standard hardware (such as modems, printers, and network interface cards), Windows 98 also supports TV-tuner cards, Universal Serial Bus (USB), IEEE 1394 (FireWire), Accelerated Graphics Port, infrared ports, and DVD.

The Universal Serial Bus is a high-speed serial connection that allows up to 127 peripherals to be connected to a single port on the PC. This is similar to using a SCSI interface card with up to seven SCSI peripherals connected to it. Unlike SCSI, however, USB allows its devices to be hot-swapped, so that no restarts are required each time a device is added or removed. The USB data transfer rate reaches 12 megabytes per second.

FireWire was introduced by IEEE 1394, and is also a high-speed serial connection. Unlike USB, FireWire was designed for devices that transfer large amounts of data. These devices would include digital camcorders and other multimedia hardware. Although these devices are not commonly used yet, Windows 98 will support both USB and FireWire hardware.

Windows 98 supports the new graphics bus slot for Intel PCs, which is the AGP. The purpose of this hardware is simply to speed up how the PC processes and displays graphics. This will allow for larger and more complex graphics to be used in multimedia games and 3D applications. AGP functions at 66 Mhz, with a data transfer rate of up to 528 Mbps. This is 3 to 5 times faster than a PCI graphics card running at 33 Mhz, with a data transfer rate of 132 Mbps.

Infrared ports are popular inclusions on laptop computers. An infrared port allows wireless data transfer between two computers, or between a computer and a printer or other infrared device. Windows 98 includes automatic detection and installation of IrDA-compatible infrared ports (IrDA: Infrared Data Association standard for wireless connectivity of printing and file transfer). Using the direct cable connection applet in Windows 98 allows data transfer between two computers. Simply mapping the infrared port to an LPT port, and installing a printer driver pointing to that port, enables infrared printing.

Windows 98 also supports the latest multimedia player, Digital Video/Versatile Disk (DVD). DVD is a successor to the CD-ROM, and a DVD player will run programs contained on CD-ROMs automatically. A DVD disk is the same size as a CD-ROM, but it can store much more data. Because of their large data capacity, movies have been released on DVD, and a DVD player can run that movie in a window under Windows 98. Who knows what DVD will do to multimedia games in the future?

GUI Reconstruction

At first glance, not much has changed on the desktop since Windows 95 debuted. The toolbar is still at the bottom, there is a Start button with the same cascading menus. Even the desktop screen, shown in Figure 1-5, is a

FIGURE 1-5

Nonactive desktop

familiar shade of aqua, but only if Active Desktop isn't turned on. What is the Active Desktop? Anyone who used Internet Explorer 4 will recognize the Active Desktop (see Figure 1-6) as a component of that part of Windows 98. Turning it on is optional.

Active Desktop includes accessing applications with a single click, floating toolbars on top of the desktop, and using an HTML page as desktop wallpaper. The Active Desktop represents an extension of the World Wide Web. There are additional toolbars, including one for an address space on the toolbar so that a URL can be accessed directly.

Networking Enhancements

Networks exist in all sorts of organizations, from the local library to high-powered financial firms. Windows 98 makes it easier than ever to log on and exchange data with many different types of network operating

Active Desktop

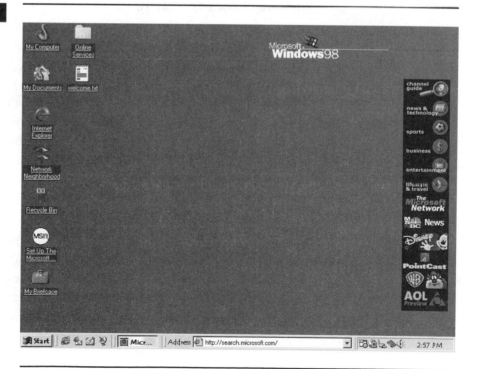

systems. Supported clients exist for Microsoft, Novell, and Banyan networks, and even include a new family logon client, so that a person can select his name from a logon list. Windows 98 supports many different protocols, such as the Internet's TCP/IP, Novell's IPX/SPX, DLC (typically used for mainframe access), fast Infrared, ISDN, and ATM networking.

exam
ⓦatch

Some of the protocols that Windows 98 supports include TCP/IP, IPX/SPX-compatible protocol, DLC, Infrared, ISDN, and ATM networking. TCP/IP is usually associated with Internet access. IPX/SPX-compatible protocol can be used to access NetWare file servers. DLC can be used for both mainframe access and HP JetDirect print-sharing devices. Infrared is used for file and printing between a Windows 98 PC with an infrared port, and another infrared device— either a PC or printer. Integrated Services Digital Network (ISDN) is a fast, digital remote access method available from many local phone companies. Asynchronous Transfer Mode (ATM) networking is a high-speed protocol used in both local area networks (LANs) and wide area networks (WANs).

Remote Access

For remote users, the addition of Multilink Channel Aggregation technology into Windows 98 is more than welcome. Multilink Channel Aggregation multiplies the total bandwidth between the remote PC and the host by combining two or more modem or ISDN lines. A potential drawback to using this technology, at least for travelers, is that there must be a separate telephone or ISDN line for each modem or ISDN device that is used, and usually a hotel room only has one line.

Logon Scripting

Windows 98 includes the new Windows Scripting Host, which is a shell that lets an administrator use more robust commands in logon scripts through ActiveX scripting. These scripts can be executed at logon or from a command line. They are language independent, and automatically support Microsoft Visual Basic Scripting (VBScript) and Microsoft Java-based

Scripting (JScript). Other scripting engines for different languages, such as Perl or REXX, can also be used, as they are provided.

Zero Administration

Windows 98 is designed to facilitate PC administration for corporations. One of the difficulties in maintaining computers is keeping the systems updated. Windows 98 includes a Web-based update program that, when the PC is connected to the Internet, can connect and be used to easily select and apply updates to the Windows 98 operating system.

CERTIFICATION OBJECTIVE 1.02

Choosing Windows 98 as a Client Operating System

There are many reasons why businesses should select Windows 98 as the client operating system for their networked PCs. There are alternatives— DOS, OS/2, UNIX, Windows 3.*x*, and Windows NT—but in most cases, the choice of a client operating system will come down to a choice between Windows 98 and Windows NT, Microsoft's two main client operating system lines.

There are several critical areas to look at when deciding between Windows 98 and Windows NT.

- Hardware
- Applications that access hardware directly
- Applications that use VXD technology
- File system
- Security

FROM THE CLASSROOM

Windows 98 or Windows NT Workstation

One of the toughest questions that I get is, "Should I use Windows 98 or Windows NT Workstation?" Microsoft isn't making this one any easier. Microsoft is trying to consolidate their desktop operating systems so that they offer one desktop operating system and one server operating system. Consequently, the hard lines that used to separate Windows versions are beginning to blur.

However, there are still some important differences between NT Workstation and Windows 98. If you need security, performance, and reliability, or if you plan single-seat administration of your NT network, then you should choose Windows NT Workstation. Single-seat administration means that you can control all of the Microsoft BackOffice server products like Windows NT Server, Systems Management Server, SQL Server, Internet Information Server, and Exchange Server from a single desktop. Not all of the administration tools for these server products can be run on Windows 98. Some require Windows NT Server or Windows NT Workstation. Think of Windows NT Workstation as your business desktop operating system.

If NT Workstation owns the business world, Windows 98 certainly owns the home desktop arena. No other operating system offers the multimedia capabilities of Windows 98. There is no better operating system for computer gaming, surfing the Internet, or general entertainment. Windows 98 provides more application compatibility than Windows NT Workstation, because Windows 98 does not have a hardware abstraction layer, as Windows NT does. The hardware abstraction layer prevents applications from directly accessing the hardware of a system. This prevents many older DOS applications and computer games that are very graphics intensive from running properly.

Windows 98 is also the best choice for mobile users. Windows 98 supports Plug and Play, advanced power management, and analog telecommunications better than Windows NT Workstation. Ask any laptop user and she will tell you that these features are essential for getting the most out of a laptop.

For people who just can't decide, my recommendation is to run both for awhile. You can dual boot a computer with both operating systems until you decide which one is right for you. Evaluate the features of each operating system and decide which are the most important to you. For example, compare the different levels of security each operating

FROM THE CLASSROOM

system offers and remember that with the NTFS file system on a Windows NT Workstation you can secure resources at the file level. With Windows 98, you only have share-level permissions.

Luckily, Microsoft uses the same interface to make it easier for users who must move back and forth between the two operating systems.

—By Robert Aschermann, MCT, MCSE

Hardware

Windows 98 supports a wider selection of hardware than Windows NT 4.0, especially among newer multimedia hardware devices. The minimum hardware requirements for Windows 98 are comparable to those for Windows NT 4.0, as shown in Table 1-1. This may be somewhat surprising, since Windows 95 supported more legacy equipment. Microsoft supplies a Hardware Compatibility List (HCL) for all equipment that has been tested and approved as compatible for both Windows 98 and Windows NT. The newest hardware supported by Windows 98, such as Accelerated Graphics Port, is not yet supported by Windows NT.

TABLE 1-1

Minimum Hardware Requirements for Windows 98 and Windows NT 4.0

Hardware Component	Windows 98 Minimum	Windows NT 4.0 Minimum
RAM	16MB	16MB
Processor	486DX2 66 Mhz	486 33 Mhz
Hard Disk Available Space	110MB	120MB
Monitor	VGA	VGA
Mouse	Bus or serial	Bus or serial

Applications That Access Hardware Directly

Windows 98 is more compatible with legacy DOS and 16-bit Windows 3.*x* programs than Windows NT. This can be a consideration for some 16-bit programs, but Windows NT does run many 16-bit programs, and both Windows 98 and Windows NT will support 32-bit programs. Windows 98 will support many legacy applications that access the PC hardware directly, rather than communicating with the operating system and having the operating system forward that communication. Windows NT will not support any application that attempts to access the hardware directly.

Applications That Use VXD Technology

Some legacy applications have been written using virtual device driver (VXD) technology. Windows 98 will support VXD technology. VXD technology is not supported by Windows NT.

File System

Either FAT or FAT32 are required by Windows 98 to run. Windows 98 does not support any other file system on the local hard disk.

FAT and NTFS file systems are both available for the hard disk under Windows NT. NTFS extends the security of the operating system, such that individual files can be protected on a user-by-user basis. Drives formatted with NTFS are only accessible to Windows 98 PCs over the network, as well as to DOS, Windows 3.*x*, UNIX, and Windows 95 client PCs. FAT tables are not proprietary, and are accessible from any boot disk. As such, security through logon is disabled on a FAT hard disk.

Security

Windows 98 is not a secure operating system. When using the FAT file system, Windows 98 can be booted from a DOS boot disk, and the files can be read. Users are able to simply escape (by pressing the ESCAPE key) out of the Logon dialog box, and then have full access to the files on the hard disk.

Security is one of the greatest pluses for Windows NT 4.0. NT 4.0 is Orange Book C2 level compliant. Orange Book C2 level security was introduced through the "Color Book Series" by the Institute of Electrical and Electronics Engineers (IEEE). It documents the specifications for a specific level of government security applied to PCs. The other "Color Books" in the IEEE series document the remaining security levels. As C2 level security has historically been implemented on servers, the use of Windows NT on the desktop greatly enhances security. In the case of laptops, and where PC equipment is exposed to public usage, this security level makes it difficult, if not impossible, to read, copy, or damage data on that hard disk. Windows 98 does not have C2 level compliance.

Windows NT has a more secure resource sharing structure than Windows 98. It allows users to set security permissions on directories, individual files, printers and other resources. Windows 98 does not support security on individual files.

When deciding between operating systems, the rule is that business requirements drive technical requirements. And the business requirements for an application take precedence over the business requirements for hardware. Hardware can always be upgraded, although changing it can be costly.

exam
ⓦatch

The exam questions on this subject tend to be tricky, listing one or two requirements that may lead a business to believe either one of the operating systems should be selected as the client. Study the following scenarios to get an idea of the approach the exam will take.

QUESTIONS AND ANSWERS

MoneyBank is a financial institution that will be upgrading all of its teller systems. The teller systems are 486 PCs that currently have 16MB of RAM and Windows 3.1 installed. A new 32-bit program that the manufacturer will only support with 32MB of RAM on NT, or with 16MB of RAM on Windows 98, will store highly confidential data on the local hard disk. The president of MoneyBank would prefer not to upgrade or replace the teller systems' hardware, but maintaining the security of the data is what is absolutely critical.	The fact that security is critical points to Windows NT as the proper operating system choice. Unfortunately, because of the application manufacturer's requirements, the hardware will not support NT, but will support Windows 98. The president must bite the bullet and upgrade the teller systems and deploy Windows NT. (In reality, the president may prefer to implement BIOS and screensaver passwords, disable booting from a floppy drive, and hope that is enough security. This does not provide the robust security that NTFS (NT's secure file system) might, and that is why the choice of Windows NT is more appropriate.)
GraphXStudio is replacing all of its Apple Computers with new Intel-based PCs. They are going to implement QuarkXpress, a 32-bit video-editing program, and DVD drives on each developer's PC. Some developers have expressed a desire for multiple monitors. The owner wishes to buy and maintain identical hardware and software for everyone, in order to cut down on administration costs.	The correct choice for this company is undoubtedly Windows 98. The DVD and multiple monitor requirements are the keys, since they are both native to Windows 98.
Bob Jones is a new administrator for a Novell NetWare network. He has been hired to do a network-wide upgrade of all the workstations. They are currently running OS/2 and DOS, with a legacy DOS application that cannot run under OS/2, since it accesses hardware directly. Bob is really interested in Windows NT, since his brother-in-law uses it on the network at his own job. Should Bob take his brother-in-law's advice and implement Windows NT?	No, he should not install Windows NT. If Bob did take his brother-in-law's advice, then the legacy DOS application would not work. Windows 98 is the appropriate operating system choice.

Planning the Environment

Microsoft has a standard methodology for deploying Windows operating systems in a networked environment. Usually this process is documented in the Resource Kit. The basic phases are:

1. Assemble resources
2. Identify the preferred client configuration
3. Prepare the planning and support teams
4. Perform lab tests of the client configuration
5. Plan and conduct the pilot rollout
6. Finalize the rollout plan
7. Conduct the final rollout

Assemble Resources

This phase starts the deployment project by gathering the information and resources required for implementation. Resources include the teams required to plan, execute, and support the deployment. Assembling resources also means gathering the Windows 98 software, Resource Kit, and training materials that will be needed.

Identify the Client Configuration

During this phase, the planning team must decide which Windows 98 applets will be installed. The team must also decide how networking will function, and which protocols, remote access features, and printing support to use. The hardware that Windows 98 will be installed on must be reviewed for compliance with minimum hardware requirements. Any hardware that must be upgraded should be identified.

Prepare the Teams

During this phase, training for Windows 98 should be provided for the planning and support teams.

Perform Lab Tests

Using a representative set of hardware and network setups, the preferred client configuration should be tested, and adjusted as necessary. This phase includes automating the installation process using the Windows 98 batch process, SMS, or third-party automation tools.

Plan and Conduct the Pilot Rollout

The pilot rollout is a small group of users who agree to have their computers deployed before the rest of the project computers. Before the pilot rollout, the users must be trained. This group should be monitored for feedback. That feedback should then be used to make any adjustments to the Windows 98 configuration.

Finalize the Rollout Plan

Depending on the feedback from the pilot group, this phase may include a revisit to the lab to change and improve the Windows 98 configuration. Once that is completed, the planning team should finalize a strategy for rolling out Windows 98 to the remaining computers.

Conduct the Final Rollout

This phase is simply the process of training the users and deploying Windows 98.

File System

Part of choosing the client configuration includes deciding which file system, FAT or FAT32, should be used.

FAT is a file system that can be used in DOS, UNIX, Windows 95, Windows 98, Windows NT, and OS/2. Any one of these operating systems can read a partition formatted in the FAT file system. FAT works by dividing the hard disk partition into clusters. Data is then filed into each cluster. When a file is being retrieved, FAT searches for the location of the clusters in which its data is stored.

A cluster is only able to store data from a single file. Any file that is larger than a single cluster will span clusters until it has been completely stored. Any space in a cluster that does not contain data is wasted. FAT cannot exist on a partition larger than 2GB. FAT clusters scale in size with the hard disk. The larger the hard disk, the larger the cluster. On a 2GB drive, a cluster is 32KB in size. With larger clusters, more disk space is wasted.

FAT32 is an upgrade to the FAT file system that is available in Windows 98. It was created to address the hard disks larger than 2GB, which have become common. FAT32 can format a hard disk larger than 2GB in a single partition. FAT32 also uses space on the hard disk more efficiently by using smaller cluster sizes. (That same 2GB drive will have 4KB clusters when formatted with FAT32.)

Converting an existing FAT hard disk to FAT32 will recover wasted free space. The only way to use FAT32 when upgrading to Windows 98 is to use the Drive Converter (FAT32) utility, shown in Figure 1-7, to convert FAT to FAT32.

FAT32 cannot be read by any operating systems other than Windows 98 and Windows 95/OSR2. The upcoming Windows NT 5.0 should be able to read a FAT32 drive, but Windows NT 4.0 cannot.

FIGURE 1-7

FAT32 converter

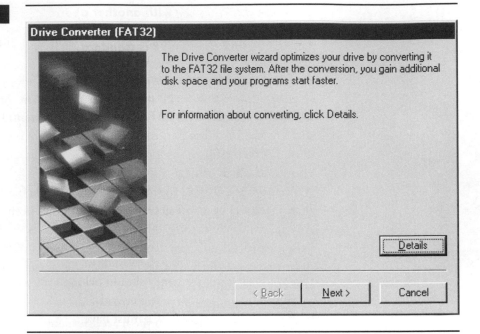

Here are two examples of the kinds of file system problems you may face on the Windows 98 exam.

QUESTIONS AND ANSWERS

After installing Windows 98, the PC can no longer be booted from a disk.	This is a symptom of installing Windows 98 on a FAT32 hard disk partition. Boot disks are formatted with the FAT system, and can only boot a FAT hard disk.
Before upgrading Windows 95 to Windows 98, the PC was able to dual boot between Windows 95 and Windows NT 4.0, which were installed on two different hard disk partitions. Files were stored on both partitions and could be read from either one of them. After upgrading the Windows 95 partition to Windows 98, and then booting into Windows NT, no files can be seen on the partition that Windows 98 is installed on. The PC can boot into Windows 98 and read all files on both partitions.	The partition with Windows 98 was converted to FAT32. Windows NT cannot read a partition formatted with the FAT32 file system. Windows 98 can read the Windows NT partition, since it must be formatted in FAT, especially if it was readable by Windows 95.

If you are dual booting with another operating system, and need access to the files on the entire hard disk, then the only choice for a file system for Windows 98 is standard FAT. This is because DOS, OS/2, UNIX, Windows 3.x, Windows 9x and Windows NT (all versions) can all access a FAT partition. If there is more than one partition, and access to the Windows 98 partition is not required from the other operating system, then FAT32 can be chosen as the file system.

Workgroup

Networking among two or more Windows 98 PCs is called Peer to Peer networking. Networking requires the PCs to have some sort of network interface and network transport. The interface and transport are provided by network interface cards and network hardware, such as cabling and hubs, or wireless ports. To enable the Windows 98 PCs to see each other in the Network Neighborhood, they should belong to the same workgroup and have the Client for Microsoft Networks installed. To share files and printers, the Windows 98 PCs must have the service installed for file and printer sharing.

The name of the Windows 98 PC must be unique on a network.

EXERCISE 1-1

Installing Networking and Identifying the Name of the Workgroup

1. Double-click the network icon in the Control Panel. Most adapters are detected by Windows 98 and automatically installed with default Client for Microsoft Networks and default TCP/IP protocols, so an adapter, protocol, and client should already be present.

2. In order to change or add a different client, adapter, service, or protocol, click the Add button.

3. Select the appropriate option (client, adapter, protocol, and services) and click Add. In the resulting dialog box, choose the correct type of client, service, adapter, or protocol. For instance, to add ATM support, select Protocol and click Add. Then select Microsoft in the left panel, and ATM LAN Emulation Client in the right panel.

To change the name of the PC or the name of the workgroup:

1. Double-click the Network icon in the Control Panel.

2. Click the Identification tab.

3. Change the names as needed.

4. Click OK and reboot.

When a Windows 98 PC participates in a Windows NT network, it also requires that the workgroup name is the same as the name of the Windows NT domain that the PC will be participating in. Also, the properties of the Client for Microsoft Networks must be changed to enable the workstation to log on to the Windows NT domain.

CERTIFICATION OBJECTIVE 1.04

Security Strategy

Another determination that must be made for the client configuration is how to implement security on the Windows 98 PCs. Windows 98 contains several options and utilities to manage the security of PCs.

- System policies
- User profiles
- File and printer sharing
- Share-level or user-level access control

System Policies

System policies allow an administrator to specify both default and individual settings for users and computers on the network. The System Policy Editor originally was introduced with Windows 95. It has been updated for use with Windows NT 4.0, and now Windows 98. System policies are not limited to individual users, but can be applied to groups of users as well.

When System Policy Editor is started, the administrator is presented with two icons, a Default Computer and a Default User. Double-clicking either of these icons presents the administrator with a tree structure of settings that can be checked off or edited. Figure 1-8 shows such a display for the Default User. Settings for specific users or computers can be added so that settings can be individualized. What the System Policy Editor does is edit the Registry (in the HKEY_CURRENT_USER hive for a user, and in the HKEY_LOCAL_MACHINE hive for a computer) to apply the settings chosen in its interface.

In order for the Registry settings to be applied to a Windows 98 PC, the PC must be configured to automatically read the policy file. System policies

FIGURE 1-8

System policies

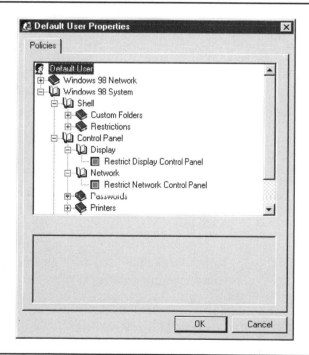

require that users have individual user profiles on the PC. The System Policy Editor can open up the local Registry and make changes directly to the Windows 98 Registry.

Note that when editing the default settings, please be careful to create a policy for the administrator, allowing Registry editing tools, before disabling Registry editing tools for default users. Otherwise, the administrator may not be able to change settings in the Registry in the future.

EXERCISE 1-2

Creating System Policies for a Specific User or Computer (Instead of Using Default Settings)

1. Open System Policy Editor.

2. Click the Edit menu, and select either Add User or Add Computer.

3. Type the name of the user or computer you want to add. An icon for each user or computer added will appear alongside the default icons.

To edit system policies for a computer or user:

1. In System Policy Editor, double-click the icon for the user or computer to be edited.

2. Expand the tree of options to view the policy options.

3. Select or clear the policy check box by clicking.

User Profiles

User Profiles is the means by which multiple users can have individual settings, such as different color schemes and wallpaper, on the same PC. In a networked environment, it is possible to configure profiles to download from a user's home directory, no matter where he logs on. These profiles are called roaming profiles.

EXERCISE 1-3

Enable User Profiles

1. Double-click the Passwords icon in the Control Panel.

2. Click the User Profiles tab. This brings up the window shown in Figure 1-9.

3. Select the option that states "Users can customize their preferences and desktop settings. Windows switches to your personal settings when you log on."

4. If the user profile should include desktop items and Network Neighborhood settings, check that selection.

5. If the user profile should include the Start menu and program groups, then check that selection.

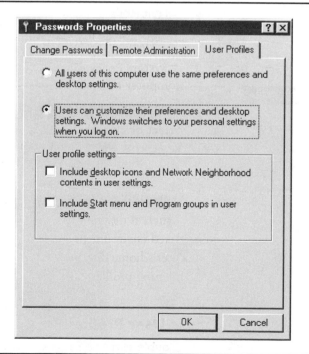

File and Print Sharing

The ability to share files and printers with other computers is the very premise of networking. Mapping a network drive or connecting to a network printer can give you access to these resources. To enable file and printer sharing, several items must be installed in the Network icon of the Control Panel:

■ **Client**   Client for Microsoft Networks or Client for NetWare Networks.

■ **Adapter**   The correct adapter for whatever network interface card is installed on the PC.

■ **Protocol**   Any protocol supported by the client will work, but if networking includes Internet access, select TCP/IP. If networking includes NetWare, select IPX/SPX-Compatible Protocol.

■ **Services**   From the window shown in Figure 1-10, select File and Printer Sharing for Microsoft Networks if using the Client for

---

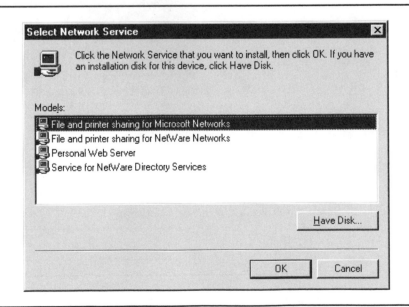

FIGURE 1-10

File and printer sharing

Microsoft Networks. Select File and Printer Sharing for NetWare
Networks if using the Client for NetWare Networks.

Sharing Out a File or a Directory

1. Open Windows Explorer or My Computer and navigate to find the file or directory.

2. Right-click on the item and select Sharing.

3. Click on the Shared As option and type in a name for the share.

4. Select Full access if network users will be granted the ability to change, add, or delete files. Select Read Only access if network users will be granted the ability to see the files and open them but not change or delete them. Select Depends on Password if some network users need read only access and others need full access.

5. Apply passwords in the Read Only Password and Full Password, if Depends on Password is selected or if a password is desired.

In order to share a printer on a network, open the Printers folder and right-click the selected printer. Choose Sharing. Type in a name, comment and password if desired.

Share-Level or User-Level Access Control

The choice of share-level or user-level access control will depend on the type of network on which Windows 98 exists. Figure 1-11 shows the Access Control tab under Network, where you make the selection.

Share-level access control can be used on any type of network, including Peer to Peer networks, where a Windows 98 PC shares files with other Windows 98 PCs. On a share-level access control share, the share can have a password applied to it. When a user accesses the shared resource, he must know the password that has been assigned to that resource.

User-level access control can be used on a NetWare network or on a Microsoft NT Domain network. In a user-level access control setup, shares can be granted to specific users (or groups) that have their own passwords in NetWare or on the NT Domain. When a user accesses the shared resource,

FIGURE 1-11

Share-level or user-level access

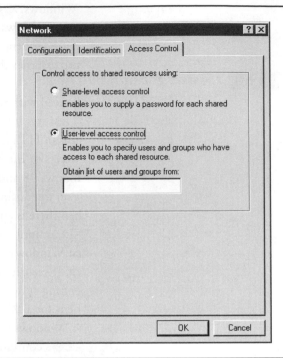

he supplies his own name and password. The PC allows access to the resource if that particular user has been granted access.

CERTIFICATION SUMMARY

On the hardware side, new Windows 98 features include support for new hardware devices such as FireWire, USB, AGP, DVD, Infrared, FAT32 and multiple monitors. Windows 98 includes drivers for these devices natively so that when the operating system or the hardware is installed, it can use the drivers in the Windows 98 source files and work "out of the box."

Maintenance features are improved for Windows 98 with the enhanced system tools and utilities, including a Registry Checker, System Configuration Utility, and a Maintenance Wizard.

Networking features in Windows 98 have been added to include more networking hardware support and improved remote access features like multilink channel aggregation.

The setup process for Windows 98 has been enhanced so that it is faster than the one that came with Windows 95. The setup process no longer includes a hardware detection sequence if upgrading Windows 95 to Windows 98. Instead, setup assumes that the Windows 95 drivers have been installed correctly.

The GUI has been enhanced with the addition of the Internet Explorer and Active Desktop. GUI features include single-click access to files and folders, the capability to use an HTML page as the desktop wallpaper, and an address box for direct access to Internet resources in the toolbar.

Choosing between Windows 98 and Windows NT as the client operating system depends on the business requirements of the enterprise making this decision. When there is a need for applications that access the hardware directly, use VXD technology. If the hardware is a type supported only by Windows 98, then Windows 98 will normally be the best choice for the client operating system. If security is critical, then Windows NT will be the appropriate client operating system choice.

Planning the environment for a Windows 98 rollout will influence the client configuration of the Windows 98 operating system. Two of the main decisions to be made about the configuration are the file system used and the networking features implemented. The file system can be either FAT or FAT32, and the decision to use one or the other is based on whether another operating system, such as DOS or Windows NT, will need to access the files on that partition in a floppy or dual-boot situation. Another factor in the FAT versus FAT32 decision is whether efficient use of space and the requirement of a single partition on a drive larger than 2GB exist. Networking features can allow the PC to access files and printers on a network or even to share local resources to other networked users.

The security strategy for Windows 98 is a combination of user profiles, system policies, file and printer sharing, and share-level or user-level access control. This will influence the client configuration, depending on the security strategy taken.

System policies allow an administrator to manage multiple networked PCs and users through the use of a System Policy Editor. Default settings can be used, or individual settings can be applied to users or computers.

User Profiles allow an individual to maintain separate settings from other users of the same PC.

Resources can be shared by installing the service for file and printer sharing. When sharing resources, share-level access can always be utilized. However, in network environments with NT domains or NetWare servers, user-level access can be used so that a user's name and password is authenticated to the appropriate server at the time the resource is being accessed.

TWO-MINUTE DRILL

❑ Windows 98 comes with a multitude of new wizards and system utilities such as:

  ❑ Update Wizard

  ❑ Maintenance Wizard

  ❑ System Information

❑ Microsoft redesigned the Windows 98 setup process.

❑ Windows 98 includes support for many new hardware devices.

❑ Active Desktop includes accessing applications with a single click, floating toolbars on top of the desktop, and using an HTML page as desktop wallpaper.

❑ The Active Desktop represents an extension of the World Wide Web.

❑ Windows 98 makes it easier than ever to log on and exchange data with many different types of network operating systems.

❑ Some of the protocols that Windows 98 supports include TCP/IP, IPX/SPX-Compatible protocol, DLC, Infrared, ISDN, and ATM networking. TCP/IP is usually associated with Internet access. IPX/SPX-compatible protocol can be used to access NetWare file servers. DLC can be used for both mainframe access and HP JetDirect print-sharing devices. Infrared is used for file and printing between a Windows 98 PC with an infrared port, and another infrared device—either a PC or printer. Integrated Services Digital Network (ISDN) is a fast, digital remote access method available from many local phone companies. Asynchronous Transfer Mode (ATM) networking is a high-speed protocol used in both local area networks (LANs) and wide area networks (WANs).

❑ There are several critical areas to look at when deciding between Windows 98 and Windows NT:

   ❑ Hardware

   ❑ Applications that access hardware directly

   ❑ Applications that use VXD technology

   ❑ File system

   ❑ Security

❑ The exam questions on this subject tend to be tricky, listing one or two requirements that may lead a business to believe either one of the operating systems should be selected as the client.

❑ Microsoft has a standard methodology for deploying Windows operating systems in a networked environment. The basic phases are:

   ❑ Assemble resources

   ❑ Identify the preferred client configuration

   ❑ Prepare the planning and support teams

   ❑ Perform lab tests of the client configuration

   ❑ Plan and conduct the pilot rollout

   ❑ Finalize the rollout plan

   ❑ Conduct the final rollout

❑ FAT is a file system that can be used in DOS, UNIX, Windows 95, Windows 98, Windows NT, and OS/2.

❑ FAT32 is an upgrade to the FAT file system that is available in Windows 98.

❑ The only way to use FAT32 when upgrading to Windows 98 is to use the Drive Converter (FAT32) utility.

❑ If you are dual booting with another operating system, and need access to the files on the entire hard disk, then the only choice for a file system for Windows 98 is standard FAT. This is because DOS, OS/2, UNIX, Windows 3.*x*, Windows 9*x* and Windows NT (all versions) can all access a FAT partition. If there is more than one partition, and access to the Windows 98 partition is not required from the other operating system, then FAT32 can be chosen as the file system.

❑ Networking among two or more Windows 98 PCs is called Peer to Peer networking.

❑ Windows 98 contains several options and utilities to manage the security of PCs:

  ❑ System policies

  ❑ User profiles

  ❑ File and printer sharing

  ❑ Share-level or user-level access control

❑ System policies allow an administrator to specify both default and individual settings for users and computers on the network.

❑ When System Policy Editor is started, the administrator is presented with two icons, a Default Computer and a Default User.

❑ User Profiles is the means by which multiple users can have individual settings, such as different color schemes and wallpaper, on the same PC.

❑ In a networked environment, it is possible to configure profiles to download from a user's home directory, no matter where she logs on. These profiles are called roaming profiles.

❑ To enable file and printer sharing, several items must be installed in the Network icon of the Control Panel:

  ❑ Client

  ❑ Adapter

  ❑ Protocol

  ❑ Services

❑ Share-level access control can be used on any type of network, including Peer to Peer networks, where a Windows 98 PC shares files with other Windows 98 PCs.

❑ User-level access control can be used on a NetWare network or on a Microsoft NT Domain network.

SELF TEST

The following Self Test questions will help you measure your understanding of the material presented in this chapter. Read all the choices carefully, as there may be more than one correct answer. Choose all correct answers for each question.

1. Which of the following is not a feature of Windows 98?

    A. Support for Digital Video/Virtual Disk

    B. Support for the IEEE 1394 specification, a.k.a. FireWire

    C. Support for NTFS file system

    D. Support for Accelerated Graphics Ports

2. FAT32 is a feature of Windows 98 that can:

    A. Be read by Windows NT 4.0 in a dual boot partition

    B. Efficiently use space on the hard disk due to the smaller cluster size

    C. Boot an OS/2 PC

    D. Be installed on a drive that is 32 times smaller in size than a typical FAT hard disk

3. In order to use two monitors to increase desktop space, how must the hardware be configured?

    A. A laptop with a monitor plugged into the Video port

    B. Two monitors plugged into the same AGP port

    C. Two monitors plugged into an AGP port and a legacy standard 16-color VGA port

    D. Two monitors plugged into two separate PCI video adapter cards

4. If Windows 98 is installed on a PC with a Universal Serial Bus, and a new USB device is added to that PC, what is the process for installing the new USB device?

    A. Simply plug in the device to the USB and power, and install the drivers.

    B. Windows 98 must be powered down, the device plugged into power and into the USB. Then, when Windows 98 is powered on again, install the drivers.

    C. First, install the drivers and power Windows 98 down. Then plug in the device into the USB and the power. Then power up Windows 98 and the drivers will select the correct settings.

    D. It can't be done. Windows 98 does not support USB devices.

5. PhysInc is a group of medical doctors networked via frame relay. They have all decided to upgrade their systems to be identical to the other doctors' systems, in order to share and reduce their administration costs. There will be no data stored on local hard disks; all critical

and secure files are stored on NetWare file servers. Some doctors have requested AGP hardware in order to implement faster video-conferencing. Some doctors want Windows NT 4.0 and others have asked about Windows 98. Which is the better client operating system?

A. Windows NT 4.0, since there are critical secure files

B. Windows 98, since it supports frame relay directly

C. Windows NT 4.0, since it supports AGP hardware

D. Windows 98, since it supports AGP hardware

6. MovieFun is a family-owned company that runs theaters across the entire state of Arizona. Each theater has a workstation that dials into the main office to update the SQL database with the day's receipts. The theater is concerned about the security of the files on the workstations in the remote theaters, since there was an incident in which one receipts file had been changed by an as-yet-unknown hacker in order to embezzle funds. MovieFun is upgrading all its workstations in order to prevent further hacker attacks. Which is the better client, Windows 98 or Windows NT 4.0?

A. Windows 98, since MovieFun will probably use DVD

B. Windows NT 4.0, since MovieFun uses a SQL database

C. Windows 98, since MovieFun uses a SQL database

D. Windows NT 4.0, since MovieFun must secure their receipts files on local hard disks

7. Gary is a new administrator with the task of upgrading all his dual-boot PCs from OS/2 and DOS to OS/2 and Windows 98 on the same partition. In the past, all files were shared between both DOS and OS/2 without a problem. Hard disks are getting crowded, and Gary wants to know if he can convert all the Windows 98 systems to FAT32 to conserve space.

A. Yes, converting the drives to FAT32 will conserve space

B. No, even though conversion will save space, OS/2 will not work

C. No, space will be wasted since OS/2 uses FAT32 differently than Windows 98

D. Yes, FAT is the same thing as FAT32 and OS/2 supports FAT

8. Ron wants to share a file with other NetWare users on his NetWare network. What must he do if he is running Windows 98?

A. Nothing, all files are shared automatically with NetWare

B. He must install the service for file and printer sharing on Microsoft networks, since Windows 98 is a Microsoft product

C. He must install the service for file and printer sharing on NetWare Networks, in addition to the Client for NetWare Networks, the appropriate adapter, and IPX/SPX protocol, and then configure user-level access control, and finally must create the shares and grant access to them

D. Ron cannot share files with NetWare users in Windows 98

9. Which of the following security strategies can edit the local Registry of a Windows 98 PC?

A. System Policy Editor

B. User Profiles

C. File and Printer Sharing

D. User-level or share-level access control

10. When accessing a Windows NT domain, where does the domain name get placed in the Control Panel?

A. In the Network icon of the Control Panel in the properties of the Protocol, and in the Workgroup space on the Identification tab of the same Network icon

B. In the Network icon of the Control Panel in the properties of the Adapter, and in the Name space on the Identification tab of the same Network icon

C. In the Network icon of the Control Panel in the properties of the Client, and in the Workgroup space on the Identification tab of the same Network icon

D. In the Network icon of the Control Panel in the properties of the Service, and in the Name space on the Identification tab of the same Network icon

MICROSOFT CERTIFIED SYSTEMS ENGINEER

2

Installing and Configuring Windows 98

Now that they have reviewed the installation procedures for Windows 98, Windows 95 experts all over the world are breathing sighs of relief, grinning, giggling, or simply laughing out loud. The minimal administration efforts promoted by Microsoft had them worried for awhile that the need for their expertise was being eliminated. But no matter how easy-to-use computers have become, they still need someone to decide the configuration that is needed, to set the configuration, to plan the deployment, to deploy and to support them. Windows 95 needed experts to handle these tasks, and Windows 98 needs them, too.

Besides, figuring out what's going on behind the installation process is part of what makes being an expert fun!

Installing Windows 98

The installation process for Windows 98 is conceptually nearly identical to that for Windows 95. It follows a hardware detection procedure, a phase for gathering information about the machine and the network to which it is attached, a phase for selecting the optional components, and the file copying phase.

Even though the installation follows the same process, enhancements have been made to the Windows 98 Setup program. Windows 95's setup program used to stop unpredictably in the middle of the hardware-detection phase or during the file copying phase. There was not much of an explanation for this behavior, and the only fix was to reboot. Windows 98 is far less likely to stop during these phases. When prompted for information, the installer is presented with fewer prompts, which speeds that phase up some. And when doing an upgrade from Windows 95 to Windows 98, hardware detection can be skipped; SETUP simply accepts the Windows 95 configuration as correct, then upgrades the hardware drivers. Figure 2-1 shows the first screen of Windows 98 Setup.

FIGURE 2-1

Windows 98 Setup

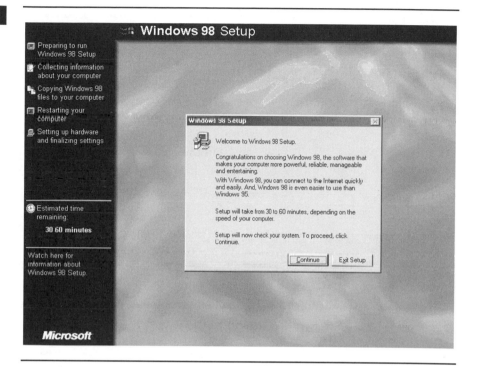

The Setup Wizard is used to manually install Windows 98. SETUP will prompt for selections and information in the wizard dialog boxes. Among other decisions, the installer must decide whether to install Windows 98 into the default directory of C:\WINDOWS, or to select a different directory. If the name of a directory that does not exist is provided, the Setup Wizard creates that directory.

The Setup Wizard includes a dialog for selecting the components that are installed as part of Windows 98. There are four types of setup that can be chosen. Each type includes a set of default optional components.

- **Typical**   Includes the set of the most common optional components.
- **Portable**   Includes options typically required for laptops.

- **Compact** Installs only the minimum required components to have the smallest possible footprint (used hard disk space). This setup option does not install optional components. The optional components can only be added after the Windows 98 installation is complete, through the Add/Remove Components icon in the Control Panel.

- **Custom** Installs whichever optional components the installer selects from the provided list. This option includes all the Typical default optional components (see Table 2-1), but proceeds directly to a screen from which the user can select the components to include or exclude.

TABLE 2-1   Default Optional Components

Group	Optional Component	Typical	Portable	Compact	Custom
Accessibility	Accessibility Options	X	X	X	X
	Accessibility Tools				
Accessories	Briefcase		X		
	Calculator	X			X
	Desktop Wallpaper				
	Document Templates	X			X
	Games				
	Imaging	X			X
	Mouse Pointers				
	Paint	X			X
	Quick View				
	Screen Savers	X			X
	Windows Scripting Host	X	X		X
	WordPad	X	X		X
Communications	Dial Up Networking	X	X	X	X

TABLE 2-1	Default Optional Components (*continued*)				
Group	**Optional Component**	**Typical**	**Portable**	**Compact**	**Custom**
	Dial Up Server				
	Direct Cable Connection		X		
	HyperTerminal		X		
	Microsoft Chat 2.1				
	Microsoft NetMeeting	X			X
	Phone Dialer	X	X		X
	Virtual Private Networking		X		
Desktop Themes	17 Desktop Themes				
Internet Tools	MS Frontpage Express	X	X		X
	MS VRML 2.0 Viewer				
	MS Wallet				
	Personal Web Server	X	X		X
	Real Audio Player 4				
	Web Publishing Wizard				
	WebBased Enterprise Mgmt				
Outlook Express	Outlook Express	X	X		X
MultiLanguage Support	Baltic				
	Central European				
	Cyrillic				
	Greek				
	Turkish				
Multimedia	Audio Compression	X	X	X	X

TABLE 2-1   Default Optional Components (*continued*)

Group	Optional Component	Typical	Portable	Compact	Custom
	CD Player	X	X	X	X
	Macromedia Shockwave Director	X			X
	Macromedia Shockwave Flash	X			X
	Media Player	X	X		X
	MS Netshow Player 2.0				
	Multimedia Sound Schemes				
	Sample Sounds				
	Sound Recorder	X	X		X
	Video Compression	X	X		X
	Volume Control	X	X		X
Online Services	America Online	X	X	X	X
	AT&T WorldNet Service	X	X	X	X
	CompuServe	X	X	X	X
	Prodigy Internet	X	X	X	X
	The Microsoft Network	X	X	X	X
System Tools	Backup				
	Character Map				
	Clipboard Viewer				
	Disk Compression Tools	X	X	X	X
	Drive Converter FAT32	X	X	X	X

| TABLE 2-1 | Default Optional Components *(continued)* |

Group	Optional Component	Typical	Portable	Compact	Custom
	Group Policies				
	Net Watcher				
	System Monitor				
	System Resource Meter				
WebTV	WaveTop Data Broadcasting				
	WebTV for Windows				

exam
ⓦatch

The Portable setup includes the optional components that are most likely to be required on a laptop, including Virtual Private Networking and Hyperterminal.

In the Custom version of Setup, the Setup Wizard includes a dialog box where the installer can select optional components. Optional components are arranged in groups. For instance, the Communications group includes both Hyperterminal and Microsoft Chat, as well as other communications components. Clicking the Details button will display the items included in a group of optional components. When selecting or deselecting an optional component, the Setup Wizard will display the space requirements for that component. The Setup Wizard will also display the total space requirements and the space available on the hard disk so that the installer may compare them.

The Setup Wizard includes a dialog box for the name of the computer. This name is called a NetBIOS name, since it is used in networks that use the NetBIOS protocol. The maximum number of characters for a computer name is 15, and it cannot include any blank spaces. This name will identify the computer on a network. Computer names should be unique on a network.

The Setup Wizard also allows the installer to create an emergency startup disk. This step copies key configuration and system files to a disk that can be used to diagnose or fix Windows 98 if there is a system error that prevents Windows 98 from booting. The emergency startup disk is a handy item to use if an error corrupts one of the configuration or system files.

After all the information has been gathered, the Setup Wizard will reboot the PC.

Preparing for the Installation

Understand how Windows 98 installs before running the installation. The prerequisites for Windows 98 installation must be considered and compared to the existing hardware and software. This will determine whether or not an installation can even occur.

The prerequisites for Windows 98 installation are:

- **Operating System**   Windows 95, Windows 3.1x, access to the DOS command prompt
- **Processor**   486DX2, 66 Mhz or higher
- **Hard Disk**   Minimum 110MB free space
- **RAM**   16MB
- **Monitor**   VGA or higher resolution
- **Floppy Drive**   high-density, 3.5-inch floppy disk drive
- **Mouse**   Microsoft mouse or compatible pointing device
- **CD-ROM or Network Drive**   For use when installing from CD or a network

The Microsoft Web site at http://www.microsoft.com/hwtest/hcl has the Windows 98 Hardware Compatibility List. This list is updated with hardware components that have been tested and that meet the Windows 98 requirements.

The Windows 98 Setup must run from a CD-ROM, floppy disk, or a network share that has the Windows 98 source files. If the installer wishes to create an emergency startup disk (a blank, high-density, 3.5-inch disk) is required.

One important preparation step is to back up the files on the PC. Backing up files is critically important in case an installation fails. The fact of the matter is that an installation's success or failure cannot be predicted, even if success had occurred on identical hardware previously. Power surges, network errors, hard disk errors and problems with the installation media are some examples of unpredictable events that can cause Windows 98 installations to fail.

There are several tools and utilities available for backing up files. If you are using MS-DOS with or without Windows 3.1, there is a backup utility included in the DOS directory. If you are using Windows 95, there is a backup utility included in the System Tools under Accessories. If the backup tool does not show up in this group, it can be added using the Add/Remove Programs icon in the Control Panel. If the PC is connected to a network drive, the files can simply be copied to the network as a form of backing them up. There are also many third-party backup utility programs available.

In order to avoid installation failures due to hard disk errors, another preparation step should be to clean out unnecessary files from the hard disk, check the hard disk for errors, and defragment the hard disk. This step is unnecessary if installing Windows 98 on a newly formatted hard disk.

And finally, before running the Windows 98 Setup, the installer should scan the PC's hard disk for viruses and clean them. Viruses can cause the installation to fail.

Installing from Windows 95

Simply placing the Windows 98 CD-ROM into a Windows 95 CD-ROM drive will prompt the user to install Windows 98. This behavior results from an AUTORUN.INF file that is included in the root of the CD-ROM. Windows 95's default behavior runs any CD-ROM or other disk with an AUTORUN.INF automatically upon access of the drive.

(NOTE: The default behavior for accessing data or audio CDs automatically can be changed through a Registry edit or through the use of Tweak UI, a Windows 9*x* utility included in the Powertoy utilities that are freely downloadable from Microsoft's Web site. If this change has been made, the workstation may not automatically prompt for the Windows 98 installation. To start the installation, double-click the CD-ROM drive in My Computer. That should run the AUTORUN.INF file.)

Information for a Windows 95 upgrade to Windows 98 can be taken automatically from the existing Windows 95 configuration. SETUP will automatically transfer the current system settings and the upgrade will allow use of existing installed applications.

The process of upgrading Windows 95 to Windows 98 is as follows:

Before starting, the files on the workstation should already be backed up, unnecessary files should be deleted, and the hard disk should be checked for errors and defragmented.

The installer should begin by booting the PC into Windows 95. Once Windows 95 is started, the installer should shut down any open programs. These programs include TSRs (Terminate and Stay Resident programs) that are started in the AUTOEXEC.BAT file, anti-virus programs, and any other applications. To view what applications are running, press CTRL-ALT-DEL to bring up the Close Program dialog box, shown in Figure 2-2. Then click any task listed that should be closed, and click the End Task button.

The next step is to gain access to the Windows 98 source files. These files can be located on the Windows 98 CD-ROM, or they may be on a set of floppy disks, or they can be located on a network drive.

From the Run dialog box located on the Start menu (shown in Figure 2-3), the installer should type the drive letter for the CD, the floppy disk, or the network drive where the Windows 98 source files are located, followed by a colon, a backslash, and SETUP. If the source files are located on drive D, the command looks like this: D:\SETUP. Clicking OK will begin the Windows 98 Setup Wizard.

exam Watch

The upgrade to Windows 98 from Windows 95 can skip the hardware detection phase. It takes existing settings and drivers and upgrades them.

Close Program dialog box

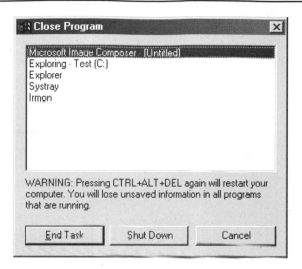

Installing from MS-DOS and Windows 3.1*x*

Windows 98 includes a Windows 3.*x* upgrade process. When upgrading from Windows 3.1 to Windows 98, the Setup Wizard presents the same screens as a fresh installation, except for the option to back up system files in case there is a need to uninstall Windows 98.

To begin the upgrade, the installer should boot into Windows 3.1*x*. All applications should be closed before starting the upgrade. Clicking the File

Run command line

Windows 3.1 Run
command line

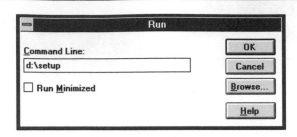

menu and the Run option in Program Manager opens the Run Command
Line dialog box, shown in Figure 2-4. The installer should type in the path
and directory structure where the Windows 98 Setup source files are
located. If installing from CD-ROM, this would most likely be D:\SETUP.
After you click OK the Setup Wizard begins.

The first screen displayed is the Welcome screen. Pressing ENTER
prompts the Setup Wizard to check the system. This is comparable to the
DOS SCANDISK, except that it runs in GUI mode.

If any programs are running, the dialog box shown in Figure 2-5
prompts the installer to close them.

The next screen displayed is the License screen. This dialog box is the
legal acceptance of the license for Windows 98. To avoid this screen, there
is a switch /IW that can be added at the end of the SETUP command.

Close Programs dialog box

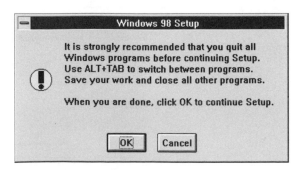

After the License screen, the installer is prompted for the directory to place Windows 98 in. The default is C:\WINDOWS, to upgrade the Windows 3.1x version.

After selecting the directory, the Setup Wizard prompts the installer to save system files in order to enable uninstalling Windows 98.

The installer is then presented with the four types of setup—Typical, Portable, Compact and Custom. Each option leads to screens allowing the installer to select which optional components to install.

The next screen presented allows the installer to name the computer and the workgroup, and provide a computer description. The computer's name must be unique on a network. In order to browse a particular NT domain, the workgroup should be named the same as the NT domain name. Since this is an upgrade, the name of the computer is taken from the username used in the computer's WIN.INI file. The default workgroup name is WORKGROUP.

Computer settings for the keyboard and language are presented next, and then the installer is prompted to create an emergency startup disk. The installer is not given the option to NOT create the disk. However, clicking the Cancel button on the Insert Disk dialog box shown in Figure 2-6 prevents the creation of one. To create a startup disk later on, the installer may use the Add/Remove Programs icon in the Control Panel and select the Startup Disk tab.

At this point, Windows 98 files are copied to the hard disk. The Setup Wizard includes an estimate of time for the file copying process.

FIGURE 2-6

Emergency startup disk prompt

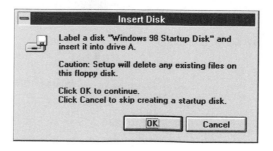

After the files are copied, the Setup Wizard restarts the computer. At reboot, the wizard searches for the hardware components on the PC. A dialog box asks if the installer is using a PCMCIA card in order to install Windows 98 over the network. The implications of this question are that if the installer is using a PCMCIA card, the PCMCIA card 32-bit drivers cannot be installed until later, since the real-mode drivers must be disabled before the 32-bit drivers can be used. If you disable them at this point in the installation, the installation will fail.

The final setup dialog box is for the installer to select the time zone, and set or verify the time, after which the Setup Wizard restarts the PC.

One advantage the Windows 98 Setup has over the Windows 95 Setup is that the installer is not requested for a name and password until after Windows 98 is completely installed. With Windows 95, the installer used to be forced to set a username and password in order to log on during installation reboots.

Windows 98 can be installed from a command prompt in DOS. In fact, it can even be installed using a freshly formatted hard disk booted from a DOS floppy disk. This method is most common in enterprise deployments of workstation operating systems. This method will also make Windows 98 the default operating system.

If running SETUP from DOS, there are no existing settings from which the setup process can gather settings. The installer is prompted with an additional dialog box for the name and organization of the user. The computer name will be created from the first name and first initial of the last name of the user placed in this box, when the dialog box for computer name and workgroup appears.

Windows Batch Setup

Microsoft Batch 98 is the program created by Microsoft to help create the files required for Windows 98 automated setup. Microsoft Batch 98 is included in the Windows 98 Resource Kit. The Microsoft Batch 98 screen is shown in Figure 2-7.

The Batch 98 program allows the installer to gather the settings on the current PC. This is significant if the installer has created the preferred client

FIGURE 2-7

Microsoft Batch 98

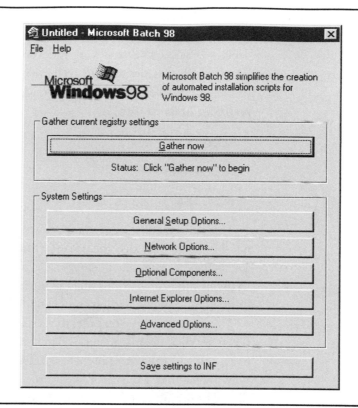

configuration that she wants to deploy enterprise-wide. If not, then the installer will need to review and change settings.

It is highly recommended that the installer review the settings. There are additional options within Batch 98 that can be turned on to enhance the deployment process. These include the ability to delete the online services icons from the desktop, turn off the Welcome screen, create different printer settings, and set Internet options that are not given as options in the standard Windows 98 setup process.

Once the settings are deemed acceptable, the installer can save them to an INF file. The default name for this file is MSBATCH.INF. The installer may wish to select a more appropriate name, especially if creating several INF files for different business units within the organization.

Multiple machine names were a problem in deploying Windows 95 enterprise-wide. The MSBATCH.INF file had to be changed for each PC deployed. Batch 98 includes an option to merge a text file that contains a list of machine names with an INF file in order to create a set of identical INF files with different machine names. The machine name text file would have a list of names such as:

BLDG1X770

BLDG1X771

BLDG2X803

This particular list of machine names represents a company with a naming convention that includes the building number concatenated with the phone extension. Each enterprise may have its own naming convention. Many naming conventions include the user's name, but that makes it difficult for moving, adding and changing users and PCs around.

To use the machine text file, the installer merely needs to have the INF file open, click the File menu in Batch 98, select Multiple Machine Name Save, and select the text file that includes the list of machine names. Batch 98 will then merge the text file with the INF file to create multiple INF files. The default text file name is MACHINE.TXT, but can be different. To create the machine name text file, the installer can use any text editor, including EDIT, or NOTEPAD.

Automated Windows Setup

Automated setup for Windows 98 uses an MSBATCH.INF file. This file can be created most easily by the Microsoft Batch 98 program, but can also be created using any text editor. A sample MSBATCH.INF file looks like this:

```
; MSBATCH.INF
;
; Copyright (c) 1995-1998 Microsoft Corporation.
; All rights reserved.
;
```

```
[BatchSetup]
Version=3.0 (32-bit)
SaveDate=04/15/98

[Version]
Signature = "$CHICAGO$"

[Setup]
Express=1
InstallDir="c:\windows"
InstallType=3
EBD=0
ShowEula=0
ChangeDir=0
OptionalComponents-1
Network=1
System=0
CCP=0
CleanBoot=0
Display=0
DevicePath=0
NoDirWarn=1
TimeZone="US Mountain"
Uninstall=0
VRC=0
NoPrompt2Boot=1

[System]
Locale=L0409
SelectedKeyboard=KEYBOARD_00000409
DisplChar=16,640,400

[NameAndOrg]
Name="Melissa Craft"
Org="Microage"
Display=0

[Network]
ComputerName="MMC188"
Workgroup="MCSA"
Description="Win98"
Display=0
PrimaryLogon=VREDIR
Clients=VREDIR
Protocols=MSTCP
```

```
Security=SHARE

[MSTCP]
LMHOSTS=1
LMHOSTPath="C:\WINDOWS\lmhosts"
DHCP=1
DNS=0
WINS=D

[VREDIR]
LogonDomain="MCSA"
ValidatedLogon=0

[OptionalComponents]
"Accessibility Options"=1
"Accessibility Tools"=1
"Briefcase"=0
"Calculator"=1
"Desktop Wallpaper"=1
"Document Templates"=1
"Games"=1
"Imaging"=1
"Mouse Pointers"=1
"Paint"=1
"Quick View"=1
"Windows Scripting Host"=1
"WordPad"=1
"Dial-Up Networking"=1
"Dial-Up Server"=1
"Direct Cable Connection"=1
"HyperTerminal"=1
"Baseball"=1
"Dangerous Creatures"=1
"Inside your Computer"=1
"Jungle"=1
"Leonardo da Vinci"=1
"More Windows"=1
"Mystery"=1
"Nature"=1
"Science"=1
"Space"=1
"Sports"=1
"The 60's USA"=1
"The Golden Era"=1
"Travel"=1
```

```
"Underwater"=1
"Windows 95"=1
"Desktop Themes Support"=1
"Microsoft FrontPage Express"=1
"Microsoft VRML 2.0 Viewer"=1
"Microsoft Wallet"=1
"Personal Web Server"=1
"Real Audio Player 4.0"=0
"Web Publishing Wizard"=1
"Web-Based Enterprise Mgmt"=1
"Microsoft Outlook Express"=1
"Baltic"=0
"Central European"=0
"Cyrillic"=0
"Greek"=0
"Turkish"=0
"Audio Compression"=1
"CD Player"=1
"America Online"=1
"AT&T WorldNet Service"=1
"CompuServe"=1
"Prodigy Internet"=1
"The Microsoft Network"=1
"Additional Screen Savers"=1
"Flying Windows"=1
"OpenGL Screen Savers"=1
"Backup"=1
"Character Map"=1
"Clipboard Viewer"=1
"TV Viewer"=0

[Printers]

[InstallLocationsMRU]
"D:\win98"
"D:\windows\"
"C:\WINDOWS\SYSTEM\PRECOPY\"
"D:\"

[Install]
AddReg=Run.Installed.Components

[Run.Installed.Components]
HKLM,%KEY_INSTALLEDCOMPS%,,,">Batch98"
HKLM,%KEY_INSTALLEDCOMPS%,IsInstalled,1,01,00,00,00
```

```
HKLM,%KEY_INSTALLEDCOMPS%,Version,,"1,0,0,0"
HKLM,%KEY_INSTALLEDCOMPS%,StubPath,,"%25%\rundll.exe
setupx.dll,InstallHinfSection Installed.Components 4 %10%\
msbatch.inf"

[Installed.Components]
AddReg=Browser.Settings

[Browser.Settings]
HKCU,%KEY_IEXPLORERMAIN%,"StartPage",,"http://home.microsoft.com"
HKLM,%KEY_IEXPLORERMAIN%,"Start
Page","http://www.microsoft.com/windows/memphis/default.asp"
HKCU,%KEY_IEXPLORERMAIN%,"Search
Page",,"http://home.microsoft.com/access/allinone.asp"
HKLM,%KEY_IEXPLORERMAIN%,"Search
Bar","http://home.microsoft.com/access/allinone.asp"
HKCU, "SOFTWARE\Microsoft\Internet
Explorer\Help_Menu_URLs",Online_Support,,"http://
support.microsoft.com/support""

[Strings]
KEY_INSTALLEDCOMPS="SOFTWARE\Microsoft\Active Setup\Installed
Components\BatchRun"
KEY_IEXPLORERMAIN="Software\Microsoft\Internet Explorer\Main"
```

FIGURE 2-8

SETUP switches and syntax

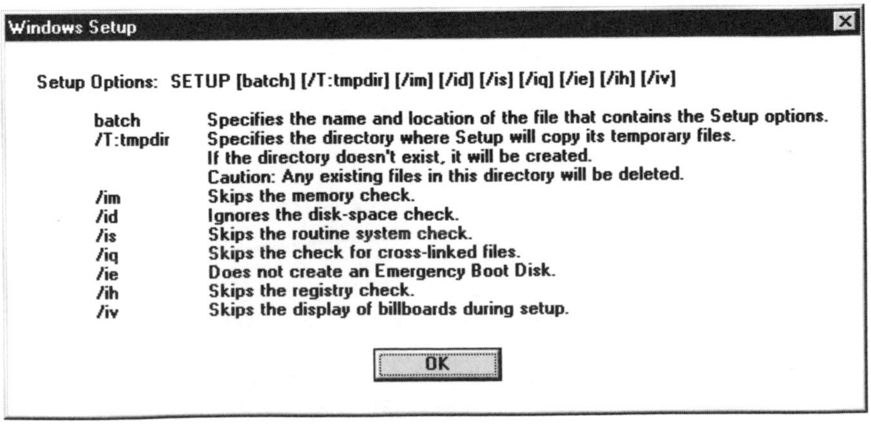

Windows Setup

Setup Options: SETUP [batch] [/T:tmpdir] [/im] [/id] [/is] [/iq] [/ie] [/ih] [/iv]

batch	Specifies the name and location of the file that contains the Setup options.
/T:tmpdir	Specifies the directory where Setup will copy its temporary files. If the directory doesn't exist, it will be created. Caution: Any existing files in this directory will be deleted.
/im	Skips the memory check.
/id	Ignores the disk-space check.
/is	Skips the routine system check.
/iq	Skips the check for cross-linked files.
/ie	Does not create an Emergency Boot Disk.
/ih	Skips the registry check.
/iv	Skips the display of billboards during setup.

OK

To invoke an automated installation, the installer must use switches with the SETUP program. The syntax is displayed in Figure 2-8. In Windows 95, there was also an undocumented switch /IW that skipped over the license agreement screen.

Here is a sample scenario of the decision making involved in setting up Windows 98. Questions on the exam might be in the form of such a scenario.

QUESTIONS AND ANSWERS

Colleen is rolling out Windows 98 enterprise-wide. Her pilot group consists of two business units: Accounting and Sales. She creates an MSBATCH.INF file and a MACHINE.TXT file, and does a multiple machine name save. Then she rolls out Windows 98. In the Accounting department she does not have to change anything. In the Sales department, however, she is forced to remove printers and add different ones, and then change the network properties on each PC, since they have a NetWare server and Accounting does not. What was the problem with the pilot?

Colleen should have created two separate INF files, one for each department with the correct settings. Then she should have created two machine name text files and merged them with the correct INF files, and deployed the PCs with the correct settings from the start.

New Install

The benefits of doing a new install as opposed to an upgrade are intangible. Windows 98 appears to work the same either way. However, if there were problems with the previous operating system that was upgraded to Windows 98, then those problems sometimes (not always) are inherited by Windows 98. Doing a fresh install allows the operating system to determine the best configuration during hardware detection, and it creates fresh Registry and INI files (WIN.INI and SYSTEM.INI), which determine Windows 98's settings.

The disadvantage of installing Windows 98 as a new install is that applications have to be installed. Developers have been creating unattended installation processes for many newer 32-bit applications. This simplifies the application installation process. The installer can create a batch file that calls each application's unattended install. Then the installer can add that batch file to the MSBATCH.INF as a Registry addition for a

RUNSERVICESONCE command. What a RUNSERVICESONCE command does is run an executable once *before* logon. Once it is run, it never runs again, because the Registry entry deletes itself. The location for this Registry key is HKEY_LOCAL_MACHINE\Software\Microsoft\ Windows\CurrentVersion\RunServicesOnce.

If the installer wants to make sure a logon occurs before the applications are installed, the Registry key to use is HKEY_LOCAL_MACHINE\Software\ Microsoft\Windows\CurrentVersion\RunOnce.

Some programs can be installed using the INFInstaller tool provided with the Resource Kit. Success with this tool can be directly related to whether the application is 32-bit.

For applications that do not include an unattended install method, and are not 32-bit, the other options for installing include:

- using third-party installation tools such as Microsoft Systems Management Server or Seagate WinInstall

- manually installing the applications

- reviewing the changes made to the PC when the application is installed, and then copying the files added and modifying any text files through string manipulation

The first option can greatly simplify the task and save time. The second option will increase the deployment time for each workstation. Installing an application across an enterprise can make this option nearly impossible, due to the time involved in visiting each PC. The last option can be difficult, depending on the complexity of the changes made to the PC, and it increases the time spent testing in the lab significantly. But if you are deploying to hundreds or thousands of PCs, it is preferable to manually installing applications.

Upgrading

Upgrading to Windows 98 in an unattended mode is the same as a new install. It can use the same MSBATCH.INF and switches.

The advantage of upgrading to Windows 98 is that applications are already installed and do not need to be installed again.

The disadvantage of upgrading to Windows 98 is that any problems with the previous operating system may remain problems with Windows 98. A second disadvantage is that if new applications, such as the latest Microsoft Office Suite, need to be upgraded after Windows 98 is installed, it requires nearly as much work as installing a new workstation.

Uninstalling Windows 98

If Windows 98 was installed over a previous version of Windows, either version 3.1 or 95, it can be uninstalled so that the older Windows version can be restored.

In order to uninstall Windows 98, the Install/Uninstall tab in the Add/Remove Programs icon in the Control Panel includes an option to uninstall, if the system files were saved during the upgrade process. Clicking this option brings up the verification dialog box shown in Figure 2-9.

After you have verified that Windows 98 should be uninstalled, the uninstall process prompts to check the hard disk for errors with the screen shown in Figure 2-10.

Windows 98 Uninstall boots to an MS-DOS mode, where it restores the disk partition table, the directory structure and files. Then it prompts to restart the PC.

FIGURE 2-9

Uninstall verification
dialog box

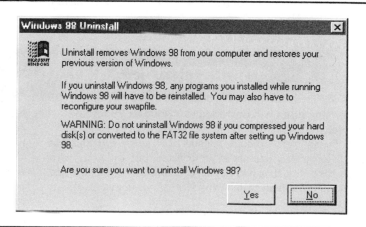

FIGURE 2-10

Check drive dialog box

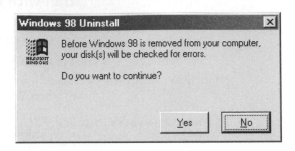

Not all files are removed from the hard disk. In the WINDOWS directory, there are several directories that are marked with system or hidden attributes. These files, because of their attributes, are not removed from the hard disk.

Uninstall will not work if compression has been implemented after installing Windows 98, or if the existing compression has been upgraded in Windows 98. FAT32 will prevent an uninstall if the hard disk has been converted after Windows 98 was installed. If the previous version of Windows 95 OSR2 had FAT32 already, then the drive *can* be uninstalled. Applications installed after Windows 98 was installed will have to be reinstalled after the uninstall.

Here is another sample scenario of installation problem solving.

QUESTIONS AND ANSWERS

Both Jerry and Susan had upgraded to Windows 98 on test systems before rolling out Windows 98 on their corporate network. Susan attempted an uninstall of Windows 98 and was successful. Jerry also attempted an uninstall, but ended up with a corrupt hard disk that had to be repartitioned and formatted before it could be used again. Why was Jerry's uninstall unsuccessful?	Jerry either had enabled compression or converted to FAT32 after he had installed Windows 98. With these changes to the file system, the uninstall process could not restore the system files.

Dual Boot Combination with Microsoft Windows NT

Dual booting with Windows NT is a common configuration. To dual boot with Windows NT, the best way to start is to install Windows 98 first. This makes Windows 98 the default operating system. Then Windows NT should be installed.

If there are two partitions, then Windows NT and Windows 98 can use NTFS and FAT32 file systems respectively, as long as they are installed on their own separate partition. Windows NT cannot use FAT32 for its boot or system partitions. However, if there is a single partition, then both Windows NT and Windows 98 must use the FAT file system. When NT 5.0 is released, it will support FAT32, and then Windows 98 will not be restricted to the FAT file system for a dual boot on a single partition.

EXERCISE 2-1

Installing Windows 98

1. Place the CD-ROM into the CD-ROM drive.
2. Type the letter of the CD-ROM drive, a colon, and a backslash. Then type **SETUP** and press ENTER. If the CD-ROM drive letter is D, the command looks like this: D:\SETUP.
3. Press ENTER to continue. The Setup Wizard will scan the hard disk for errors.
4. The Welcome To Setup screen appears. Press ENTER to continue.
5. Click I Accept on the License screen shown in Figure 2-11, and Next to continue.
6. Type in a name and organization and press ENTER to continue.
7. Accept C:\WINDOWS as the directory by pressing ENTER to continue.
8. Select the Custom type of setup, and press ENTER to continue.
9. Verify the components and press ENTER to continue.
10. Enter the name, workgroup, and description for this PC, then press ENTER to continue.
11. Accept the computer settings by pressing ENTER.

12. Create the disk by providing a freshly formatted disk when prompted.

13. Press ENTER to allow Windows 98 Setup Wizard to start copying files to the hard disk.

14. The PC will restart after the file copying process is complete. Then it will begin the hardware detection process with the PCMCIA Wizard, if there are PCMCIA slots in the PC. Take the default answers for each of the three PCMCIA wizard screens.

15. When hardware detection is complete, Windows 98's settings are finalized. The Time Zone will be displayed for confirmation. Click Apply and then OK.

16. The PC will restart, and Windows 98 Setup is complete.

FIGURE 2-11

License screen

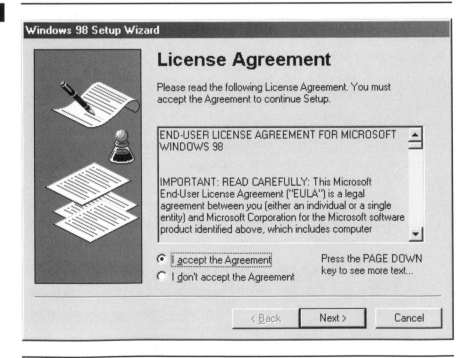

FROM THE CLASSROOM

Dual Booting a Windows 98 System

Many times people are unprepared to give up the comforts of an operating system that they have been using for a long time. Yet they want all of the new features of the latest and greatest Microsoft operating system. Or maybe they just want a chance to play with and evaluate a beta version of an operating system while still using a safe version in their production environment. These are just a couple of the reasons for dual booting a system.

The most common combination of operating systems that I am asked about is Microsoft Windows NT Workstation and Microsoft Windows 98. You'll be happy to know that these two Microsoft operating systems can be loaded on the same system, and you will be able to dual boot them. In fact, the process is not that much different from dual booting a Windows NT system and a Windows 95 system.

However, there is one big catch. Windows 98 gives you the option of using the FAT32 file system. This file system offers many advantages over the FAT file system. It also offers one big disadvantage: A Windows NT system can't read a FAT32 file system. There are no FAT32 drivers for Windows NT, and it is unclear whether there ever will be.

There are two places where FAT32 can really cause you headaches if you are dual booting Windows 98 and Windows NT. First, if you convert your hard disk to FAT32, you can no longer use dual booting to run earlier versions of Windows (Windows 95 [Version 4.00.950], Windows NT 3.*x*, Windows NT 4.0, and Windows 3.*x*). Second, if you convert a drive to FAT32 and you were using that drive to share data between two operating systems, that data will now only be available to the Windows 98 operating system.

However, all is not lost. If you are on a network, earlier versions of Windows can still gain access to your FAT32 hard disk through the network. When you share a directory, other systems are able to access that information through redirector and server services, regardless of the underlying operating system and file system drivers.

The simple solution to the compatibility problem is to partition your hard disk. Load Windows NT on an NTFS file system, so you have all of the features available that NTFS offers. Convert your Windows 98 partition to FAT32 to take advantage of the new features of FAT32, and keep a small partition as a FAT file system, so that you have a place that both

FROM THE CLASSROOM

operating systems can use to move data back and forth.

Partitioning a hard disk can be done through a DOS utility such as FDISK, or during the installation of Windows NT. My personal preference is to do the partitioning and formatting before doing the install. That way, I don't have to abort an install if I decide to change the partitioning scheme.

—*By Robert Aschermann, MCT, MCSE*

CERTIFICATION OBJECTIVE 2.02

Troubleshooting SETUP

Nothing is perfect. Sometimes Windows 98 Setup will fail. There are some mechanisms for troubleshooting the SETUP included with Windows 98.

Windows 98 creates log files during the setup process. These can help in determining the errors that led to setup failure. Some of these files are marked as hidden, and using the ATTRIB command with the –H switch is required to "see" them in DOS. The most helpful log file is DETLOG.TXT. This is the hardware detection log, which displays whether hardware successfully installs. NETLOG.TXT logs all the network drivers and devices discovered and installed. The SETUPLOG.TXT is the entire log of all the installation files and components. Another file to explore is BOOTLOG.TXT, which displays whether the system files load successfully the first time Windows 98 starts.

SETUP can stop if interruption to the network connection or power occurs. If SETUP stops for any reason, or if the PC hangs, the best course of action is to hard boot the PC. When the PC restarts, and the system has sufficient correct files copied, the Windows 98 Setup Wizard will offer to start the setup process in safe recovery mode.

Checking for viruses is recommended. Also, running SCANDISK can fix problems with the hard disk or file system. If the system was not checked for hardware compatibility prior to the installation, it should be checked now, since an incompatible hardware component can cause a SETUP failure. If an error message references a file, the installer should check to see if that file is missing or damaged. A new file extracted from the Windows 98 CAB files using the EXTRACT utility can replace the missing or damaged file.

When installing from a network share, it is best to verify that the installation server is up and running, and that the logged-on user has been granted access to the source files. A logon script, or even the AUTOEXEC.BAT file can load TSRs that can consume memory and prevent SETUP from running properly. When using the DOS client for Microsoft networks, check to make sure that the name of the PC on the disk is unique. Using the same disk to start multiple installations will lead to failure. Also, check to make sure that when using TCP/IP, the IP address is unique and has the correct subnet mask and default gateway.

CERTIFICATION OBJECTIVE 2.03

Configuring Windows 98 Components

Much of Windows 98 configuration can be done during the setup process. When SETUP is complete, the user will want to change things to suit his purposes. Additional hardware devices can also be set up at this point. For example, configuring multiple monitor support is done after SETUP has been completed.

Server components used to share printers and files can be added through the Network icon in the Control Panel. The file and printer sharing services will allow other users to connect over the network to specifically shared resources. The installer may also add the Personal Web Server component to share information via an intranet.

Using Control Panel

Configuration is done through the Control Panel most of the time. Only on extremely rare occasions will a user configure items directly through the Registry. See Figure 2-12 for the icons used in configuration.

FIGURE 2-12

Control Panel

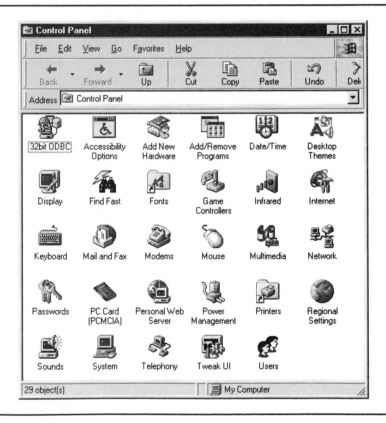

If you are not installing with an MSBATCH.INF file, networking capabilities and hardware settings will most likely need to be examined and changed. Networking configuration is done through the Network icon in Control Panel. The System icon is used to review and change hardware settings. The Add New Hardware icon is used to add hardware components. The Display icon is used for changing the monitor settings, such as color depth and refresh rate.

Hardware Settings

The Add New Hardware icon in Control Panel allows the installer to add hardware that was not automatically detected in the hardware detection process of Windows 98 Setup. Windows 98 will automatically look for new Plug and Play hardware. If none is detected, it then allows the installer to select the appropriate hardware devices from a list. If no hardware drivers exist in this list, then the installer can click the Have Disk icon and point to a disk or network share where the driver for the newly added device exists.

The PC Card icon's Socket Status tab displays the cards currently inserted in a PCMCIA slot. The Global Settings tab can configure the memory address that is used by the PC Card. Modems can be added or removed through the Modems icon in Control Panel.

To review hardware settings, Windows 98 includes a new utility called System Information, which is in the Start menu under Programs | Accessories | System Tools. System Information can display any hardware conflicts. To reconfigure the Windows 98 settings, the System icon in Control Panel can be utilized. As shown in Figure 2-13, devices are grouped under the type of hardware components. Clicking an item, and then clicking the Properties button will enable the user to configure the properties of that device.

FIGURE 2-13

System settings

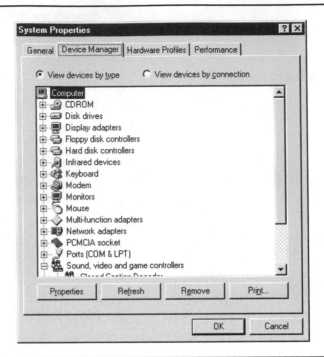

EXERCISE 2-2

Configuring Hardware Profiles

1. Click Start, then Settings, then Control Panel, then double-click the System icon. (Alternatively, right-click My Computer and select Properties.)

2. Click the Hardware Profiles tab.

3. Click the name of one of the existing hardware profiles.

4. Click Copy.

5. Type the name for the hardware profile that is being created.

6. Reboot the PC and select the new hardware profile.

7. Open the System icon in Control Panel again.

8. Click the devices that are not desired for this profile, and click the Remove button.

9. When prompted, select the option to remove the device from the current profile only.

System Settings

Other system settings that may need reconfiguration can be accessed through the System icon in Control Panel as well. These settings are located in the Performance tab.

The File System button leads to options for configuring how Windows 98 works with the hard disk, the floppy disk, the CD-ROM drive, and removable disk drives. It also contains a troubleshooting tab for configuring advanced file system options.

The Graphics button leads to options to configure how Windows 98 handles graphics acceleration. The defaults for this tab are usually correct.

The Virtual Memory button leads to the configuration options for the page file. This file is, by default, dynamically expanded or reduced as needed. Changing this page file setting can cause unpredictable results on the PC.

Software Settings

Software can be added or removed from within the Control Panel, using the Add/Remove Programs icon. Also, Windows 98 components can be installed or removed through the same icon.

Most 32-bit programs will register themselves correctly in the Registry, such that they can be removed from the Add/Remove Programs icon even if their standard installation is run from a command line. However, older programs will not necessarily do this. In order to ensure that a program will register itself so that it can be removed from Windows 98, it should be installed using the Install button on the first tab in the Add/Remove Programs dialog box.

The second tab in the Add/Remove Programs icon enables the installer to add or remove Windows 98 optional components. Adding or removing a

Windows 98 component requires access to the Windows 98 source files. If the source files only exist on a network share, but the network share is not accessible because the networking components are not working correctly, there will be problems.

Adding and Removing Programs

1. Click the Start button, click Settings, and then click Control Panel.

2. Double-click the Add/Remove Programs icon.

3. Click the Install button.

4. Click the Next button.

5. Type in the path to the application being installed. Alternatively, click Browse and navigate through the file system until the setup executable is located.

6. Click Finish to begin the setup process.

7. To remove the program, click Start | Settings | Control Panel.

8. Double-click Add/Remove Programs.

9. Select the name of the program from the list in the dialog box, then click the Add/Remove button.

CERTIFICATION OBJECTIVE 2.05

Using the Registry to Configure Settings

The Registry is actually a set of two files: SYSTEM.DAT and USER.DAT. SYSTEM.DAT contains hardware and global settings. The USER.DAT file contains user settings, and can also be located in each user profile directory. REGEDIT, the Registry Editor, is the program used to manipulate Registry entries. It is not located in the Start menu. Instead, the user must click Start | Run and type REGEDIT in the Run dialog box, then click OK. The Registry Editor is shown in Figure 2-14.

FIGURE 2-14

Registry Editor

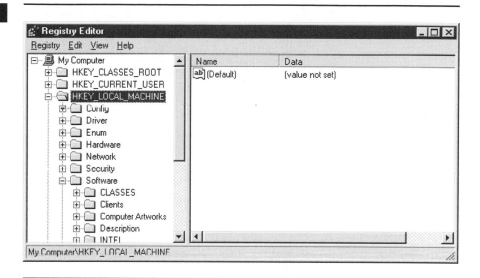

Viewing and Modifying the Registry

1. Click Start | Run and type REGEDIT. Then click OK.

2. Navigate through the keys, first expanding HKEY_LOCAL_MACHINE, then Software, then Microsoft, then Windows, then CurrentVersion.

3. Find Winlogon and click on it to highlight it.

4. Click the Edit menu and the New option, then select the String Value option. Name the new string value DontDisplayLastUserName and give it a value of 1. This Registry key keeps the last user ID from appearing in the logon screen.

5. Exit the Registry Editor, and reboot.

CERTIFICATION OBJECTIVE 2.06

Configuring the Desktop

The easiest method to change the way the desktop looks is to install and apply desktop themes. The Desktop Themes icon in Control Panel allows the user to select an entire look for the desktop, including matching sounds and screensaver—something like a full wardrobe complete with accessories.

With the new Active Desktop and Web integration, there are other options available to customize the desktop look and functionality. The Control Panel has the Display applet, which contains all the video settings, wallpaper and colors for the desktop look.

User Interface Enhancements

New to Windows 98 is the ability to use an HTML page as wallpaper. To enable this functionality, the user should click Start | Settings | Active Desktop, then select View As Web Page from the menu. To change the HTML page that is used, the user can right-click the desktop and select Properties. Then the user should simply click the Browse button and navigate to the correct HTML page.

Folder options can significantly change what a user will see when using Explorer or My Computer. To change the way files are displayed, the user should open either Explorer or My Computer, then click the View menu and select Folder Options. On the View tab, the most helpful changes for an administrator are to uncheck the box for Hide File Extensions For Known File Types, and to select the Show All Files radio button.

Additional toolbars can add functionality to the desktop. To display these toolbars, the user can right-click the existing toolbar and select Toolbars from the popup menu. If the user chooses the Address option, an Internet address box will appear in the existing toolbar. The user can also click and drag the toolbar to any side of the screen.

exam
ⓦatch

To use an HTML page as the desktop wallpaper, the Active Desktop settings must be set to View As Web Page.

Web Integration

Windows 98 has integrated the World Wide Web (WWW) and the desktop using Microsoft's Internet Explorer technology. This makes the desktop and file directories act like a browser and Web-based objects. From any Windows 98 Explorer or open window, there is a Go and Favorites menu that can be used to browse.

To use the desktop and explore the computer the same as browsers access Web-based objects, there are two items to enable.

1. Make sure the desktop is set to be viewed as a Web page. Click Start | Settings | Active Desktop. View As Web Page should be checked.

2. Enable single-click access to icons. Open My Computer. Click the View menu, and select Folder Options. The button for Web Style should be checked.

Active Desktop View

The Active Desktop is the biggest change to the Graphical User Interface (GUI). Active content is information that is periodically updated on the World Wide Web and then updated on the PC "behind the scenes." Active content is sometimes called a "channel." A channel is simply a link to a specific Web site for particular types of information. For example, a stock ticker is considered active content. And it might originate from the CNN channel.

A channel bar, such as the one shown in Figure 2-15, is displayed on the Active Desktop, and includes some default channels. This bar can be customized. First, the user must be connected to the World Wide Web. Then, the user should click the Channel Guide button at the top of the bar. This will prompt a Web page to be displayed, and from there the user can select or change the content that is desired.

FIGURE 2-15

The channel bar

CERTIFICATION SUMMARY

Windows 98 can be installed over a network, from CD-ROM, or from floppy disks. The installer can upgrade previous versions of Windows—both Windows 3.1x and Windows 95—using the SETUP.EXE program, as well as begin a new installation.

Upgrading from Windows 95 can shorten the installation time, since SETUP will use existing hardware settings and upgrade drivers rather than go through the hardware detection phase. Existing information, such as the machine name, is also inherited from the older Windows version.

The Compact setup installs the fewest optional components in order to conserve space on the hard disk. All the online services are installed in each setup type.

Microsoft Batch 98 is used to create INF files that can automate setup of Windows 98 in large deployments. For each workgroup that has separate settings, the installer should create a separate INF file. Multiple machine name save can be used to create a separate INF file for each PC, in order to use unique computer names.

SETUP includes switches that can automate the installation. The syntax is: SETUP MSBATCH.INF /T:TMPDIR /IM /ID /IS /IQ /IE /IH /IV. The MSBATCH.INF file contains the setup options. /T:TMPDIR is the directory where SETUP will create temporary files. /IM ignores the memory check. /ID ignores the disk space check. /IS ignores the system check. /IQ ignores the crosslinked file check. /IE ignores the creation of an emergency startup disk. /IH ignores the Registry check. /IV ignores the view of billboards while SETUP runs.

Checking for viruses and disk errors are two options to use in troubleshooting SETUP. The workstation should be reviewed with the Hardware Compatibility List (HCL) from Microsoft. The log files that Windows 98 creates during setup should be reviewed for errors. If a particular file is causing an error, it should be checked to see if it is missing or damaged, and a new file extracted from the Windows 98 CAB files.

The file and printer sharing services allow the user to share resources on the computer for use by other networked computers. The Personal Web Server component enables the user to share information via an intranet.

Windows 98 configuration occurs mostly in the Control Panel. To add software, the installer should use the Add/Remove Programs icon. To add hardware devices, the installer should use the Add New Hardware icon. To configure hardware settings, the installer can use the System icon. PC cards and modems each have their own icon in Control Panel. Networking components are configured in the Network icon.

It is rare to use the Registry Editor to configure settings on the Windows 98 computer. Some Registry changes are not available in the Control Panel, and those require the use of REGEDIT to change, delete or add keys to create the desired configuration.

The desktop can be configured using the Active Desktop option in the Settings menu. Also, Folder Options and the Display properties can change the way the desktop is used. Active content can be changed through the Channel Guide icon on the channel bar.

TWO-MINUTE DRILL

❑ The installation process for Windows 98 is conceptually nearly identical to that for Windows 95.

❑ Enhancements have been made to the Windows 98 Setup program.

❑ The Setup Wizard is used to manually install Windows 98.

❑ The Portable setup includes the optional components that are most likely to be required on a laptop, including Virtual Private Networking and HyperTerminal.

❑ The prerequisites for Windows 98 installation must be considered and compared to the existing hardware and software.

❑ Information for a Windows 95 upgrade to Windows 98 can be taken automatically from the existing Windows 95 configuration. SETUP will automatically transfer the current system settings and the upgrade will allow use of existing installed applications.

❑ The upgrade to Windows 98 from Windows 95 can skip the hardware detection phase. It takes existing settings and drivers and upgrades them.

❑ Windows 98 includes a Windows 3.x upgrade process.

❑ Microsoft Batch 98 is the program created by Microsoft to help create the files required for Windows 98 automated setup.

❑ Automated setup for Windows 98 uses an MSBATCH.INF file.

❑ There are some mechanisms for troubleshooting the SETUP included with Windows 98.

❑ Much of Windows 98 configuration can be done during the setup process. Server components used to share printers and files can be added through the Network icon in Control Panel.

❑ Configuration is done through the Control Panel most of the time. Only on extremely rare occasions will a user configure items directly through the Registry.

❑ The Add New Hardware icon in Control Panel allows the installer to add hardware that was not automatically detected in the hardware detection process of Windows 98 Setup.

❑ Other system settings that may need reconfiguration can be accessed through the System icon in Control Panel as well.

❑ Software can be added or removed from within the Control Panel, using the Add/Remove Programs icon. Also, Windows 98 components can be installed or removed through the same icon.

❑ The Registry is actually a set of two files: SYSTEM.DAT and USER.DAT. SYSTEM.DAT contains hardware and global settings. The USER.DAT file contains user settings, and can also be located in each user profile directory.

❑ The Desktop Themes icon in Control Panel allows the user to select an entire look for the desktop, including matching sounds and screensaver.

❑ To use an HTML page as the desktop wallpaper, the Active Desktop settings must be set to View As Web Page.

❑ Windows 98 has integrated the World Wide Web (WWW) and the desktop using Microsoft's Internet Explorer technology.

❑ The Active Desktop is the biggest change to the Graphical User Interface (GUI).

SELF TEST

The Self Test questions will help you measure your understanding of the material presented in this chapter. Read all the choices carefully, as there may be more than one correct answer. Choose all correct answers for each question.

1. Which of the following are the types of setup presented in Windows 98?

   A. Standard, Laptop, Minimum, Complete

   B. Standard, Portable, Minimum, Custom

   C. Typical, Portable, Compact, Custom

   D. Default, Laptop, Compact, Custom

2. Which type of setup will install the Games components?

   A. Typical

   B. Portable

   C. Compact

   D. None of the above

3. What does the switch /IE do?

   A. Ignores the creation of the emergency disk

   B. Ignores extended memory check

   C. Ignores crosslinked files

   D. Skips the License Agreement screen

4. What does the HCL do?

   A. It helps in troubleshooting hardware problems

   B. It is used in preparation for deploying Windows 98

   C. It lists hardware compatible with Windows 98

   D. All of the above

5. What program(s) can be used to create MSBATCH.INF files?

   A. EDIT

   B. NOTEPAD

   C. Batch 98 or any text editor

   D. WORDPAD

6. What is the minimum processor that Windows 98 will support?

   A. Pentium II 300 Mhz

   B. 486DX2 66 Mhz

   C. 286

   D. 386DX 33 Mhz

7. Which icon in Control Panel would an installer use to change a graphics card's properties?

   A. Add New Hardware icon

   B. Add/Remove Programs icon

   C. PC Card icon

   D. System icon

8. If an installer wants to add WebTV support after Windows 98 is installed, what does he do?

   A. He uses the EXTRACT utility to obtain the WebTV drivers, and copies them to the Windows\System directory.

B. He obtains the WebTV software and runs SETUP from the Start | Run command dialog box.

C. He uses the Add/Remove Programs icon and selects WebTV components from the Windows Setup tab.

D. He cannot do this. Windows 98 does not support WebTV.

9. If a setting has to be changed in the Registry, how does the installer make the change?

A. He uses SYSEDIT

B. He uses REGEDIT

C. He uses System Information

D. He opens the SYSTEM.DAT and USER.DAT files in WORDPAD

10. How can a user change his settings to use an HTML page as wallpaper?

A. He cannot do this, since Windows 98 doesn't support this feature.

B. He must edit the Folder Options from within Explorer.

C. He can change to an HTML page using the Internet Explorer settings.

D. He must click Start | Settings | Active Desktop and check View As Web Page. Then he must select an HTML page using the Control Panel Display icon.

3

Managing Files, Hard Disks, and Applications in Windows 98

Windows 98 continues the refinement found in Windows 95 for managing your computer. Large hard disks can be utilized much more efficiently than before. It's also easier than ever to keep your system files up to date and in order. Applications run more quickly, and it's never been easier to maintain your computer. It is important to know how these new features work and how they can make a Windows 98 system run more quickly, efficiently, and safely.

Windows 98 File Systems

Windows 98 offers a lot of improvements over previous versions of Windows, and one of the most invisible, yet important, ones is the file system. The file system is what determines how Windows 98 stores data on your hard disk. File systems work at such a low level that they can even limit how much of your hard disk the computer can see. This can be a very big problem, especially with today's hard disks being several gigabytes in size.

Previous versions of Windows used a file system called FAT. (It stands for File Allocation Table, a set of detailed information about the hard drive.) The FAT file system was originally developed for use with MS-DOS, almost 20 years ago! The maximum size of hard disk that FAT can understand is 2048MB (2GB). Twenty years ago, a large hard disk was 5MB, so the possibilities FAT offered seemed endless. While you can use FAT with a hard disk larger than 2GB, you will have to use multiple partitions, otherwise all the space over 2GB is wasted!

FAT is also very inefficient with larger hard disks. FAT has a limited amount of space to keep track of the whole hard disk, so it chops the disk up into manageable blocks, called *clusters*. A cluster is the smallest amount of disk space that the computer can use. It is set when the drive is formatted, and cannot be changed. Table 3-1 shows the block sizes used by the FAT file system, depending on the size of the drive.

Drive Size	FAT Cluster Size
< 32MB	512 bytes
32 – 63MB	1KB
64 – 127MB	2KB
128 – 255MB	4KB
256 – 511MB	8KB
512 – 1023MB	16KB
1024 – 2048MB	32KB

If you have a 2GB hard drive formatted using FAT, it will use 32KB clusters. If you store a 3KB file on this drive, it will waste 13KB. A drive with mainly large files won't be affected much. But if there are many small files, it will increase the amount of wasted space, inefficiently using the hard drive.

Windows 98 introduces an updated version of FAT called FAT32 (32-bit File Allocation Table). FAT32 is usually no faster than FAT, but it is much more efficient, and it can understand hard disks as large as 2048GB (that's 2 terabytes!). Table 3-2 shows the FAT32 cluster sizes.

If you have a 2GB hard disk formatted using FAT32, it will use 4KB clusters. If you store a 3KB file on this drive, it will waste only 1KB. While there is still some waste, it is a great deal more efficient than FAT drives.

FAT32 also allows you to format hard drives larger than 2GB as one partition, since FAT32 recognizes individual drives as large as 2TB. This makes hard disk management much simpler. Unless you have special needs that require special partitions, you can use FAT32 to format a monster 7GB hard disk as one 7GB C: drive.

Drive Size	FAT Cluster Size
< 260MB	512 bytes
260MB – 8GB	4KB
8 – 16GB	8KB
16 – 32GB	16KB
> 32GB	32KB

It would seem that it would be a no-brainer to choose FAT32, right? Well, not quite. Other operating systems such as DOS, Windows 95, and even Windows NT cannot read FAT32 drives. DriveSpace disk compression does not work on FAT32 drives. Older disk administration utilities (such as disk editors and defragmenters) also cannot make sense of FAT32 drives, since they store information on the hard disk differently than FAT drives. FAT32 only offers increased efficiency on drives larger than 512MB, so if you still use a smaller hard disk, there is no advantage to using FAT32.

In general, you will want to use FAT32 as your file system with Windows 98. Only if you have the sort of requirements outlined previously should you consider sticking with FAT. Of course if you have multiple drives, you may choose FAT or FAT32 on a case-by-case basis. You might find it useful to use FAT on a small boot drive for backward compatibility, but store all your Windows 98 files and programs on a nice fat FAT32 drive. (Sorry, I couldn't resist!)

Viewing System Information

Whether you are trying to track down a problem, or are just curious about the computer, Windows 98 offers many new ways to look at your computer's configuration. On the Start | Programs | Accessories | System Tools menu you will find over a dozen tools for viewing and configuring your system.

Previous to Windows 98, the only way to modify your system and see how it was configured was to trudge through INI files or the Registry. A trained technician could make good use of this information, but it was a mystery to the average user. For a novice to relay the configuration information to a technician was a challenging endeavor. What's worse, it was very easy for the novice (or professional for that matter) to accidentally modify those settings, possibly making the computer unusable.

Microsoft System Information Utility

The Microsoft System Information utility (MSI) provides easy Read Only access to detailed information regarding the Windows 98 operating system, computer hardware, and even third-party software. MSI can be very useful in trying to determine potential problems.

The Microsoft System Information utility allows you to take the information and print it or save it to disk (in both MSI's proprietary NFO format and plain text), making it a very helpful utility for technical support professionals. Even novice users can run MSI, simply pointing and clicking where a support person guides them. Then they only have to click the Print or Save button and send the results in for detailed help, without having to recite pages and pages of tech-babble over the phone.

The Microsoft System Information utility breaks down information into four categories: System Information, Resources, Components, and Software Environment. Figure 3-1 shows MSI in its default view, System Information. This view gives a general overview of the computer, including operating system version, browser version, memory, processor type, and resources. The three sub-views, Resources, Components, and Software

---

FIGURE 3-1

Microsoft System
Information main screen

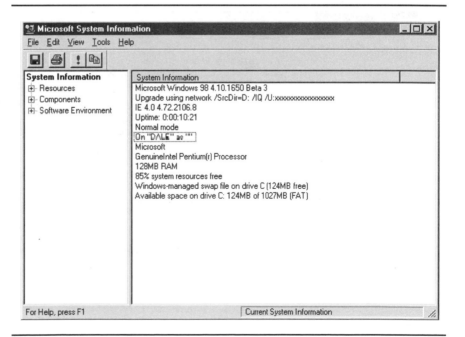

Environment, offer a much more detailed look at the inner working of the computer.

The Resources view gives details on how the computer resources—items such as IRQs, memory maps, and I/O ports—are configured. If you were installing legacy hardware (for example, an ISA card that you had to configure with jumpers) into a Windows 98 computer, the Resources view would be extremely helpful in determining which IRQs and I/O ports are available. Figure 3-2 shows the IRQs found under Resources. If we were installing an ISA network card in this computer, we can see that the IRQs 5, 9, and 12 are available for that card to use.

The Components view gives detailed information on the hardware devices installed in your computer, such as video cards, modems, and sound cards. This is another helpful view when troubleshooting a specific hardware device. Figure 3-3 shows the Components view, giving brief information on the ports installed in our computer.

FIGURE 3-2

System Information
Resources view

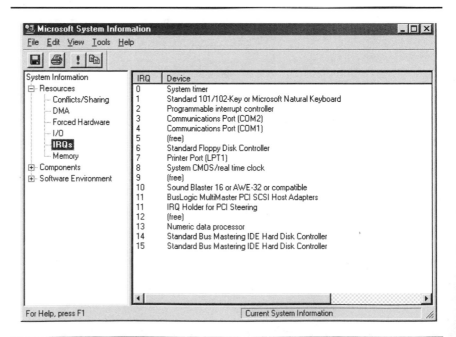

FIGURE 3-3

System Information
Components view

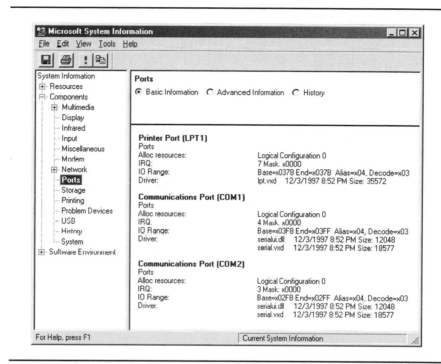

Notice the Basic Information, Advanced Information, and History radio buttons above the information on the ports. Basic Information gives the configuration the component is currently using. Advanced Information gives the current configuration as well as all the known configurations that component could use. History gives information on configuration changes, such as new drivers being loaded.

The Software Environment view gives detailed information on all software running on the computer. Not just programs like Word and Excel, but all the DLLs, VXDs, and drivers that make it possible to load Word and Excel. The MSI Software Environment view gives information such as driver filename, version, manufacturer, and more. This sort of information can be helpful in tracking down a modified or corrupt software component. Figure 3-4 shows the Software Environment and all the currently running software. (You can see Word in there, but just look at all the other junk Windows needs!)

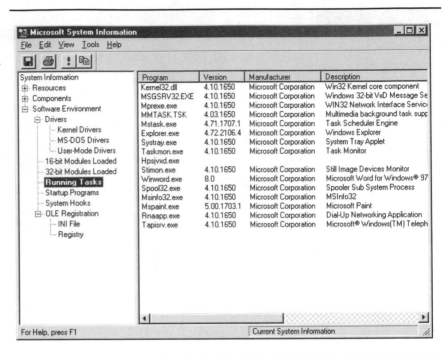

FIGURE 3-4

System Information
Software Environment view

The Microsoft System Information (MSI) utility is an extremely useful tool for configuring and troubleshooting Windows 98 computers. MSI can give a full scope of information, from general system information to detailed configuration information, and the history of the information. Learn to use MSI well if you ever expect to provide technical support for Windows 98!

Examining System Files

When running a complex operating system such as Windows 98, there are literally thousands of files needed to make it run properly. Just one key file becoming corrupt can cause the system to freeze or even lose data. It becomes important to take a proactive approach to maintaining these system files, rather than waiting for a possible disaster.

Microsoft System Information can be useful for examining system files that are currently running on a Windows 98 computer.

Troubleshooting File System Problems

The big weapon against file system errors is the venerable ScanDisk. ScanDisk has been around since MS-DOS 6.0, upgraded to fully support each version of Windows. Windows 98 still has this standby, in both GUI and text mode versions. The latter is useful in case a file system error prevents the system from booting.

ScanDisk can be run from any command line by simply entering ScanDisk, or from the Start | Programs | Accessories | System Tools menu. ScanDisk allows you to choose a drive and run either a Standard or Thorough check. The latter adds on to the Standard by performing a surface test, a test of every single point on the disk. Obviously this adds a substantial amount of the time required to complete the scan. Figure 3-5 shows ScanDisk hard at work.

System File Checker

The System File Checker (SFC) is a tool for automatically checking that all system files are in order, and that none is corrupt. You can use SFC to verify the integrity of your operating system files, to restore them if they are corrupted, and to extract compressed files (such as drivers) from your installation disks.

If you choose to restore your original driver files, System File Checker can back them up before restoring the originals. You can also customize search criteria based on folder and file extension, choose a different verification data file, or restore the default verification data file. Figure 3-6 shows SFC asking what to do after finding a corrupt system file.

When restoring a file, SFC will ask where to get the file from (your CD drive for instance) and where to put it. SFC will automatically fill in the destination (which is good, since few people know where every file goes!) so you will not need to change that unless you have a special situation. Figure 3-7 shows SFC restoring a file.

FIGURE 3-5

ScanDisk running
on drive C:

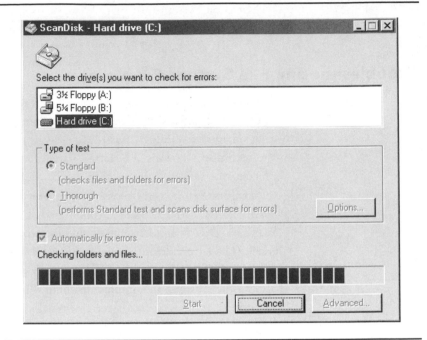

FIGURE 3-6

System File Checker finding
a corrupted file

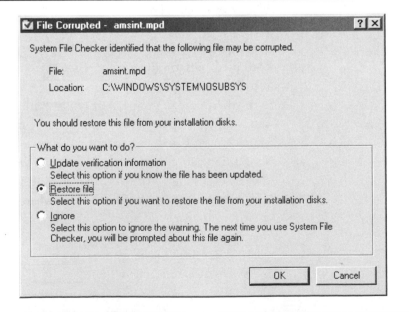

FIGURE 3-7

System File Checker
restoring a corrupted file

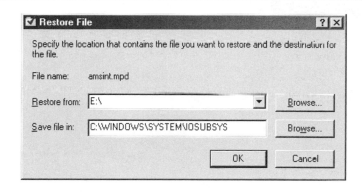

SFC will ask you where you would like to back up the file being overwritten, just in case. By default, SFC will store the file in \WINDOWS\HELPDESK\SFC. When it has finished scanning your system files, SFC will display a summary detailing what it did, as in Figure 3-8.

You can also use SFC to restore original files manually from the Windows 98 install CD. If you are having trouble with Windows 98 and you suspect a certain file, you can select the Restore One File From Installation Disk option and enter the filename, or click Browse and choose the file via GUI. Figure 3-9 shows the file KERNEL32.DLL being selected for manual restoration of the original file.

FIGURE 3-8

System File Checker results

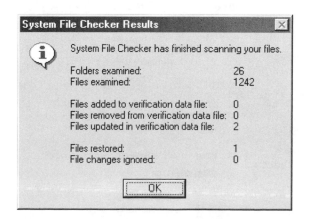

FIGURE 3-9

Using System File Checker
to manually restore a
system file

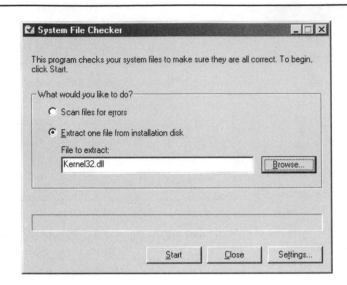

CERTIFICATION OBJECTIVE 3.02

Partitioning a Hard Disk

When setting up a hard disk in virtually any operating system, you must
tell the operating system about the hard disk: how big it is, what type of file
system is used, and how the hard disk is divided up. The last part, dividing
the disk up, is known as partitioning the hard disk. The process of
partitioning takes a large hard disk and divides it into smaller drives. The
words "disk" and "drive" are often used interchangeably, but usually a hard
disk is the physical unit, while a hard drive is a logical unit in the physical
unit. For instance, you may have a 4GB hard disk with two 2GB drives, the
C: and D: drives.

exam
ⓦatch

*You must know how to partition a hard disk into one or more
disk drives.*

Before Windows 98, hard disk partitioning had become very important in trying to make efficient use of large hard disks. As discussed earlier, the limits of the FAT file system required large disks to be partitioned into smaller drives so the cluster size would be smaller. With the introduction of FAT32, it is now possible to keep the cluster size at an efficient size for drives as large as 8GB (although FAT32 supports drives as large a 2TB).

The FDISK program is used to partition hard disks in Windows 98. FDISK is a text-mode program that can be run from a command prompt or from Run on the Start button. When you run FDISK on a disk that can be formatted with FAT32, it will ask you whether you would like Large Disk Support (LDS). If you enable LDS support, any drives you create will format using FAT32.

If you have no need to access a FAT32 drive from an operating system other than Windows 98, and are not going to be using older disk utilities, then you should enter **Y** on the FDISK screen. (Figure 3-16 shows this screen.) After you get into FDISK, a simple text menu allows you to create and delete partitions. After making any changes to a drive (whether creating, deleting, or deleting and creating), you must reboot Windows 98 for those changes to take effect.

CERTIFICATION OBJECTIVE 3.03

Disk Compression

Windows 98 includes DriveSpace, a disk drive compression software package. With DriveSpace, you can take all or part of a hard drive, and create a new, compressed drive. All data stored on the compressed drive is automatically compressed, giving you more free space. DriveSpace is not for everyone, however. It requires a traditional FAT partition. FAT32 is not supported.

With hard disk prices at all-time lows, fewer people compress their hard drives, but there are situations where it can be useful. Obviously, it can help get some more life out of a smaller hard disk if you are being thrifty. If you have a FAT partition and cannot convert it to FAT32 for one reason or another, DriveSpace can give you more efficient use of the drive.

To compress a drive, you must run DriveSpace. If it is not installed on your computer, use the Control Panel Add/Remove Software applet to install the files from your original Windows 98 disk. DriveSpace will ask you to choose an existing drive that you want to compress, as shown in Figure 3-10. You may compress any floppy drive or hard drive, and you may select part or all of the drive to be compressed.

You may also compress a drive using the drive's Properties sheet and choosing the Compression tab, as shown in Figure 3-11.

Once you choose to compress a drive, DriveSpace allows you to choose how to compress the drive. You may want the entire drive and its data compressed (using the Drive I Compress menu). Or you may want only a portion of the drive's free space compressed to create a new, empty compressed drive (using the Advanced I Create Empty menu). After a lengthy check to make sure the drive is error-free, DriveSpace will create a file on the original drive that is the size you specified.

FIGURE 3-10

DriveSpace3

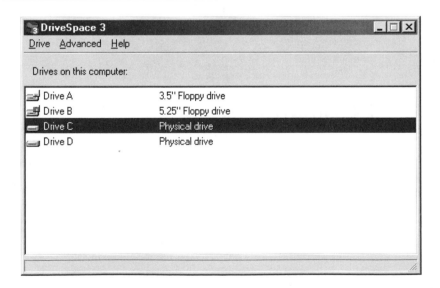

FIGURE 3-11

Drive Properties
Compression tab

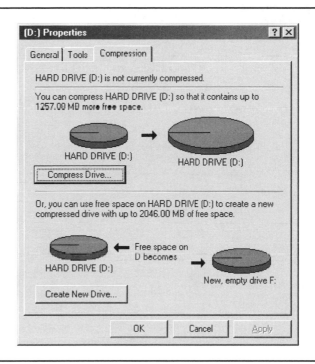

DriveSpace then maps a new drive letter that is the compressed drive. (Usually H: or the first available drive letter. You can configure it to any unused drive letter.) The original drive is called the *host drive.* The host drive stores a file that contains all the data on the compressed drive. The DriveSpace3 software takes all data sent to the compressed drive letter, compresses that data, and places it in the compressed volume file (.CVF) on the host drive. If the two drives are confusing, the host drive may be hidden so only the compressed drive is visible to the user. This is generally the less confusing method.

Windows 98 also includes Compression Agent, a tool for tweaking the compression and performance of compressed drives. Figure 3-12 shows the Compression Agent.

By default DriveSpace tries to be in the middle of the road when it comes to the amount of compression it uses on files (the more compressed the files, the longer it takes) versus the performance level the user sees.

FIGURE 3-12

Compression Agent

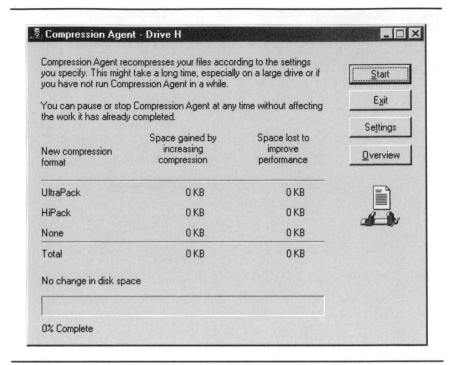

Compression Agent allows you to move DriveSpace closer to one side of the road. If you desire the maximum amount of compression (and therefore space available to you), you could tell it to increase compression. On the other hand, if you need speed, you can set it to improve performance (which is just less compression).

Compression Agent even allows you to change the compression settings based on filename, folder name, or file extension. For instance, a folder containing your Word documents could be set to use maximum compression, while a folder containing ZIP files (which are already compressed) could be set to never use compression. Figure 3-13 shows the exception list and the settings used on different files.

Compression Agent provides a simple interface that gives you complete control of your DriveSpace drives. It is just another example of the many

FIGURE 3-13

Configuring compression
exceptions via
Compression Agent

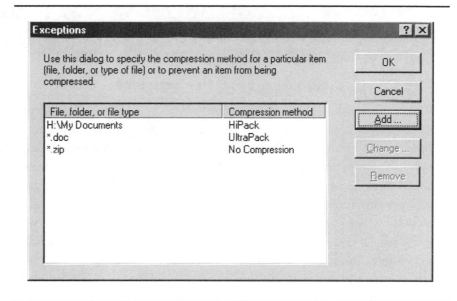

utilities Windows 98 includes that allow users to take control of their
computers.

Maintaining a Hard Disk

A hard disk should be regularly maintained in any operating system, just
like an automobile must regularly have its oil changed. Failure to maintain
the hard disks properly won't cause immediate problems, but problems will
creep up over time. The most minor problem is decreased performance.
Programs load more slowly. It takes longer to start or shut down the
computer. Over longer periods of time, errors can even creep into the hard
disk that cause you to lose data. If one of those errors should creep into
critical system areas, your computer could freeze up.

There are several utilities included with Windows 98 that prevent
performance degradation and errors that affect any hard disk over time.

FROM THE CLASSROOM

The Compression Agent and Performance

With Compression Agent, you can save disk space by compressing files, or improve performance by changing the level of compression on your files. There's no doubt about it: compression does affect the performance of your system. Luckily, it probably won't be noticeable, especially if you have a fast processor.

Compression in Windows 98 is done by intercepting file read and write operations, and running the data through a compression algorithm before it is written to the disk, and before it is read into memory. The data is compressed on the hard disk and uncompressed when it is stored in memory.

DriveSpace3 is the utility used to compress both hard and floppy disks to create more free space for files. You can also use DriveSpace3 to configure disk drives that you have already compressed by using DoubleSpace or DriveSpace3. The compression options available are:

- HiPack Compression
- Standard Compression
- No Compression, unless drive is at least ___% full (you set the percentage)
- No Compression

Once you have created a compressed drive, you will have a chance to specify what type of compression you would like to use. HiPack compression will give you the most disk space after files have been compressed, but it is also the most CPU-intensive compression method. Consequently, HiPack is not recommended for 486-class machines. Standard compression is the default, and it provides a balance between gaining additional disk space and not affecting CPU performance.

While files on your drive are being recompressed after you have changed your compression settings, Compression Agent updates information in a table to reflect how your disk space changes as files are moved from one compression method to another.

One more thing to remember: You should be aware that FAT32 drives can't be compressed. The DriveSpace utility only supports compression for drives with FAT file systems. This can be very frustrating if you had planned to compress a FAT32 drive. Microsoft (or a third party) may include a compression agent for FAT32 drives in the future, along with a number of other file system utilities.

—By Robert Aschermann, MCT, MCSE

ScanDisk will check the drive for logical and physical defects in the hard disk(s). It checks to catch file system errors and fix them before they can cause serious system problems. If file system problems are not fixed for a long time, they can prevent the system from functioning at all.

Disk Defragmenter will make sure the files on your hard disk are arranged in a contiguous fashion, allowing them to be loaded faster. When programs and data files are arranged on the disk all in a row, the hard disk can read them much more quickly than if it had to jump all over the place.

Disk Cleanup helps you track down and delete temporary files and unused programs to free up valuable disk space. All three of these programs should be used on a regular basis to avoid problems and keep your system running at its best.

EXERCISE 3-1 ### Using Disk Defragmenter

1. Open Disk Defragmenter from the Start | Programs | Accessories | System Tools menu.
2. Choose the hard disk you want to defragment.
3. Click OK to start.
4. Click Yes to exit Disk Defragmenter when finished.

Automating Maintenance Tasks

As mentioned earlier, it is important to run certain system maintenance utilities on a regular basis to keep system performance up, and to avoid data loss. Most of us are rather forgetful when it comes to actually running these programs. To simplify these tedious tasks, Microsoft has included the Scheduled Tasks utility, which allows you to schedule various programs to run unattended at any time. You can also schedule programs to run on a regular schedule, say every week. (Kind of like automating that 3000-mile oil change.)

Further simplifying things, Windows 98 has a Maintenance Wizard. Maintenance Wizard simply takes those three most important system utilities mentioned earlier (ScanDisk, Disk Defragmenter, and Disk Cleanup) and makes it easy to set them up in the Scheduled Tasks.

Maintenance Wizard allows you to control the settings of each utility, as well as changing the schedule to suit your needs and habits. Figure 3-14 shows the Maintenance Wizard after setting everything up.

Keep several things in mind when scheduling these tasks. Obviously, your computer must be turned on for them to work. If you schedule things to happen in the middle of the night, then you have to remember to leave the computer on. You will want to make sure you have a good surge protector (better yet, an uninterruptible power supply) in case a storm comes through in the middle of the night.

Also, complex disk maintenance programs like ScanDisk and Disk Defragmenter don't like to have changes made to the hard drive while they are running. So you shouldn't be loading or saving files while they are working. If you do work while they are running, they will start over every time they detect a change. This could cause them to run several times longer than usual.

FIGURE 3-14

Maintenance Wizard

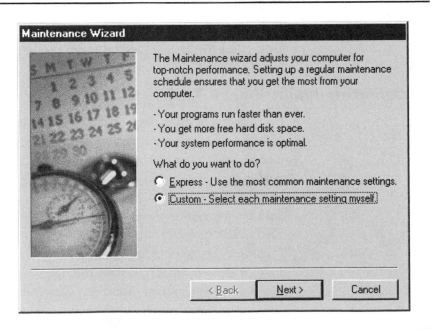

EXERCISE 3-2

Using the Maintenance Wizard to Automate Maintenance at Night

1. Open the Maintenance Wizard from the Start | Programs | Accessories | System Tools menu.

2. Select Change My Maintenance Settings Or Schedule and click OK.

3. Select Express and click OK.

4. Select Nights and click OK.

5. Notice the list of tasks that the computer will automatically do beginning at midnight, then click Finish.

EXERCISE 3-3

Using the Scheduled Tasks

1. Open the Scheduled Tasks from the Start | Programs | Accessories | System Tools menu.

2. Double-click Add Scheduled Task.

3. Click Next.

4. Select ScanDisk from the list and click Next.

5. Select Weekly and click Next.

6. Change the start time to 12:00 A.M. every week on Sunday and click Next.

7. Click Finish and then OK to add ScanDisk to the scheduled tasks.

Updating Windows 98

As with any software, it is very important to make sure you have the most current version of the software available. Even after you buy a software product, companies often enhance it or fix problems with it. Microsoft is no exception.

In previous versions of Windows, Microsoft has provided what it calls Service Packs, a collection of bug fixes and product enhancements. You could order the update on CD or (if you are very patient) download the fixes online. When the fix is extremely urgent, Microsoft provides what it calls a Hotfix, a temporary fix to an urgent problem, such as a network security problem.

With the release of Internet Explorer 4.0, Microsoft introduced a new way to update its product: active online upgrades. You simply point Internet Explorer to a special Microsoft Web site and it lets you compare your Internet Explorer to the most recent one available, allowing you to update any pieces that are behind.

Microsoft has extended this concept to the entire operating system with Windows 98. Now, rather than ordering a CD or waiting for a single large file to download, you can have Windows 98 automatically update its older components via the Internet with the Windows Update tool.

Windows Update Tool

The Windows Update tool lets you use the Internet to update Windows components. When you run the Windows Update, it takes you to a special Microsoft Web site. Once there, the Update tool will compare your current Windows 98 configuration with the most recent one available from Microsoft. You can then decide whether or not you want the Update tool to download and install all, some, or none of the updates.

In addition to product updates, the Update tool will allow you to download optional components that Microsoft makes available to Windows 98 users. Things like new Active Desktop applets, screen savers, and trial products are likely to pop up.

To run the update tool, open Start | Settings | Windows Update. This will actually open a special link to Microsoft's Web site, where the updates are available. You are initially presented with two choices: Update and Restore. Update allows you to search for updates, download, and install them. Restore lets you undo a previous update, just in case it created more problems than it solved. Figure 3-15 shows the main Windows Update screen.

Once you go into the Product Updates section, you can pick and choose the updates you need. So if there is an update for a problem with video capture cards, and your system does not have video capture, then you can skip it, since you obviously don't need it. It's sort of like updates *a la carte!*

FIGURE 3-15

Windows Update

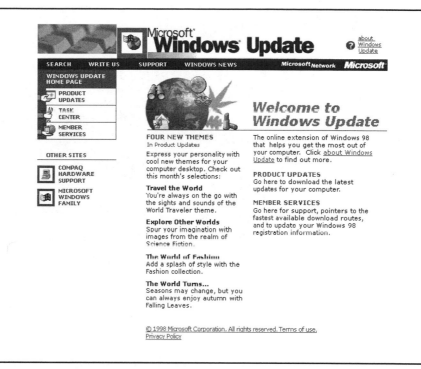

CERTIFICATION OBJECTIVE 3.04

Enabling Large Disk Support

Large Disk Support allows Windows 98 to format hard disks with the new FAT32. In order to use LDS and FAT32, a partition must be created using Windows 98 Fixed Disk Setup Program (FDISK) with Large Disk Support enabled.

When FDISK is first started in Windows 98, it immediately asks whether you want to enable large disk support. If you want to create a FAT32 drive, enter **Y**. If you want to create a traditional FAT drive, enter **N**. Figure 3-16 shows the FDISK screen that will greet you and allow you to enable large disk support.

FDISK enabling large
disk support

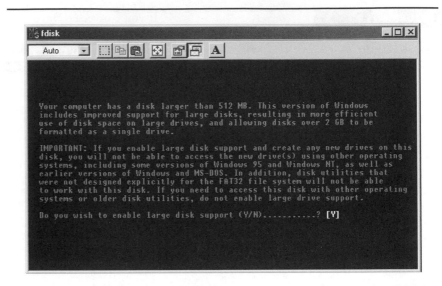

 Know how and why to enable large disk support.

CERTIFICATION OBJECTIVE 3.05

Converting to FAT32

If you upgraded from a previous version of Windows, or you installed using
standard FAT, you will want to consider converting that drive to FAT32.
The new file system included with Windows 98 is FAT32, an enhanced
version of FAT.

Before converting to FAT32, you should keep the following points
in mind:

■   Once you convert your hard drive to the FAT32 format, you cannot
return to using the FAT16 format unless you repartition and format

the FAT32 drive. If you converted the drive on which Windows 98 is installed, then you must reinstall Windows 98 after repartitioning the drive.

- If you have a compressed drive, or want to compress your drive in the future, you should not convert to FAT32.

- If you have a removable disk that you use with another operating system, don't convert to FAT32.

- Hibernate features (Suspend To Disk, for example) will not work on a FAT32 drive.

- If you convert your hard drive to FAT32, then you cannot uninstall Windows 98.

- Although most programs are not affected by the conversion from FAT16 to FAT32, some disk utilities that depend on FAT16 do not work with FAT32 drives. Contact your disk utility manufacturer to see if there is an updated version that is compatible with FAT32.

- If you convert your hard drive to FAT32, you can no longer use dual boot to run earlier versions of Windows (Windows 95 [version 4.00.950], Windows NT 3.*x*, Windows NT 4.0, and Windows 3.*x*). However, if you are on a network, earlier versions of Windows can still gain access to your FAT32 hard drive through the network.

You need to weigh these issues carefully, but for the majority of users, FAT32 is the way to go. Few people use disk utilities other than the ones that come with Windows 98, and these work with FAT32 just fine. With hard disk prices holding steady while their capacities continue to climb, it just doesn't make sense to compress your data in most situations. And apart from your average power user, few people want to be able to access their Windows 98 drives from DOS or Windows NT.

exam
Watch

Understand FAT32 and its advantages. Know how to convert a FAT drive to FAT32 and what the limitations are.

Once you have worked out all the details and decide to switch to FAT32, it is a very easy process. Simply run the Drive Converter (FAT32) from the

Start | Programs | Accessories | System Tools menu. Drive Converter will remind you of the issues concerning FAT32, check for any old software that will not work with FAT32, allow you to make a backup before proceeding (a very good idea when making such drastic changes to your system), and finally, it will start the conversion.

The conversion is actually a two-step process. First, Drive Converter will boot into DOS Mode and do two things: run ScanDisk to make sure the drive isn't corrupt, then run Microsoft FAT to FAT32 Converter, a DOS Mode program that actually performs the conversion. Figure 3-17 shows Drive Converter just before it boots into DOS Mode to perform those two steps.

Finally, the system will reboot back into Windows 98 and automatically perform a defragmentation, a critical step. It is critical because although the drive has been converted, it has not been optimized with its new format. Stopping the defragmentation process from completing can have a severe impact on performance.

Converting to FAT32 can give you huge gains in hard drive space, even though the size of your drive has not changed. Figures 3-18 and 3-19 show

FIGURE 3-17

Drive Converter

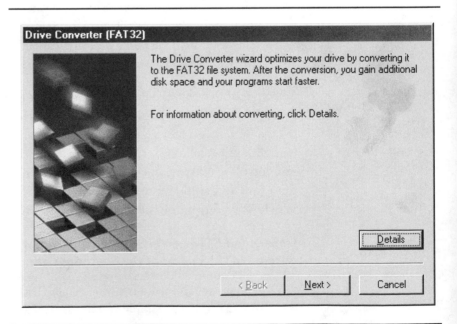

FIGURE 3-18

ScanDisk before FAT32
conversion

a 1GB drive as a FAT drive, and after being converted to FAT32, respectively. Although the number of files has gone up between the times these snapshots were taken, there is still a 30 percent increase in space—300MB of newly usable drive space!

It's not that that space wasn't there before; it was simply wasted by the 32KB allocation units used by the FAT file system. When those allocation units were shrunk down to 4KB by FAT32, a lot of that wasted space

FIGURE 3-19

ScanDisk after FAT32
conversion

became available again. It is true that there is some waste with 4KB allocation units as well, but much less.

Converting to the FAT32 file system using the Drive Converter is a relatively simple task that can net huge gains in hard disk space. Anyone who meets the requirements to use it should convert and reap the benefits!

| EXERCISE 3-4 |

Converting from FAT to FAT32

1. Open the Drive Converter utility from the Start | Programs | Accessories | System Tools menu.

2. Click the Next button.

3. Click OK to accept warning about being able to access FAT32 from older operating systems.

4. Select the FAT drive you wish to convert and click Next.

5. Click Next after Drive Converter searches for old software that is incompatible.

6. Click Create Backup if you want to back up any files before continuing, or simply click Next to continue.

7. Drive Converter will boot to DOS Mode to actually perform the conversion. This may take several hours. Click Next to proceed.

8. After converting the drive, Windows 98 will automatically reboot. It will immediately defragment the converted drive. Wait for this to complete. Once it's done, you are all ready to go with your new FAT32 drive!

CERTIFICATION OBJECTIVE 3.06

Backing Up and Restoring Data

Windows 98 comes with its own data backup tool, called, simply, Backup. It was developed by Seagate Software, the same company that made the backup program for Windows NT. Seagate also retails its own backup software for all versions of Windows. The backup program that comes with Windows 98 allows for simple backups and restores of your data. Backup allows you to copy some or all of your files from your hard drive(s) to your backup device(s). Supported devices include floppy disks, hard disks, network drives, and tape drives.

exam
ⓦatch

You will need to know how to install, configure, and use the Backup application to back up your data.

Backup should be installed in most default installations. If you don't see it under the Start | Programs | Accessories | System Tools menu, you will need to install it manually. To do so, open the Control Panel and select Add/Remove Programs. Click the Windows Setup tab, select System Tools, and click the Details button. Check the Backup box and click OK. Figure 3-20 shows the dialog to select the Backup utility.

When started, Backup gives you the options to create a new backup job, load a previous backup job, or restore a previous backup, as shown in Figure 3-21. The New Job Wizard is a good choice for the novice user. The wizard will guide you through each step of the backup process.

FIGURE 3-20

Installing the Backup utility

FIGURE 3-21

Backup startup

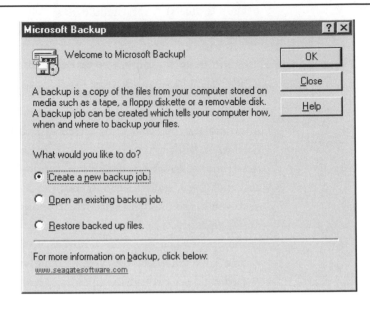

If you press the Close button or ESCAPE key, it will bring you to the Backup main menu so that you can manually create a backup job. The more accomplished user will probably prefer the full Backup interface, shown in Figure 3-22.

Backup's interface is very simple. It allows you to simply check off the drives you wish to back up, and which types of files you want backed up (all, or just new and changed files). Then you select the media to back up to (tape, floppy, removable media, even other hard disks or network connections) and how to perform the backup (use verification afterward, compression, or do it all without asking for any verification). Then you can save all your choices to a file for easy recall in the future.

Backing Up System Configuration Files

It is very important to back up the Windows 98 system files on a regular basis. In particular, the Registry file should always be backed up in case of a system problem. In order to make sure the Registry is always backed up, you must make sure Backup is configured to do so. Figure 3-23 shows the Tools | Preferences screen from the backup application.

Backup interface

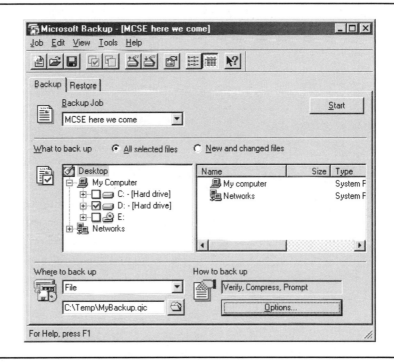

Make absolutely sure the middle option, "Back up or restore the Registry when backing up or restoring the Windows directory" is selected. This way, every time you back up your system files, the Registry will be properly

Backup preferences

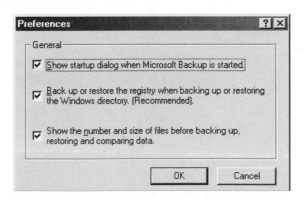

backed up as well. Backing up the Registry in conjunction with the entire Windows subdirectory structure (C:\WINDOWS\) will ensure that your computer can live through almost any catastrophe.

CERTIFICATION OBJECTIVE 3.07

Running Applications in Windows 98

Windows 98 provides a robust, extensible environment for Windows applications. Windows 98 is a preemptive multitasking system, which means several Windows 98 programs can run at the same time without having to completely wait for one or the other to finish. Before Windows 98, it was very difficult to format a floppy disk and do anything else at the same time. Now you can format a disk and play a game with no noticeable load on the system.

Even older legacy software can run on Windows 98. The system can even be tuned to make older software run more efficiently. MS-DOS programs have a great deal of flexibility. After creating a shortcut to a DOS program, you can fine-tune its running parameters via the shortcut's Properties sheet. Figure 3-24 shows the MS-DOS prompts memory properties.

Windows 98 also protects programs from one another in memory. When one program crashes, it's less likely to bring down the whole system. Instead, just that program is stopped, while the rest continue to run. If your application locks up, you can press CTRL-ALT-DEL to bring up the Close Program dialog, making it easy to take care of ill-behaved programs.

Older, 16-bit Windows applications may not be so easy to tame. All 16-bit Windows programs are assigned the same resources to use, much like they were under Windows 3.1. Since they are all sharing, if one 16-bit Windows program crashes, it can cause all the other 16-bit applications to crash as well. 32-bit Windows applications do not suffer this fate.

FIGURE 3-24

MS-DOS memory
properties

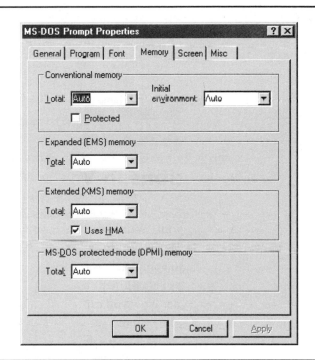

CERTIFICATION OBJECTIVE 3.08

Troubleshooting Tools

For all the technical support people in the world, Windows 98 is a heavily
armed operating system. Compared to previous versions, Windows 98 has
several more troubleshooting utilities at its disposal. Nearly all can be found
in the Start | Programs | Accessories | System Tools menu. There are several
automated tools to help the novice user try to figure out problems on his
own. If he still can't figure it out, nearly every tool allows its findings to be
dumped to a file and sent to more experienced troubleshooters.

exam
ⓦatch

*You will need to know what troubleshooting tools are available in
Windows 98, and when each one is appropriate.*

Registry Checker

Windows 98 stores nearly all of its configuration information in the Registry. This includes user account information, software settings, operating system settings, protocol bindings, and user preferences. Obviously, the Registry is vitally important to Windows 98.

Windows 98 always keeps a backup copy of your Registry. You can use the backup copy if your current Registry encounters a problem. Registry Checker checks your Registry for errors, and if everything is OK, it makes a backup copy of the Registry. If there is a problem with your current Registry, Registry Checker will allow you to restore the current backup copy.

Registry Checker runs automatically each time that you restart your computer. If it notices a problem, it automatically replaces the Registry with the backup copy. Registry Checker can also be started by clicking Start | Run, typing **scanreg** in Open, and then clicking OK.

Registry Checker is a very simple program that requires no user input to get started. Once it completes its check, it will prompt you to use a backup copy if the Registry is corrupt, or ask if you want to make a new backup, if everything is OK. Figure 3-25 shows the Registry Checker doing its thing.

There are actually two versions of the Registry Checker: ScanReg and ScanRegW. ScanReg is a DOS version, which is useful when Registry problems prevent the system from booting properly. ScanReg can be used after booting to a Windows 98 DOS prompt using a boot disk. ScanReg doesn't back up the Registry, and runs in Real mode.

ScanRegW is the Windows version of the Registry Scanner, running in Protected mode. Even if you run ScanReg in Windows 98, it will automatically run ScanRegW, since you are already running in Windows mode. Just remember: ScanReg for DOS, ScanRegW for Windows.

The two versions are basically the same, except:

- ScanReg uses MS-DOS environment, while ScanRegW uses Windows.
- ScanReg uses Real mode, while ScanRegW uses Protected mode.
- ScanRegW doesn't fix or restore the Registry.

FIGURE 3-25

Windows Registry Checker

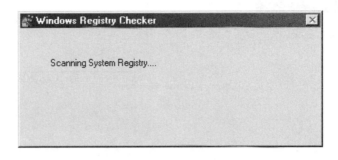

- ScanReg doesn't back up the Registry or run in Safe mode.

Dr. Watson

Dr. Watson is useful for detecting errors and logging them for technical support. It can be run manually to simply take a system snapshot, or if you are encountering regular problems, it can be run in the background. When you encounter the problem, Dr. Watson will detect it and attempt to log a system snapshot at the time of the error.

Dr. Watson is not loaded by default when Windows 98 starts. To load Dr. Watson, click Start | Run and type **drwatson** in Open, and then click OK. To launch Dr. Watson automatically, you must create a shortcut in your Startup group to \WINDOWS\DRWATSON.EXE. When Dr. Watson is running, it only shows up as an icon in the task bar. This illustration shows Dr. Watson while in its ready state on the task bar:

The diagnosis view allows you to see the results of the Dr. Watson snapshot. By default this view only shows information on any problems encountered. When you are manually running a Dr. Watson snapshot, it is very unlikely that it will find any problems. The advanced view allows you to see more information, even when Windows 98 is running great. It

FIGURE 3-26

Dr. Watson diagnosis

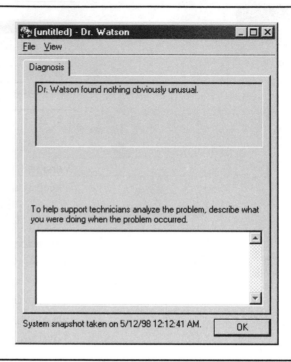

includes the diagnosis from the basic view, as well as system, tasks, startup, kernel drivers, user drivers, MS-DOS drivers, and 16-bit modules. Note that all the information gathered by Dr. Watson when the system is running fine can also be viewed by the Microsoft System Information utility. Figure 3-26 shows a typical Dr. Watson report.

Automatic Skip Driver Agent

The Automatic Skip Driver (ASD) allows you to find devices that are failing to initialize during Windows 98 startup, and isolate them from future bootups. Devices that are failing often have trouble loading their device drivers, the software that makes them function under Windows 98. Such problems may simply be annoying because the device doesn't work, or they could be the cause of unexplained system crashes and possible data loss.

All devices that have failed to start are listed by ASD. You can enable any device previously disabled by ASD, and Windows 98 will attempt to use the device on the next startup attempt. Figure 3-27 shows ASD on a well-behaved computer.

FIGURE 3-27

Automatic Skip Driver

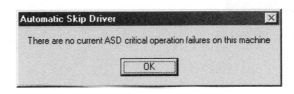

Version Conflict Manager

Windows 98 also features Version Conflict Manager, a behind-the-scenes part of Windows that helps keep your system file versions at the most recent. If a program copies a system file, Version Conflict Manager will check to see which is more recent, the file being copied or the existing file. Whichever is newer is put into place, while the older file is copied to \WINDOWS\VCM. If problems erupt with the new file, the old one can be copied back.

If you want to restore an older version of a driver, you can pull up the Version Conflict Manager via System Information. Click Start | Programs | Accessories | System Tools | System Information and select the Tools | Version Conflict Manager menu. The Version Conflict Manager will appear and show a list of drivers that have been copied to \WINDOWS\VCM. Simply select the driver(s) you want to restore and click the Restore Selected Files button. Figure 3-28 shows the Version Conflict Manager.

System Configuration Utility

The Microsoft System Configuration tool is very useful when troubleshooting. System Configuration allows you to control how Windows is configured. Load System Configuration from Start | Programs | Accessories | System Tools | System Configuration. Figure 3-29 shows the System Configuration utility.

After starting System Configuration, you will find six tabs: General, Config.sys, Autoexec.bat, System.ini, Win.ini, and Startup. These tabs allow you to edit the configuration of Windows 98. The General tab allows you to control how Windows 98 boots up, as well as making backups of critical system files CONFIG.SYS, AUTOEXEC.BAT, SYSTEM.INI, and WIN.INI.

FIGURE 3-28

Version Conflict Manager

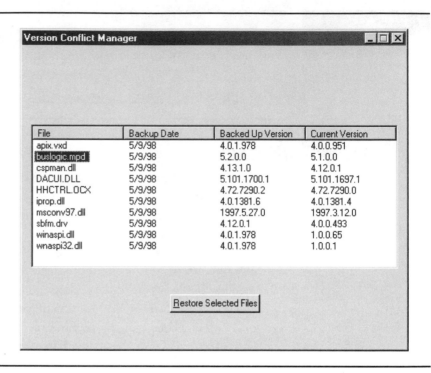

Now, you may be thinking, "SYSTEM.INI? WIN.INI? Weren't those replaced with the Registry back in Windows 95?" Well, mostly. The SYSTEM.INI and WIN.INI files, as well as CONFIG.SYS and AUTOEXEC.BAT are still there for legacy Windows 16-bit applications to use. Since these applications don't know about the Registry, they still use the INI files to set themselves up on the system. System Configuration makes it easier than ever to manipulate these files to troubleshoot unruly applications. Sections can be disabled or even deleted as necessary.

The Startup tab makes it easy to enable or disable background tasks that load at startup. There are a lot of small support programs that load when Windows 98 starts, even though there may be no icons in your STARTUP folder. They are set to load at startup in the Registry. Clicking the Startup tab shows a list of programs currently loading at startup. Simply uncheck those you do not want to load.

FIGURE 3-29

System Configuration utility

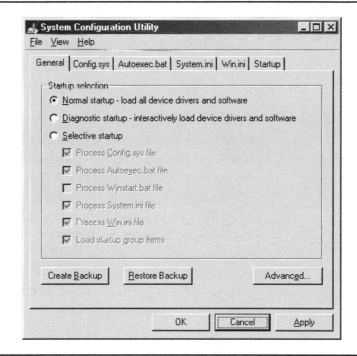

Web-Based Troubleshooting Tools

One of the best uses of the Internet by computer makers has been for support. Most allow you to browse Web sites for technical support and download updates and fixes online, without racking up long distance phone and modem calls. Microsoft and Windows 98 are no exception.

Windows 98's principal Internet-based troubleshooting tool is Windows Update. This tool will automatically compare your system configuration to the most recent available from Microsoft, and allow you to easily download and install any updates and fixes. Run Windows Update from Start | Settings | Windows Update.

To search for help on your own, open Start | Programs | Accessories | System Tools | Welcome to Windows. Here you will find Web links to Windows 98, Microsoft, Microsoft Technical Support, and Microsoft Press.

Microsoft Technical support allows you to search their Knowledge Base, a database of known problems and solutions. When you call Microsoft for support, this is what they use to help you. Cruise on over to http://www.microsoft.com/support and click Support Online.

Controlling the Boot Process

Sometimes you need more control while the system boots up. If the computer fails during the boot process and never makes it to the GUI, how are you going to figure out where it failed? Use Step-by-Step Confirmation during the boot process to verify each component as it loads.

To use Step-by-Step Confirmation, boot the computer, and when the text "Starting Windows 98" appears on screen, press F8. A menu will appear with several options. Press the number for Step-by-Step Confirmation and press ENTER. As Windows boots up, it will prompt you before it loads each command. For each command you want to run, press Y. To skip a command, press N. If the command runs successfully, you are prompted with the next command. If the command does not run successfully, you will receive an error message. Any commands that give an error are suspect and should be corrected or removed.

You may need to boot Windows 98 in Safe mode in order to correct a boot error. To do this, boot the computer, and when the text "Starting Windows 98" appears on screen, press F8. A menu will appear with several options. Press the number for Windows 98 Safe Mode and press ENTER. Windows 98 will load with limited options known to work on most computers.

Signature Verification Tool

All files shipped with Windows 98 will be digitally "signed" by Microsoft. This signature makes it possible to verify that the system files have not been altered, either accidentally or intentionally. Such alterations to system files may be harmless, but some could result in data loss.

The Signature Verification Tool allows administrators to view the digital certificates assigned to files, and to search for signed or unsigned system

FIGURE 3-30

Signature Verification Tool

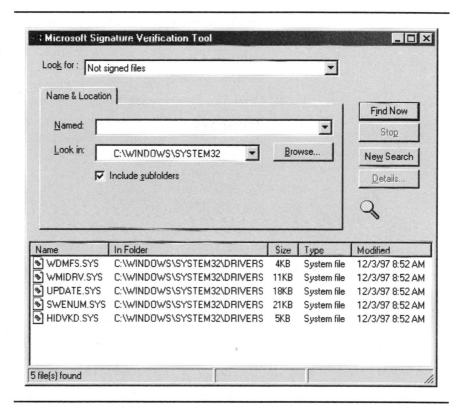

files. To start the Signature Verification Tool, load Start | Programs | Accessories | System Tools | System Information and select the Tools | Signature Verification menu. Use the search option to find the signed or unsigned files you want to check, highlight the file(s), and click the Details button. Figure 3-30 shows the Signature Verification Tool.

Windows 98 can also be set to use digital signatures to allow or disallow files to be installed on the system. By default, this feature is disabled, but it can be turned on via the Registry. Use REGEDIT to locate the HKEY_LOCAL_MACHINE\SOFTWARE\ MICROSOFT\DRIVER SIGNING\POLICY key. The Policy may be set to one of three levels:

- **Level 0** disables digital signature checking. The dialog box that identifies a digitally signed driver will not appear, and all drivers will be installed on the system, whether they are signed or not. Set Policy="00 00 00 00."

- **Level 1** determines if the driver has passed WHQL testing. A message appears whenever a user tries to install a driver that fails the signature check. Set Policy="01 00 00 00."

- **Level 2** blocks the installation of a driver that fails the signature check. A dialog box appears with a message informing the user that the driver cannot be installed because it is not digitally signed. Set Policy="02 00 00 00."

QUESTIONS AND ANSWERS

I have a 6GB hard disk. How would I make all of it my C: drive?	Enable Large Disk Support (FAT32) and format the drive, or use the Driver Converter.
How would I make my programs load faster?	Run Disk Defragmenter.
How do I back up my Registry?	Run Registry Checker and tell it to make a backup when done.
How can I get detailed information on my computer?	Use the System Information tool.
How can I make a FAT drive store more information?	Compress it with DriveSpace3.
How can I easily make copies of all my files?	Use the Backup tool to copy the entire system to tape or another hard drive.
How can I control the boot process?	Press F8 when "Starting Windows 98" appears.
How can I automatically get a report on a program that frequently crashes?	Start Dr. Watson before loading the offending program.
How can I easily check my system files for integrity?	Run System File Checker.
What is the easiest way to maintain my computer?	Run Maintenance Wizard to run ScanDisk, Defragmenter, and Disk Cleanup once a week.

While it may seem wise to turn the digital signature feature on, it could result in your not being able to install third-party software that must modify or replace certain Windows 98 files to function properly.

CERTIFICATION SUMMARY

Windows 98 offers a much wider variety of ways to manage your hard disks, files, and applications than ever before. When taking the Windows 98 certification test, you must know how to install and use the Backup application. When dealing with hard disks, understand partitioning, large hard disk support, and FAT32. Also know how to convert existing FAT drives to FAT32. Understand how to use disk compression, and don't forget how FAT32 impacts disk compression!

When working on Windows 98 systems, know how to use all of the following tools: Disk Defragmenter, SCANDISK, DriveSpace3, System Configuration Utility, Windows Update, Maintenance Wizard, System File Checker, Scheduled Tasks, ScanReg, and ScanRegW. Knowing what these utilities do, when they are needed, and how to use them is crucial.

 # TWO-MINUTE DRILL

- ❏ Windows 98 offers a lot of improvements over previous versions of Windows, and one of the most invisible, yet important ones, is the file system.

- ❏ On the Start | Programs | Accessories | System Tools menu you will find over a dozen tools for viewing and configuring your system.

- ❏ The Microsoft System Information utility (MSI) provides easy Read Only access to detailed information regarding the Windows 98 operating system, computer hardware, and even third-party software.

- ❏ Microsoft System Information can be useful for examining system files that are currently running on a Windows 98 computer.

- ❏ The big weapon against file system errors is the venerable ScanDisk.

- ❏ The System File Checker (SFC) is a tool for automatically checking that all system files are in order, and that none is corrupt.

❑ When setting up a hard disk in virtually any operating system, you must tell the operating system about the hard disk: how big it is, what type of file system is used, and how the hard disk is divided up.

❑ You must know how to partition a hard disk into one or more disk drives.

❑ Windows 98 includes DriveSpace, a disk drive compression software package.

❑ Failure to maintain the hard disks properly won't cause immediate problems, but problems will creep up over time.

❑ ScanDisk will check the drive for logical and physical defects in the hard disk(s).

❑ Disk Defragmenter will make sure the files on your hard disk are arranged in a contiguous fashion, allowing them to be loaded faster.

❑ Disk Cleanup helps you track down and delete temporary files and unused programs to free up valuable disk space.

❑ Microsoft has included the Scheduled Tasks utility, which allows you to schedule various programs to run unattended at any time.

❑ Maintenance Wizard simply takes the three most important system utilities, ScanDisk, Disk Defragmenter, and Disk Cleanup, and makes it easy to set them up in the Scheduled Tasks.

❑ Microsoft provides what it calls Service Packs, a collection of bug fixes and product enhancements.

❑ The Windows Update tool lets you use the Internet to update Windows components.

❑ Large Disk Support allows Windows 98 to format hard disks with the new FAT32.

❑ Know how and why to enable Large Disk Support.

❑ You will want to consider converting your existing drive to FAT32.

❑ Understand FAT32 and its advantages. Know how to convert a FAT drive to FAT32 and what the limitations are.

❑ You will need to know how to install, configure, and use the Backup application to back up your data.

❑ It is very important to back up the Windows 98 system files on a regular basis. In particular, the Registry file should always be backed up in case of a system problem.

❑ Windows 98 is a preemptive multi-tasking system, which means several Windows 98 programs can run at the same time without having to completely wait for one or the other to finish.

❑ You will need to know what troubleshooting tools are available in Windows 98, and when each one is appropriate.

❑ Registry Checker checks your Registry for errors, and if everything is OK, it makes a backup copy of the Registry.

❑ Dr. Watson is useful for detecting errors and logging them for technical support.

❑ The Automatic Skip Driver (ASD) allows you to find devices that are failing to initialize during Windows 98 startup, and isolate them from future bootups.

❑ Windows 98 also features Version Conflict Manager, a behind-the-scenes part of Windows that helps keep your system file versions at the most recent.

❑ The Microsoft System Configuration tool is very useful when troubleshooting. System Configuration allows you to control how Windows is configured.

❑ Windows 98's principal Internet-based troubleshooting tool is Windows Update.

❑ Use Step-by-Step Confirmation during the boot process to verify each component as it loads.

❑ The Signature Verification Tool allows administrators to view the digital certificates assigned to files, and to search for signed or unsigned system files.

SELF TEST

The following questions will help you measure your understanding of the material presented in this chapter. Read all the choices carefully, as there may be more than one correct answer. Choose all correct answers for each question.

1. What are two advantages of using FAT32?

   A. Use of only SCSI disks and faster performance

   B. Supports larger hard disks and faster performance

   C. Supports larger hard disks and more efficient use of large hard disks

   D. Use of only SCSI disks and more efficient use of large hard drives

2. Which one of the following would prevent you from using DriveSpace?

   A. FAT

   B. FAT32

   C. A small hard disk

   D. A large hard disk

3. You are having trouble reading a data file from your hard drive. Which tool would be most helpful in fixing this problem?

   A. Disk Defragmenter

   B. DriveSpace

   C. System File Checker

   D. ScanDisk

4. What does Enable Large Disk Support do?

   A. Makes Windows 98 SCSI drive compatible

   B. Allows you to format a drive using FAT32

   C. Allows you to format a drive using FAT

   D. Enables Iomega ZIP drives under Windows 98

5. After converting a FAT drive to FAT32, how can you convert back to FAT?

   A. You cannot convert back

   B. Run Disk Converter with the /U option

   C. Right-click the drive and select Undo

   D. Download the FAT32 to FAT conversion utility from Microsoft's Web site

6. How can you control what commands Windows 98 runs during the boot process?

   A. Press F5

   B. Press F8 and select Safe Mode

   C. You cannot control the boot process

   D. Press F8 and select Step-by-Step

7. What utility would you use to make your applications open faster?

   A. Disk Defragmenter

   B. ScanDisk

   C. FDISK

   D. Automatic Skip Driver utility

8. What utility would you use to automatically find and delete files that are wasting disk space?

   A. ScanDisk

   B. Disk Defragmenter

   C. Disk Cleanup

   D. FDISK

9. How would you update your Windows 98 system?

   A. ScanDisk

   B. Automatic Skip Driver

   C. Registry Checker

   D. Windows 98 Update

10. You suspect your Registry is corrupt. How would you fix this problem?

    A. ScanDisk

    B. Registry Checker

    C. Windows 98 Update

    D. REGEDIT

11. Where can you find nearly all of Windows 98 tools for maintaining your system?

    A. Start | Settings

    B. Start | Programs | Accessories | System Tools

    C. C:\WINDOWS\SYSTEM TOOLS

    D. http:\\www.microsoft.com\ systemtools.htm

12. What does the Automatic Skip Driver do?

    A. Skips drivers that are not necessary on your computer

    B. Skips Windows 98 drivers to use a manufacturer driver

    C. Detects any drivers that are failing to load and allows you to disable them

    D. Skips unnecessary system prompts

13. What is the largest drive size supported with FAT32?

    A. 2GB

    B. 2TB

    C. 8GB

    D. 512MB

14. What system utility is useful for finding out more details about a computer?

    A. Registry Checker

    B. REGEDIT

    C. ScanDisk

    D. Microsoft System Information

15. What provides an easy-to-use interface for making copies of system and user data files?

    A. Backup Wizard

    B. Registry Checker

    C. Drive Converter

    D. Automatic Skip Driver

MICROSOFT CERTIFIED SYSTEMS ENGINEER

4

Printing in Windows 98

CERTIFICATION OBJECTIVES

Printing in Windows 98 has not really changed all that much from printing in Windows 95. In all honesty, that's really not a bad thing, because printing in Windows 95 worked fairly well. Microsoft has more or less just tweaked printing. The basic features of printing in Windows 98 include:

- **32-bit print subsystem** This means that jobs print faster. The printer is fed the data as it needs it, as opposed to data being fed whether the printer is ready or not. The print spooler is consolidated into a single architecture.

- **EMF (Enhanced MetaFile) spooling** This allows you to print faster, and it also returns you back to your application faster.

- **Deferred (Offline) Printing** You can create a print job even though you are not connected to a printer. Once you are connected to a printer, you can print the deferred print job.

- **Point and Print Support** This allows you to install and print to shared network printers.

- **Support for Image Color Matching 2.0 (ICM)** The ICM 2.0 standard preserves original colors from input devices (scanners, digital cameras) and ensures that the colors, when output (monitors, printers), will be consistent with the colors from the original input.

New additions to printing in Windows 98 include:

- Support for more printers.
- Improved printing from the Internet.

Web printing is probably where the biggest improvement has been made. You can now background print Web pages, which means you can get back to surfing, while your Web pages print. Another Internet enhancement is the ability to recursively print hyperlinks. This means that you can print all pages that are hyperlinked to the page you're currently printing, and print the pages that are hyperlinked to *those* pages, and so on. Last, but not least, you also have the ability to print a specific frame or all frames from Web pages designed with frames.

CERTIFICATION OBJECTIVE 4.01

Installing a Local Printer

In contrast to Windows 3.1, Windows 95 and Windows 98 have a 32-bit print subsystem. This is significant because the new 32-bit print subsystem consolidates print spooling functionality that was spread across several Windows components into a new single architecture made up of virtual device drivers (VXDs) and dynamic-link libraries (DLLs).

The advantages of this new print spooler include smoother background printing, and return-to-application time that is quicker and more flexible. With Windows 3.1, print jobs were spooled to the printer in fixed blocks of information, regardless of whether the printer was ready to receive it. The new spooler dynamically sends data to the printer as the printer is able to receive the data.

exam
Watch

The print subsystem is 32-bit, provides smoother background printing, and returns you to your application faster.

Printer Considerations

Before you go out and buy a printer, look over the following considerations.

Considerations in General

Look for printers that support Extended Capabilities Port (ECP). These ports are bi-directional, that is, they allow Windows 98 to identify the printer and have the printer send status messages to Windows 98. For example, your printer can send your computer messages when it's out of paper, or when its ink cartridges are low on ink. ECP also improves your printing performance, because the port sends data from your computer to the printer faster and more consistently. It won't make your printer print any faster, but the print job as a whole will finish faster than if it was printed with Windows 3.1. To actually take advantage of these enhancements, though, your computer's printer port (LPT1) must have

ECP capabilities, your printer cable must be IEEE 1284-compliant to support bi-directional communication, and your printer must be Plug and Play.

Another consideration is font cartridges. If you have a printer that uses one, the fonts will also have to be installed on your computer as well.

Considerations for Networks

In order to share a printer, whether it is on a Microsoft or Novell network, you must use the 32-bit, Protected mode client, with file and printer sharing enabled.

You can also configure computers for Point and Print. This means that a computer can browse across a network to find a printer shared over a network and have the printer driver automatically installed on the computer, if one isn't already installed.

Installing a Printer

Printers in Windows 98 are right where they were in Windows 95—in the Printers folder.

Essentially, there are three ways to access the Printers folder:

■ From the Settings menu (seen in Figure 4-1)

■ From the Control Panel

■ From inside My Computer

Furthermore, there are four ways that a printer can be installed:

■ Using Plug and Play

■ Using Point and Print on a network

■ Using Add Printer in the Printers folder

■ Using a custom setup script during a Windows 98 installation

If you upgrade your computer from Windows 95 to Windows 98, all previously installed printers are migrated over during the upgrade. If you didn't have a printer previously installed, but connected one during the Windows 98 upgrade, Setup will automatically run the Add Printer Wizard to install the printer.

FIGURE 4-1

One way of opening the
Printers folder in
Windows 98

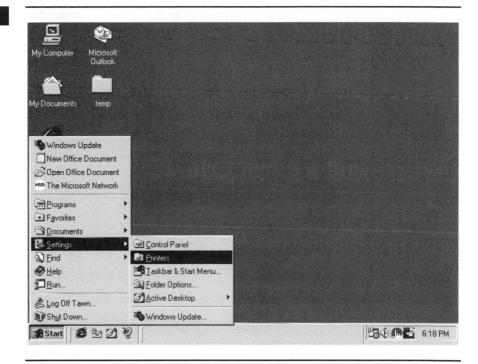

EXERCISE 4-1

Manually Install a Printer Using the Add Printer Wizard

1. Double-click the Add Printer icon.

2. Click Next.

3. If you are connected to a network, the wizard will ask you whether the printer is local or on a network. Choose Local. (For installing a printer on a network, see Chapter 5, Windows 98 Networking Components.)

4. In this screen, select your printer manufacturer and model. Click Next. If your printer does not appear on the list, you can either choose the Generic manufacturer and Generic/Text Only printer, or slide your driver disk into the floppy drive, click the Have Disk button, and follow the instructions supplied.

5. Select the printer port to which the printer is connected. Click Next.

6. In the Printer Name box, keep the name that shows up by default, or type in a different one. The printer name is the name that

appears below the icon in your Printers folder. Also, select whether you want this printer to be the default printer for Windows programs. Click Next.

7. Choose whether or not you want to print a test page with your newly connected printer. Click Finish. If you click Yes, you may be asked for the Windows 98 CD-ROM to finish installing the printer driver.

If you print a test page and it does not print correctly, you can click No on the dialog box that asks you if the test page printed correctly. This will bring up the Print Troubleshooter. It will walk you through a series of questions that will try to resolve your printer problem. If the Print Troubleshooter does not appear, or you need it at some later time, you can start it by clicking Start/Help. Once the Help window appears, click the Contents tab, click Troubleshooting, and click Print. See Figure 4-2.

FIGURE 4-2

Windows 98 Print Troubleshooter

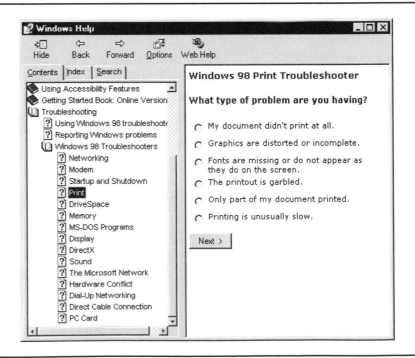

EXERCISE 4-2

Install a Printer via Plug and Play

1. With your computer turned off, plug the printer cable into your computer and into the printer.

2. Turn your computer on.

3. Windows will do the rest, though you may be instructed to insert a driver disk into your floppy drive. If you do not have a disk with a printer driver on it, Windows will provide you with a list of printers that have a compatible driver.

ECP Support

As we mentioned earlier, an Extended Capabilities Port provides high-speed printing and support for ECP-compliant devices. You may have to enable ECP through you computer's BIOS. Refer to your computer's manual if you are unsure if your computer supports ECP, or if you are unsure how to enable ECP support. Enabling ECP does not mean your devices have to be ECP compliant, though. You can connect either ECP or non-ECP devices to the port. In either case, using an ECP parallel port will enhance your port's input and output (I/O), for faster printing. If you have ECP enabled, you will see something like Figure 4-3 in Device Manager.

exam
ⓦatch

ECP allows printers to send unsolicited messages to Windows 98 and other applications, such as "Low ink" or "Out of paper."

EXERCISE 4-3

Verify ECP Support

1. Consult your computer manual to determine if your computer's BIOS supports ECP.

2. Click Start.

3. Click Settings.

4. Click Control Panel.

5. Double-click System. Click the Device Manager tab. If you have ECP and it is enabled, your Printer Port will reflect this.

Using Device Manager to
verify ECP support for your
parallel port

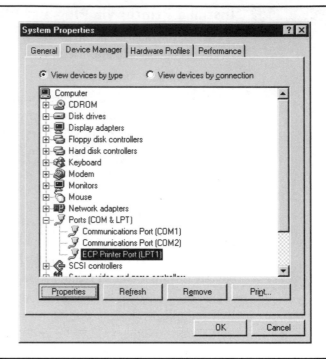

If your computer supports ECP and you do not see something similar to
Figure 4-3, refer to your computer's manual on how to access your
computer's BIOS to make the necessary change. Once you enable ECP
support, Windows 98 should auto-detect the ECP port on bootup.

CERTIFICATION OBJECTIVE 4.02

Configuring a Local Printer

We've looked at installing a printer. Now let's move on to configuring it for
use. If you have more than one printer (perhaps a color printer for graphics
and a laser for high-quality output), you'll want to set one as the default.
That is, set up one printer (let's say the laser) to print everything, until you
need the other printer (the color) to print. To set a printer to be the default,

just open the Printers folder, right-click the printer you want to make the default, and select Set As Default. You can tell which printer is currently the default by opening the Printers folder. The default printer will have a small check mark in the upper-left corner of the icon.

There are two basic ways to configure your printer:

- From the Printers folder
- From inside a Windows application by selecting File | Print | Properties.

To configure the printer from the Printers folder, open the Printers folder and right-click the icon of the printer you want to configure. Select Properties from the context menu. This brings up the Printer Properties dialog box. In general, a Printer Properties dialog box contains the two constant tabs and a mixture of the other five varying tabs. See Table 4-1 for a description of the properties of each tab.

Sharing is another tab in the Properties dialog box, but it only appears when the printer is shared.

To configure your printer from inside a Windows application, click File, then click Print. The Print dialog box opens. Next to the printer that you are printing to is a Properties button. Click the Properties button and the Printer Properties dialog opens up. You can make the changes you want, click OK, and continue printing.

| TABLE 4-1 | | Tabs Found In a Printer's Properties |

Appearance	Tab	Properties
Constant	General	Enter any comments about the printer; select a separator page between each print job; print a test page.
	Details	Select the port and driver the printer will use; select timeout settings (how long the printer will wait for the computer to send it data before it displays an error message); set the spool settings to determine how quickly control of the computer is returned to you.

TABLE 4-1		Tabs Found in a Printer's Properties (*continued*)
Appearance	**Tab**	**Properties**
Vary	Paper	Choose the default paper size, orientation, source (tray fed or manual fed), and number of copies to print.
	Graphics	Determine how the printer will print graphics. Typically this goes from coarse to fine, but higher resolution requires more printer memory.
	Fonts	Choose how to handle TrueType fonts.
	Color Management	Allows you to add and remove profile associations with a printer.
	Device Options	Depending on the printer driver, this tab allows setting specific options for your printer.

exam
ⓦatch
Printer Properties can be accessed by right-clicking a printer in the Printers folder, or through an application by clicking File/Print.

The tabs in printers' Properties windows can vary by printer, because the tabs reflect the different capabilities of different printers. Typically, two of the tabs, General and Details, remain constant. Refer to Table 4-1.

For example, look at Figure 4-4 and Figure 4-5, which show the Printer Properties for two color ink jet printers. The Lexmark 5700 printer gives you extended control over what kind of paper you can use (greeting card stock, iron-on transfers, transparencies, plain paper) on the Document/ Quality tab. The Epson 800, on the other hand, does not have the same tab. If you want to print on transparencies, you need to go to the Main tab, and then the Advanced Settings button. So, you can see that two tabs remain constant, the Sharing tab appears when the printer is shared, and the other tabs are dependent on the printer driver.

FIGURE 4-4

Printer Properties for a
Lexmark 5700 printer

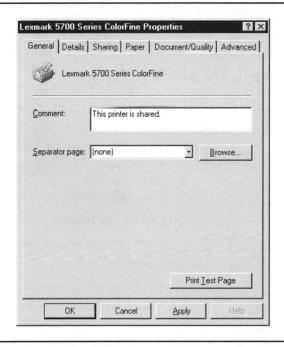

FIGURE 4-5

Printer Properties for an
Epson 800 printer

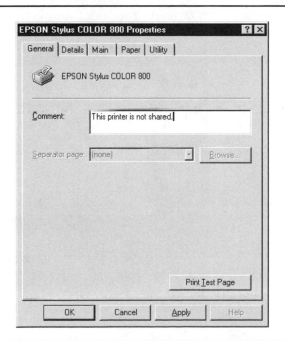

CERTIFICATION OBJECTIVE 4.03

Managing Local Printing

Once the printer is installed and working properly, we have to grapple with the everyday issues of managing the printer. The first thing you may want to do is to create a shortcut to your printer. There are a couple of ways to do this, but probably the easiest way is to do the following:

1. From the Desktop, double-click My Computer.

2. Double-click Printers.

3. Right-click and drag to the Desktop the printer you want the shortcut for.

4. Click Create Shortcut Here. See Figure 4-6.

FIGURE 4-6

Creating a shortcut for your printer on the Desktop

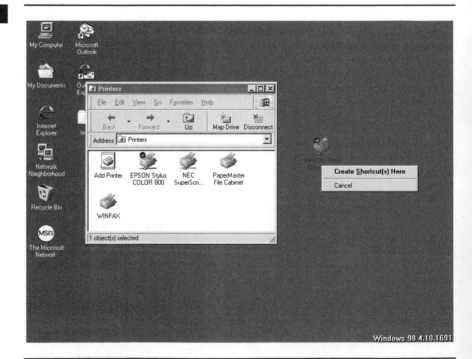

You can either keep the shortcut on your desktop, or drag it to the Quick Launch toolbar.

Managing printers also means that you'll have to dispose of printer drivers and other associated files that you no longer need when you delete a printer.

EXERCISE 4-4

Delete and Rename a Printer

To delete a printer:

1. Open the Printers folder.
2. Right-click the printer icon you want to delete. Select Delete.
3. Click Yes if you are sure.
4. Windows then asks if it can remove all of the files associated with this printer. Click Yes. If you plan to reattach the printer to this computer, select No to preserve the files.

To rename a printer:

1. Open the Printers folder.
2. Right-click the printer icon you want to rename. Click Rename.
3. Type in a new name for the printer. Press ENTER.

Windows 98 does allow you to rename the printer during the installation process, but sometimes it isn't necessary to rename the printer until later. For example, you may have different printers located in each corner of the office. The default name of the icon won't help you figure out where the printer is. In this case, you could rename each printer ColorNorth, LaserSouth, DotEast, and ColorWest to help everyone determine which printer is where. This means that if someone wanted to print in color, all he needs to think about is whether or not the north printer is any closer than the west printer.

If others use your computer and you do not want them to change the printer settings on your computer, you can use the System Policy Editor to restrict their ability to change the settings. (See Chapter 8 for more on the System Policy Editor.) See Table 4-2 for a list of printer settings that can be restricted with the System Policy Editor.

TABLE 4-2	Restriction	Effect
Printer Settings That Can Be Restricted with the System Policy Editor	Hide General and Details Page	Hides the General and Details page from the printer's properties page.
	Disable Deletion of Printers	Prevents a user from deleting an installed printer.
	Disable Addition of Printers	Prevents a user from installing a printer.

Printing a Document

There are four different ways to print a document. The first three are the most commonly used methods:

■ From inside an application, click File and then click Print.

■ From inside an application, click the Printer icon on the toolbar.

■ Right-click a file and select Print from the Context menu.

■ Select your document by clicking it, dragging it to the icon of the printer you will print from, and dropping the document on the printer. This will send the document automatically to the printer.

The fourth method might seem like a lot of work. One way to make things easier is to create a shortcut to your printer on your desktop, as described at the beginning of this section. You can then drag your document to the shortcut, which will then send it to the printer.

Using Print Manager

Print Manager lets you control print jobs that have been sent to the printer. Print Manager can be opened two different ways:

■ During printing, a Printer icon appears in the System Tray (next to the clock). Double-click the Printer icon and Print Manager opens, showing a list of all print jobs and their status.

■ From the Printers folder, double-click the printer you are printing to. Print Manager will open. Depending on the size of the print job, you may not have enough time to bring up Print Manager using this method. It is probably easier to use the first method described.

In either case, when Print Manager opens, you will see a window like Figure 4-7.

Once Print Manager is open, you can see the status of all print jobs, or you can control specific print jobs by selecting one or more print jobs from those displayed. Each printer installed on your computer has its own manager. Table 4-3 shows the functions of Print Manager.

To pause or cancel a specific print job, click Document from the Print Manager toolbar and select Pause or Cancel. To pause all print jobs, click Printer and select Pause. To purge or resume printing, click Printer from Print Manager's toolbar.

When you cancel a print job, any pages that have been spooled to the printer will continue to print until finished. You can also reorder the list of print jobs in Print Manager. All you have to do is click the document you want and drag it further up the list of documents waiting to be printed. The only exception is that a document already printing may not be moved, and may not have another document put in front of it.

exam
ⓦatch

Print Manager allows you to check the status of print jobs as well as reorder the print jobs. However, you cannot move or put a print job in front of a document that is already printing.

Printing without a Printer

Windows 98 supports deferred (offline) printing. This is especially useful for mobile users who are not always connected to a printer, for network users who may not have a network printer immediately available, or for users working from a remote site. Deferred printing means that even though you are not connected to a printer, you can still print to the printer. The

---

Print Manager with
documents spooling
to print

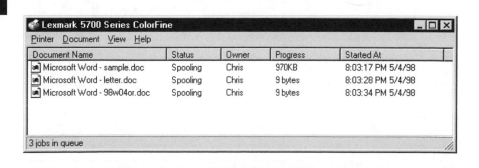

Function	Description
Check the status of a print job	Opening Print Manager allows you to see if a particular document is spooling yet, and its progress.
Pause a specific print job	If you have multiple print jobs, you can pause a print job, keeping it in the list, but allowing other print jobs to print first.
Pause all print jobs	Pauses all printing.
Resume a paused print job	Starts printing a job that has been paused.
Cancel a print job	Stops printing a print job.
Purge print job	Removes all print jobs from Print Manager.

print job will be stored on your hard disk until you are connected to a printer. To check on the status of a printer, open the Printers folder. If a printer is not available, the printer icon will be dimmed and it will be set to Offline. Figure 4-8 shows a network printer that is unavailable and has been set to work offline.

FIGURE 4-8

Examining the properties of
a printer that has been set
to work offline

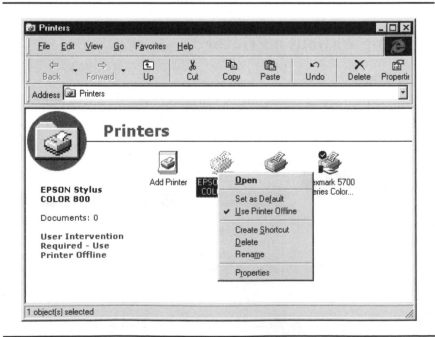

FROM THE CLASSROOM

Taking It Offline

Offline printing allows you to use a printer that you are not currently connected too. When you send a document to this printer, it will be stored until you switch the printer online by clicking the Use Printer Offline command again. This option is very handy for laptop users who are not always connected to the network.

To use a printer that is not currently connected:

1. Click Start, point to Settings, and then click Printers.
2. Click the icon for the printer you want to use offline.
3. On the Printer menu, click Use Printer Offline.

The Use Printer Offline command is available only for portable computers or for computers using a network printer. For local printers, you can still work with the printer offline, but the procedure is a little different. Instead of selecting the Use Printer Offline command, use the Pause Printing command.

If you have a laptop computer with a docking station and you start Windows while the computer is undocked, your print jobs are automatically saved. If you then start Windows while your computer is docked, the documents are sent to the printer automatically.

Offline printing uses the print spooler in Windows 98 to accept print jobs from applications and to store them until the printer is available. So if you have turned off spooling, you cannot print offline. If you are not sure whether spooling is enabled for a printer, open the Properties dialog box for the printer and go to the Details tab. On the Details tab, click the Spool Settings button. If the radio button next to Print Directly To The Printer is filled in, then print spooling for that printer has been disabled. By default, print spooling is enabled.

It is generally a good idea to leave print spooling turned on. Not only does it allow you to use printers offline, it improves the performance of most applications. About the only time I turn off print spooling is when I am troubleshooting a printer connection and I want to rule out a problem with the spooling system.

— *By Robert Aschermann, MCT, MCSE*

Printing from DOS

Printing from DOS-based applications in Windows 98 has been improved for smoother background printing and increased printing performance. DOS-based applications print directly to the 32-bit print spooler. Through programming magic, Windows 98 actually takes output sent to a printer in MS-DOS and puts it into the Windows 98 print spooler. This means that you can use Print Manager to control your DOS print jobs, and that you are returned to your application more quickly.

It is also possible to print a file from the MS-DOS prompt without opening the file. You do this via the COPY command. The syntax is as follows:

```
copy /b filename lpt1:
```

The /B switch allows the printing of binary files.

For more information on copying files to the printer port, type **copy /?** at a DOS prompt. This will give you the syntax of the command and a listing of all the switches.

Printing via an Infrared Connection

Windows 98 also supports Microsoft Infrared version 3.0 for printing to printers via an infrared connection. Microsoft Infrared version 3.0 supports the Infrared Data Association (IrDA) standard 1.0 and the IrDA for Serial Infrared Devices (SIR) standard, as well as the IrDA 2.0 for Fast Infrared Devices (FIR). Before you print, first make sure the infrared communications driver is installed correctly.

You can give printers that do not have an infrared port the capability to use an infrared port by connecting an infrared adapter made for printers to the parallel port of the printer.

Image Color Matching

Windows 98 also uses Kodak's Image Color Matching (ICM). ICM adheres to InterColor 3.0, an industry standard for color matching, created by

Kodak, Microsoft, Apple Computer, Sun Microsystems, and Silicon Graphics. It ensures that colors displayed on a monitor match those printed on output devices such as printers.

The color-matching profiles are stored in the <systemroot>\SYSTEM\ COLOR folder. These profiles are used by Windows 98 to adjust the colors as "seen" by an input device so that they match as closely as possible when output to a monitor or printer.

CERTIFICATION OBJECTIVE 4.04

Configuring Printing

Printers can be individually configured, and then there are those settings that affect printers globally. In this section, we'll look at the printer driver model, go over options to optimize printing, and look over the Registry keys that pertain to printing.

Printer Driver Support

Windows 98 has a modular architecture that makes it easier for peripherals manufacturers to write device drivers for the Windows operating system, and printers are no exception. There are two components in the printer driver model, the universal driver and the minidriver.

The universal driver is the component that communicates with parts of the Windows operating system and contains information common to all printers. There is only one universal driver. However, between the universal driver and the printer is the minidriver. The minidriver is the driver written by the device manufacturer. For example, the PostScript minidriver for PostScript printers was written in cooperation with Adobe systems. A minidriver is added each time you install a new printer. Because the Windows 98 print subsystem is compatible with the Windows NT print subsystem, minidrivers written for Windows 98 will work with Windows NT 3.51.

Optimizing Printing

The major trade-off to consider when printing is "How much hard disk space do I have?" as opposed to "How quickly do I want to get back to work?" If you have a large amount of hard disk space, you can adjust your printer's spool settings to write the print job to your hard disk, and spool the print job from your hard disk. This way you are returned to your application more quickly, though total printing time is increased. If you have a not-so-large hard disk, you can spool the print job directly to the printer. This takes longer to return you to your application, but it does not require as much hard disk space, and the total print time is not as long. See Table 4-4 for a comparison of the two methods.

To tweak your spool settings:

1. Open the Printers folder.

2. Right-click a particular printer. Click Properties.

3. Click Details. Click Spool Settings.

4. Click Spool Print Jobs So Program Finishes Printing Faster, then click one of the following:

   ■ Start Printing After Last Page Is Spooled
   This option returns you to your application faster. You also need more disk space and more print time.

   ■ Start Printing After First Page Is Spooled
   This option returns you to your application more slowly. You will need less disk space and print time is quicker.

TABLE 4-4	Start printing after last page is spooled.	Start printing after first page is spooled.
The Effects of Adjusting the Print Spooler Settings		
Return-to-application time	Faster	Slower
Disk space used	More	Less
Print time	Slower	Faster

We've talked quite a bit about the print spooler and spooling, but what exactly are we talking about? Think of it as a queue. It's where the data from a print job is stored while the print job is being processed. The local spooler on your machine does all printing, unless you print to a network. On a network, the local print spooler passes the print job to the network printer spooler. The spool file is actually stored on your hard disk in the *<systemroot>*\SPOOL\PRINTERS folder.

You'll note in Figure 4-9 that the spooler settings are set to return the user to the application faster. Start Printing After First Page Is Spooled is the default for the print spooler.

Also note the pull-down for Spool Data Format: EMF. EMF stands for Enhanced MetaFile. All non-PostScript printers spool two types of data: RAW and EMF. Windows 3.1 spools RAW data. The difference is that by using RAW data, the application is busy and will not release control until all RAW data is spooled by the printer driver for printing and submission to Print Manger. This takes longer to print.

EMF, on the other hand, is created quicker, so it prints quicker—up to two times quicker. An EMF is a set of commands that tell the printer how to print the document. Using EMF allows you to return to your application

---

FIGURE 4-9

Spool Settings options

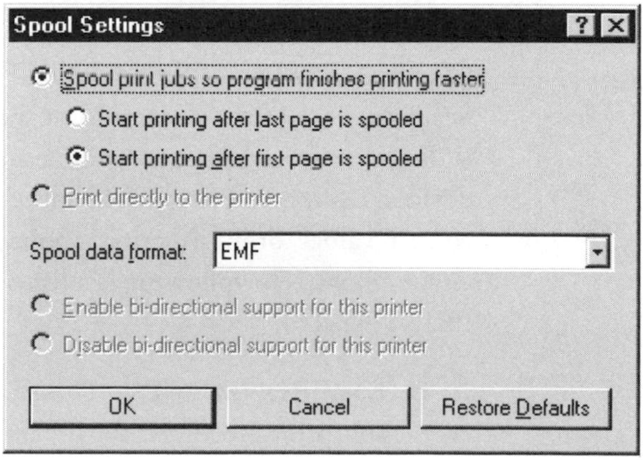

faster, because the application is freed up after the EMF is created. The print job is then translated into raw printer data by the 32-bit print subsystem and spooled in the background, allowing you to continue working while the document prints. The EMF is created by the Graphical Device Interface (GDI), which controls all of the windows that appear on your screen.

PostScript printers spool PostScript-language printer data. Print jobs from MS-DOS cannot take advantage of EMF; only Windows applications can benefit from EMF. MS-DOS programs are spooled in RAW format.

exam
Watch

Only Windows applications spool in EMF data format to non-PostScript printers.

Registry Keys

The Registry is the repository for configuration information for Windows 98. Before you make any changes to the Registry, be sure to back it up.

CAUTION: Wherever possible, use the printer's Properties sheet to make configuration changes, rather than using Registry Editor. If you make errors while changing values with Registry Editor, you will not be warned, because Registry Editor does not understand or recognize errors in syntax or other semantics.

Printers that have been installed on your computer can be found in the Registry under the HKEY_LOCAL_MACHINE\SYSTEM\ CURRENTCONTROLSET\CONTROL\PRINT\PRINTERS Key. See Figure 4-10 for a closer look at the PRINT Key in the Registry.

From inside the Registry you have direct access to all settings of all devices. Under the PRINTERS subkey are several more subkeys that contain values, or information, about installed printers and the printing environment. The following is a list of subkeys contained in the PRINT Key:

- **ENVIRONMENTS** Contains even more subkeys defining drivers and print processors for system environments.

- **MONITORS** Can contain subkeys that contain data for specific network printing monitors.

- **PRINTERS** Can contain subkeys that describe printer parameters for each installed printer.

- **PROVIDERS** Contains subkeys describing DLLs for network print services.

Once again, we would like to reiterate the seriousness of attempting to edit the Registry. This should only be done as a last resort.

FIGURE 4-10

Using the Registry Editor to look inside the Registry at the PRINTERS subkey

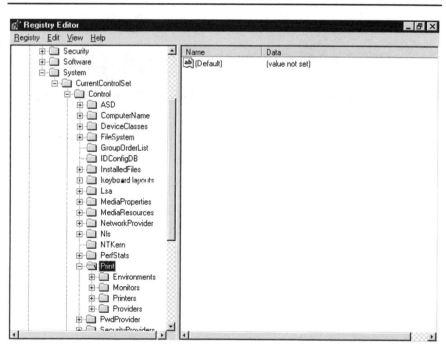

Troubleshooting Printing Problems

As mentioned earlier in the chapter, Windows 98 provides a Print Troubleshooter to help you resolve certain issues that might arise when you are installing or using a printer. This troubleshooting section covers issues that the Print Troubleshooter cannot resolve. As always, check with your printer manufacturer to make sure you have the latest version of your printer driver for Windows 98. There is also a PRINTERS.TXT file on the Windows 98 compact disc that provides information on the latest printer models, as well as other troubleshooting issues for Windows 98.

You may also want to refer to this chart of common printing problems and the best places to start looking for solutions.

QUESTIONS AND ANSWERS

I want to install a new printer...	Use the Add Printer Wizard in the Printers folder.
What do I need to have the best possible print performance from my system?	A computer with an ECP parallel port, an IEEE 1284-compliant cable, a Plug and Play printer, and the spool data format set to EMF.
I want to upgrade from Windows 95 to Windows 98, but how will it affect installed printers?	When you upgrade to Windows 98, all printer settings are migrated over. You do not have to worry about doing anything special to your printers.
My printer has stopped printing...	Use the Print Troubleshooter to try to determine the cause. Print Troubleshooter can be accessed via the Help button on the Start menu. If your problem persists, contact your printer manufacturer.
My computer does not have an ECP port. How will this affect my printing?	You will be unable to take advantage of the enhanced performance of the port, so your print job will not print as fast, otherwise there will be no noticeable difference.

QUESTIONS AND ANSWERS

I need to stop a document from printing, and check the status of another document in the queue…	Open Print Manager. It allows you to check the status of all documents in the queue as well as cancel, pause, purge, and reorder documents in the queue.
I don't always have a printer connected to my laptop…	Use deferred (offline) printing. This will save the print job to the hard disk and allow you to print it next time you are connected to a printer.
After printing a document, I need to be returned to my application as quickly as possible…	From the printer's Properties window, click the Details tab and click the Spool Settings button. Make sure that Spool Print Jobs So Program Finishes Printing Faster is checked and that Start Printing After First Page Is Spooled is also checked.
I don't have a lot of free space on my hard disk…	To make the spool file written to your hard disk as small as possible, open the printer's Properties window, click the Details tab and click the Spool Settings button. Make sure that Spool Print Jobs So Program Finishes Printing Faster is checked and that Start Printing After First Page Is Spooled is also checked.

Fixing Printer Installation Problems

Despite the Add Print Wizard, things still do go wrong sometimes. This next section describes some common problems when installing a new printer, and ways to work around the problems.

File-Copy Error Happens During New Printer Installation

If you are installing a printer driver from a floppy disk with the Add Printer Wizard and an error occurs, specific error information will be displayed showing the name of the file being copied and the destination of the file. Verify the name, origin, and destination of the file in the error message, and try again.

Another strategy is to look at the floppy disk with Windows Explorer. This will verify that the disk is readable and that there are files on it. If the installation still fails, copy the contents of the floppy disk into a temporary folder and then, during the printer installation, point the wizard to the temporary directory as the source with the printer driver files.

Print Dialog Box Does Not Contain Any Printers

If no printers appear in the Print dialog box, go to the INF directory and make sure there is a PRTUPD.INF file. This file contains the information displayed in the Manufacturer and Model lists.

Setup Can't Find Printer Driver Files

If the Add Printer Wizard can't find the necessary printer driver files, it checks the installation drive and directory. If the needed files can't be located, a dialog box appears that asks you to specify the path to where the driver is located. You have the choice of typing the location into the box, or navigating to it using the Browse button.

Fixing Printing Problems

This section describes fixes to some specific problems with printing.

You're Unable to Print to a Printer

Often, we overlook the obvious when we have a problem. The following is a list of some common sources of problems. Always check these features first.

- Make sure the printer is online.

- Open the Properties for the printer that is not printing and attempt to print a test page.

- Turn the printer off, wait a few seconds, and turn the printer back on. This clears the printer's buffer.

- Verify that there are no problems with the printer, such as a paper jam or inadequate toner.

- Run the printer's self-diagnostic.

- Double-check that the printer cable is securely fastened at both ends.

Check the Printer Driver

As we noted before, you should always be using the latest version of your printer driver. Here's how to find out if you are.

1. In the Printers folder, right-click the printer you are interested in.

2. Click the Paper tab. Click About.

If you do not have a Paper tab, or the Paper tab does not have an About button, check the other tabs. My Lexmark 5700 has a Paper tab, but the About button is located on the Document/Quality tab.

Fixing the Registry Description of the Printer Driver

Delete the printer from the Printers folder. When prompted to delete any additional files associated with the printer, click Yes. Then reinstall the printer.

If you are still unable to print, there might be a conflict between the printer driver and an application.

There is a Conflict with an Application

Sometimes the application that we are printing from is the culprit. Try the following to rule out any interference caused by an application:

1. Try printing from a different application.

2. If successful, check the configuration of the conflicting application, and reinstall it if necessary.

If you are still unable to print, there could be a spooling problem.

There Is a Spooling Problem

To see if spooling is the problem, we need to disable spooling and print directly to the printer port.

1. Open the Printers folder. Right-click the printer you are printing with and select Properties.

2. Click the Details tab.

3. Click the Spool Settings button.

4. Click Print Directly To The Printer.

Bi-directional Printing Support Problems

If you believe that you are having problems because of bi-directional printing, first check to make sure your printer cable is IEEE 1284-compliant. If it is, disable bi-directional printing to see if the problem clears up.

1. Open the Printers folder and right-click the printer you are having problems with. Click Properties.

2. Click the Details tab.

3. Click the Spool Settings button.

4. Click the Disable Bi-directional Support For This Printer.

Problems Printing Graphics

If your graphics are not printing properly, try the following techniques.

- Disable EMF spooling.

- If your printer is a PostScript printer, print with the PostScript driver. If this prints successfully, the problem is with UNIDRV.DLL.

- If printing in PostScript fails, the problem is either with the Graphical Device Interface or with the application you're printing from. To rule out the application, try printing a different document, or from an entirely different application.

- If you are printing a large document or several documents, try printing fewer or shorter jobs.

- If the graphic is an Encapsulated PostScript (EPS) file, try copying the file to the printer.

- For PostScript printers, switch from vector to raster graphics. Raster graphics use less memory.

- On a PostScript printer, try adjusting the virtual memory settings.

Partially Printed Pages

If your pages do not print completely, try the following techniques.

- If graphic images are only partially printed, your printer may have insufficient memory. Try reducing the print resolution.

- Try printing the graphic image from a different document and application.

- Make sure you are printing within the printer's printable region.

- If a section of text is missing, make sure the font is correctly installed.

- Try printing from a different document with the same font.

- Try printing from the same document with a different font.

- If your printer's Properties sheet has a Fonts tab, try enabling Print TrueType As Graphics.

- Streamline your document by reducing the number of objects and fonts.

Slow Printing

If you notice that your printer is printing slowly, or you believe it could print faster, try the following techniques.

- Hard disk fragmentation can slow printing down. Run the Disk Defragmenter utility.

- Since printing is spooled to your hard disk, you could be running out of space. Check your hard disk for available disk space.

- Your system could be low on resources. Check available system resources.

- If you are printing with a PostScript printer, it could be low on virtual memory. To adjust its memory settings:

  1. Open the Printers folder.

  2. Right-click your PostScript printer. Click Properties.

3. Click the Device Options tab. In the Available Printer Memory box, increase the value.

■ Verify that the correct printer driver is installed. If not, reinstall it.

■ Check to see if you have Print TrueType As Graphics enabled. If so, disable it using the following procedure:

1. Open the Printers folder.

2. Right-click the printer you are printing to and click Properties.

3. Click the Fonts tab.

4. Click Print TrueType As Graphics. Click OK.

You're Unable to Print More than 256 Copies of a Document

This is actually a documented problem with some printers. Consult your printer's manual to see if it has this limitation. Among the models that have this limitation are:

■ Canon Bubble-Jet BJ-230

■ CoStar LabelWriter Pro

■ HP LaserJet4, 4MV PostScript

■ HP LaserJet Series II

Your Computer Locks Up While Printing

If your computer stops responding while you are printing, try the following techniques.

■ Check the video and printer drivers and reinstall either or both if necessary.

■ Since printing is spooled to your hard disk, you could be running out of space. Check your hard disk for available disk space.

■ Sometimes spool files written to your hard disk are not automatically deleted. Use the following procedures to delete those files:

1. Double-click My Computer.

2. Double-click the C: drive.

3. Double-click Windows.

4. Double-click Spool.

5. Double-click Printers.

6. Delete all files with an SPL extension (*.SPL).

7. Click the Up button on the toolbar twice.

8. Double-click the Temp folder.

9. Delete all files that have a TMP extension (*.TMP) or begin with a tilde (~df7409.TMP). Those are both indications of temporary files.

10. Try restarting your computer. Windows 98 should delete spool and temporary files on bootup.

An Application Prints a Document, But Nothing Gets Printed

If it appears that your document spooled to the printer, yet nothing printed, try the following techniques.

- Verify the amount of free space on your hard disk so that the spool file can be written.

- Disable EMF spooling.

- Check the Spool folder to make sure the print job was spooled to the printer.

CERTIFICATION SUMMARY

Printing in Windows 98 includes some basic features: 32-bit print subsystem, EMF print spooler, bi-directional printer support, EPP/ECP support, Point and Print support, Image Color Matching, and improved Web printing. The Printers folder can be opened three ways: through My Computer, through Settings, and through Control Panel. A printer can be installed in four ways: automatically, if it's Plug and Play; with the Add Printer Wizard; using Point and Print; or using a custom setup script during Windows 98 installation. Plug and Play printers use bi-directional communication to let Windows 98 query the printer for information, and to send unsolicited information such as "low ink" warnings to the operating system.

Besides printing a document from within an application, you can also right-click on the document and select Print from the Context menu.

You can configure a printer by adjusting its properties. Either right-click the printer, or when printing from an application, click the Properties button. You have six basic tabs in the Properties window: General, Details, Paper, Graphics, Fonts, and Device Options. You can print a test page from the General tab. The spooler is adjusted via the Details tab/Spool Settings button. By adjusting the spooler, you can be returned to your application quickly, or you can print your document quickly. To print quickly, make sure the spool file is an EMF. MS-DOS printing is also done through the Windows 98 print spooler, but keep in mind that MS-DOS prints in RAW format. When printing, the GDI creates an EMF, the application releases control back to the user, and the print job is spooled to the printer in the background.

Windows 98 supports the Infrared Data Association (IrDA) standard 1.0, the IrDA for Serial Infrared Devices (SIR) standard, and the IrDA 2.0 for Fast Infrared Devices (FIR). You don't necessarily have to have a printer connected to your computer in order to print. You can defer printing, storing the print job on your hard disk until the computer is hooked up to a printer. The print job is then despooled.

Print jobs can be managed with Print Manager. Print Manager allows you to check the status of a print job, pause printing, cancel printing, purge one or all print jobs, and resume printing. You can open Print Manager by double-clicking the printer you are printing to, or double-clicking the Printer icon in the system tray. You can also reorder documents waiting to be printed.

The System Policy Editor can be used to restrict changes made to printers. Printers can only be shared when File and Print Sharing are enabled.

✓ TWO-MINUTE DRILL

❏ The basic features of printing in Windows 98 include:
  ❏ 32-bit print subsystem
  ❏ EMF (Enhanced MetaFile) spooling
  ❏ Deferred (Offline) Printing
  ❏ Point and Print Support
  ❏ Support for Image Color Matching 2.0 (ICM)

❏ New additions to printing in Windows 98 include:
  ❏ Support for more printers.
  ❏ Improved printing from the Internet.

❏ The print subsystem is 32-bit, provides smoother background printing, and returns you to your application faster.

❏ Look for printers that support Extended Capabilities Port (ECP).

❏ In order to share a printer, whether it is on a Microsoft or Novell network, you must use the 32-bit, Protected mode client, with file and printer sharing enabled.

❏ Printers in Windows 98 are right where they were in Windows 95—in the Printers folder.

❏ There are four ways that a printer can be installed:
  ❏ Using Plug and Play
  ❏ Using Point and Print on a network
  ❏ Using Add Printer in the Printers folder
  ❏ Using a custom setup script during a Windows 98 installation

❏ Extended Capabilities Port provides high-speed printing and support for ECP-compliant devices.

❏ ECP allows printers to send unsolicited messages to Windows 98 and other applications, such as "Low ink" or "Out of paper."

❏ There are two basic ways to configure your printer:
  ❏ From the Printers folder
  ❏ From Inside a Windows application by selecting File | Print | Properties

❑ Printer Properties can be accessed by right-clicking a printer in the Printers folder, or through an application by clicking File/Print.

❑ You will want to create a shortcut to your printer.

❑ When managing printers you'll have to dispose of printer drivers and other associated files that you no longer need when you delete a printer.

❑ There are four different ways to print a document:

   ❑ From inside an application, click File and then click Print.

   ❑ From inside an application, click the Printer icon on the toolbar.

   ❑ Right-click a file and select Print from the Context menu.

   ❑ Select your document by clicking it, dragging it to the icon of the printer you will print from, and dropping the document on the printer. This will send the document automatically to the printer.

❑ Print Manager lets you control print jobs that have been sent to the printer.

❑ Print Manager allows you to check the status of print jobs as well as reorder the print jobs. However, you cannot move or put a print job in front of a document that is already printing.

❑ Windows 98 supports deferred (offline) printing. The print job will be stored on your hard disk until you are connected to a printer.

❑ Printing from DOS-based applications in Windows 98 has been improved for smoother background printing and increased printing performance.

❑ Windows 98 also supports Microsoft Infrared version 3.0 for printing to printers via an infrared connection.

❑ Windows 98 also uses Kodak's Image Color Matching (ICM).

❑ There are two components in the printer driver model, the universal driver and the minidriver.

❑ Only Windows applications spool in EMF data format to non-PostScript printers.

❑ The Registry is the repository for configuration information for Windows 98. Before you make any changes to the Registry, be sure to back it up.

❑ Printers that have been installed on your computer can be found in the Registry under the HKEY_LOCAL_MACHINE\SYSTEM\ CURRENTCONTROLSET\CONTROL\PRINT\PRINTERS Key.

❑ The following is a list of subkeys contained in the PRINT Key:
  ❑ ENVIRONMENTS
  ❑ MONITORS
  ❑ PRINTERS
  ❑ PROVIDERS

❑ Windows 98 provides a Print Troubleshooter to help you resolve certain issues that might arise when you are installing or using a printer.

❑ Despite the Add Print Wizard, things still do go wrong sometimes.

SELF TEST

The following questions will help you measure your understanding of the material presented in this chapter. Read all the choices carefully, as there may be more than one correct answer. Choose all correct answers for each question.

1. John buys a new computer and a new printer that are both Plug and Play. He connects the printer and turns the computer on, but the printer is not automatically installed. What could be the problem?

   A. The printer is out of ink

   B. The computer's hard disk is full

   C. There is no such thing as a Plug and Play printer

   D. His printer cable is not IEEE 1284 compliant

2. Your computer supports ECP, your printer cable is IEEE 1284 compliant, and your printer is Plug and Play. You would like to take advantage of the enhanced performance that the ECP provides. How do you know if the computer's ECP has been enabled?

   A. Call your computer's manufacturer.

   B. Check the Details tab of the printer's Properties window.

   C. Check the Ports (COM and LPT) in Device Manager.

   D. Print a test page. The port details are on the test page.

3. You have just installed a new printer. How can you make sure that the printer is

properly installed and that everything works correctly?

   A. Pull the printer cable to see if it comes loose

   B. Knock on the printer

   C. Call Bill Gates and ask him

   D. Print a test page

4. You have two Epson 800 printers in your organization. One is color and one is black and white. What can you do to help your coworkers distinguish between the two?

   A. Rename each printer with a name that corresponds to its ink type.

   B. Nothing. Printers can't be renamed.

   C. Install a different printer driver.

   D. Make one printer the default printer.

5. You want to use drag-and-drop printing. What should you do first?

   A. Enable drag-and-drop printing

   B. Disable EMF spooling

   C. Install the proper printer driver

   D. Make the printer the default printer

6. Which of the following cannot be accomplished in Print Manager?

   A. Check the status of a print job

   B. Rename a print job

   C. Cancel a print job

   D. Pause a print job

7. You have accidentally sent a document to the printer. You open Print Manager to

delete the document, and you see several other documents waiting in the queue. How do you remove the one document you accidentally printed from Print Manager?

A. Highlight the print job, click Document and then click Purge

B. You can't remove just one document; all documents have to be removed

C. Highlight the print job, click Document, and then click Cancel

D. Highlight the document, click File, and then click Delete

8. You have several documents waiting to be printed in Print Manager. You would like to place a print job ahead of the document that is currently printing. From inside Print Manager, how do you do this?

A. You can't put a print job ahead of one that is currently printing

B. Click and drag the waiting document ahead of the printing document

C. Click Printer, then Print Now

D. Click Document, then Print Now

9. You can print a document even though there is no printer connected to your computer. What is this feature called?

A. Deferred printing

B. Print Pausing

C. Offline printing

D. None of the above

10. What does ICM stand for?

A. Interprocess Control Manager

B. Integrated Color Management

C. Image Color Matching

D. Image Color Management

11. How many minidrivers does Windows 98 have?

A. Two: EMF and RAW

B. It depends on how many printers you have installed

C. One: the universal minidriver

D. It depends on whether or not your printer is PostScript

12. When you print a document on your laser printer, it takes some time before control of the application is returned to you. How could you speed up the return of control?

A. Buy an IEEE 1284-compliant cable

B. There is no way to speed up return of control

C. From Print Properties, click Details, click Spool Settings, click Start Printing After First Page Is Spooled

D. From Print Properties, click Details, click Spool Settings, click Start Printing After Last Page Is Spooled

13. Your printer is printing slowly. You suspect that older spool files have not been deleted. Where is the spool file?

A. *<systemroot>*\SYSTEM\SPOOL

B. *<systemroot>*\SYSTEM\

C. *<systemroot>*\SYSTEM\PRINTERS\ SPOOL

D. *<systemroot>*\SPOOL\PRINTERS

14. You are printing a file that is not using EMF spooling. When does the application release control back to you?

A. When the EMF spooling is done

B. As soon as you click OK on the Print dialog box

C. When the RAW file has been sent to the printer

D. After you quit the application

15. What Windows component generates an EMF file during the print process?

A. The Kernel

B. The GDI

C. Print Manager

D. Print Spooler

16. A PostScript file will not print correctly on a PostScript printer. You disable EMF spooling, but the file still doesn't print correctly. Why not?

A. EMF spooling can't be disabled

B. EMF has nothing to do with printing

C. For PostScript printing, Windows 98 does not generate an EMF file

D. EMF spooling is only available on Windows 3.1

17. Why would you want to remove a printer driver for an existing printer?

A. Never. You should never remove a printer driver.

B. The printer needs to be taken in for repairs.

C. To install a new toner or inkjet cartridge.

D. To troubleshoot a printing problem.

18. You are running out of disk space as you try to print from Windows 98. What is the best solution to fix this problem?

A. Delete temporary files and archive older files to make more room

B. Turn the printer off and then on again

C. Enable the ECP port

D. Reinstall the printer driver

5

Windows 98 Networking Components

With a focus on lowering the total cost of ownership per PC, Windows 98 brings many new and exciting networking features to the desktop. Several new utilities have been introduced to aid in the installation and configuration of the networking components on a Windows 98 workstation. This chapter will concentrate on these new additions as they relate to the networking certification objectives for the Windows 98 MCSE test.

CERTIFICATION OBJECTIVE 5.01

Installing and Configuring Windows 98 Network Components

You can perform automated installations of Windows 98 by either push or pull methods. In a pull installation the user performs the upgrade, whereas in a push installation, the administrator performs the upgrade.

Push installations can be performed via some sort of script that outlines the configuration you want. These scripts can be deployed by several methods: through systems management software (like Microsoft's SMS), by launching a batch file in a user logon script, or as an attachment in an e-mail message.

Setup scripts can be created with Microsoft Batch 98, the utility that comes with the Windows 98 Resource Kit. Microsoft Batch 98, shown in Figure 5-1, gives a GUI interface to creating a script file that follows the MSBATCH.INF file format. By copying the CAB files from the installation subdirectory along with this file to a server, automated installations can be performed across a network.

EXERCISE 5-1

Installing and Running BATCH.EXE

1. Install Windows 98 on a computer with the exact configuration you wish subsequent installations to follow.
2. Run BATCH.EXE setup from the Resource Kit CD.

3. Click the Start button and select Programs | Microsoft Batch 98.

4. Click the Gather Now button to retrieve the required information from the Registry.

5. You can then use the other tabs to display dialog boxes for customization of the Display, Printers, MRU Locations, Setup Prompts, User Information, Desktop, and Regional Settings.

Windows 98 as a Client

Windows 98 provides native support as a 32-bit Protected mode client on a wide variety of networks, as well as a 16-bit client on several Real mode networks. A Windows 98 client can bind multiple network protocols,

Microsoft Batch 98 is a utility for creating automated installation scripts

services, and clients simultaneously. The following networks have built-in support in Windows 98.

- Microsoft Windows NT
- Novell NetWare, version 3.11 or later
- Microsoft LAN Manager
- Banyan VINES, version 7.0 or later
- DEC Pathworks 32
- Solstice NFS client, version 3.1 or later
- Artisoft LANtastic, version 7.0
- Peer to Peer fashion with Windows for Workgroups, Windows 95, and other Windows 98 computers

Network Adapters

A network interface card (NIC) is installed in a computer to allow it to communicate with other computers over a network. Windows 98 supports most network adapters, and supplies 32-bit Real mode drivers, which it can install and configure. When considering network adapters, you want to make sure you find one that matches the media type of your network, and that you purchase one based on the fastest interface your PC supports. For instance, a 32-bit PCI adapter card will outperform an equivalent 16-bit ISA.

If you are installing a Plug and Play card, Windows 98 should set it up for you once you turn the PC on. If your card is non-Plug and Play (a legacy adapter) you will need to manually configure the hardware settings with either jumpers or software, and use the Add New Hardware Wizard to find and install the drivers.

Network Printers

You learned earlier about printing to a locally attached printer. You can also connect to a remote printer that is either directly attached to your network, or managed by another PC or server.

Installing a Network Printer

1. Click the Start button and select Settings | Printers.

2. Double-click the Add Printer icon.

3. Click Next to begin the installation process.

4. Choose Network Printer and click Next.

5. Click Browse and find the print server and printer you wish to install. Press OK.

6. There will then be a prompt asking whether you are planning on printing from MS-DOS-based applications. If you are, make sure Yes is selected before pressing Next. (If you have selected Yes, choose an open LPT port to map the printer to.)

7. If the drivers are stored on the print server, you will be prompted to select the printer you are installing. When you have found it, click Next.

8. Decide the printer name and whether or not this should be your default printer. Click Finish when you are ready.

9. Windows 98 also has a feature called deferred printing. If a network printer is not available, the printer will be grayed out and set to offline, and the jobs will be stored on the user's PC until the network connection to the printer is re-established.

Installing and Configuring Hardware Devices

Every part of your computer is considered a device, and every device allocates resources. Windows 98 keeps track of devices by categorizing them and putting them into different subkeys within the Registry. All devices are managed with Device Manager, which can be found under the System icon in the Control Panel.

Device Manager lists all devices in a hardware tree, where each branch is a category, and within each category is the listing of applicable devices. Each device has a unique identification code that Windows 98 uses internally, a list of allocated resources, and information on whether the device is functional. Different errors will be shown if any of the following conditions are not met: the device is not present, all the required devices are not loaded or installed, or the resources the device is trying to use are conflicting with the resources being claimed by another device.

Windows 98 is compatible with (and works best with) devices that are considered Plug and Play. Plug and Play devices are devices that, after installation, can be configured without any user intervention. These devices have the capability to dynamically load and unload drivers, allocate and release resources, and be detected automatically.

Windows 98 also supports non-Plug and Play devices, also known as *legacy devices*. These devices, however, must be manually added and configured. The resources allocated can be configured with either jumper/dip switches located on the card itself, or through a software configuration utility. Windows 98 does have a utility to aid in installation, called the Hardware Installation Wizard. It will scan the buses and resource ranges available, and try to find legacy devices automatically. If it finds them, it will try to reallocate the resources being used by the Plug and Play devices already in the machine the device is set for. If this is not possible, it will make recommendations of what resources the legacy device should be configured for. If at any time you do not want to use the resources Windows 98 has configured devices to have, you have the ability to override them and force any device to any resource available. Keep in mind, however, that this is not recommended, since by forcing the allocation of certain resources, you limit Windows 98's capabilities to configure future devices.

Modems

The word modem is a contraction of the words "modulate" and "demodulate." Modems are devices used to allow computers to communicate over standard phone lines. Computers transmit data digitally, but phone lines only transmit analog signals. Modems, through modulation and demodulation, translate and convert from one type of signal to the other, to allow communication among computers through phone lines.

Windows 98 natively supports a wide variety of modems and ISDN adapters. ISDN, which stands for Integrated Services Digital Network, allows connectivity at speeds up to 128 Kbps. You can install a Plug and Play modem by simply inserting the internal card or plugging in the external modem. If it is a legacy modem, you must first use the Add New Hardware option in Control Panel, and add the COM port. After Windows 98 detects the new port, it is best to click Modem in Control Panel and have Windows 98 auto-detect the installed modem.

Once Windows 98 detects the modem, a wizard will launch, asking you to define your location. Windows 98 uses this information to analyze phone numbers you need to dial and to insert the proper prefixes. For instance, if the number you wish to dial is outside your area code, but still in the US, the system will know to insert a 1 before the number, and to dial the area code next. If you travel with a laptop, you can set up new locations for each place you frequent. When you tell the system you are at your new location, it may not need to dial the 1 + area code, if the number is now a local number.

Universal Serial Bus (USB)

Universal Serial Bus (USB) is an external bus standard that brings all the positive features of Plug and Play and standardized connectivity outside of the PC. With this feature, devices can be added, and will be installed and configured automatically, without the need for user intervention or rebooting. USB allows up to 127 simultaneous connections, with connection speeds up to12 Mbps. This slower speed makes USB suitable for devices such as keyboards, mice, and joysticks.

Multiple Display Support

Windows 98 brings a new enhancement to the traditional display found up to this point. Now, with one or more of the following video cards, you can expand your desktop to cover up to nine displays, without regard to resolution, size, or refresh rates.

- S3-ViRGE series
- S3-Trio64V+
- S3 Aurora
- Cirrus 5436, 5446, 7548
- ET6000

- ATI Mach64, Rage I, II
- Imagine i128(2)

(The preceding list was taken from the *Windows 98 Resource Kit*, Beta Release, © 1998 Microsoft Press.)

Multiple Display works by creating a virtual desktop, with each monitor customized to view a certain portion of it. Each monitor has a coordinate for each corner, with your primary monitor's upper left coordinates being 0,0. This cannot be altered, for backward compatibility reasons. You can customize and change any of the secondary monitors' coordinates to whatever you wish, as long as all the monitors touch each other on the virtual desktop. For example, let's say your primary monitor has a resolution of 800x600, and your secondary monitor, which is sitting to the right of the primary, has the same resolution of 800x600. Under this configuration, the primary monitor's bottom right coordinate would be 799,599, and the secondary monitor's bottom right coordinate would be 1439,599.

exam
ⓦatch

The primary VGA display will be whichever comes first in the PCI slot order.

IEEE 1394 FireWire

Another external connection standard, similar to USB, is IEEE 1394. Also known as FireWire, it is geared more toward higher-speed devices than USB is. Capable of supporting videodisk players and external storage boxes, it is a very promising addition to future computers.

IEEE 1394 is capable of supporting up to 63 devices per bus, with a maximum of 1023 interconnected buses. It was designed for high-bandwidth devices, with speeds ranging from S100 at 98.304 Mbps, to S400 at 393.216 Mbps.

Both IEEE 1394 and USB support both isochronous and asynchronous connections as their transfer protocols. An isochronous connection is a guaranteed delivery at a fixed rate. Asynchronous data can be transferred whenever there is no isochronous traffic on the bus.

Infrared Data Association (IrDA)

Windows 98 comes with support for Microsoft Infrared, version 3.0. Infrared is a wireless transmission used for network connectivity, and for printing to infrared-ready printers. Infrared devices can now be used in Windows 98, just like devices that are normally connected directly with a cable. IrDA 1.0 is a supported standard for Serial Connected Devices (SIR), and IrDA 2.0 is for Fast Infrared Devices (FIR). SIR devices can send and receive up to 115.2 Kbps, and FIR devices can communicate at up to 4 Mbps. The next two exercises explain how to install both Plug and Play and non-Plug and Play Infrared devices.

EXERCISE 5-3

Installing a Plug and Play Infrared Device

1. Either insert the card, or plug the device in.
2. Windows 98 should install the Infrared 3.0 software.
3. Click the Start button and choose Settings | Control Panel.
4. Double-click the Infrared icon.

EXERCISE 5-4

Installing a Non-Plug and Play Infrared Device

1. Either insert the card, or plug the device in.
2. Click the Start button and choose Settings | Control Panel.
3. Double-click Add/Remove Programs, and select the Windows Setup tab.
4. Under Installed components, click Communications, and select Details.
5. Select the Infrared check box, and press OK.
6. Click Apply.
7. Double-click the Infrared icon that will appear in the Control Panel.
8. When the Add Infrared Devices Wizard launches, it will prompt you for the communications port the device is connected to.

Multilink

Multilink refers to Windows 98's capability to combine two or more dial-up devices to act as one single link. It is an inexpensive way to increase the bandwidth of your dial-up PPP connections, but this service is not available for the dial-up server. Multilink is accomplished by connecting two modems or ISDN adapters to two separate phone lines, and combining the bandwidths. There are two things you need to keep in mind in order to implement PPP multilink. First, the Internet Service Provider (ISP) you are using must support multilink in order for it to function properly. Second, to avoid performance problems, you need to make sure both devices are configured to run at the same speed.

EXERCISE 5-5

Configuring Multilink for Dial-Up Connections

1. Click the Start button and choose Programs | Accessories | Communications | Dial-Up Networking.

2. Right-click the Connection icon you wish to use and select Properties.

3. Select the Multilink tab (shown in Figure 5-2).

4. Click Use Additional Devices.

5. Select Add.

6. Choose the additional device you wish to use.

When you are finished, double-click the icon you set up for multilink, and choose Connect. Windows 98 will establish a connection, first with the original device you set the connection to use, followed by any additional devices configured within multilink.

Power Management Scheme

Power Management (PM) sends the computer and/or monitor into standby mode after there has been no keyboard or mouse activity for a specified amount of time. Windows 98 has two different Power Management schemes that allow you to easily configure these and other related settings. If

FIGURE 5-2

Configuring multilink allows you to increase your bandwidth by using multiple ISDN adapters or modems with multiple phone lines

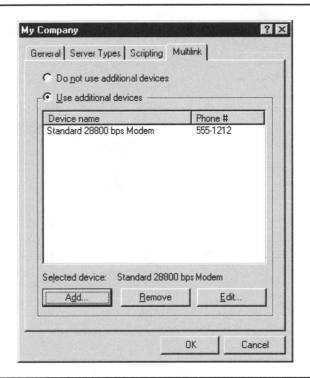

neither of the schemes listed seems to fit your needs, it even allows you to design and customize your own.

Under Control Panel, you will find an icon named Power Management. After double-clicking it, you will see a window like the one in Figure 5-3.

Under Power Schemes, you can choose between Home/Office Desk and Portable/Laptop. Each of these has a default time setting for turning off the monitor and the hard disks. When you click the arrows following each time selection, other times are available, incrementing by both minutes and hours. If you only want one of the devices' power to be managed by Windows 98, each has a selection marked Never, to disable PM.

Power Management allows you to conserve power on your laptop or desktop PC

Microsoft Personal Web Server 4.0

Microsoft Personal Web Server (PWS) version 4.0 is a Web server that runs on the Windows 98 platform. PWS can be used on a small intranet to share documents and information, or it can be used for testing and development of Web sites. PWS supports Active Server Pages as well as drag-and-drop publishing capabilities. Figure 5-4 shows the Main page of Personal Web Server.

The following are some add-on features included within PWS 4.0.

- FrontPage 98 Server Extensions
- Microsoft Message Queue
- Transaction Server
- Visual InterDev RAD Remote Deployment Support

FIGURE 5-4

Personal Web Server is
used to share information
on an intranet

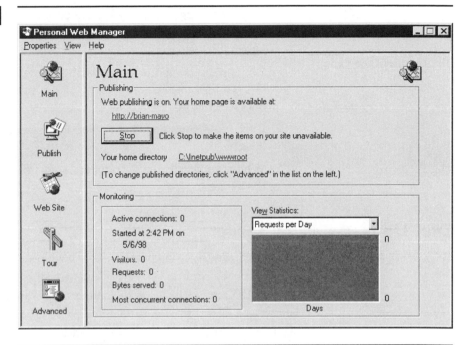

The following exercise will explain how to install and use Microsoft
Personal Web Server. After installation you will find the added
components in Program Files under the headings Internet Explorer |
Personal Web Server.

Installing Personal Web Server

1. Click the Start button and choose Run.

2. Select Browse and go to the \ADD-ONS\PWS directory on the
   Windows 98 CD.

3. Click SETUP.EXE and select OK.

4. In the Installation dialog box, select Next.

5. If you have a previous version of PWS running, a dialog box will
   appear informing you that the new version no longer supports FTP.
   Click OK.

6. If this is an upgrade, you have the option of upgrading only the existing components, or adding new components as well. Click Upgrade Plus.

7. Choose the components you wish to install and select Next, or if this is a new installation, select Custom and choose the desired components.

8. Click Next, and then Finish when the selected components are installed.

9. When the installation is complete, select Finish, and Yes to restart the system.

Dial-Up Networking Server

The Dial-Up Networking Server allows Windows 98 to host a single dial-up network connection. Any client with support for PPP can dial in using IP, IPX, or NetBEUI as the connection protocol. Windows 98 can then act as a server, sharing its files and printers just as it does on a LAN, or it can act as a gateway for an IPX or NetBEUI network. Windows 98 cannot, however, act as an IP router and allow access to an internal TCP/IP network.

EXERCISE 5-7

Configuration of the Dial-Up Networking Server

1. Click the Start menu and choose Programs | Accessories | Communications | Dial-Up Networking.

2. From the Connections menu, select Dial-Up Server.

3. In the Dial-Up Server window, click Allow Caller Access.

4. If you have share-level security enabled, you will have a Change Password button available for setting security. If you are implementing user-level security, you will have an Allow Caller Access button.

Asynchronous Transfer Mode (ATM)

Asynchronous Transfer Mode (ATM) is a switching technology that runs on high-bandwidth media such as FDDI. ATM is unique among other switching technologies in that it has a fixed length (53-byte cells), as opposed to frames that vary in length. Because of this fixed length, devices that employ ATM operate very efficiently and result in high throughput.

As its name indicates, ATM is asynchronous, meaning transmission times do not occur in fixed intervals. Through a process known as Label Multiplexing, time slots are allocated on demand. This allows time-insensitive traffic, such as data requests, not to be a hindrance to high-priority transmissions, such as video and sound. Other technologies, such as a T-1 line (1.544 Mbps), use time division to divide up the channels so that each channel gets to transmit at a fixed interval for a fixed amount of time. The problem with this is that an idle channel won't yield its bandwidth for the other channels that need it.

ATM differs from most other protocols in that it uses virtual circuits on virtual paths for communications on a network. Unlike TCP/IP and IPX/SPX, which simply send data out onto a network, ATM establishes this virtual connection before transmissions occur. Obviously these dissimilar LANs would be unable to communicate without some sort of bridge linking them together. Through a process known as LAN emulation, Windows 98 can be configured to allow communication with ATM devices.

EXERCISE 5-8

Configuring LAN Emulation

1. Click the Start button and choose Settings | Control Panel.
2. Double-click the Network icon.
3. Click the Add button.
4. Choose Protocol and then Add.
5. Under Manufacturers, select Microsoft.

6. Under Network Protocols, choose ATM Call Manager and press OK.

7. Repeat steps 3 through 5.

8. Under Network Protocols, choose ATM Emulated LAN and press OK.

9. Repeat steps 3 through 5

10. Under Network Protocols, choose ATM LAN Emulation Client and press OK.

ATM networks can be configured with several emulated LANs running on the same physical network. These emulated LANs can be set up for different departments or for different groups of users. Even when this is the case, all ATM networks will have a default emulated LAN to which all computers will belong, unless specifically configured otherwise. Windows 98 will automatically join the default emulation LAN, but this can be changed and configured for it to take part in any emulated LAN running.

Virtual Private Network (VPN) and PPTP

Communication between two computers on a network occurs by protocols establishing a connection using the physical medium for transmission. Virtual Private Networks (VPNs) use the connections already established by the protocols as their medium for transmission. They do this through a process known as tunneling. Tunneling occurs via PPTP (Point-to-Point Tunneling Protocol) to establish a secure connection with a server over a public-type network, such as the Internet. PPTP encapsulates, encrypts, and compresses PPP packets into IP datagrams for transmission.

If you will recall, PPP packets are protocol independent, so IPX, NetBEUI, and TCP/IP can all be used as the tunneled protocol.

exam
⍥atch

To use the Internet as your network for establishing PPTP connections, the PPTP server must have a valid, registered IP address for use on the Internet. The encapsulated packets, however, can be addressed to computers on the private network, since the PPTP server disassembles the PPTP packet and forwards the PPP portion to the correct computer.

Sharing Windows 98 Resources

Windows 98 has the capability to simulate a server by sharing its files, drives, and printers across a network. Peer Resource Sharing, as it is called, allows you to add a secure method of storage and printing to your network at a very nominal cost. If a user wishes to make resources available to others, that user must choose between user-level and share-level security implementation.

Share-level security protects each individual resource with a password. This method requires the File and Printer Sharing for Microsoft Networks service, and is only available for use on Microsoft Networks. If a user wishes to retrieve a file or print a document from this peer or peer-level server, she must know the appropriate password for the share. If a password is not assigned, any user with access to the network will be able to access that resource.

User-level security protects the resources on the computer by using pass-through authentication to a security provider. The user then makes her shares secure by choosing, from a list provided by the security authenticator, which individual users and which groups get access. Before a Windows 98 system will grant access to a share, it first verifies that the user's name and password are the same as those stored by one of the following types of servers.

- Windows NT Server 3.5 or later
- Windows NT Workstation 3.5 or later
- NetWare 3.x server
- NetWare 4.x server running bindery emulation

File and Printer Sharing for Microsoft Networks

The File and Printer Sharing for Microsoft Networks service supports any network device that utilizes the SMB protocol, such as LAN Manager,

Windows for Workgroups, Windows NT, SAMBA, LAN Manager for UNIX, DOS, and OS/2. This service must be installed before you will be able to share any resources on your computer. (One important thing to note is that File and Printer Sharing for Microsoft Networks cannot run concurrently with File and Printer Sharing for NetWare Networks.) The following exercise explains the installation of this service.

EXERCISE 5-9

Installing File and Printer Sharing for Microsoft Networks

1. Click the Start button and choose Settings | Control Panel.
2. Double-click the Network icon.
3. Click the Add button on the Configuration tab.
4. Choose Service and then Add.
5. Under Manufacturers, select Microsoft.
6. Under Network Services, choose File and Printer Sharing for Microsoft Networks.
7. Press OK three times. When you are prompted to reboot, choose Yes.

The default settings for this service are correct unless you need to manually control the designation of Browse Master, or if you want LAN Manager 2.*x* clients on your network to access your system's shares. In such cases, clicking the service's Properties can modify each setting.

Passwords

If you are using share-level access, passwords can be assigned to shares by right-clicking the resource and selecting Sharing. A dialog box will appear like the one in Figure 5-5.

As you can see, passwords can be independently assigned for either Read Only or Full Access.

FIGURE 5-5

Sharing tab as it
appears when using
share-level access

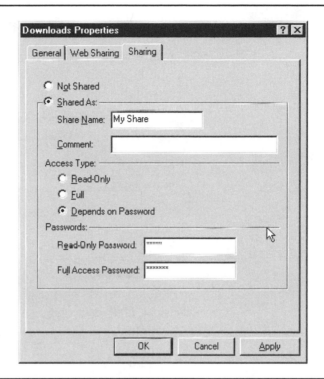

User and Group Permissions

If you are using user-level access as your security method, after right-clicking a resource you wish to share, you will see a dialog box like the one in Figure 5-6.

You can at this point click the Add button, and it will download a list of users and groups from your network authenticator. You can then customize the types of access available to each user, group, or to "the world."

FIGURE 5-6

FIGURE 5-6

Sharing tab as it appears when using user-level access

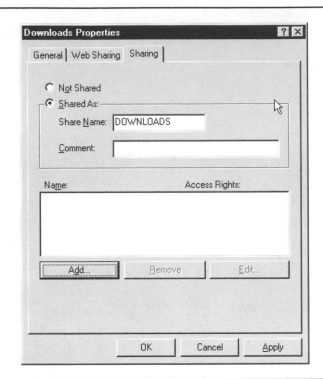

Configuring the Browse Master

Whenever a Windows computer wishes to browse the network to view available resources, it will make a request for the list to a computer that has been designated as either the Browse Master or the Backup Browse Server. There is only one Browse Master computer per protocol per workgroup, but there can be multiple Backup Browse Servers on each. A good estimation is one browse server per 15 computers in a workgroup.

When a Windows 98 computer starts up, it checks to see if a Master Browse Server already exists in the workgroup. If it doesn't, an election is performed and a Master Browse Server is created. If a Master already exists,

Windows 98 checks the ratio of Browse Servers to workstations. If the ratio exceeds the predefined amounts, another election is performed to add another Backup Master Browser.

A Windows 98 station can, by default, serve as either a Master or a Backup Browse Server. This can, however, be changed from automatic to either enabled or disabled. If you select File and Printer Sharing for Microsoft Networks, and select Properties, you will see the Browse Master property and its current value. If you change it to Enable, that workstation will automatically become a Browse Server, regardless of whether or not the ratios are met. If you choose Disable, it will never become a Browse Server, even if one is needed. Unless you are having problems with network browsing, it is best to leave this setting alone.

CERTIFICATION OBJECTIVE 5.04

Remote Access

Windows 98 has really put forth some effort to cut down on the total cost of ownership per PC. Several remote management tools have been included to help you troubleshoot and repair PCs on a network, without having to dispatch someone from IT.

- **System Policy Editor** Allows you to edit a subset of the Registry keys of remote computers. You can also manage system policies individually, or for groups of computers or users, all in real time.

- **Registry Editor** Grants you access to the entire Registry for editing. It is very flexible and allows for the creating, deleting, and searching of Registry keys.

- **System Monitor** Allows you to view, in real time, the performance of remote computers. This allows you to diagnose and troubleshoot a wide variety of performance issues by monitoring the virtual device drivers on the remote computer.

■ **Net Watcher** Allows you to manage and monitor remote shares on Windows 98 computers. You can create, edit, and delete shared resources, as well as managing the users who are connecting to them.

To enable the first three administration methods listed, remote administration, remote Registry, and user-level security must be enabled on each workstation you wish to administer. If you are using one or more of these three utilities, File and Printer Sharing does not have to be enabled. It does, however, need to be loaded if you wish to use Net Watcher to manage and monitor remote shares.

EXERCISE 5-10

Installation of Microsoft Remote Registry Service

1. Click the Start button and choose Settings | Control Panel.
2. Double-click the Network icon.
3. Click the Add button.
4. Choose Service and then Have Disk.
5. Under the Install From Disk box, enter the path to the TOOLS\RESKIT\NETADMIN\REMOTREG directory on the Windows 98 installation CD.
6. Press OK.
7. Under Select Network Service, choose Microsoft Remote Registry.
8. Press OK twice. When you are prompted to reboot, choose Yes.

EXERCISE 5-11

Enabling of Remote Administration

1. Click the Start button and choose Settings | Control Panel.
2. Double-click the Passwords icon.
3. Select the Remote Administration tab.
4. Verify that Enable Remote Administration Of This Server is checked.
5. Add or remove any users or groups that will have rights to remotely administer your computer.

CERTIFICATION OBJECTIVE 5.05

Network Protocols

In order for two computers on a network to communicate with each other, they must be using identical protocols. Even though two computers may have multiple protocols bound to their respective network adapters, as long as they share one in common, they will be able to communicate. Windows 98 provides Protected mode drivers for most protocols you will encounter, and can run multiple protocol stacks simultaneously. The next few sections will outline the features and benefits of the more widely adopted protocols today.

Two devices whose functions need to be understood for the next few sections are bridges and routers. Both bridges and routers, through different methods, filter data to different LAN segments.

A bridge forwards data, based on a table it constructs of the MAC address directly accessible by each of its ports. A MAC address is a unique sequence of letters and numbers that is hard-encoded into each network interface card. By monitoring the headers of packets, the bridge adds to its table data on where each packet comes from and where it goes. Then, if it gets a packet whose destination it recognizes, it forwards the packet to the appropriate place, or does not allow it to pass.

A router makes its decision on what to do with a packet based on the protocol being used and the network address. A router keeps a table of known networks, and forwards a packet to the appropriate place, if it is known, or sends it to the default gateway. The default gateway is just what it sounds like. If there is no appropriate place to send a packet, it will send it to the default gateway, and this process will continue until a router that knows where the network destination is can send the packet to the appropriate place. The basic difference to remember is that a bridge forwards a packet based on the MAC address, and a router forwards a packet based on its network address.

NetBEUI

The NetBIOS Extended User Interface (NetBEUI) protocol is probably the easiest to implement. The only configuration requirement is to specify a computer name and either a domain or workgroup name. It is very fast in terms of performance, and is dynamically self-tuning. One drawback to NetBEUI is that although it can be bridged, it cannot be routed.

exam
ⓦatch

Remember that NetBEUI is nonroutable. Bridges are the only mechanism NetBEUI can use to communicate between LAN segments.

IPX/SPX Compatible Protocol

The Internetwork Packet Exchange and Sequenced Packet Exchange protocols (IPX/SPX) are the default protocols for, and required for, NetWare networks. IPX is an OSI Network Layer protocol that is used as a transporter for SPX and a few other higher-level protocols. Microsoft's version, named NWLink IPX/SPX, is NetWare compatible and supports automatic frame type detection. IPX/SPX is both bridgeable and routable.

TCP/IP

The Transmission Control Protocol/Internet Protocol (TCP/IP) is a generic term for a suite of protocols developed by the Department of Defense as a method of communication between many different types of computers. It has since become the standard protocol for UNIX operating systems, as well as for communication across the Internet. TCP/IP is harder to implement and maintain than the other protocols listed here, but it is much more powerful and robust. TCP/IP is routable.

In order for TCP/IP to function properly, several pieces of information must be supplied. First, each computer must be supplied its own unique identifying network address. This address is a 32-bit number comprised of four octets of up to three digits each, separated by periods. The first part of the address signifies the network on which the computer is located. The second part is what uniquely identifies the host on the network. The division of an IP address in this way helps routers by decreasing the size of their routing tables.

(You can think of the network address as the street you live on, and the host address as your house number. You may have the same house number as dozens of other people in your town, as long as you live on different streets. If you didn't have street names to divide up your city, every house would have to be given a unique number. It would require an awfully good memory to recall the number and location of every house in town, or even just the houses of people you know. The division of TCP/IP addresses into network and host addresses provides a similar sense of order.)

You can determine where the network ID ends and the host ID begins in an address by examining the subnet mask associated with it. A subnet mask starts with one, two, or three of its octets being 255, and usually ends with the remaining octets being 0. For most network addresses, the point where the 255s end and the 0s begin corresponds to where the network ID ends and the host ID begins. Let's say we have an address of 190.22.1.10 with a subnet mask of 255.255.0.0. If we take what we just learned, this means 190.22 is the network ID, and 1.10 is the host ID.

There are five classes of IDs, but you will most likely only encounter three of them. Each class is listed in Table 5-1, with its corresponding number of networks and number of hosts available.

If you noticed, the 127 network is missing from the table. This is because 127.0.0.1 is reserved for use as a loopback. You can ping the loopback address of 127.0.0.1, and it will send a ping to the adapter card in the computer you are using. This is for testing purposes, so if you are

TABLE 5-7	The Three Most Common Classes of Network IDs		
Address Class	**First Octet Range**	**Number of Networks Available**	**Number of Hosts Available**
Class A	1-126	126	16,777,214
Class B	128-191	16,384	655,534
Class C	192-223	2,097,152	254

having connectivity problems, this technique will allow you to make sure the problem doesn't lie within the computer itself.

Occasionally you may run across a subnet mask like 255.255.255.224. A subnet mask similar to this indicates that some of the digits from the host ID have been borrowed for use on the network ID. The only way to determine the host ID for this address is to convert the last octet to its binary equivalent. Where the 0s begin is where the host ID begins. This process of comparing the network address to the subnet mask is called ANDing.

These two sets of numbers, the host ID and the network ID, are required to implement TCP/IP. This information must be supplied manually unless you have a Dynamic Host Configuration Protocol (DHCP) server. A DHCP server will dynamically allocate and assign IP addresses from a given range for hosts on the network.

exam
ⓦatch

Learn which addresses are reserved for specific purposes. You cannot assign these addresses to a computer.

Microsoft DLC

The Data Link Control protocol (DLC) provides an interface for connectivity with IBM Mainframes and Hewlett-Packard's network-attached printers. Windows 98 has a 32-bit driver, which not only supports native 32-bit applications, but is also backward compatible with most 16-bit applications. If, however, you have an application that will not work with Windows 98, it also supplies a Real mode, 16-bit driver that loads itself when the AUTOEXEC.BAT is executed.

Fast Infrared

Fast Infrared is the newest part of Microsoft Infrared 3.0. Windows 98 can transfer data with Fast Infrared Devices (FIR) at up to 4 Mbps. You can send and receive files with the Microsoft Infrared Transfer application, and you can use Infrared Monitor to verify connectivity and transmission speeds.

QUESTIONS AND ANSWERS

I need to select a protocol for my network that can be routed across multiple segments...	Choose TCP/IP or IPX/SPX. With its widespread use across the Internet, TCP/IP is by far the most common choice.
Since my company has a fairly high turnover rate, I need the most secure way for users to protect their shared resources across the network...	Select user-level access. If you use share-level, you have to assign a password that can be compromised when an employee leaves. If you use user-level, once the user is removed from the authenticating server, there is no security threat.
I am trying to decide which class of address I should assign to my new TCP/IP network. I am anticipating around 10,000 users across 300 different networks...	Use a Class B schema. Class B networks support 16,384 networks with 65,534 possible hosts. A Class A schema wouldn't allow for enough networks, whereas a Class C wouldn't allow for enough hosts.
I am trying to decide which class of address I should assign to my new TCP/IP network. I am anticipating around 10,000 users across 300 different networks. I also want to connect to the Internet...	Class B is not the right schema if you are connecting to the Internet, because the IP address won't be legitimate. (You have to get an address assigned from InterNic at www.internic.org). In this case, you would have to get two Class C addresses (since Class B addresses aren't available).
I am redoing my company's backup routine. As of now, we do a full backup every weeknight. My boss has decided a full backup is taking too long to do every night, and in the event of a restore, we need to be able to accomplish it rapidly...	Start by performing a full backup, and on each subsequent night make a differential backup. A differential will back up the files that have changed since the last full. In the worse case scenario, only two tapes will be needed for a complete restore. (Thus a faster restore time.)
I need to perform an automated upgrade of Windows 98 for around 200 users. The times when their laptops are connected vary, and scheduling a time with them is very difficult...	Perform a push installation with a script that is launched through their logon batch file. This way, whenever they log on to the network, it will perform it automatically.
My company only has eight employees, who share a dial-up connection through a gateway to the Internet. I want to increase the throughput without the expense of upgrading to ISDN...	Find a provider who supports multilink, and purchase another line plus modem. In most cities, this is quite a bit cheaper than the high costs associated with ISDN.

CERTIFICATION OBJECTIVE 5.06

The Backup Application

Microsoft Backup is a utility provided with Windows 98 for backing up and restoring files from your hard disk to both removable and non-removable disks or tapes. The backup devices supported can be IDE/ATAPI, SCSI, or even the parallel forms like Iomega Zip drives. This backup utility adheres to the QIC 113 tape specification, which supports long filenames. Important to note for systems that are upgrades: Microsoft Backup will not restore backup sets created by MS-DOS 6.*x* utilities.

Microsoft Backup allows full, differential, and incremental backups. Full backups back up every file every time a backup is performed. Differential backups only back up the files that have changed since the last full backup. Incremental backups back up the files that have changed since the last full or the last incremental backup. Incremental backups take less time than differentials since they have less to back up per tape, but they are harder to restore, because a restore must be done for each incremental tape made since the last full backup was performed.

Windows 98 can keep track of these backups, since every file contains an attribute called an archive bit. Whenever a file is created, Windows 98 sets the bit to On. When a full backup is run, the backup utility changes the bit to Off after it backs up each file. Then, if and when the file is altered, the bit gets set back to On.

EXERCISE 5-12

Installation of Microsoft Backup

1. Click the Start button and choose Settings | Control Panel.
2. Double-click the Add/Remove Programs icon.
3. Select the Windows Setup tab.
4. Double-click System Tools.
5. Check the box next to Backup if one is not present. (If there is already a check mark in the box, Microsoft Backup has been installed already, and you can skip this section.)
6. Click the OK button and then Apply.
7. Click OK one final time to finish installation.

8. Now the device can be found in the System Tools folder under Programs | Accessories.

FROM THE CLASSROOM

The New and Improved Backup Utility

The new Backup utility is one of the most useful new features in Windows 98. It provides improved backup and restore capabilities, including support for more tape drives. Besides backing up to a tape drive, you now have the option to back up files from your hard disk to floppy disks, to another hard disk, or to another computer on your network. It's now much easier for you to protect your data.

I strongly recommended that you perform a full backup of your system regularly, so you have a current backup of your entire system available to restore, if hard disk failure should occur. The new Backup utility allows you to do this in just a few easy steps. The utility will even back up the Windows 98 Registry.

To make a full system backup:

1. On the Job menu, click New.

2. Expand My Computer and select the check box next to each drive.

3. Click Options, then the Advanced tab in the Backup Job Options dialog box.

4. Select the Back Up Windows Registry check box, and then click OK.

5. Click Start.

Any backup settings you select can be saved as a backup job. Jobs allow you to select different sets of information, and different options to apply to those sets, so that you can develop a backup scheme for your system. For example, you might do a full system backup once per week, and incremental or differential backups every day between full system backups, to save time and space.

Other new features that users will find beneficial include the capability to back up network drives, and the capability to back up to a file on another drive. Network drives are backed up simply by selecting the drives and files you need in the backup window, just as if they were located on your local system.

I use Windows 98's capability to back up to a file on another drive, for backing up files to my home directory, located on a fileserver. I set a password on the backup file to make sure my files stay safe, and I set the option to compress data during backup, to make sure I don't take up too much space on the server. On a system that I had connected to the network all of the time, I could also schedule my backup to happen automatically.

—By Robert Aschermann, MCT, MCSE

CERTIFICATION SUMMARY

Windows 98 provides native support for, and can serve as, a client on virtually any network you will encounter today. Windows 98 can not only act as a client, but also serve as a server by sharing its resources. In order to share a Windows 98 system's resources across a network, you need to decide between user-level and share-level access. User-level protection allows you to decide which group or individual has which particular types of access. Share-level security, on the other hand, allows you to assign passwords to resources for access control. To implement share-level security, a user list is obtained from a network authenticator, such as an NT or Novell server.

When it comes to network protocols, TCP/IP and IPX/SPX are both routable, whereas NetBEUI can only be bridged. Since TCP/IP is the most common protocol used today, make sure you know all aspects of how it is configured and implemented. If you see any questions about DLC on the exam, they most likely concern printing and probably referencing HP printers.

Devices within Windows 98 are managed with Device Manager. New devices can be detected and installed automatically (if they are Plug and Play), or added manually (if they are non-Plug and Play). Two new standards for the connection of external devices being introduced with Windows 98 are Firewire and USB. USB is for slower-input devices such as keyboards and mice. Firewire is for higher-speed and -bandwidth devices, like videodisc players and external storage.

 ## TWO-MINUTE DRILL

❑ You can perform automated installations of Windows 98 by either push or pull methods. In a pull installation the user performs the upgrade, whereas in a push installation, the administrator performs the upgrade.

❑ Windows 98 provides native support as a 32-bit Protected mode client on a wide variety of networks, as well as a 16-bit client on several Real mode networks.

❑ Windows 98 supports most network adapters, and supplies 32-bit Real mode drivers, which it can install and configure.

❑ You can connect to a remote printer that is either directly attached to your network, or managed by another PC or server.

❑ Windows 98 keeps track of devices by categorizing them and putting them into different subkeys within the Registry. All devices are managed with Device Manager, which can be found under the System icon in Control Panel.

❑ Plug and Play devices are devices that, after installation, can be configured without any user intervention.

❑ Windows 98 also supports non-Plug and Play devices, also known as legacy devices.

❑ The primary VGA display will be whichever comes first in the PCI slot order.

❑ Microsoft Personal Web Server (PWS) can be used on a small intranet to share documents and information, or it can be used for testing and development of Web sites.

❑ The Dial-Up Networking Server allows Windows 98 to host a single dial-up network connection.

❑ Asynchronous Transfer Mode (ATM) is a switching technology that runs on high-bandwidth media such as FDDI.

❑ Virtual Private Networks (VPNs) use the connections already established by the protocols as their medium for transmission.

❑ To use the Internet as your network for establishing PPTP connections, the PPTP server must have a valid, registered IP address for use on the Internet. The encapsulated packets, however, can be addressed to computers on the private network, since the PPTP server disassembles the PPTP packet and forwards the PPP portion to the correct computer.

❑ Windows 98 has the capability to simulate a server by sharing its files, drives, and printers across a network.

❑ The File and Printer Sharing for Microsoft Networks service supports any network device that utilizes the SMB protocol, such as LAN Manager, Windows for Workgroups, Windows NT, SAMBA, LAN Manager for UNIX, DOS, and OS/2.

❑ Whenever a Windows computer wishes to browse the network to view available resources, it will make a request for the list to a computer that has been designated as either the Browse Master or the Backup Browse Server.

❑ Several remote management tools have been included in Windows 98 to help you troubleshoot and repair PCs on a network, without having to dispatch someone from IT.

  ❑ System Policy Editor

  ❑ Registry Editor

  ❑ System Monitor

  ❑ Net Watcher

❑ Windows 98 provides Protected mode drivers for most protocols you will encounter, and can run multiple protocol stacks simultaneously.

❑ The NetBIOS Extended User Interface (NetBEUI) protocol is probably the easiest to implement.

❑ Remember that NetBEUI is nonroutable. Bridges are the only mechanism NetBEUI can use to communicate between LAN segments.

❑ The Internetwork Packet Exchange and Sequenced Packet Exchange protocols (IPX/SPX) are the default protocols for, and required for, NetWare networks.

❑ The Transmission Control Protocol/Internet Protocol (TCP/IP) is a generic term for a suite of protocols developed by the Department of Defense as a method of communication between many different types of computers. It has since become the standard protocol for UNIX operating systems, as well as for communication across the Internet.

❑ Learn which addresses are reserved for specific purposes. You cannot assign these addresses to a computer.

❑ The Data Link Control protocol (DLC) provides an interface for connectivity with IBM Mainframes and Hewlett-Packard's network-attached printers.

❑ Fast Infrared is the newest part of Microsoft Infrared 3.0. Windows 98 can transfer data with Fast Infrared Devices (FIR) at up to 4 Mbps.

❑ Microsoft Backup is a utility provided with Windows 98 for backing up and restoring files from your hard disk to both removable and non-removable disks or tapes.

SELF TEST

The following questions will help you measure your understanding of the material presented in this chapter. Read all the choices carefully, as there may be more than one correct answer. Choose all correct answers for each question.

1. Which of these are viable solutions for deploying an installation script to upgrade a Windows 95 workstation to Windows 98?

   A. Microsoft Deployment Manager

   B. Microsoft Systems Management Server

   C. Attaching a batch file to an e-mail message

   D. Modifying the logon script

2. Which of the following statements are true?

   A. USB can support up to seven devices with single channel, and up to 14 devices with dual channel

   B. With the high speeds supported by USB, it is an ideal choice for videodisc players and external storage

   C. Both FireWire and USB support both isochronous and asynchronous as their transfer protocols

   D. USB is Plug and Play, but FireWire must be configured manually

3. Which feature of Microsoft's Personal Web Server is no longer supported in version 4.0?

   A. Active Server Pages

   B. FTP Server

   C. RAD—Remote Deployment Support

   D. Drag-and-drop capabilities

4. Which of the following would be a valid reason for implementing ATM across your network?

   A. Not quite as fast as 10baseT, but much easier to implement and manage

   B. Uses Time-Division for allocating bandwidth

   C. Integrates seamlessly with standard TCP/IP LANs

   D. Use of Label Multiplexing

5. PPTP in a Virtual Private Network supports which of the following protocols?

   A. TCP/IP

   B. IPX/SPX

   C. NetBEUI

   D. All of the above

6. Which two statements here are correct?

   A. Share-level access assigns a password to each resource

   B. User-level access assigns a password to each resource

   C. Share-level access requires each user or group to be granted individual rights

   D. User-level access requires each user or group to be granted individual rights

7. Which of the following utilities are included with Windows 98 for remote access management?

   A. System Policy Editor

   B. Microsoft Remote Console

   C. Registry Editor

   D. System Monitor

8. Which of the following protocols are routable?

   A. TCP/IP

   B. IPX/SPX

   C. NetBEUI

   D. All of the above

9. Which classification of address is 127.72.101.80?

   A. Class A

   B. Class B

   C. Class C

   D. None of the above

10. Which of the following statements about the filtering performed by routers and bridges are true?

    A. Routers use network addresses, and bridges use MAC addresses

    B. Routers use MAC addresses, and bridges use DNS resolution

    C. Routers use DNS resolution, and bridges use MAC addresses

    D. Routers use MAC addresses, and bridges use network addresses

6

Windows 98 on a Windows NT-Based Network

There were many complaints about the original Windows 95 exam. Not only did it not follow the Windows 95 course material very well, but a large portion of it concerned Novell integration. There was a good reason for the number of Novell questions at the time: the majority of corporations were running Novell with Windows 95. This has dramatically changed in the last year or so. That is one of the reasons why the Windows 95 exam was updated.

On the Windows 98 exam, expect to see even more questions about interoperability with Windows NT than were on the Windows 95 update exam. Whatever topic you are studying, you should strive to learn several methods to achieve the same results. This chapter is designed to supply the information needed to be successful on the exam and in the real world.

Prior to taking any Microsoft exam, be sure to go to their Web site (www.microsoft.com/train_cert) and check the skills being measured on the exam you are about to take.

CERTIFICATION OBJECTIVE 6.01

Windows NT Interoperability

The evolution of Windows has been amazing. Windows NT is quickly becoming the network operating system of choice for organizations. Windows market share continues to grow. When Windows first came out, most organizations were using Novell NetWare. Windows was designed to integrate with Novell. Even when Windows 95 came out, Windows NT was just beginning to gain recognition. The corporate computer environment quickly became Windows 95 on the desktop and Novell on the servers. As Windows 98 becomes available, there is a new leader among network operating systems: Windows NT. Windows 98 has been designed to interoperate with Windows NT more than the previous version. Remember, when Windows 95 was released to media frenzy, Windows NT was just beginning to make a name for itself. That's why Windows 95 seemed to integrate better with Novell than it did with NT. On the surface, Windows 98 looks like Windows 95 with IE 4 loaded. But in the background, things are different.

Although Microsoft would like for corporations to use Windows NT Workstation 5.0 for the desktops, many corporations will upgrade to Windows 98 because of the hardware requirements of Windows NT.

Since Microsoft is the corporation that produces the Windows product, whether it is Windows 98 or Windows NT, it just makes sense to think they would work together more harmoniously than competing products. For example, if you own a VCR and a TV made by RCA, the setup is easier than it would be if the two components were competing brands. Not only because the terminology in the manuals is the same, but also because they have corresponding input/output connectors. They were made to work together. If one of the components is from a different manufacturer, there may be some setup differences in the input/output connectors and in the terminology.

On the software side, there is no competition for the desktop market. Microsoft has almost complete dominance. If you already have one component by a manufacturer, it makes sense to buy additional components from the same manufacturer.

Windows 98 as a Client

Windows 98 as a client simply means that Windows 98 can be a part of something bigger than a single workstation. Whether this is a workgroup of two machines or a worldwide enterprise, Windows 98 will integrate. It can be a client to multiple systems, including Novell, Banyan VINES, Windows NT, and others. It is designed to coexist in multiple environments. It is a simple process to make Windows 98 act as a client to a Windows NT domain. The steps are discussed in more detail later in this chapter, in the Logging on to a Windows NT Domain section.

Distributed File System

Microsoft Distributed File System (DFS) is a way of simplifying the task of sharing and finding resources for users. It also makes it easier for the administrator to manage the data on a network. DFS is a way to group files from different servers into a single namespace. It provides a way of building a single, hierarchical view of multiple servers and shares on a network. Before DFS, it was very difficult to find resources needed. Browsing through Network Neighborhood would display countless servers, each with its own separate directory structure. A user would first have to know what server a resource was located on, and then what share it was in. The user also had to know what directory it was in. DFS simplifies this process. With DFS, users see a few logical directories that include all of the important servers and shares. The shares appear in the most logical place, regardless of what server they are actually located on. DFS makes it easier for a large corporation to manage and utilize its resources. DFS can be thought of as a share of other shares.

With UNC naming (universal naming convention), a user specifies the physical server and share in order to access the file information. An example would be \\FILESERVER1\DOCUMENTS\WORD\RESOURCE.DOC. Now imagine an organization that contains a large number of file servers, each with its own directory structure. How easy would it be to find the file RESOURCE.DOC? The user has to know what server it was located on. DFS eliminates that need and makes it easier for the user to find the file.

Most organizations use drive mapping to try to simplify the process for the end users. To continue the preceding example, a user might have a logon script that maps drive X to \\FILESERVER1\DOCUMENTS. The user then looks at drive X and sees the directory structure within the Documents share. One folder would be the Word folder that contains the needed file. As networks continue to grow, the idea of mapping a single drive letter to individual shares scales poorly. And even though a user could still directly reference UNC naming, the problem is that a user could become overwhelmed by the increasing amount of locations that need to be accessed in order to gather the necessary data to perform his or her duties. Also, imagine the time it would take for a user to locate a file. This explains the need for DFS.

DFS permits the joining of servers and shares into an easier, navigable namespace. The new DFS volume allows the shares to be hierarchically connected to other Windows NT shares. Subsequently, the actual location of the data becomes transparent to the users and applications, because the physical storage is now logically represented.

Organizing Network Resources

DFS is simple to manage, because there are no new tools required for most management tasks. DFS does include a user-friendly Administration tool that makes it simple for network administrators to maintain and build DFS directories. File security is managed using the Windows NT Server security model via the Windows Explorer.

Replacing servers is easy for network managers with DFS. Each node in the DFS directory tree is assigned a logical name that points to a file share. The DFS node can be switched to point to a new server, while the old server is taken offline. This process will be transparent to the users. They will never know that they are using a different server, since the DFS directory tree does not change.

DFS support for Windows 98 is included in the DFS release and Client for Microsoft Networks. DFS can make Windows 98 desktops easier to use by eliminating the need for multiple persistent network connections to individual physical servers.

DFS also simplifies file maintenance tasks such as Enterprise backups. Since a single DFS tree can be built to cover a large number of servers, the backup software only needs to back up this single tree, no matter how many servers or shares are part of the DFS. In addition, DFS can make it easy to back up data on end-user systems. This has always been a problem in Enterprise environments. In most organizations, if end users want to have data backed up, they would have to put the data on a network server. This was due to the fact that it was too time consuming to back up individual

FROM THE CLASSROOM

Using DFS Effectively

The Microsoft Distributed File System makes it easy to create a single directory tree that includes file servers and shares from many different groups within an enterprise. If you come from the UNIX world, you'll recognize that DFS is very similar to the Network File System (NFS) that is so popular in UNIX environments. DFS gives a user a single directory that can span an almost unlimited number of file servers and file shares. This single directory allows the user to "browse" the network to find data and files. Browsing the DFS directory is easy, because DFS sub-directories can be assigned logical, descriptive names, no matter what the name is of the actual file server or share.

The file search tools included in Windows 98 can now search for a specific file that can be located on any server in the DFS directory tree. DFS support is already included in Windows NT Workstation 4.0, and support for Windows 98 is included in the DFS release. One of the biggest benefits of DFS is that it eliminates the need for multiple persistent network connections. Each user only needs one persistent network connection to his DFS tree.

DFS also makes enterprise backups easy. A DFS tree can be built to cover an entire enterprise. The backup software can then back up the tree, no matter how many servers or shares are involved. DFS makes backups of data on end-user systems easy as well, since Windows 98 systems can be leaves in a DFS tree. A DFS tree can be built that includes all of the directories on users' desktops that network managers want backed up. DFS is also useful for other management tasks, like scanning for viruses across an entire network and content indexing all data for use with search tools such as Microsoft Index Server.

DFS even simplifies deployment of Internet and intranet solutions. A webmaster can now build a logical DFS directory that includes the default Web pages of each department's Web server as a subdirectory of the main Internet or intranet Web. This allows each department or group to retain control over its unique intranet content and applications, while the user only sees a single, unified Internet site or intranet.

If you aren't already getting familiar with DFS, you should. Expect to see a lot more of DFS in the future. DFS is one of Microsoft's new and emerging technologies. In the future, especially with Windows NT 5, you should expect DFS to take an even more important role in network administration and user support.

You may also hear DFS referred to as data hiding, since the resulting directory tree

FROM THE CLASSROOM

represents a logical view of data storage on the network, hiding the actual physical layout of servers and shares from the user. Once the user is in the tree, he has no idea what server he is

accessing to get his data. In fact, he may access multiple servers for a single file search.

—*By Robert Aschermann, MCT, MCSE*

workstations. Since Windows 98 systems can be leaves in a DFS tree, a DFS tree can include all of the directories on users' desktops that administrators want to back up.

Other file maintenance tasks that DFS can help simplify include scanning for viruses across an entire network, and content indexing of data for use with search tools, such as Microsoft Index Server.

DFS is an exciting new technology that Windows 98 can participate in. It is another item that Microsoft has created to give organizations a lower total cost of ownership, by allowing users to focus on doing their jobs instead of worrying about their computers.

exam
ⓦatch

Look for questions about the new technology being introduced with the product. Look for questions about DFS and Windows NT interoperability.

CERTIFICATION OBJECTIVE 6.03

Logging on to a Windows NT Domain

Logging on to a Windows NT domain has not changed very much from Windows 95. Logging on to a Windows NT domain enables a user account to be authenticated once. This authentication process predetermines what rights a user will have, based on what groups the user's account belongs to, or what rights have been granted to the user account. Microsoft's philosophy is, "one user account, one logon." This logon process eliminates the need for a user account and password to be entered multiple times to access different resources. Think of logging on to a Windows NT domain as receiving a backpack full of keys and tokens to access various resources. When a user tries to access a resource, he will be granted access if his backpack contains the appropriate key or token. If it does not, the user will be prompted for a password to access the resource.

exam
ⓦatch

The network components of Windows 98 in a Microsoft environment include: Client for Microsoft Networks and File and Printer Sharing for Microsoft Networks.

Before a user can log on to a Windows NT domain, the Windows 98 machine has to be set up properly. This can be done several ways, but in the following exercise, we demonstrate using the Control Panel. Follow these steps to set up a Windows 98 computer that will log on to a Windows NT domain.

EXERCISE 6-1

Participating in a Microsoft NT Domain

1. Select the Start button on the task bar, and then Settings | Control Panel. This will generate the Control Panel window, which contains several configuration icons.

2. Click the Network icon to produce the Network dialog box, shown in Figure 6-1. There are three tabs on this dialog box, Configuration, Identification, and Access Control.

3. Select the Configuration tab. This page displays four sections: Network Components, Primary Network Logon, File and Print Sharing, and a Description section.

4. The Network Components section should contain, at a minimum, a client (represented by a little computer icon), an adapter (an icon that looks like a network card), and a protocol (an icon that looks like two pieces of cable being joined). If the client listed is the Client for Microsoft Networks, click Properties and continue on to Step 8.

FIGURE 6-1

Network dialog box

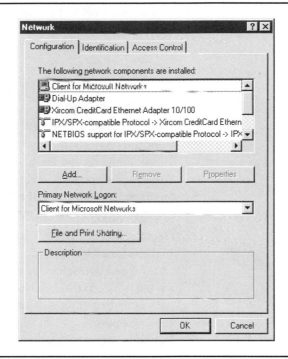

5. If a different client is listed, you will have to add Client for Microsoft Networks. Select the Add button to bring up the dialog box shown in Figure 6-2. Select Client, click Add.

FIGURE 6-2

Network Component dialog box

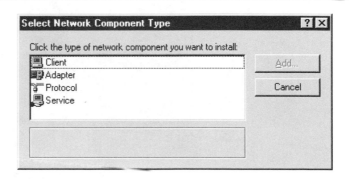

6. Select Microsoft and Client for Microsoft Networks on the dialog box in Figure 6-3. Click OK. You are now returned to the Configuration tab. In the Network Components section, select the Client for Microsoft Networks, then click the Properties button.

7. You now see the Client for Microsoft Networks Properties dialog box, shown in Figure 6-4. There are two sections to this dialog box: Logon Validation and Network Logon Options.

8. Click the open check box next to Log On To Windows NT Domain. Next, type the name of the domain under Windows NT Domain. This process will bring up the correct logon prompt when the user first logs on to the Windows 98 machine.

9. Select the best option for the situation in the Network Logon Options section. There are two choices, Quick Logon and Logon And Restore Network Connections. The first option logs the user on to the network, but doesn't restore any drive mappings until they are used. The second option logs the user onto the network and verifies that each network drive mapping is ready for use. After you make the selection, click the OK button. This will bring back the Network dialog box.

FIGURE 6-3

Network Client
dialog box

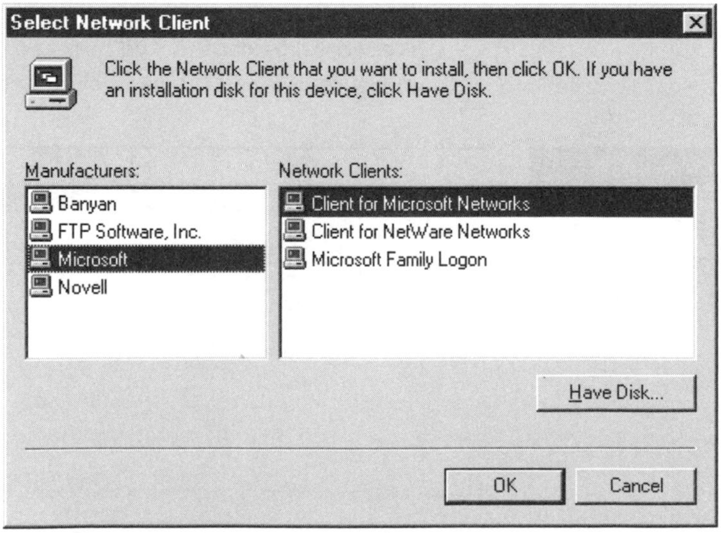

FIGURE 6-4

Client for Microsoft
Networks dialog box

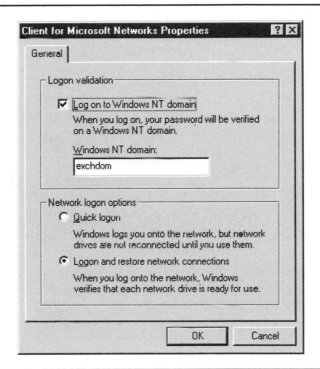

10. Check to make sure that Client for Microsoft Networks is the Primary Network Logon. If not, click the drop-down arrow and select it.

11. Make sure that the appropriate protocol is listed, then click OK. You might need to have the CD-ROM available, as Windows 98 may need to load drivers for the changes made.

The system will then need to be rebooted for the changes to take effect. When the computer restarts, there will be a new Logon dialog box (actually called Enter Network Password). It will contain three areas for information: the user name, the password, and the domain to log on to. This dialog box is shown in Figure 6-5.

Note: If the computer is a laptop and the user travels between organizations (as a lot of consultants do) there is an easy way to log on to different domains. As long as there is a common network protocol, like NWLink or IP with

FIGURE 6-5

Enter Network Password
dialog box

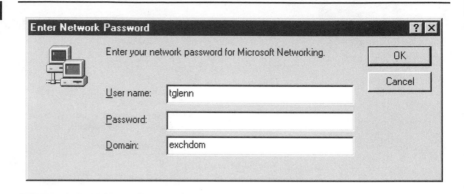

DHCP enabled, the user can simply type the name of the domain, along with the valid user name and password, at the Logon dialog box.

CERTIFICATION OBJECTIVE 6.04

Sharing and Managing Resources

Sharing of resources is the reason for having a network. If this need didn't exist, we could save the cost of cabling and network cards. However, not having a network card would cause several problems for an organization. The organization would have to purchase printers for every computer that needed to print documents. Files would have to be carried to other machines on disks to share or collaborate on information. Without networks, productivity levels would drop dramatically.

Sharing of resources is a necessity for any organization, whether it takes the form of e-mail, printers, or applications. Windows 98 has the capability to share not only data, but also printers that might be attached to the computer. It is this capability to share resources that allows Windows 98 to be a contributing operating system in the network environment. Enabling File and Print Sharing, and choosing which type of security to implement, utilizes the capabilities of Windows 98.

File and Print Sharing

File and Print Sharing allows resources to be utilized, no matter where they are located. If you want to share resources, File and Print Sharing must be enabled. It gives the user the ability to share printers or folders, and to collaborate with colleagues. Sharing also enables network administrators to look at the files on a machine without ever having to travel to its physical location. This is especially helpful in a help desk environment.

File and Print Sharing is set up using the Network dialog box. Exercise 6-2 takes you through the necessary steps.

EXERCISE 6-2

Setting Up File and Print Sharing

1. Right-click the Network Neighborhood icon on the desktop, then select Properties. This displays the Network dialog box.

2. Click the Configuration tab. Click the File and Print Sharing button. This brings up the File and Print Sharing dialog box, shown in Figure 6-6.

3. There are two check boxes. If there is a printer attached that you want to share, check both boxes. Otherwise, select the check box next to I Want To Be Able To Give Others Access To My Files. Click OK. This brings back the Network dialog box.

4. Click OK in the Network dialog box. Be prepared to have the Windows 98 CD ready, as drivers might be needed. You will be prompted to restart the system.

FIGURE 6-6

File and Print Sharing dialog box

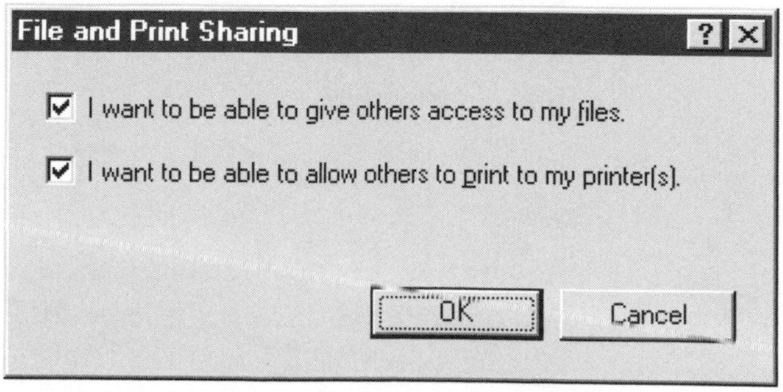

The system now has the capability to share resources, but there are not any resources being shared. In order to allow other users to access resources, a share must be created. Before creating a share, the security level needs to be determined. The process of creating a share will be discussed later in this chapter.

Network Printers

Windows NT has a point-and-click method for adding new printers from the network. All that is necessary is to select the printer to attach to, and Windows NT will automatically configure the system to use it. This includes installing the proper driver for the printer. Attaching to a shared printer is very similar to setting up a printer that is physically connected to the Windows 98 machine.

1. Select the Printers folder in Control Panel.

2. Double-click the Add Printer icon and the Add Printer Wizard shown in Figure 6-7 will be launched.

3. The wizard will ask how the printer is attached to the computer. Choices are Local or Network Printer.

4. Now the location of the printer that is being shared needs to be entered. Type the UNC path or use the Browse button. This is shown in Figure 6-8.

When the server is a Windows NT server that has been set up for the various operating systems to share the printer to, the drives will automatically be downloaded and set up. The end user doesn't even need to know what type of printer is being used. This is another feature that lowers the total cost of ownership.

Security Levels

As with any sharing of resources, there needs to be some form of security. Windows 98 has two security levels for File and Print Sharing with Windows 98: One is User Level (also known as pass-through security) and the other is Share Level.

FIGURE 6-7

Add Printer Wizard
dialog box

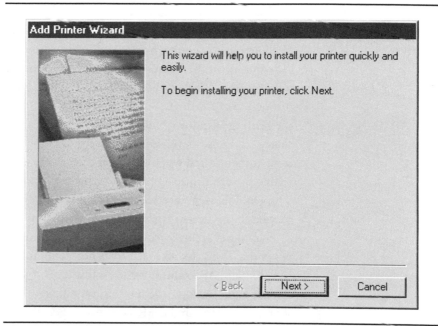

FIGURE 6-8

Enter the network path in
the Add Printer Wizard
dialog box

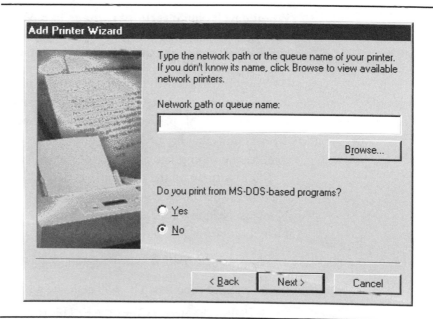

User-level is the security level that should be chosen when the Windows 98 machine participates in a Windows NT domain. This allows the user to choose user accounts from the domain accounts when giving access to resources on the Windows 98 machine. When a user tries to access a resource, the Windows 98 machine passes the authentication request through to a Windows NT server (or Novell). User-level security leverages the existing Windows NT security. Accessing a resource that has been shared using user-level security is a simple process. The user has already been authenticated when she logged on to her own machine. Based on her rights, she can utilize any resource that her account has the authority to use. This eliminates the need for her to enter a password when accessing a share that has been created with user-level security.

Share-level security requires more work. This security level is usually used when the Windows 98 machine is not going to participate in a Windows NT domain. An example of when this level of security would be used is in a workgroup setting. The user creates a share, then assigns a password to the share. The share can be a Read Only or a Full Control option. Based on the password a user enters, she will get Full Control or Read Only access.

exam
ⓦatch

When developing a security strategy in a Microsoft environment, strategic considerations include: file and printer sharing, and share-level access control versus user-level access control.

A problem exists with the maintenance of passwords. Most users have a hard enough time remembering their own password without having to remember multiple passwords for multiple resources. When a user tries to access a share that has been created using share-level security, she is required to enter the appropriate password for the share.

It is easy to set up the security level desired. As with Windows 95, there are usually multiple ways to get to the same result. Either Control Panel or Network Neighborhood can be used. Follow these steps if you use Network Neighborhood:

1. Right-click the Network Neighborhood icon located on the desktop.

2. Select Properties. This will generate a Network dialog box.

3. Select the Access Control tab. This is shown in Figure 6-9.

The Access Control tab
on the Network
dialog box

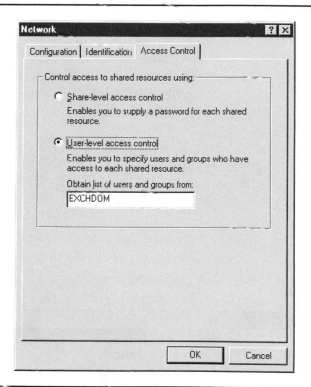

4. If share-level is the desired security type, click the appropriate radio button. If user-level is the desired security type, after clicking the appropriate radio button, select the source of the accounts. (This is usually the domain to which the user and the machine belong.) Then click OK. Have the CD handy.

Now that the process of adding File and Print Sharing and choosing the security level has been completed, the workstation is ready to create shares. To create a share, open Windows Explorer. Do this by right-clicking on the Start button and selecting Explore. Once Windows Explorer is open, follow these steps to create a share:

1. Select the desired folder to share by right-clicking it. Then select Sharing from the list of options.

2. A Properties dialog box for that folder is displayed (Figure 6-10). Click the Sharing tab.

3. Click the Shared As button. The share name is the name other users are going to see when connecting to the folder selected to share. By default this will be populated with the name of the folder. It is a good idea to keep the share 12 characters or less.

4. After the Share Name and Comment fields have been filled in, users and/or groups and their access rights need to be added. Click the Add button. This brings up an Add Users dialog box, shown in Figure 6-11. This box has four main sections: Name, Read Only, Full Access, and Custom.

5. Select the users and/or groups that should have access to the share, and what permissions they should have.

6. Click the OK button on the Add Users dialog box.

FIGURE 6-10

Folder Properties |
Sharing

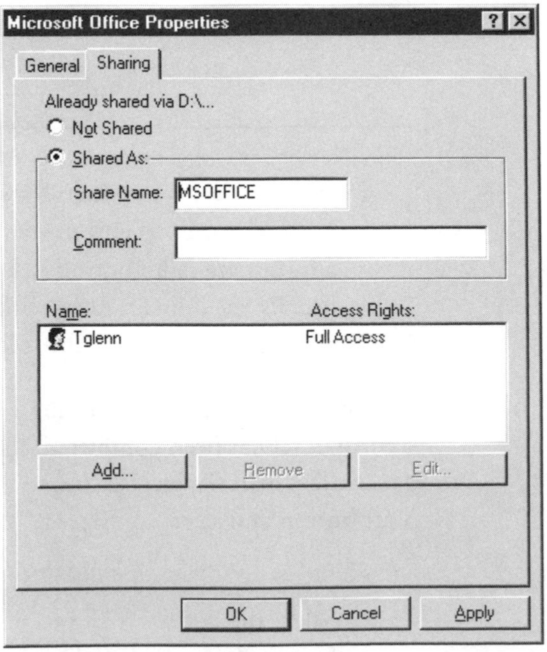

FIGURE 6-11

Add Users dialog box

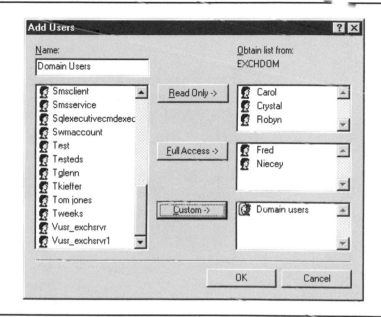

7. Click OK on the Folder Name Properties dialog box.

A share has now been created. Users given access can now use your shared resources. Sharing a printer is much the same. All that is necessary is to select the printer from the Printers folder by double-clicking the My Computer icon on the desktop. After double-clicking the Printers folder, the printers that are connected to the Windows 98 workstation are displayed. Simply select the printer that is to be shared by right-clicking the icon. Then select Sharing from the drop-down list to bring up the Printer Property dialog box. Click the Sharing tab, shown in Figure 6-12.

The process of sharing a printer is almost identical to sharing a folder, with the exception of rights. The Add Users dialog box is a little different. See Figure 6-13.

exam
ⓦatch

Be prepared for security questions in which you are given scenarios about various organizations and their security needs. As a rule, if there is a need for security, Windows NT is a better option.

FIGURE 6-12

The Sharing tab on the
Printer Properties
dialog box

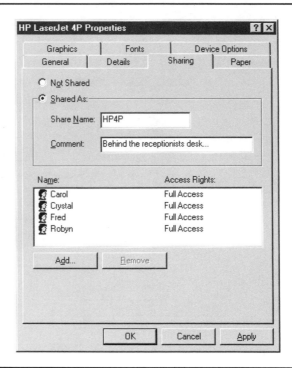

FIGURE 6-13

Add Users dialog box

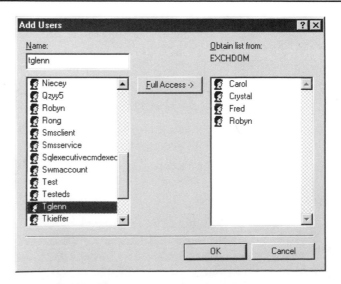

Remote Computers

Dial-Up Networking allows Windows 98 to access resources on the network as if the computer were still at the office, although the Windows 98 machine can be anywhere, as long as there is a phone line available.

Windows 98 Dial-Up Networking provides support for a single-client Point to Point Tunneling Protocol (PPTP) connection, and for internal ISDN adapters. Windows 98 treats the Dial-Up Networking software and modem combinations as just another instance of a network adapter. Looking at the Network dialog box, you can see this. Double-clicking the Network icon in Control Panel can access this dialog box. Windows 98 supports the notion of multiple, concurrently operating network adapters, clients and protocols. If one protocol, adapter or client cannot satisfy the network request, Windows 98 tries each component in turn. If there is no physical adapter that can resolve the network request, such as is the case when a user is mobile, Windows 98 then tries a Dial-Up Networking adapter. Windows 98 will create a Dial-Up Network connection whenever the user's action implies that one is needed. These automatic connections are referred to as implicit connections.

Establishing a remote connection works the same as establishing a connection in the office. This is due to the support in Windows 98 for implicit connections. Windows 98 will take whatever steps necessary to establish a connection.

With mobile computing there is a process called deferred printing. Users can generate print jobs regardless of where they are located. If the user is not currently connected to the network printer, jobs are spooled to the hard disk by the system until a printer becomes available. Windows 98 detects the connection to a printer and automatically prints the jobs as a background process.

Whenever an installed printer is not available, Windows 98 switches to deferred printing mode. The printer could be unavailable due to a network failure or printer hardware problem. Once the deferred print mode has been enabled, Windows 98 periodically checks the connection to the printer to see if it has been re-established. If the printer is once again available, Windows 98 switches out of deferred printing mode and begins spooling any documents that are in the queue. Windows 98 will prompt the user to start printing so that the user has the option of staying in the deferred printing mode.

QUESTIONS AND ANSWERS

I want to log on to a Windows NT domain...	Use the Network dialog box and add Client for Microsoft Networks and select Log On To Windows NT Domain.
I want to change from user-level security to share-level security...	Use the Access Control tab in the Network dialog box.
I want to share a folder but sharing doesn't appear as an option when I right-click on the folder...	File and Print Sharing needs to be enabled. Use the Network Dialog box.
I need to change my password...	Use the Password icon in Control Panel.
I need to connect to a printer on the network...	Use the Add Printer Wizard and be sure that the user account has access to the printer.
I need to ensure that I got the appropriate IP configuration information from the DHCP server...	Use the WINIPCFG.EXE utility from the start run or DOS prompt.

CERTIFICATION OBJECTIVE 6.05

Troubleshooting the Windows NT Interoperability

Troubleshooting is an important part of network administrators' responsibilities. As the administrator gains more experience, his trouble-shooting skills will be greatly enhanced. Troubleshooting ultimately comes down to a person's attitude, ability to use logic, the process of elimination, and experience.

Attitude is probably the most important. Treat the process like a game, a mystery that needs to be solved. If a person can maintain a positive, sometimes humorous, attitude, he or she will do well in this industry. Things do break, and the network administrator cannot just put off dealing with the problem until the next day, even if it is five o'clock. Hardware or software being down costs business big money. Some manufacturers can lose thousands of dollars a minute if an entire production line is down. It's at these times that the pressure is high and the main thing that is going to get an administrator through is attitude. Maintain a positive attitude in every troubleshooting situation. There is a resolution to any problem; it's just a matter of finding it.

Troubleshooting is always a process of elimination. There are so many different things that could be the cause of the same problem; it is unlikely that the first guess will be the right one. A user not being able to log on in the morning could be due to a router being down, a duplicate IP address, an incorrect password, or the cleaning crew knocking the network cable out of the wall. All of these, and many more, would cause the same result. The process of elimination is the only way to find the resolution.

Of course, logic is important to troubleshooting. In the preceding example, if only one user is having a problem logging on, then the router must be working properly. This is a logical conclusion. Logic can save time in finding the resolution.

The more experience and exposure a network administrator has, the easier it is to troubleshoot problems. Retention of knowledge is greatly enhanced when the knowledge is acquired through hands-on experience.

Problems with interoperability of Windows NT can usually be attributed to two main factors, network problems and user rights. Network problems could be due to duplicate IP addresses, user error when entering the IP information, or physical problems with network components such as hubs, routers, and gateways.

As you can see from Figure 6-14, computers need more than just unique IP addresses to locate and communicate with each other. There must also be a subnet mask, a default gateway, a WINS server and a DNS server.

A subnet mask helps a computer determine its own network number and host ID, and those of the computer it is trying to communicate with

FIGURE 6-14

TCP/IP Properties
dialog box

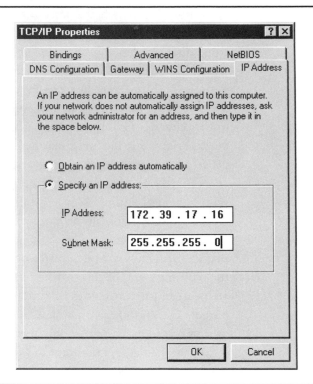

The process resolves whether another computer is local (on the same subnet) or remote (on a different subnet) via a mathematical process involving the IP address and subnet mask of both computers.

If the computer is remote, the default gateway is used. The DNS and WINS servers provide name resolution. DNS usually resolves Fully Qualified Domain Names (for example, www.microsoft.com) and WINS usually resolves NetBIOS names (for example, Server1) to an IP address. There are many numbers that have to be entered correctly in order for IP to work properly. If the subnet mask is incorrect, a remote computer may appear to be local.

exam
Watch

Jot down any memory aids on the scratch paper that will be provided at the exam. A good one to memorize is: WINS is to LMHOSTS as DNS is to HOSTS (referring to name resolution).

DHCP is a service that can be added to a Windows NT server that eliminates the potential for human error. DHCP automatically dispenses IP configuration information to client machines.

There are several utilities that can be used to help troubleshoot IP problems. They are WINIPCFG.EXE, PING.EXE, NETSTAT.EXE, and TRACERT.EXE. WINIPCFG, shown in Figure 6-15, displays the IP information for a Windows 98 machine.

This is the quickest way to determine if the information was entered properly. PING (Figure 6-16) allows the user to send a test message to another computer to ensure that IP is loaded properly and working.

NETSTAT, shown in Figure 6-17, is used to display statistics on, and the state of, current TCP/IP connections.

TRACERT, shown in Figure 6-18, is used to determine the route to a host.

FIGURE 6-15

IP Configuration dialog box

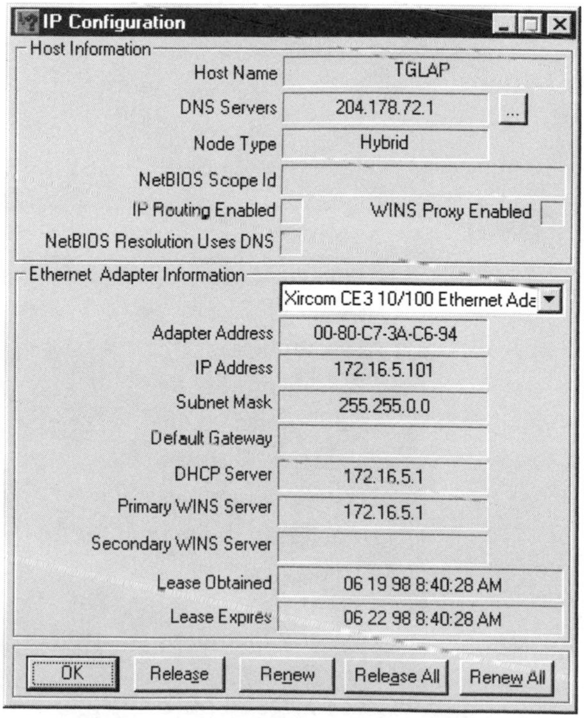

FIGURE 6-16

PING utility

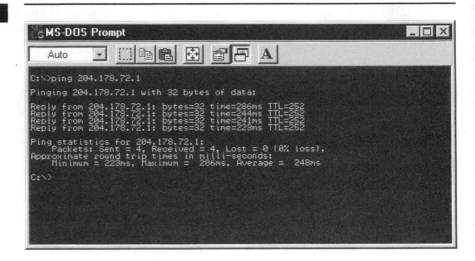

Another area that presents problems is user and group rights. If a user is trying to connect to a share or to a printer, then he must have the appropriate permissions. Rights are more of a user-training issue than a chronic

FIGURE 6-17

NETSTAT utility

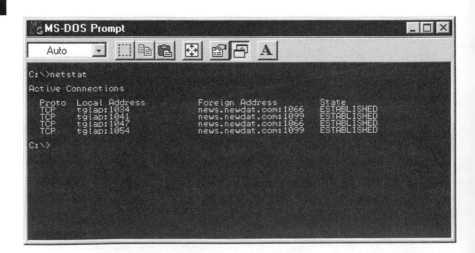

FIGURE 6-18

TRACERT utility

```
C:\>tracert www.microsoft.com

Tracing route to www.microsoft.com [207.46.130.165]
over a maximum of 30 hops:
  1    164 ms    143 ms    164 ms  acas24.ght.ladfw.net [206.66.0.24]
  2    166 ms    165 ms    152 ms  206.66.0.254
  3    241 ms    232 ms    212 ms  sl-gw14-fw-9-0-T3.sprintlink.net [144.228.138.17
]
  4    234 ms    295 ms    239 ms  sl-bb11-fw-3-3.sprintlink.net [144.232.1.149]
  5    222 ms    234 ms    250 ms  sl-bb10-sea-0-0.sprintlink.net [144.232.8.54]
  6    235 ms    240 ms    273 ms  sl-gw4-sea-0-0-0.sprintlink.net [144.232.6.50]
  7    239 ms    264 ms    334 ms  sl-mic-3-0-T3.sprintlink.net [144.228.96.22]
  8    225 ms    291 ms    273 ms  207.46.129.5
  9    __
```

problem. The more users are aware of rights, the fewer problems they will
encounter in the future.

CERTIFICATION SUMMARY

The acceptance of Windows NT continues to grow, as will the importance
of Windows NT interoperability. Windows 98 is an important part of the
make-up of a network. It has been designed to work better with NT than
the previous versions, and is the culmination of several advancements.
There is a closer tie-in with DFS (Distributed File System), and with the
new Client for Microsoft Networks. Windows 95 had to have a separate
DFS client loaded.

But as some things change, some things remain the same. This is evident
in configuring a Windows 98 machine to log on to a Windows NT
domain. The dialog boxes are almost identical to the previous version. The
majority of the configuration is handled with the Network dialog box,
which can be accessed by right-clicking on the Network Neighborhood icon
and selecting Properties.

In order to share resources, File and Print Sharing must be enabled. This is done through the Network dialog box also. After File and Print Sharing has been enabled, simply right-click on the folder or printer to be shared. Remember to use a share name that conforms to the 8.3 settings, to elevate any other clients from having trouble accessing the share.

The exam might have quite a few questions on troubleshooting, so be prepared. Be familiar with the utilities used to check the configuration of TCP/IP on a Windows 98 machine (WINIPCFG). Also the PING utility is used to verify a connection to another machine. TRACERT is used to find the hops being taken in connecting to another machine.

Another important area is security levels. There are two levels, User Level and Share Level. User-level is when validation of a user account is passed on to the NT server. This is the preferred security level when an NT domain environment exists. Share-level is where a password is assigned to each share created. This can be fine for a small workgroup, but an administration nightmare for a larger group. Users have a hard enough time remembering their own password. The last thing needed is for them to remember a password for each resource they need to access.

Certification is not an easy process, but if you set your goals, stay committed and utilize the resources provided, you will be able to get certified on Windows 98.

 # TWO-MINUTE DRILL

- ❑ On the Windows 98 exam, expect to see even more questions about interoperability with Windows NT than were on the Windows 95 update exam.

- ❑ Prior to taking any Microsoft exam, be sure to go to their Web site, www.microsoft.com/train_cert, and check the skills being measured on the exam you are about to take.

- ❑ Windows NT is quickly becoming the network operating system of choice for organizations.

- ❑ It is a simple process to make Windows 98 act as a client to a Windows NT domain.

❑ Microsoft Distributed File System (DFS) is a way of simplifying the task of sharing and finding resources for users.

❑ DFS does include a user-friendly Administration tool that makes it simple for network administrators to maintain and build DFS directories.

❑ DFS support for Windows 98 is included in the DFS release and Client for Microsoft Networks.

❑ Look for questions about the new technology being introduced with the product. Look for questions about DFS and Windows NT interoperability.

❑ Logging on to a Windows NT domain enables a user account to be authenticated once.

❑ Microsoft's philosophy is, "one user account, one logon."

❑ The network components of Windows 98 in a Microsoft environment include: Client for Microsoft Networks and File and Printer Sharing for Microsoft Networks.

❑ Windows 98 has the capability to share not only data, but also printers that might be attached to the computer.

❑ Enabling File and Print Sharing, and choosing which type of security to implement, utilizes the capabilities of Windows 98.

❑ File and Print Sharing allows resources to be utilized, no matter where they are located.

❑ Windows 98 has two security levels for File and Print Sharing with Windows 98: One is User Level (also known as pass-through security) and the other is Share Level.

❑ When developing a security strategy in a Microsoft environment, strategic considerations include: file and printer sharing, and share-level access control versus user-level access control.

❑ Be prepared for security questions in which you are given scenarios about various organizations and their security needs. As a rule, if there is a need for security, Windows NT is a better option.

❑ Windows 98 Dial-Up Networking provides support for a single-client Point-to-Point Tunneling Protocol (PPTP) connection, and for internal ISDN adapters.

❑ Windows 98 treats the Dial-Up Networking software and modem combinations as just another instance of a network adapter.

❑ Problems with interoperability of Windows NT can usually be attributed to two main factors, network problems and user rights.

❑ Jot down any memory aids on the scratch paper that will be provided at the exam. A good one to memorize is: WINS is to LMHOSTS as DNS is to HOSTS (referring to name resolution).

❑ There are several utilities that can be used to help troubleshoot IP problems. They are WINIPCFG.EXE, PING.EXE, NETSTAT.EXE, and TRACERT.EXE.

SELF TEST

The following questions will help you measure your understanding of the material presented in this chapter. Read all the choices carefully, as there may be more than one correct answer. Choose all correct answers for each question.

1. Fred did not install and configure all networking options during Windows 98 Setup. How can he configure networking support after installing Windows 98?

   A. By using the System option in Control Panel

   B. By using the Network option in Control Panel

   C. By restarting Windows; all networking options will be configured automatically

   D. By using the Add New Hardware option in Control Panel

2. Carol is adding Windows 98 computers to her existing network. She wants to protect shared network resources on the computers running Windows 98 with individually assigned passwords. Which of the following types of security would be appropriate?

   A. Pass-through security

   B. System security

   C. User-level security

   D. Share-level security

3. What is a TCP/IP subnet mask?

   A. Another name for the IP address

   B. The address of the DHCP server for the subnetwork

   C. A value that allows a computer to distinguish the network number from the host ID

   D. The network number

4. Crystal did not install TCP/IP when she installed Windows 98. How can she install TCP/IP now?

   A. By using the Add New Hardware Wizard

   B. By using the Network option in Control Panel

   C. By using the Modems option in Control Panel

   D. By using the Mail and Fax option in Control Panel

5. You cannot use TCP/IP to establish a connection. One of your friends suggested you use the TCP/IP diagnostic utilities to isolate network hardware problems. Which utility should you use if you want to check the route to a remote computer?

   A. PING.EXE

   B. NBTSTAT.EXE

   C. NETSTAT.EXE

   D. TRACERT.EXE

6. You want to use the PING command to check the TCP/IP configuration.

However, you cannot use the command successfully. What are some of the possible causes of this problem?

A. The IRQ setting is invalid

B. The IP address of the default gateway is invalid

C. The local computer's IP address does not appear correctly in the TCP/IP Properties dialog box

D. The IP address of the remote host is invalid

7. Robyn wants to share her printer with other users. What should she do?

A. Use the Add New Hardware option in Control Panel

B. Edit the Sharing tab on the printer's property sheet

C. Drag the Printer icon to her desktop

D. Use the Add Printer Wizard

8. Your Windows 98 computer is protected with user-level security. Which of the following access rights can be assigned to the folders on your computer?

A. Read Only

B. Custom

C. Full

D. Execute

9. IP addresses are assigned by a DHCP server. You are curious to see what IP address and other IP information was assigned to your computer. How would you do this?

A. Open a DOS prompt and type **IPINFO**

B. Open a DOS prompt and type **WINIPCFG**

C. Use the START/RUN command and type **IPCONFIG /all**

D. Select TCP/IP Properties from the Network dialog box

10. Which of the following statements are NOT true of deferred printing in Windows 98?

A. When deferred printing is enabled, the printer will be dimmed in the Printers folder

B. When deferred printing is enabled on a network, print jobs are stored in the print queue, and will be printed when the computer is reconnected to the network

C. Deferred print jobs are stored on the local computers

D. Deferred printing only works with print jobs generated by Win32-based applications

7

Interoperating with NetWare

Working on a network is a fact of business life. People need to share information and resources in an increasingly group-ordered workplace. The group working on Project X needs to access the "X-files." Those workgroup users have to connect to the X-files server. And sometimes, that server is a Novell NetWare server.

For Windows 98 developers, the trick was to make Windows 98 access to the NetWare-based files transparent. That is, to let the user log on, connect, print and transfer files to and from a PC, without having to do anything odd or excessive. This seamless transition from local to network resources is something that Windows 98 excels at, not just with Windows NT servers, but even with NetWare servers.

CERTIFICATION OBJECTIVE 7.01

NetWare Interoperability

Support for Novell NetWare connectivity is native to Microsoft Windows 98. This is an improvement over Windows 95. When Windows 95 first came out, it also supported Novell NetWare connectivity, except it was limited to a "Bindery" connection. The Bindery is the name given to the server-centric database of users, printers, and resources on a NetWare server. The Bindery exists on a Novell NetWare 2.*x* or 3.*x* server.

Novell NetWare 4.*x* and IntranetWare servers do not have a Bindery. Instead, they use Novell Directory Services (NDS), which is a network-wide database for network resources, based on the X.500 directory service standard created by the International Telecommunications Union Standardization Sector (ITU-T). Since Windows 95 was limited to Bindery connections, it did not work well with later versions of NetWare. It was still possible to use them, by creating a Bindery context on the server itself. But it was not easy, nor a native functionality for Windows 95 to access those servers. Great news! NDS compatibility is included in Windows 98.

Installing and Configuring IPX/SPX-Compatible Protocol

Every client/server network requires at least four things:

■ **A physical medium** This is the transport vehicle by which the communications travel. A good comparison to a network physical medium is the phone wire used to connect telephones to the telephone network. Examples of network physical media are copper wire and fiber optic cable.

■ **A client** The client is the workstation that requests the use of resources on the network. It may need to access data on another PC, or use a printer connected to another PC. PC workstations and terminals are clients.

■ **A server** The server is the station that controls the resources to the network. It grants access to client workstations so that they can use the resources shared by the server. The server could be a PC server or a mainframe, for example.

■ **A protocol** A protocol is the method of communication. This is how TCP/IP is used for the Internet. For NetWare, the protocol is IPX/SPX.

IPX/SPX stands for Internet Packet Exchange/Sequential Packet Exchange. It represents the two main protocol types used for NetWare. These protocols provide network and transport services. In order to connect completely with NetWare servers, another protocol must also be used, called NetWare Core Protocol (NCP).

The IPX/SPX protocol can be used with Microsoft networking to connect Windows NT and/or Windows 98 PCs together. Although they use the same transport and network protocols, they do not use the NetWare Core Protocol, which is why simply adding that protocol to a workstation will not let it "talk" to a NetWare server. This is due to NCP being required to implement the core services for shared resources, such as file and printer sharing.

In order to connect to a NetWare network, the client workstation requires the full protocol stack, including NCP. This is provided by a NetWare client. Windows 98 supports both of the DOS clients for Novell NetWare. The NETX and the VLM stacks are the DOS clients provided by Novell.

The problem with using a monolithic 16-bit DOS client is that only one network client can be used at a time. This problem does not exist with 32-bit clients, where multiple 32-bit clients may be used simultaneously.

There is only one 32-bit network client for NetWare that is provided as part of Windows 98. This 32-bit client is located in the Microsoft set of network clients, since Microsoft created it. See Figure 7-1 for the location of this client.

FIGURE 7-1

Selecting the
NetWare client

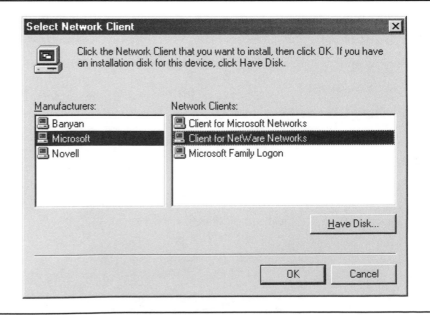

exam
ⓦatch

Windows 98 supports the NETX and VLM clients from Novell for connecting to NetWare servers. It also includes a 32-bit client for NetWare. (What will not be on the exam, but is good to know, is that Novell created a 32-bit client for NetWare, too, but it is not part of Windows 98.)

Client for NetWare Networks

If the user needs access to even a single printer on a NetWare network, the Client for NetWare Networks should be installed to provide that access.

The following exercise shows you how to connect a Windows 98 workstation to a Novell NetWare network using the Microsoft Client for NetWare Networks.

EXERCISE 7-1

Installing the Microsoft Client for NetWare Networks

1. Open the Control Panel Network icon by clicking Start | Settings | Control Panel. Then double-click the Network icon. Alternatively, right-click the Network Neighborhood icon on the Desktop and select Properties. Both these methods bring up the screen in Figure 7-2.

2. Click the Add button and select Client from the list of options, as shown in Figure 7-3.

3. Click Add and select the Microsoft option in the left pane under Manufacturers.

4. Select the Client for NetWare Networks in the right pane under Network Clients.

5. Click OK. If the source files are not available from their original source location, Windows 98 will prompt for the Windows 98 CD in order to access the source files. If the source files are located in a directory other than the one listed in the window, simply change the directory location.

There are several configuration options available to the Client for NetWare Networks. In order to configure the client portion, click the

FIGURE 7-2

The Network dialog box

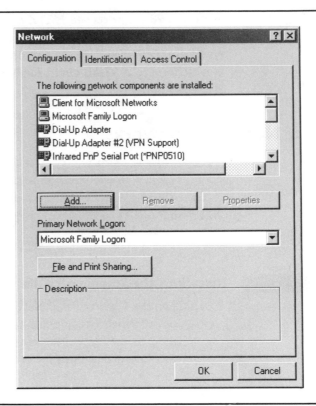

FIGURE 7-3

Network options

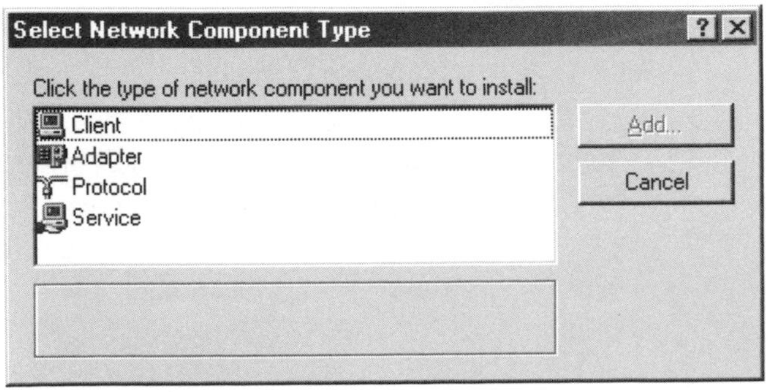

Client for NetWare Networks and then click the Properties button. The dialog box in Figure 7-4 will appear.

The General tab allows the selection of a Preferred Server. A Preferred Server is the server chosen to log on the user. Older versions of NetWare used a server-centric database of users called the Bindery. This meant that the user ID had to exist on each server to which a user needed access. The results of this Bindery system meant increased administration and multiple user IDs and passwords for each user. It became somewhat confusing. The Preferred Server parameter was used to manage which server a workstation would use as the default to log on to.

The General tab also allows the user to select the first network drive letter. Since some drives are mapped by default to the first available drive letter in NetWare logon scripts, it may be preferable to manage which drive

FIGURE 7-4

Properties for the
NetWare Client

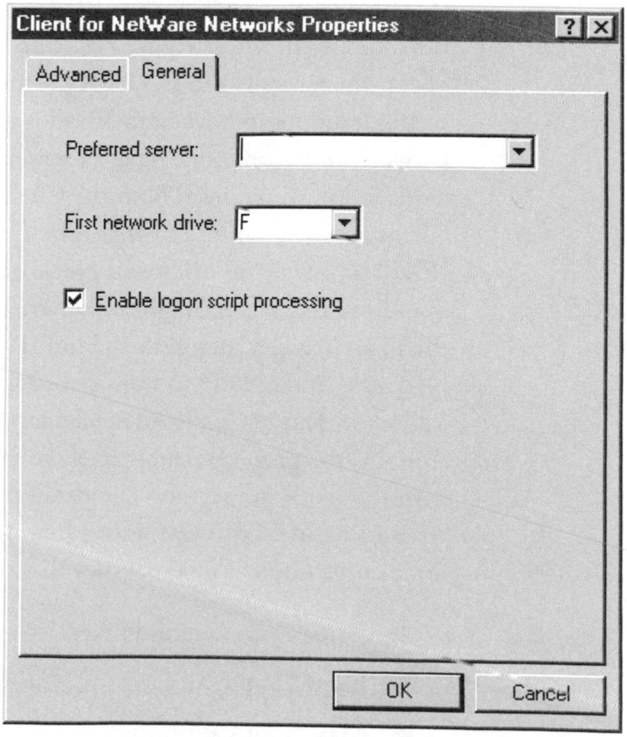

letter is the first available. The General tab also allows the user to enable logon script processing.

The Advanced tab has a single option to Preserve Case. NetWare is mostly case insensitive, but since using capitalization is easier for users to read, this can be helpful.

IPX/SPX-Compatible Protocol Properties

The protocol requirement of the Client for NetWare Networks is the IPX/SPX-Compatible Protocol. There are many properties available to configure the protocol. From the Network dialog box, click the IPX/SPX-Compatible Protocol and click the Properties button. If there is more than one adapter in the PC, there will be multiple cases of the IPX/SPX-Compatible Protocol—each bound to a separate adapter. Some properties for IPX/SPX can be configured independently for each network interface.

There are three tabs for the IPX/SPX-Compatible Protocol. The first is Bindings, shown in Figure 7-5. The Bindings tab allows the user to select which clients the IPX/SPX protocol will be used with. A common configuration is to have both Windows NT and NetWare servers on a network. To access both types of servers simultaneously, the Windows 98 workstation would need both the Client for NetWare Networks and the Client for Microsoft Networks. The Client for NetWare Networks needs IPX. The Client for Microsoft Networks only requires TCP/IP. Since the Windows NT servers might only have the TCP/IP protocol installed on them, an installer may wish to bind IPX only to the Client for NetWare Networks and only IP to the Client for Microsoft Networks.

The second tab is the Advanced tab, shown in Figure 7-6, which contains the properties most likely to be required to make the client work with the NetWare servers. The default properties are usually fine for connecting to a NetWare server, but in some networks, the protocol needs to be customized. The properties that can be configured are:

- Force Even Length Packets
- Frame Type
- Maximum Connections

■ Maximum Sockets

■ Network Address

■ Source Routing

The Force Even Length Packets option has a value of Yes, No, or Not Present (default). This option is only used for the Ethernet 802.3 frame type on older NetWare networks that were implemented in a configuration that cannot handle odd-length packets.

The Frame Type option is critical to the network connection. NetWare versions 3.11 or older, use the Ethernet 802.3 by default, although different frame types could be configured for them. The Ethernet 802.2 frame type was added to NetWare and became the default protocol for versions 3.12 and later. The frame type must match the server's on the workstation. Windows 98 has a catchall frame type option called Auto. When the Auto

FIGURE 7-5

IPX/SPX Bindings tab

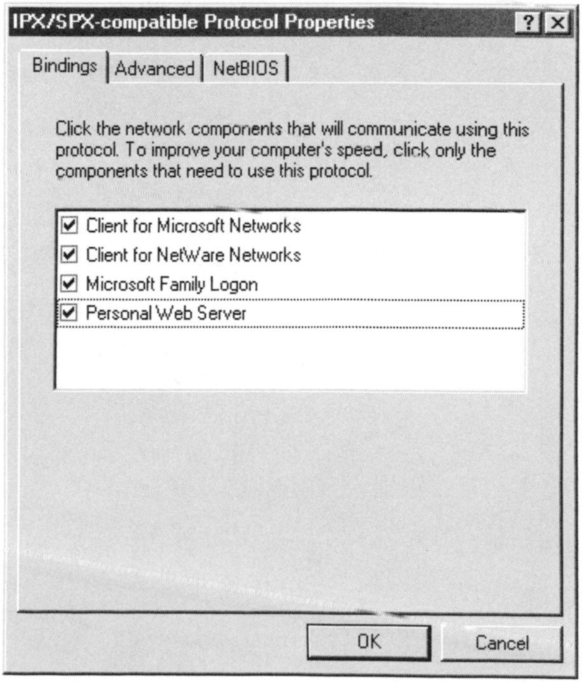

option is selected, the Client will listen on the network for the frame types being used. Then it will use the first frame type it encounters. The behavior of the Ethernet 802.2 protocol is such that the Windows 98 client always uses Ethernet 802.2 first, when both 802.2 and 802.3 are on a network.

e x a m
ⓦatch

When configuring the IPX/SPX protocol, the frame type on the workstation must match the frame type that is used on the server.

The Maximum Connections option refers to the connections that can be made from the workstation to the resource. The number of connections can manage whether the Windows 98 PC can use a network resource reliably. When printing is unstable and disconnects in the middle of a print job, creating garbled output, an old trick is to increase the connections to 60. The Not Present value allows connections to be configured dynamically.

FIGURE 7-6

Frame Type options

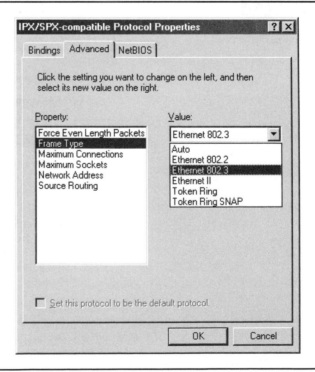

Maximum Sockets is an option used when connecting to applications. Some applications require specific socket connections to be available in order to work correctly. The Not Present value allows sockets to be configured dynamically.

The Network Address option is used to specify the address of the network. This is normally configured dynamically through the IPX/SPX protocol determining the address from packets on the network. It is not usually necessary to use this option, except when troubleshooting a network connection.

Source Routing is a function of token ring networks. If a token ring network uses source routing, then the client workstation must also use it in order to connect. This is not necessary if the NetWare server is on the same ring as the client. The values for Source Routing specify the cache size used for source route entries. The value of 16 entries is the most efficient.

The final tab in the IPX/SPX-Compatible Protocol Properties dialog box is the NetBIOS tab. It enables NetBIOS traffic to run over IPX/SPX. Some applications require NetBIOS over IPX/SPX, but most do not.

The following problem-solving scenarios are presented to help you understand what's involved in choosing a network client service.

QUESTIONS AND ANSWERS

Fred has installed the Client for NetWare Networks on his Windows 98 PC. His network consists of a NetWare 3.11 server and a Windows NT server, both of which use the IPX/SPX protocol. Fred has no problem connecting to the Windows NT server, but cannot see the NetWare server in the Network Neighborhood, nor does the Windows 98 PC log on to that server, even though it is configured as the Preferred Server. What is the problem?

NetWare 3.11 uses the Ethernet 802.3 frame type by default. The Windows NT server is probably configured to use the Ethernet 802.2 frame type and possibly other frame types. The Windows 98 PC is defaulted to Auto, which means that it will use the first frame type it senses, and the 802.2 frame type is consistently sensed first. The way to fix this is to configure the Windows 98 PC's IPX/SPX-Compatible Protocol with the Ethernet 802.3 frame type for the binding to the Client for NetWare Networks. There is no need to reconfigure the protocol for its binding to the Client for Microsoft Networks, since connectivity has already been established.

QUESTIONS AND ANSWERS

George has installed the Microsoft Client for NetWare Networks on 20 Windows 98 PCs in order to connect to his NetWare server, which is on a different ring on his token ring network. None of the PCs can access the NetWare server, and none of them "sees" the server in the Network Neighborhood icon. What can be done to fix this?	George probably has Source Routing configured on his token ring network. He simply has to enable this feature in the IPX/SPX-Compatible Protocol Properties on the Windows 98 client PCs and then reboot in order to connect.

CERTIFICATION OBJECTIVE 7.03

Logging on to a NetWare Server

Windows 98 has a method of logging on clients such that a single logon will provide access to multiple network types. This typically requires that the passwords are identical on each network, and that 32-bit network clients are used.

Windows 98 uses a password list file that ends in the extension .PWL. The password list file saves any passwords, in an encrypted format. The primary network logon determines which network will be accessed first. When the primary network logon is the Windows logon, or the Microsoft Family Logon, the user is first logged on locally to the Windows 98 PC, and then each subsequent network logon is presented. These logons are transparently passed the user's password, if it is identical and saved in the .PWL file, and the user is automatically logged on.

The Microsoft Family Logon is a client added for easy selection of a user from a list of configured users on the local Windows 98 PC. The family logon will log the selected user onto the local PC the same as the Windows logon will. It is intended for use in a home environment, not in a network.

To specify the primary network logon, the Network dialog box from the Network icon in the Control Panel contains a drop-down list of the available client logons.

CERTIFICATION OBJECTIVE 7.04

Connecting to NetWare Servers

It is common for a NetWare logon to involve a logon script that maps network drives to drive letters so that commonly accessed resources are immediately available. Sometimes, and especially in large networks consisting of many servers, the user must manually connect to the resources that are needed.

Mapping a network drive is the most common way to connect to a NetWare server. This is how the client workstation accesses shared files and directories on the NetWare server. Exercise 7-2 shows how to map a network drive.

EXERCISE 7-2

Mapping a Drive to a NetWare Resource

1. Right-click My Computer and select Map Network Drive. (Alternates: Right-click Network Neighborhood and select Map Network Drive, *or* open Windows Explorer, click the Tools menu and select Map Network Drive.)
2. In the Map Network Drive dialog box, shown in Figure 7-7, select an available drive letter in the Drive drop-down box.

FIGURE 7-7

Mapping a network drive

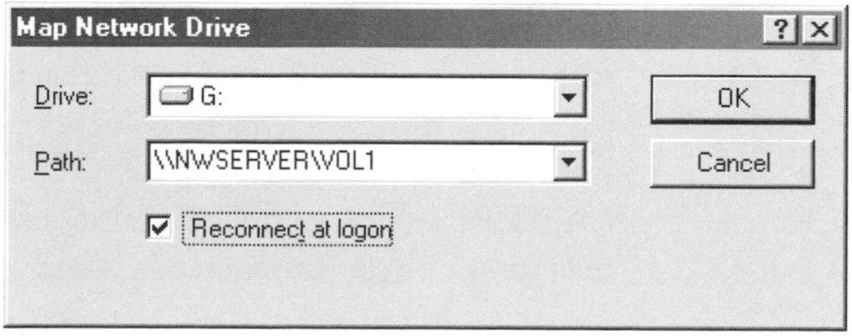

3. In the Path field of the Map Network Drive dialog box, type in the UNC (universal naming convention) for the path to the NetWare path. This would be in this format: \\NetWareServerName\ VolumeName.

4. If you wish to have a persistent drive mapping to this path, the box for Reconnect At Logon should be checked.

5. Click OK.

Once a drive has been mapped, the user can open the My Computer icon or Explorer, and drag and drop files between the local workstation and the network server. The user can also save files to the mapped drive from within applications running under Windows 98.

The Network Neighborhood is provided to enable browsing of the servers and resources on the network. The user can double-click the Network Neighborhood icon on the desktop and browse until the resource is found. Or the user can browse the Network Neighborhood in the Windows Explorer, which provides a tree structure of network resources.

In order to disconnect from a NetWare server, the user can right-click the Network Neighborhood icon and select the Who Am I option. Then, from the resulting list, the user may select the server and click Detach.

There are two different methods of connecting to NetWare printers. Historically, DOS PCs were only able to print to their logical printing ports (LPT1, LPT2, and LPT3), even if there was only hardware supporting LPT1, the LPT2 and LPT3 ports were "available" for use. NetWare included the ability to *capture* a print queue to any one of the LPT ports. (A print queue in NetWare is a holding place on the NetWare server hard disk for print jobs.) When a user submits a print job by printing to an LPT port that has been captured to a print queue, the job stays in that queue until any previously submitted jobs or higher-priority jobs have been printed. In fact, the command is called CAPTURE. Many logon scripts include CAPTURE commands that enable users to focus on productivity, rather than computer configurations. In Windows 98, if there is a local printer driver installed to one of the LPT ports, the CAPTURE command can still work exactly as it did in DOS.

Windows 98 includes an updated printing engine that enables users to connect directly to a print queue without requiring CAPTURE commands. It works this way: The user (or the installer) creates a printer. But instead of using a local port, the printer is connected directly to a print queue using a Browse button or the UNC name for that printer. The UNC name for a NetWare printer is \\NWServer\PrintQueueName.

| EXERCISE 7-3 | ### Printing to a NetWare Print Queue |

1. Open the My Computer icon by double-clicking it. (Alternatively, click Start | Settings | Printers. Or double-click the Printers icon in the Control Panel.)

2. Double-click the Printers folder to open it.

3. Double-click the Add Printer Wizard icon.

4. On the Add Printer Wizard, shown in Figure 7-8, click Next.

5. Select the Network Printer radio button and click Next.

| FIGURE 7-8 |

Add Printer Wizard

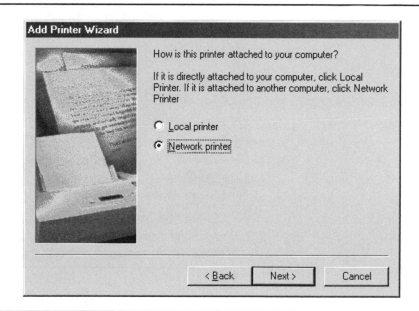

6. You now see the window shown in Figure 7-9. Type in the UNC name, in the form of \\NWServer\PrintQueueName, in the Network Path Or Queue Name field. (Alternatively, click the Browse button and scan through the network until the print queue is located.)

7. If the need to print from DOS-based programs exists, then select Yes in the radio button dialog. (This enables printing to an LPT port, and works as though the DOS CAPTURE command was used.)

8. Click Next.

9. The Add Printer Wizard will attempt to connect to the printer and will alert you if it is not online. Click Next.

10. You now see the window shown in Figure 7-10. Select the manufacturer of the printer in the left pane and the model of the printer in the right pane of the dialog box. Click Next.

FIGURE 7-9

Path to NetWare queue

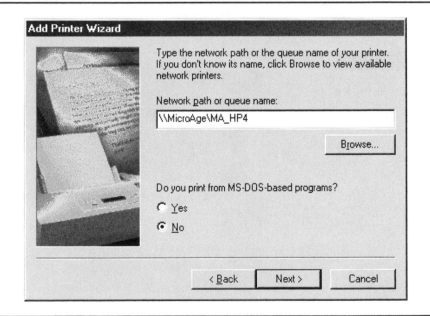

FIGURE 7-10

Printer driver choices

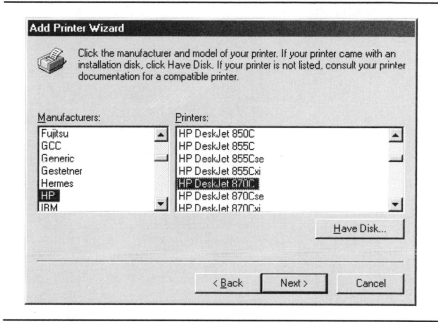

11. Type in an appropriate name for the printer in the final dialog box, or accept the default printer name. Select whether this workstation will use this print queue as its default printer. Then click Finish.

12. To print to the new printer, open up WordPad by clicking Start | Programs | Accessories | WordPad.

13. Type something into WordPad.

14. Click the File menu and select the Print option. The Print dialog box, shown in Figure 7-11, will appear.

15. Click the down arrow on the Name list box and select the printer name just created. Note that the Where line in this dialog will state the UNC name of the printer (or the LPT port, or other port, depending on the printer location).

16. Click OK.

FIGURE 7-11

The Print dialog box displays the path to a network printer

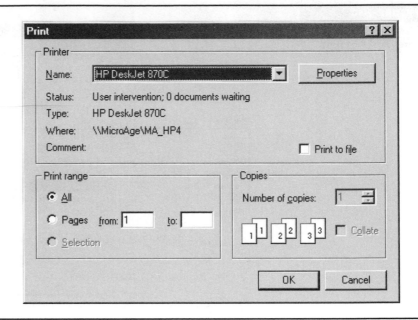

Security is often an issue on a network. One way for administrators to maintain security is to force a password change on a periodic basis. To change a password manually:

1. Connect to the preferred NetWare server's SYS volume.

2. Open the DOS prompt by clicking Start | Programs | MS-DOS Prompt.

3. Change to the drive mapped to the NetWare SYS volume.

4. Open the PUBLIC directory, or another directory that contains the NetWare SETPASS utility program.

5. Type **SETPASS** and then type in the old password, the new password, and the new password a second time, to confirm it.

FROM THE CLASSROOM

Selecting the Right NetWare Client

For a Windows 98 system to participate in a Novell NetWare network, the Windows 98 computer must have a NetWare client installed. Both Microsoft and Novell provide a Client for NetWare Networks. Microsoft's version is included with Windows 98 and Novell's version must be purchased separately.

To install the Microsoft Client for NetWare Networks:

1. Open the Network dialog box.
2. Click Add.
3. Click Client, and then click Add.
4. Select Microsoft in the Manufacturers window.
5. Select Client for NetWare Networks in the Network Clients window.
6. Click OK.

With the Microsoft Client for NetWare Networks that is included in Windows 98, you can connect to Novell NetWare 3.*x* and 4.*x* servers. Two versions of the Novell NetWare workstation shell are also available.

I've found that when connecting to a NetWare network, the majority of the problems occur because of an incorrect frame type. To find out what frame types are being used on the network, ask your network administrator. If only one frame type is being used, then you can set the Frame Type property of the IPX/SPX-Compatible Protocol, found on the Advanced tab, to Auto. The system will detect and use the appropriate frame type. If multiple frame types are being used, then you will have to specify which frame type to use for your client, and you will be unable to communicate with servers using a different frame type. A good indication that multiple frame types are being used, or that you have specified the wrong frame type, is being able to see some servers in Network Neighborhood, but not others.

Once you have the correct frame type set, if you are still having trouble communicating with the NetWare servers, you may need to check with the network administrator to make sure that IPX routing is enabled on all of the routers between your client and the NetWare servers. If IPX routing has been disabled on any of the routers, you will not be able to establish a connection.

—*By Robert Aschermann, MCT, MCSE*

Service for NetWare Directory Services (NDS)

NetWare Directory Services (NDS) is a database that catalogs all NetWare resources, including the user IDs, printers, servers, volumes and any other network resources. NDS provides a single logon access to any resource in the entire database structure, called the NDS tree. The NDS tree structure is organized much like files and directories. The path from the NDS tree root to the location of the resource is called the resource's *context*.

When a Windows 98 client needs to access IntranetWare and NetWare 4.*x* servers, the Service for NetWare Directory Services should be installed. The Microsoft Service for NetWare Directory Services is available in the Network icon of Control Panel.

Once the Network icon of Control Panel is open, the user should click the Add button and select Service from the next dialog. In the Services box, the user should select the Service for NetWare Directory Services, then click OK.

After Windows 98 reboots, it will prompt to log on to the NDS tree. The dialog box will require the correct context and NDS tree name.

When the Service for NetWare Directory Services is installed, it adds a line to the AUTOEXEC.BAT file in order to run _NWNDS.BAT. This line should be removed manually after the service has been installed. The Service for NetWare Directory Services install process uses the _NWNDS.BAT file, but does not remove it from the AUTOEXEC.BAT file. The only way to remove the line is by manually editing the AUTOEXEC.BAT.

The properties for the Service for NetWare Directory Services, shown in Figure 7-12, are available in the Network icon in the Control Panel. Click the Service line and then click the Properties button.

To configure a default tree and context for the Windows 98 workstation, the Service for NetWare Directory Services Properties can be edited and saved. After the workstation reboots, the properties will be inherited.

FIGURE 7-12

Service for NDS
properties

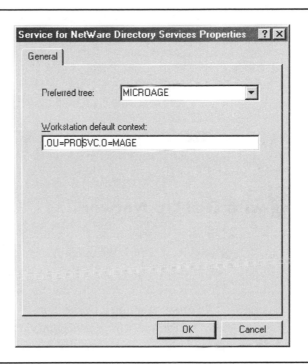

exam

atch

To log on to a NetWare 4.x server, the Service for NetWare Directory
Services should be installed and configured with an NDS tree name
and a default context.

EXERCISE 7-4

Logging on to NetWare 4.x

1. Once the Service for NetWare Directory Services is installed, reboot.

2. At the logon screen, enter the user ID in the User Name box, and
   the password in the Password box.

3. If the Windows 98 PC has a different context than that of the user ID, the user ID must include the context that the ID is located in. This is called a fully distinguished name. The format for a fully distinguished name looks like this for a user MCRAFT in the PROSVC Organizational Unit, which is in the MAGE Organization: .CN=MCRAFT.OU=PROSVC.O=MAGE.

The NDS tree can be browsed in the Network Neighborhood by opening the Entire Network icon.

Connecting with Dial-Up Networking

Novell has a remote access product for NetWare servers called NetWare Connect. It is possible to connect to a NetWare Connect remote access server via Windows 98's Dial-Up Networking. Once connected, a user will have remote node access to the NetWare resources.

In order to set up a connection to a NetWare Connect server, the workstation must have a modem, the Client for NetWare Networks, and Dial-Up Networking installed. Dial-Up Networking can be configured with individual icons for different types of connections, including connections to Internet Service Providers, Windows NT servers, and Novell NetWare servers.

The user must also know whether the NetWare server provides PPP (Point to Point Protocol) connections, which are common to Internet Service Providers and in newer NetWare Connect servers, or if the NetWare server uses the older NRN (NetWare Remote Node) connection type.

To create a Dial-Up Networking connection to a NetWare server, the user should:

1. Open up the Dial-Up Networking folder, which is located both in the My Computer icon, and in the Start menu under Programs | Accessories | Communications folder.

2. Dial-Up Networking includes a wizard icon called Make New Connection. The user should invoke the wizard by double-clicking this icon to bring up the screen shown in Figure 7-13.

3. Name the connection and click the Next button.

4. Enter the phone number and click the Next button.

5. Click the Finish button.

6. If the NetWare server is an older version of NetWare Connect, right-click the New Connection icon and select Properties.

7. Click the Server Types tab.

8. In the drop-down box for Type Of Dial-Up Server, select NRN, NetWare Connect version 1.0 and 1.1. The default setting of PPP is correct for newer NetWare Connect versions.

FIGURE 7-13

Dial-Up Networking Make
New Connection Wizard

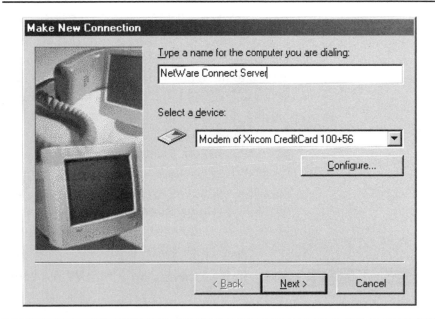

CERTIFICATION OBJECTIVE 7.05

Sharing Resources

In a traditional NetWare network, the NetWare servers are the only computers on the network that share resources. Those resources include files, printers, other network-connected equipment, and intranet information.

Windows 98 is a client/server platform. It is capable both of accessing network resources and sharing them out. Microsoft included the capability to share the local printer and files on a NetWare network as part of Windows 98.

File and Printer Sharing for NetWare Networks

In order to share resources on a NetWare network, the Service for File and Printer Sharing for NetWare Networks must be installed. This is only half the equation, since the resources must be shared out, and permissions granted to the appropriate users, or passwords must be placed on those resources. File and Printer Sharing for NetWare Networks cannot be installed together with File and Printer Sharing for Microsoft Networks.

The properties for File and Printer Sharing enable or disable the type of advertising that the Windows 98 PC will perform. Advertising is the function that allows a Windows 98 PC to be browsed in the Network Neighborhood icon from other workstations. As is shown in Figure 7-14, the SAP advertising is disabled automatically, since it has been known to cause problems in some networks. The Workgroup advertising is enabled.

EXERCISE 7-5

Sharing Resources on a NetWare Network

1. Click Start | Settings | Control Panel and double-click the Network icon.

2. Click the Add button.

3. Select Service.

4. Select File and Printer Sharing for NetWare Networks.

5. Click OK.

6. If a dialog box prompts you to change the Access Control in order to change the provider of the user and group lists, click OK.

7. Click the Access Control tab of the Network icon dialog box, and select User-Level Access Control.

8. Type the name of the server in the box to Obtain List Of Users And Groups From.

9. Click OK.

10. When prompted to Restart, click Yes.

11. When the Windows 98 workstation reboots, log on.

FIGURE 7-14

Advertising properties

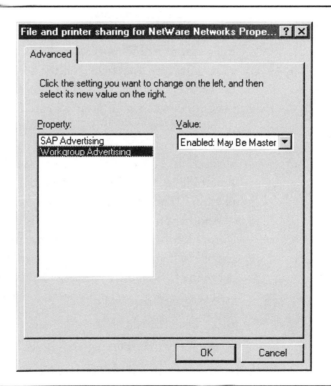

12. Open My Computer and select the C: drive, or a printer from the Printers folder, as the resource to share.

13. Right-click the resource and select Sharing.

14. Select the Shared As radio button and type in an appropriate Share name.

15. Click the Add button and select a user or group and grant access rights.

CERTIFICATION OBJECTIVE 7.06

Troubleshooting NetWare Interoperability

Several things can happen to cause the network access to malfunction. One of the first things to determine is whether the NetWare access is the only thing that is malfunctioning, or if all network resources are inaccessible. If all resources are unavailable on the network, then the problem resides with the network interface card, the physical network connection, the drivers for the card, or a common protocol used for all the network clients. Usually, a problem like this will appear when some change has been made to the workstation, such as the addition of hardware, or another service or application. To troubleshoot, remove the latest addition to the workstation. If nothing has been added or changed, then it is best to examine the physical connections and the hardware to determine if it is functional.

Another problem that can occur is the password list file may become corrupt, or in some cases the user has forgotten the Windows Logon password. If either is the case, the user can open the Windows directory and delete the *.PWL file (replacing the * with the Windows Logon user ID).

If the Network Neighborhood does not display any NetWare servers, the user should:

■ verify that there are active NetWare servers on the network

■ verify that the Client for NetWare Networks or another appropriate client is installed

- verify the frame type used on the server and configure it on the Windows 98 workstation, if using Ethernet
- verify whether source routing is used and configure it on the Windows 98 workstation, if using token ring
- check whether the adapter is functioning
- check the physical network connection

If the Windows 98 workstation cannot connect to a specific NetWare server, the user should:

- check the frame type for that particular server
- verify that the user ID exists on that server
- verify that the workstation can connect to other NetWare servers
- verify that other workstations can connect to that NetWare server using that particular user ID
- check the context or the preferred server statement

If the Windows 98 workstation cannot connect to a server on a different router segment on the network, the user should verify that the workstation is using the correct network address number. If there are no servers on the same segment as the Windows 98 PC, the network address may need to be specified in the IPX/SPX-Compatible Protocol properties.

If other users cannot connect to the resources shared out by the Windows 98 workstation, the user should verify that:

- the shares have been created
- the users have been granted appropriate access rights to the shares
- the File and Printer Sharing for NetWare networks service has been installed
- the passwords being used are correct

If the NetWare 4.x server logged onto is not the preferred server set in the Client for NetWare Networks properties, the user should check to see if the NetWare Directory Services (NDS) tree is correctly specified. If the preferred server is set to a NetWare server that is version 3.*x*, or to a server in a different NDS tree, then the preferred server parameter is ignored.

CERTIFICATION SUMMARY

Windows 98 includes native IPX/SPX-Compatible Protocol support, and a 32-bit Client for NetWare Networks. Windows 98 also supports the monolithic 16-bit DOS NETX and VLM clients distributed with NetWare. A single 16-bit client can be installed on Windows 98, or multiple 32-bit clients may be used.

The IPX/SPX-Compatible Protocol is a protocol stack provided in Windows 98 to be used with 32-bit clients, including the Client for NetWare Networks and the Client for Microsoft Networks. This protocol is installed from the Network icon inside the Control Panel. The IPX/SPX-Compatible Protocol alone does not provide a complete NetWare connectivity. In order to access NetWare networks, the IPX/SPX-Compatible Protocol must be installed in conjunction with the Microsoft Client for NetWare Networks.

The properties for the IPX/SPX-Compatible Protocol manage how Windows 98 connects to the NetWare network. The Frame type is critical for connecting to the NetWare network, especially when multiple frame types are used on a network.

The Client for NetWare Logon is presented first if the Client for NetWare Networks is selected as the Primary Network Logon. Logging on to a NetWare server is prompted automatically at the workstation boot. In order to configure the Windows 98 workstation to log on to the correct server, the properties for the Client for NetWare Networks allows the user to configure the Preferred Server, along with whether a logon script will be processed.

The Network Neighborhood allows a user to browse the resources available on the NetWare network. Mapping a network drive is available by right-clicking the My Computer or Network Neighborhood icons, or from the Tools menu in Explorer. NetWare printers can be connected to through the Add Printer Wizard, by selecting the Network Printer option and typing the UNC name for the NetWare print queue.

To share resources on a NetWare network, the Service for File and Printer Sharing on a NetWare Network must be installed. Access control must be changed to user-level, with the NetWare server specified as the provider for user and group lists. Then the resources must each be shared out, and rights granted to the appropriate users.

The fundamental things to check when troubleshooting a NetWare connection problem are: the physical connection, the network interface card, the frame type or source routing status for the network, and whether the correct properties for the client and the protocol have been set.

✓ TWO-MINUTE DRILL

❑ Support for Novell NetWare connectivity is native to Microsoft Windows 98.

❑ NDS compatibility is included in Windows 98.

❑ Every client/server network requires at least four things:

  ❑ A physical medium

  ❑ A client

  ❑ A server

  ❑ A protocol

❑ Windows 98 supports the NETX and VLM clients from Novell for connecting to NetWare servers. It also includes a 32-bit client for NetWare. (What will not be on the exam, but is good to know, is that Novell created a 32-bit client for NetWare, too, but it is not part of Windows 98.)

❑ If the user needs access to even a single printer on a NetWare network, the Client for NetWare Networks should be installed to provide that access.

❑ The protocol requirement of the Client for NetWare Networks is the IPX/SPX-Compatible Protocol.

❑ When configuring the IPX/SPX protocol, the frame type on the workstation must match the frame type that is used on the server.

❏ Windows 98 has a method of logging on clients such that a single logon will provide access to multiple network types. This typically requires that the passwords are identical on each network, and that 32-bit network clients are used.

❏ Mapping a network drive is the most common way to connect to a NetWare server.

❏ NetWare Directory Services (NDS) is a database that catalogs all NetWare resources, including the user IDs, printers, servers, volumes and any other network resources.

❏ To log on to a NetWare 4.x server, the Service for NetWare Directory Services should be installed and configured with an NDS tree name and a default context.

❏ Novell has a remote access product for NetWare servers called NetWare Connect. It is possible to connect to a NetWare Connect remote access server via Windows 98's Dial-Up Networking.

❏ Windows 98 is a client/server platform. It is capable both of accessing network resources and sharing them out. Microsoft included the capability to share the local printer and files on a NetWare network as part of Windows 98.

❏ In order to share resources on a NetWare network, the Service for File and Printer Sharing for NetWare Networks must be installed.

❏ One of the first things to determine if there is a network access problem is whether the NetWare access is the only thing that is malfunctioning, or if all network resources are inaccessible.

SELF TEST

These questions will help you measure your understanding of the material presented in this chapter. Read all the choices carefully, as there may be more than one correct answer. Choose all correct answers for each question.

1. What are the three clients that Windows 98 supports natively?

   A. VLM

   B. NetBIOS

   C. NETX

   D. Microsoft Client for NetWare Networks

2. What client can be used with the Client for Microsoft Networks?

   A. VLM

   B. NetBIOS

   C. NETX

   D. Microsoft Client for NetWare Networks

3. Roger has a Windows NT server, a NetWare 4.11 server, and a NetWare 2.15 server on his network. He is upgrading all his OS/2 PCs to Windows 98. What protocols must he install?

   A. TCP/IP and IPX/SPX

   B. IPX/SPX-Compatible Protocol

   C. TCP/IP, and NETX or VLM

   D. NetBIOS and NCP

4. What needs to be configured if the administrator wants all the Windows 98 PCs to log on to a particular NetWare 3.12 server?

   A. Preferred Server

   B. IPX/SPX-Compatible Protocol

   C. Service for NetWare Directory Services

   D. Frame type

5. In a large enterprise Ethernet network with over 50 NetWare servers of various versions, Georgette is installing Windows 98 using a batch method. The business unit that she is creating the batch for uses only NetWare 4.1 servers. What options should Georgette specify in the batch file?

   A. Source Routing should be Yes

   B. Frame Type should be Ethernet 802.3

   C. File and Printer Sharing for NetWare Networks should be installed

   D. Service for NetWare Directory Services should be installed

6. Alice installed a new printer on the queue HPQ on her NetWare 4.1 server, NWS312 in the NDS tree NDSTREE. What does she need to type in the Add Printer Wizard dialog box when prompted to specify the printer or queue name?

   A. \\NDSTREE\NWS312\HPQ

   B. .CN=HPQ.O=NDSTREE

C. NWS312:\HPQ

D. \\NWS312\HPQ

7. Julie is visiting from Houston and is borrowing a PC in the New York branch office. All the Windows 98 PCs in New York have been set with the default context, .OU=NY.O=MAGE. Julie's ID JULIEM is in the HOU organizational unit. What must she type in for the username when logging on?

A. JULIEM

B. .O=MAGE.CN=JULIEM

C. .CN=JULIEM.OU=HOU.O=MAGE

D. HOU

8. Kelly installed the Service for File and Printer Sharing for NetWare Networks on her Windows 98 PC, but other users can't "see" any resources in their Network Neighborhood icons. What went wrong?

A. Kelly installed the wrong service

B. Kelly did not share out any resources yet

C. Kelly does not have IPX/SPX-Compatible Protocol installed

D. Kelly did not set up a Preferred Server

9. Frank is a new administrator for a NetWare network with 50 Windows 98 PCs. On his second day, he received numerous phone calls, pages, and voice messages complaining that no one could log on. Everyone was able to log on the day before. What should Frank check first?

A. That the server is up and running

B. The protocol properties

C. The client properties

D. The service properties

10. Greg has a NetWare 3.11 network consisting of seven servers. He is gradually upgrading them all to NetWare 4.11. His pilot NetWare 4.11 server went online, but soon afterward, users found that they couldn't log on to the network if they rebooted. Users who didn't reboot were able to continue working. What should Greg check first?

A. That the NetWare 3.11 servers are up and running

B. The Frame Type settings

C. The Preferred Server settings

D. The default Context settings

8

User Profiles and System Policies in Windows 98

I magine having to share your Windows 98 system with another person whose idea of the perfect color scheme and icon placement is opposite of yours. It could make your work on that system become tedious very quickly. Luckily, Microsoft has built a mechanism into Windows 98 that allows this situation to be avoided. It is called user profiles.

In the first section of this chapter, we discuss user profiles. The second and third sections discuss how to enable and implement user profiles. The fourth section details how to troubleshoot user profiles.

User profiles are very useful in helping to keep your desktop settings the way that you like them, but what about controlling how a computer is set up and used? This is where system policies can be used.

In the fifth section of this chapter, we discuss system policies; in the sixth section, the system policy editor. In the seventh section, we cover implementing system policies on a network. And in the final section, we discuss troubleshooting system policies.

CERTIFICATION OBJECTIVE 8.01

User Profiles

As we mentioned, sharing a single computer with multiple users can be a problem, since each individual will customize the desktop to meet his needs. User profiles allows the system to be set up with each user having his own custom environment.

Loading and Updating User Profiles

Each user profile can consist of several different items including a USER.DAT file, a My Documents folder, a Recent folder, a Desktop folder, a Start Menu folder, and a Programs folder on the Start menu, as well as other items. These files are stored in the user's profile folder that is located within the C:\WINDOWS\PROFILES folder structure. Figure 8-1 shows the PROFILES folder of a system used by two people, Marissa and sdc. Marissa's profile folder structure is expanded to show every folder that is in her profile. If Marissa changes any of the settings when she is logged on, they will only apply to her profile and not the profile of sdc.

If a third user joins the same system as Marissa and sdc, he will have his own user profile folder created under the C:\WINDOWS\PROFILES folder, just like the folders of Marissa and sdc.

The Registry is made up of two files, USER.DAT and SYSTEM.DAT. If user profiles are not used, then all users have the same preferences and desktop settings. These settings are stored in the USER.DAT portion of the Windows 98 Registry, located in the C:\WINDOWS directory. In this case, any change that Marissa makes to her desktop will also affect sdc.

FIGURE 8-1

Expanded view of Marissa's user profile folders

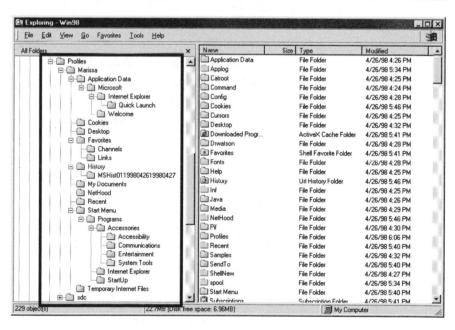

Mandatory User Profiles

Windows 98 supports mandatory user profiles, which can be created for use on Microsoft Windows NT or Novell NetWare networks. Mandatory user profiles can be used to create a standardized user profile for each computer on your network, and to ensure it is implemented at every logon. Creating a mandatory user profile is an easy task. Create a USER.DAT file with the settings you want, and rename it to USER.MAN. Place the USER.MAN file in the network directory for each user you want to have that profile. The type of network you use dictates where the USER.MAN file needs to be located. If your network is Windows NT based, then place the USER.MAN in the user's home directory. If your network is Novell NetWare based, then place it in the user's MAIL directory. While Windows 98 copies required files for normal user profiles, it does not copy them for mandatory user profiles.

When a Windows 98 user logs on to a network that uses mandatory profiles, the settings in USER.MAN are loaded into his Registry, instead of the data in the local USER.DAT. Any changes that the user makes to his Windows 98 desktop configuration while using a mandatory user profile are not saved to the master copy located on the server.

Mandatory user profiles are useful for novice users, who cannot manage the settings of their own desktop. Since novice users won't need to worry about their desktop settings, mandatory profiles can increase their productivity, and also reduce the training and support requirements for the Information Systems department.

Roaming User Profiles

A roaming user is defined as a user who moves from computer to computer while doing his work. Typically, a roaming user is going to be someone from the technical or support staffs. A roaming user can become very frustrated having to set up a desktop every time he moves to a different computer. This is where roaming user profiles can be extremely helpful. Roaming user profiles are similar to mandatory user profiles in that they exist on a network server. However, they allow the user to customize his desktop environment as he sees fit, and to map persistent network drives. We will discuss implementing roaming user profiles in a later section of this chapter.

exam
ⓦatch

It is very important that the clocks on all the computers on your network are synchronized when using roaming user profiles. Windows 98 keeps two copies of the USER.DAT file when roaming user profiles are used. One copy stays on the local machine and one exists on the server. The two USER.DAT files are compared, and the copy with the newest time is the one that is used. The easiest way to synchronize the clocks on all systems is to use the NET TIME command from the user's logon scripts. For example, NET TIME \\MAINSERVER /SET /Y.

Now that you are familiar with the different types of user profiles available within Windows 98, here is a quick reference for possible scenario questions, and the appropriate answer.

QUESTIONS AND ANSWERS

John calls the help desk daily with questions about how to fix something he has changed on his desktop…	Implement a mandatory user profile so that changes John makes to his desktop are not saved when he shuts his system down. This should eliminate some of the help desk calls. Mandatory user profiles are not saved to the master copy in the user's network directory when the user shuts down.
Kevin is very irritated that he must share a computer with James. James keeps changing the wallpaper and shortcut locations, which offends Kevin…	Implement user profiles so that Kevin and James can configure the computer with their own preferences, which they can use without disturbing each other.
James must be available to troubleshoot the computers in any office in the four buildings of the company that he works for…	Implement a roaming profile for James so that he can access his desktop no matter what computer he is using. This is especially handy, since his roaming profile can include the mapping to a network drive that holds his diagnostic tools.

CERTIFICATION OBJECTIVE 8.02

Enabling User Profiles

Within Windows 98 there are two methods of enabling user profiles. In this section we will discuss both methods. The first method involves using the Passwords applet from within Control Panel, as shown in Figure 8-2.

The User Profiles tab on this applet determines whether user profiles are enabled for the Windows 98 system. For the system shown in Figure 8-3, profiles are not enabled. Clicking the second radio button would enable user profiles. After enabling using profiles and clicking the OK button, the system will prompt you to restart.

FIGURE 8-2

Passwords applet highlighted in the Control Panel

FIGURE 8-3

User Profiles tab of
Passwords Properties

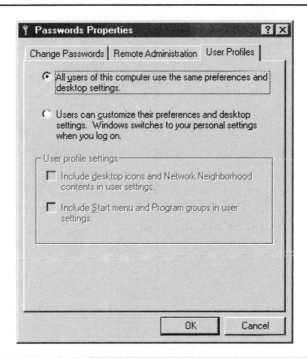

The second method of enabling user profiles for a system is to use the
Users applet that is located in the Control Panel, as shown in Figure 8-4.

Clicking the Users applet prompts you with the Multi-User dialog box
shown in Figure 8-5.

When you click the Next button, you are prompted for a User Name, as
shown in Figure 8-6.

After you select a username and click the Next button, information is
displayed (as shown in Figure 8-7), that Windows 98 will restart, and that
you need to use the username that you just created to log on. Once you log
on, Windows 98 will automatically save your desktop settings for you.

In essence, the Users applet toggles the radio button in the User Profiles
tab of Passwords Properties, while at the same time creating a user who will
have a user profile. If you enable user profiles via the User Profiles tab of
Passwords Properties, then you will have to create a user once the system
restarts.

FIGURE 8-4

Users applet highlighted in the Control Panel

FIGURE 8-5

Enable Multi-User Settings dialog box

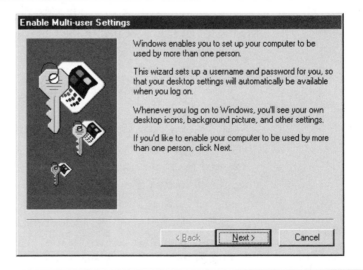

FIGURE 8-6

Add a user to the
Multi-User settings

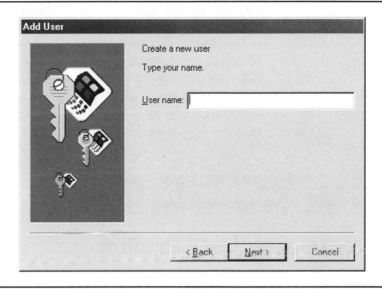

FIGURE 8-7

Dialog box showing that
Windows 98 will restart
when the Finish button
is clicked

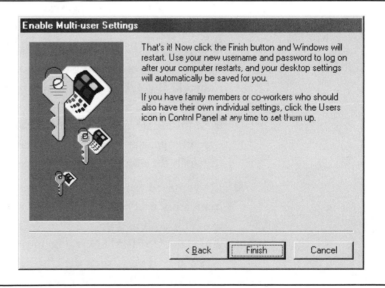

exam
Watch

Application installation becomes a different matter after user profiles are enabled with the option to include the Start menu and Programs in the profile. Any application that is installed from that point on will have an entry for that application on the Programs menu only for the user who was logged on when the application was installed. If other users of the system want access to the application, they will have to create shortcuts to the application on their Programs menus when they are logged on.

CERTIFICATION OBJECTIVE 8.03

Implementing User Profiles

There are several issues that you need to consider before you implement user profiles. Some of these issues are:

- What items should you include in user profiles? Do you want to include desktop icons and Network Neighborhood contents, or the Start menu and Program groups? You may decide to include all of those items, depending on your requirements.

- Are the user profiles going to support roaming users on your network? If you decide to support roaming users, the computers have to use a 32-bit, protected-mode network client, and have access to their profile from the network. Since each user needs access to his own unique user profile, he must have a home directory established, in which the user profile can reside.

- Do you need to use mandatory user profiles? If you do need to use mandatory user profiles, you must make sure that a home directory exists for each user on the Windows NT network, since this is where the USER.MAN will be located. If you are using a Novell NetWare network, then the USER.MAN needs to be placed in the MAIL/USER_ID directory.

It's time for you to practice implementing user policies on a standalone computer system. Exercise 8-1 will take you through the appropriate steps.

Implementing User Policies on a Standalone Computer System

1. Click the Start button and choose Settings | Control Panel.
2. Double-click the Passwords applet.
3. Select the User Profiles tab.
4. Click the radio button located to the left of "Users can customize their preferences and desktop settings. Windows switches to your personal settings whenever you log on."
5. After you click the radio button in step 4, the two check boxes become unghosted, with a check mark already in the first box. Click the check box located to the left of "Include Start menu and Program groups in user settings."
6. Click the OK button.
7. The system will prompt you to restart the system before the new settings will take effect. Click the Yes button to restart your system.
8. After the system has restarted, it will prompt you to log on. Use the logon name **sdc** with **sdc** as your password. Retype the password to verify it.
9. After successfully logging on to Windows 98, click the Start button and select Programs | Windows Explorer.
10. Navigate to the Profiles folder located in your Windows folder. You will see a new folder called SDC, where your profile exists. Any changes you make while logged on as sdc will be updated in the SDC folder hierarchy.

But what happens if sdc decides that he no longer wants to have the Start menu personalized in his user profile? He can turn off the Start menu by removing the check mark from the "Include Start menu and Program groups in user settings." But then it will affect all the users of that computer system and not just him. To affect only his user profile he needs to adjust the setting using the Users applet in Control Panel. As shown in Figure 8-8, all users of the system are displayed in the User List window after the Users applet is double-clicked.

If the user sdc wants to change the settings for his profile, he should highlight his username and click the Change Settings button. He will be presented with the dialog box shown in Figure 8-9. Since he no longer wants the Start menu personalized, he simply needs to click the check box located to the left of Start Menu to deselect it.

FIGURE 8-8

User List window showing the users Marissa and sdc

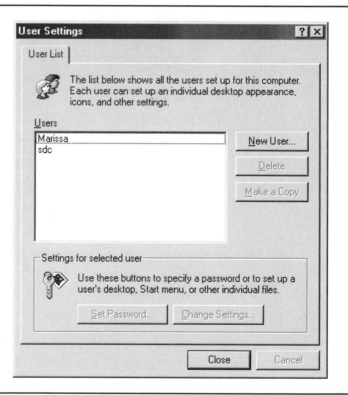

FIGURE 8-9

Personalized Items Settings
for the user sdc

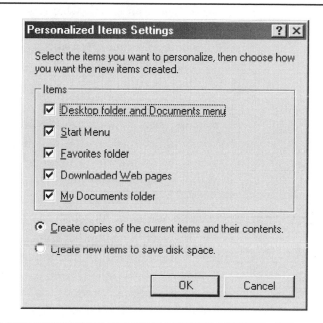

CERTIFICATION OBJECTIVE 8.04

Troubleshooting User Profiles

User profiles can be handy items when more than one user is on the same computer system, or if you need to support roaming users. But what about when something goes wrong with the user profiles? How you have user profiles implemented will dictate how you need to troubleshoot them.

If a user is having problems with a user profile that is located on a standalone system, you may need to delete his profile from the C:\WINDOWS\PROFILES folder and have the user re-create it. Sometimes this is the fastest way to get a user back into being productive—better than trying to figure out exactly what is wrong in the profile. I once sent a technician out on a service call and he spent over four hours trying to fix the existing profile for a user. The profile could have been rebuilt in a few minutes, which would have saved both the user and technician valuable time.

If you are using mandatory user profiles, it is likely that more than one user will be affected if something goes wrong with the USER.MAN file. Supporting roaming users can also become interesting to troubleshoot, because you never know what system they may be using.

One to watch for when troubleshooting both mandatory and roaming user profiles is that every computer on your network has the same names for the folder and the hard disk drive in which Windows 98 is installed. For example, if Windows 98 is installed in C:\WINDOWS on one computer, and in C:\WIN98 on another computer, then it is very possible that some components of the user profile will not function correctly. Keep in mind that not only do the folders need to be identical, but also the hard disk drives. (For example, Windows 98 is installed on C:\WINDOWS on some machines and D:\WINDOWS on others.) Another item that can affect user profiles on a network is an inability of a user to get into her home directory. If she cannot get to her user profile, it cannot be incorporated into the system she is presently using.

Mandatory user profiles are very good for controlling every user-specific setting. But what if you want to selectively determine a subset of user settings to control? How can it be done? This is what we will discuss in the next section of the chapter.

CERTIFICATION OBJECTIVE 8.05

System Policies

System policies are settings that get applied to the Registry as soon as someone logs on to a computer system. Hey, wait a minute! Isn't that the same thing a mandatory user profile does? Well, yes and no. A mandatory user profile affects only users, whereas system policies can be utilized on users, groups of users, and machines.

System policies allow accurate control of the computer system and network by combining policies for users, the machine that they are logging onto, and any groups that they are members of.

Policy Files

In order to successfully use system policies you will need to make use of two types of files, an .ADM file and a .POL file.

.ADM File

The .ADM file is a template that is used to create the .POL file. The .ADM file is an ASCII-based file that determines the limits available to policies that are created in the .POL file. Even though Windows 98 comes with the ADMIN.ADM file, you are free to create your own. This is very handy in case there is a policy that you want to implement that is not covered by the default Windows 98 ADMIN.ADM file.

The template can affect anything in the Windows 98 Registry. To create a template you must use the appropriate keywords in the appropriate format. The template can consist of many different sections, and each section follows the same structure.

```
CLASS
      CATEGORY
             POLICY
                    PART
                    END PART
             END POLICY
      END CATEGORY
```

Okay, now we have seen how a section is supposed to look, but what does it all mean?

- **CLASS** is defined as either MACHINE or USER, depending on what the section affects.
- **CATEGORY** is the main heading. For example, MSClient or NWClient.
- **POLICY** signifies an entry under the CATEGORY. For example, LogonDomain or PrefServer. Entries under POLICY can often consist of multiple PARTs.
- **PART** signifies a single setting such as DomainName or DomainLogonConfirmation.
- **END CATEGORY**, **END POLICY**, and **END PART** are used to signify the end of each of the respective sections.

You do not have to indent each portion of an .ADM file, but it is easier to locate sections of the code in case you need to modify it, if you do indent it. To give you a better perspective, here is a real .ADM file—an excerpt of the ADMIN.ADM file that ships with Windows 98. The !! indicates a string value.

```
CLASS MACHINE
CATEGORY !!MSClient
        POLICY !!LogonDomain
        KEYNAME Network\Logon
        VALUENAME "LMLogon"
                PART !!DomainNameEDITTEXT REQUIRED
                MAXLEN 15
                KEYNAME System\CurrentControlSet\
                  Services\MSNP32\NetworkProvider
                VALUENAME AuthenticatingAgent
                END PART

                PART !!DomainLogonConfirmation CHECKBOX
                KEYNAME Network\Logon
                VALUENAME DomainLogonMessage
                END PART

                PART !!NoDomainPwdCaching CHECKBOX
```

```
                    KEYNAME Network\Logon
                    VALUENAME NoDomainPwdCaching
                    END PART
              END POLICY

POLICY !!Workgroup
KEYNAME System\CurrentControlSet\Services\VxD\VNETSUP
        PART !!WorkgroupName EDITTEXT REQUIRED
        VALUENAME "Workgroup"
        MAXLEN 15
        END PART
END POLICY

POLICY !!AlternateWorkgroup
KEYNAME System\CurrentControlSet\Services\VxD\VREDIR
        PART !!WorkgroupName EDITTEXT REQUIRED
        VALUENAME "Workgroup"
        MAXLEN 15
        END PART
END POLICY

END CATEGORY; Microsoft Network
```

.POL File

System policy information is stored in the .POL file. The .POL file consists of binary data, and is read during system startup. The information in the .POL file is merged with the existing Registry information. The .POL file is created using the System Policy Editor and an .ADM template.

In order for the .POL file to be integrated into the Registry of a user's machine, that user's system needs to know that it exists. By default, Windows 98 looks in three different locations for the .POL file.

- On a computer that is not located on a network, Windows 98 looks in the \WINDOWS folder.

- On a computer that belongs to a Windows NT network, Windows 98 looks in the NETLOGON folder of the server that validates its logon.

■ On a computer that belongs to a Novell NetWare network, Windows 98 looks in the SYS:PUBLIC directory of the preferred server.

If Windows 98 cannot find the .POL file, it cannot load the system policies. If you are using a .POL file on a Windows NT or Novell NetWare network, then the file must be named CONFIG.POL.

Figure 8-10 shows the portion of the .ADM file that we looked at earlier in the chapter, but this time in .POL format.

FIGURE 8-10

Microsoft Client for
Windows Network
Policies Settings

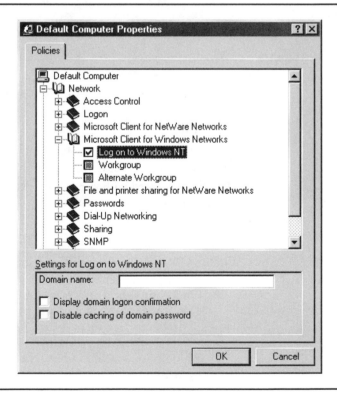

FROM THE CLASSROOM

Policy and Profile Tips and Tricks

Policies and profiles are two of the most powerful, and least understood, features of Windows 98. Let's look at policies first. A policy is a collection of Registry settings stored in a file called CONFIG.POL. When a user logs on, the policy file is downloaded to the local Registry of the computer the user logged on to. Policy Registry settings enable or disable certain features of Windows 98. Access to some desktop items like My Computer, and some Control Panel items like Network and Display, can be controlled on a user, group, or network-wide basis. Policies can also be used to maintain a standard desktop configuration in an organization by resetting display characteristics like desktop wallpaper and color schemes every time a user logs on.

Profiles, on the other hand, are usually kept on a per user basis, and maintain a user's personal settings. A personal profile is a copy of all of the Registry settings that affect what a user sees, what network connections to printers and shares a user has, and some application settings. Since all of this information is kept on a per user basis, multiple users can use the same computer and have that computer reflect their personal preferences. A mandatory profile is like a Read Only profile. When a user has a mandatory profile, he can't save any changes to the environment. Changes can still be made, just not saved. Consequently, the user sees the same desktop configuration every time he logs on. The way to tell the difference between a personal profile and a mandatory profile is by looking at the file extension. The name of the file you are looking for is the name of the account used to log on, followed by either a .DAT or .MAN extension. Personal profiles use the .DAT extension; mandatory profiles use the .MAN extension.

The most difficult part of implementing policies and profiles is figuring out what settings are stored where. Some settings can even be stored in more than one place. You'll need a good reference book and a lot of lab time to properly implement these features. The Windows 98 Resource Kit and TechNet both offer a wealth of information about policy and profile settings, but you may still have to play detective to find all of the settings you need.

FROM THE CLASSROOM

One approach used by many administrators to find the Registry settings they need is to take a snapshot of the Registry, and then install an application or make a change to the system configuration. Then they take another snapshot of the Registry, and use a file comparison utility to see what changed. You can take a snapshot of the Registry by using the Export Registry File option in the Registry

Editor. The result is a text file with a .REG extension. To compare the before and after snapshots, download a DOS version of a UNIX utility called DIFF. This utility will compare two text files line by line and display, or write to a log file, the lines that are different.

—*By Robert Aschermann, MCT, MCSE*

CERTIFICATION OBJECTIVE 8.06

Using System Policy Editor

The System Policy Editor can be used to create a .POL file, and also as a menu-driven interface for accessing the Registry of the computer it is running on. The System Policy Editor is not loaded during installation of Windows 98, but it can be installed from the Windows 98 CD-ROM using the Add/Remove Programs applet from within Control Panel, as shown in Exercise 8-2. The System Policy Editor is located in the \TOOLS\ APPTOOLS\POLEDIT folder of the Windows 98 CD-ROM. Once it is installed on your system you can find it by clicking the Start button and looking in Programs | Accessories | System Tools. The first time that the System Policy Editor is run, it will prompt you for the .ADM file it will use, as shown in Figure 8-11. It will not ask again for the .ADM file as long as the System Policy Editor is run from the same computer. If you run the System Policy Editor from a different computer, it will ask for a template file again.

FIGURE 8-11

Open Template File dialog box prompting for an .ADM file to use

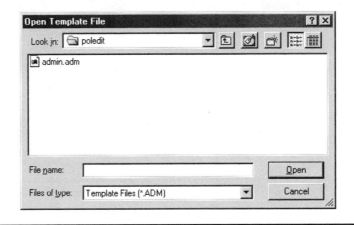

EXERCISE 8-2

Installing the System Policy Editor

1. Click the Start button and choose Settings | Control Panel | Add/Remove Programs.

2. Click Windows Setup.

3. Click Have Disk.

4. Click Browse and go into the TOOLS\APPTOOLS\POLEDIT directory from the Windows 98 CD.

5. Select POLEDIT.INF and click the OK button.

6. Click the OK button.

7. Place a check mark in the box to the left of System Policy Editor, then click Install.

8. Click the OK button.

After you select an .ADM file, the System Policy Editor is ready for use. As mentioned earlier, it can be used to develop a .POL file, or as a menu-driven interface for the Registry. Choosing Open Registry from the File menu displays two icons in the System Policy Editor, Local User and Local Computer, as shown in Figure 8-12.

Any changes made after opening the Local Registry apply only to that machine, and a .POL file is not created. Using the System Policy Editor to open the Local Registry is advantageous for standalone computers,

FIGURE 8-12

Opening the Local Registry
using the System Policy
Editor

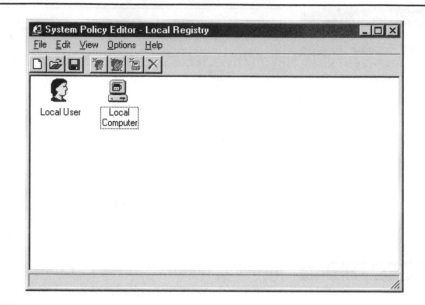

troubleshooting, and computers that do not utilize a .POL file. Exercise 8-3
gives you a chance to modify the Local Registry of your computer.

EXERCISE 8-3

Using the System Policy Editor to Modify the Local Registry

1. Install the System Policy Editor as described earlier in the chapter.
2. Click the Start button and select Programs | Accessories | System Tools | System Policy Editor.
3. Choose ADMIN.ADM and click the Open button.
4. Select Open Registry from the File menu.
5. Double-click the Local User icon.
6. Click the + located to the left of System.
7. Click the + located to the left of Restrictions.
8. Place a check mark in the box located to the left of Disable Registry Editing Tools.

9. Click the OK button.

10. Select Save from the File menu. Now it is time to see if your change is applied to the Windows 98 Registry.

11. Click the Start button and choose Run.

12. Type **REGEDIT** in the dialog box and click the OK button.

13. You will see a dialog box that states, "Registry editing has been disabled by your administrator."

Creating a .POL file is similar to working with the Local Registry. Instead of choosing the Open Registry menu item, you use either the New File or Open File menu items. If a .POL file does not already exist, then you need to use the New File option. Once a new file is open, the System Policy Editor displays the Default User and Default Computer icons, as shown in Figure 8-13.

A policy control can be in one of three states. Those states are:

■ **Selected**   When the box has a check mark, the function is turned on.

■ **Cleared**   When the box is empty, the function is turned off.

■ **Dimmed**   When the box is grayed, the availability of the function is not determined by the policy. The state the function is in will not be changed.

Figure 8-14 shows all three states being applied to policies in a new .POL file that is being created. The Restrict Network Control Panel box is grayed, so it will stay the same as it already is for the system. This policy does not turn it on or off. The Restrict Passwords Control Panel box is empty, so this policy does not restrict that function for the default user. The Restrict System Control Panel has a check mark in the box, so this policy will enforce that function. Notice at the bottom of the Default User Properties window that there are many settings that can be configured for the Restrict System Control Panel function.

The settings you make to the .POL do not have to apply to only the Default User and the Default Computer. It is possible to create unique settings for different users by adding them to the .POL file. Figure 8-15 shows the menu where users can be added to the policy file.

FIGURE 8-13

Creating a new .POL file
using the System Policy
Editor

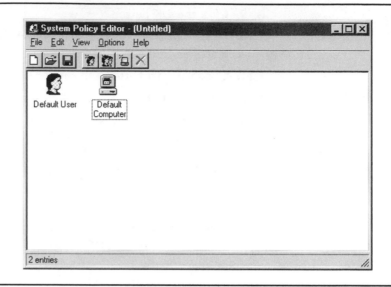

FIGURE 8-14

Modifying the Default User
Properties using System
Policy Editor

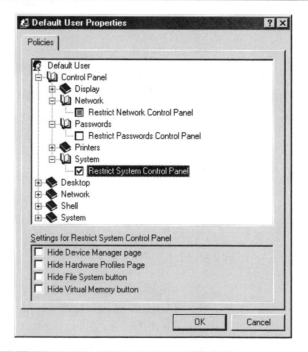

FIGURE 8-15

The Add User item located on the Edit menu

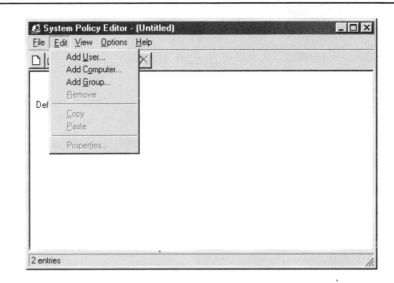

CERTIFICATION OBJECTIVE 8.07

Implementing System Policy on a Network

Implementing system policies on a network is easily accomplished. You create a .POL file and place it in the NETLOGON folder of all Windows NT servers that validate user logons. If your network is Novell NetWare, then you place the .POL file in the SYS:PUBLIC directory of the preferred server. However, creating a .POL file for a network can be a daunting task, since there can be many hundreds of users, each with his or her own needs in regards to system permissions. Since networks support the concept of groups, it would be nice to create profiles based upon groups. Luckily, the System Policy Editor supports groups, as shown in Figure 8-16. New groups cannot be created using the System Policy Editor; you can only use groups that already exist on your Windows NT or Novell NetWare network.

Adding a group to a .POL file using the System Policy Editor

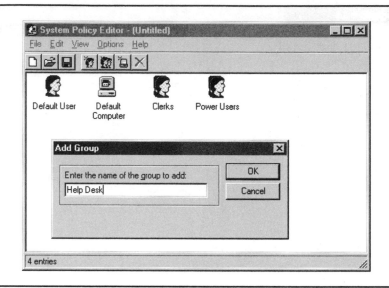

Getting group policies to work properly involves more work than just adding an existing group to the .POL file. The GROUPPOL.DLL must be installed on each Windows 98 computer system so that they all can honor the group policies. The GROUPPOL.DLL can be added to Windows 98 by using the Windows Setup tab of the Add/Remove Programs applet located in the Control Panel. Group Policies are located under the System Tools option, as shown in Figure 8-17.

exam
Watch

If a policy exists for a specific named user, then the group policies are not applied to that user.

Group Priorities

It is possible that you have users who belong to multiple groups, and that you have defined a policy for each of those groups. It's not good if you try to enable a function for a group of users, and some of them do not receive that function because it is overridden by the policies for another group they

FIGURE 8-17

Installing Group Policies from the Add/Remove Programs applet of the Control Panel

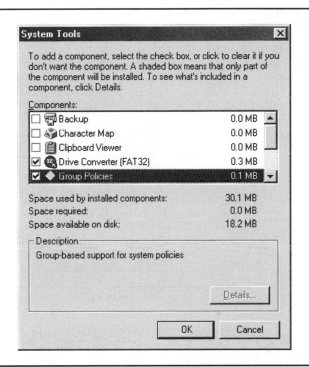

System Tools

To add a component, select the check box, or click to clear it if you don't want the component. A shaded box means that only part of the component will be installed. To see what's included in a component, click Details.

Components:

☐ 📦 Backup		0.0 MB
☐ 📇 Character Map		0.0 MB
☐ 📋 Clipboard Viewer		0.0 MB
☑ 💾 Drive Converter (FAT32)		0.3 MB
☑ ◆ Group Policies		0.1 MB

Space used by installed components: 30.1 MB
Space required: 0.0 MB
Space available on disk: 18.2 MB

Description
Group-based support for system policies

Details...

OK   Cancel

belong to. How are the priorities determined for multiple groups? Group policies are downloaded to the Windows 98 computer in order from the lowest priority group to the highest priority group. Every group that you have created in the .POL file is processed. The group that has the highest priority is processed last, so that any of its settings are applied that may be different from the settings that are in other, lower-priority groups. The priority levels for groups are set using the Group Priority selection of the Options menu in the System Policy Editor, as shown in Figure 8-18. The Help Desk group will be processed last because it is highest on the priority list.

exam
ⓦatch

Windows 98 computers that are not configured to use Group Policies (GROUPPOL.DLL) ignore the group policies in the .POL file.

FIGURE 8-18

Group Priority settings for
three groups in a .POL file

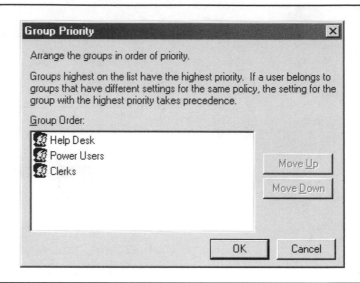

CERTIFICATION OBJECTIVE 8.08

Troubleshooting System Policies

As you can imagine, several things can go wrong when implementing
system policies. A few of the more common items to look at are:

- That the .ADM file is using the correct Registry keys

- That the .POL file has the functions set correctly

- That the .POL file is located in the proper folder on the network
  server(s)

- For group policies, that the username, group name, and computer
  name are correct, and that the user is a member of the group that is
  specified

If you implement a policy and it does not do what you thought it would
do, check to see if it involves a setting that can be exploited by a user. If a

policy involves a setting that a user can exploit through the Control Panel, the best way to stop enforcing that policy is to make sure that the policy setting is grayed. This gives the user the chance to make his or her own choices.

If a Windows 98 computer that is running the Microsoft Client for NetWare Networks cannot utilize the policies from a CONFIG.POL file on the NetWare server, then check the following items.

- Make sure that the Windows 98 computer can successfully log on to the preferred server.

- Make sure that the Windows 98 computer has its preferred server set to the Novell NetWare server that contains CONFIG.POL.

- Make sure that there is a CONFIG.POL in the PUBLIC directory on the SYS: volume of the Novell NetWare server.

If a Windows 98 computer that is running the Client for Microsoft Networks cannot utilize the policies from a CONFIG.POL file on the Windows NT domain, then check the following items.

- Make sure that the Windows 98 computer is successfully logging on to the Windows NT domain.

- Make sure that there is a CONFIG.POL file in the NETLOGON directory on the domain controllers that validate all logons on the Windows NT network.

CERTIFICATION SUMMARY

User profiles allow multiple people to use the same computer system, while having it set up to match their own unique tastes. Besides user profiles, there are two special types of profiles, mandatory user profiles and roaming user profiles. The two special profiles exist on network servers, either Windows NT servers or Novell NetWare servers.

User profiles are enabled using either the Passwords applet or Users applet located in the Control Panel. Several different items can be configured for user profiles, including whether or not the Start menu,

Program groups, desktop icons, and the Network Neighborhood are included in the user settings.

System policies allow accurate control of the computer system and network by combining policies for users, the machine that they are logging onto, and any groups that they are members of. System policies use two different files, the .ADM file and the .POL file. The .ADM file is a template file that is used to create the .POL file. The .POL file contains the system policy information, and is read by the Windows 98 computer when it is first started. The .ADM file is ASCII, whereas the .POL file is binary.

The System Policy Editor is used to create the .POL file and it is also used as a menu-driven interface to the Local Registry. There are three states that can be toggled for a function using the System Policy Editor: selected, cleared, and dimmed.

System policies can be used on a network by placing the CONFIG.POL file in the appropriate folder or directory, which will depend on whether it is a Windows NT-based network or a Novell NetWare-based network. Group policies can also be used on the network, as long as the Windows 98 computers have Group Policies (GROUPPOL.DLL) installed.

TWO-MINUTE DRILL

❑ User profiles allows the system to be set up with each user having his own custom environment.

❑ Each user profile can consist of several different items including a USER.DAT file, a My Documents folder, a Recent folder, a Desktop folder, a Start Menu folder, and a Programs folder on the Start menu, as well as other items.

❑ Windows 98 supports mandatory user profiles.

❑ Mandatory user profiles can be used to create a standardized user profile for each computer on your network, and to ensure it is implemented at every logon.

❑ Roaming user profiles are similar to mandatory user profiles in that they exist on a network server.

❑ It is very important that the clocks on all the computers on your network are synchronized when using roaming user profiles. Windows 98 keeps two copies of the USER.DAT file when roaming user profiles are used. One copy stays on the local machine and one exists on the server. The two USER.DAT files are compared, and the copy with the newest time is the one that is used. The easiest way to synchronize the clocks on all systems is to use the NET TIME command from the user's logon scripts. For example, NET TIME \\MAINSERVER /SET /Y.

❑ Within Windows 98 there are two methods of enabling user profiles. The first method involves using the Passwords applet from within Control Panel. The second method is to use the Users applet that is located in the Control Panel.

❑ Application installation becomes a different matter after user profiles are enabled with the option to include the Start menu and Programs in the profile. Any application that is installed from that point on will have an entry for that application on the Programs menu only for the user who was logged on when the application was installed. If other users of the system want access to the application, they will have to create shortcuts to the application on their Programs menus when they are logged on.

❑ How you have user profiles implemented will dictate how you need to troubleshoot them.

❑ System policies allow accurate control of the computer system and network by combining policies for users, the machine that they are logging onto, and any groups that they are members of.

❑ In order to successfully use system policies you will need to make use of two types of files, an .ADM file and a .POL file.

❑ The System Policy Editor can be used to create a .POL file, and also as a menu-driven interface for accessing the Registry of the computer it is running on.

❑ Implementing System Policies on a network is accomplished by creating a .POL file and placing it in the NETLOGON folder of all Windows NT servers that validate user logons.

❑ If your network is Novell NetWare, then place the .POL file in the SYS:PUBLIC directory of the preferred server.

❑ If a policy exists for a specific named user, then the group policies are not applied to that user.

❑ Group policies are downloaded to the Windows 98 computer in order from the lowest priority group to the highest priority group.

❑ Windows 98 computers that are not configured to use Group Policies (GROUPPOL.DLL) ignore the group policies in the .POL file.

❑ Several things can go wrong when implementing system policies. A few of the more common items to look at are:

   ❑ That the .ADM file is using the correct Registry keys

   ❑ That the .POL file has the functions set correctly

   ❑ That the .POL file is located in the proper folder on the network server(s)

   ❑ For group policies, that the username, group name, and computer name are correct, and that the user is a member of the group that is specified

SELF TEST

The following questions will help you measure your understanding of the material presented in this chapter. Read all the choices carefully, as there may be more than one correct answer. Choose all correct answers for each question.

1. How can you prevent a user from using the MS-DOS prompt?

   A. Implement a roaming user profile for the user

   B. Restrict it from the default user with the System Policy Editor

   C. Implement user profiles

   D. Restrict it from the user with the System Policy Editor

2. What file is the template used by the System Policy Editor?

   A. The .AMD file

   B. The .PLO file

   C. The .ADM file

   D. The .POL file

3. You want to implement a mandatory user profile for a troublesome user. What file do you need to place in his home directory on the Windows NT server?

   A. USER.NAM

   B. USER.MAN

   C. USER.DA0

   D. USER.DAT

4. You encounter a Windows 98 computer in your IS department, on which System Policy Editor is open, with the Local User and Local Computer icons displayed. What can you determine about the state of the System Policy Editor?

   A. The System Policy Editor has opened the Registry of the Windows 98 computer

   B. The System Policy Editor has opened the .POL file of the Windows 98 computer

   C. The System Policy Editor has closed the Registry of the Windows 98 computer

   D. The System Policy Editor has closed the .POL file of the Windows 98 computer

5. In what order are group priorities downloaded to a Windows 98 computer?

   A. From highest priority to lowest priority

   B. From lowest priority to highest priority

   C. The highest priority is processed first

   D. The lowest priority is processed last

6. Where are user profiles stored for a standalone Windows 98 computer?

   A. In the NETLOGON folder

   B. In the SYS:PUBLIC directory

   C. In the USER PROFILES folder

   D. In the PROFILES folder

7. How are profiles enabled on a Windows 98 computer?

   A. From the Profiles applet in Control Panel

   B. From the Users applet in Control Panel

   C. From the System applet in Control Panel

   D. From the Passwords applet in Control Panel

8. What state does a grayed-out box signify for a function in the System Policy Editor?

   A. Selected

   B. Cleared

   C. Dimmed

   D. Complete

9. What type of file includes the statement CLASS MACHINE?

   A. A .POL file

   B. A .MAN file

   C. A .DAT file

   D. An .ADM file

10. Several Windows 98 computers on your network don't seem to be implementing group policies correctly. What can cause this to happen?

   A. The GROUPPOL.EXE file is not installed on the Windows 98 computers

   B. The GROUPPOL.EXE file is not installed on the network servers

   C. The GROUPPOL.DLL file is not installed on the Windows 98 computers

   D. The GROUPPOL.DLL file is not installed on the network servers

11. System policies are not being implemented for any of the users on your Windows NT network. What can be causing this problem?

   A. The ADMIN.ADM file is not located in the SYS:PUBLIC directory

   B. The CONFIG.POL file is not located in the SYS:PUBLIC directory

   C. The ADMIN.ADM file is not located in the NETLOGON folder

   D. The CONFIG.POL file is not located in the NETLOGON folder

12. How is a string value displayed in an .ADM file?

   A. ??

   B. !!

   C. ?

   D. !

13. You have enabled roaming user profiles for the Windows 98 computers on your network. What must you ensure to keep the roaming profiles working correctly?

   A. That the clocks for all computers on the network are synchronized

B. That the directories for all computers on the network are the same size

C. That the amount of RAM is the same for all computers on the network

D. That the computers on the network all have sound cards

14. Marissa has not had any problems using her roaming profile until today, when she could not use it correctly on a machine on the second floor. What could have caused her problem?

A. Windows 98 is installed in the WINDO98 folder on that system

B. Windows 98 is installed on the D: drive on that system

C. She is not set up to use a roaming profile

D. She did not log on to the Banyan VINES server correctly

15. What must the system policy file be named if you plan on using it on a Windows NT or Novell NetWare network?

A. CONFG.POL

B. ADMIN.POL

C. CONFIG.POL

D. ADMN.POL

MCSE
MICROSOFT CERTIFIED SYSTEMS ENGINEER

9

Internetworking and Intranetworking Windows 98

CERTIFICATION OBJECTIVES

By far, the biggest change from Windows 95 to Windows 98 is the integration of the Web browser with the Windows operating system. While Windows 98 looks unassumingly familiar, several changes and enhancements have been made to (among other things) make getting on the Internet as seamless as clicking a link on your Desktop. If you're using Windows 95, you can download Internet Explorer 4 and experience the interface changes that have been incorporated into Windows 98.

In this chapter we'll take a closer look at Internet Explorer: how to set it up and use it on an intranet as well as the Internet, how to personalize it by customizing its configuration, and how to take advantage of the new features of Internet Explorer 4.

CERTIFICATION OBJECTIVE 9.01

Internetworking and Intranetworking

The Internet is a global network of networks. To communicate with each other, all computers must use the protocol TCP/IP (Transmission Control Protocol/Internet Protocol). The distinction between the Internet and an intranet is simply that, on an intranet, you run the many Internet protocols over your own internal network. For example, TCP/IP is the transport protocol, HTTP (Hypertext Transport Protocol) is the protocol for the World Wide Web, NNTP (Network News Transport Protocol) is the protocol used for USENET News. These protocols can be run internally on your own network, allowing everyone in your company to use his or her Web browser on your network. Even better, the protocols work cross-platform. That is, they work on PCs, Macs, and UNIX, so your network can consist of more than one type of computer. This is convenient, because a lot of companies already have a LAN (local area network). Setting up an intranet is just a matter of installing the protocols to run on the LAN.

Many companies are finding an intranet linked to the Internet to be very valuable. Sales people working remotely (on their laptops, not connected to the network) can dial in to the Internet and access their company's intranet. This means that salesman Sam, at a prospective client, can dial up the Web, connect to the company intranet, browse available inventory, trade e-mail with the Sales department for delivery times, and file an online credit application to give his prospect an instant line of credit. This makes for a very convincing sales pitch. Of course, there is a great deal of concern for security, but that is where programs like Proxy Server come in. (I will touch upon proxy servers later in this chapter.)

Connecting Windows 98 to an intranet, the Internet, or both is easy. All Windows 98 needs is to have the TCP/IP protocol installed on it with the correct configuration. Windows 98 will install the TCP/IP protocol by default if you are installing, as opposed to upgrading, your operating system and you have a network card installed. If you are upgrading, Windows 98 will preserve your network settings.

exam
ⓦatch

Remember that TCP/IP is loaded by default only if it is a new install and there is a network card installed in the machine.

To check if TCP/IP is installed:

1. Click Start | Settings | Control Panel.
2. Double-click Network.
3. Scroll through the Installed Network Components box and check for the TCP/IP protocol in the list. (See Figure 9-1.)

   If it is there, great! If TCP/IP isn't installed:

1. Click Add.
2. Click Protocol to highlight it, click Add.
3. Click Microsoft, click TCP/IP, click OK.

You'll be prompted to restart your machine.

FIGURE 9-1

Checking the Network
Components for TCP/IP

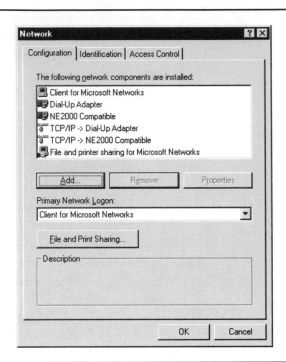

Now that your machine has the TCP/IP protocol installed, it has to be configured. Every computer using TCP/IP can be identified by a unique 32-bit IP address. An IP address is a series of four 3-digit numbers separated by periods. Here's an example: 10.215.56.156. Each set of 3-digit numbers is called an octet, and each octet is eight bits. Thus, an IP address is 32 bits. The IP address contains two pieces of information: the network ID and the host ID. Both IDs are used to determine which messages should be received and which should be ignored.

Windows 98 offers three ways to implement IP addressing. We can have the server do all of the work for us, we can have Windows 98 do all of the work for us, or we can do the entire configuration manually. To have the server do all of the work, we need to use one of its services, called Dynamic Host Configuration Protocol (DHCP). When the service is running on the server, DHCP assigns IP addresses on the fly, and reuses addresses as computers connect and disconnect from the network. You need to ask your network administrator if DHCP is being used or not. When Windows 98 installs TCP/IP, DHCP is enabled by default.

Configure Internet Explorer 4 to Use DHCP

1. Click Start | Settings | Control Panel.
2. Double-click Network.
3. Click the TCP protocol that is bound to your network card to highlight it.
4. Click Properties to bring up the screen in Figure 9-2.
5. Click the IP Address tab if you are not already there, and select Obtain An IP Address Automatically.

FIGURE 9-2

TCP/IP Properties dialog

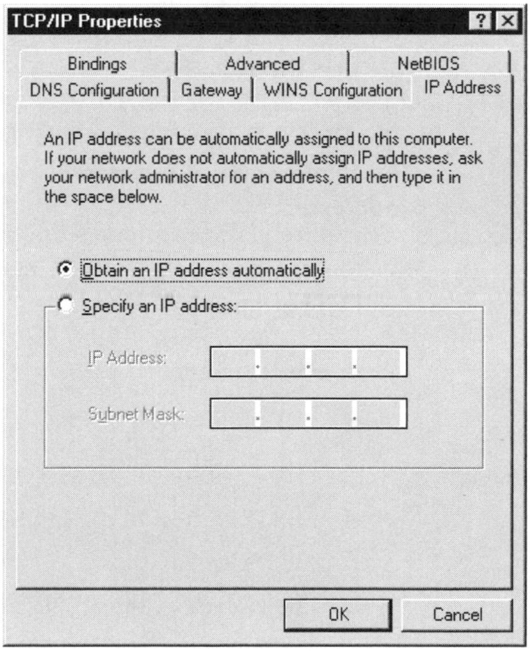

6. Go to the DNS Configuration tab and make sure it is disabled.

7. If you had to make any changes, you'll have to restart your machine.

Once you have rebooted, you should be able to open your Web browser and access your company Web server.

When Windows 98 is installed, DHCP is enabled by default.

If your company does not use or have a DHCP server, you can use a new feature of Windows 98, Automatic Private IP Addressing. If a DHCP server is not present, Windows 98 machines will assign themselves IP addresses even though Windows 98 machines cannot be DHCP servers. Automatic Private IP Addressing assigns an IP address called a net 10 address. This is because the IP address takes the form of 10.*x.x.x.* The net 10 addresses have been set aside for internal use and are not valid on the Internet. Once each computer has a net 10 address, it can communicate with other computers using the net 10 address scheme. If a DHCP server is found later, the local computer stops private addressing, and the addresses provided by DHCP are used instead.

If a DHCP Server is not available to assign IP addresses, Windows 98 machines can use Automatic Private IP Addressing to assign IP addresses.

You can also set up TCP/IP manually. You'll need the following pieces of information.

■ An IP address

■ The subnet mask

■ The IP address for the default gateway

■ The IP address of the DNS server, if DNS (Domain Name System) will be used

■ The address of the WINS (Windows Internet Naming Service) server, if WINS servers are being used

Once you have this information, follow these steps:

1. Click Start | Settings | Control Panel.

2. Double-click Network.

3. Click TCP/IP in the box and click Properties.

4. Click the IP Address tab if you are not already there, and select Specify An IP Address. Type in the IP address and the subnet mask in their respective boxes. (You should receive these addresses from your network administrator.)

5. Click the Bindings tab and make sure there is a check mark next to the TCP/IP protocol bound to the network adapter.

6. Click the Gateway Configuration tab, type in at least one IP address for the default gateway (router), and click Add.

7. If there is an additional router, type the IP address in the New Gateway box and click Add.

8. Click OK.

Restart your machine. Once you have rebooted, you should be able to open your Web browser and access your company's intranet. If you have a large network to deal with, you could distribute Internet Explorer 4 over the intranet.

If you would like to make changes to Internet Explorer on a company-wide basis, you can also customize Internet Explorer 4 installations within your company by using the Internet Explorer Administrator's Kit (IEAK) from Microsoft. The IEAK allows you to create automatic configuration files, create custom setup cabinets with only those components of Internet Explorer 4 you want installed, and set a default home page and links.

Instead of showing the rotating "e" in the upper right-hand corner of Internet Explorer 4, you could insert your company's logo, or you could create a setup file that includes a default home page welcoming employees to the company Web site. You can also create a setting file to automatically configure Internet Explorer 4 to use a proxy server. (Read about proxy servers later in this chapter.) However, you do not have to use IEAK before you distribute Internet Explorer 4. A file can be created that, once the browser is pointed to it, automatically configures Internet Explorer 4. IEAK can also be used to customize Security Zones, and even to restrict NetMeeting activities like transferring files.

exam
ⓦatch

Be familiar with the IEAK. Create custom setup files, set a default home page and proxy server, and you can choose which components get installed.

Dial-Up Networking

If you don't have access to the Web via a LAN, you need to use the computer's modem and Dial-Up Networking. In contrast to the Windows 95 Dial-Up Networking, Windows 98 provides easier access to the Internet. You can use a commercial online service such as America Online (AOL), or an Internet Service Provider (ISP).

Windows 98 creates an Online Services folder that contains convenient access to five commercial online services. To subscribe to one of these online services, open the Online Services folder, double-click the service of your choice and have a credit card handy. (See Table 9-1.)

The alternative is to use an ISP. You can use the Internet Connection Wizard (ICW) to connect to your ISP. If you do not have an ISP, you can let the ICW download a list of ISPs that you can choose from. (See Table 9-2.)

TABLE 9-1	Service	Phone Number
Commercial Services in the Online Services Folder	America Online	800-827-3338
	AT&T WorldNet	800-967-5363
	CompuServe	800-336-6823
	Microsoft Network	800-386-5550
	Prodigy Internet	800-213-0992

ISP	Phone Number	Web Site
MCI	800-550-0927	www.mci.com
GTE	800-363-8483	www.gte.net
Earthlink Network	800-395-8425	www.earthlink.com
Concentric Network Corp.	800-939-4262	Home.concentric.net
Sprint Internet Passport	800-359-3900	www.sprint.com

The ICW makes creating a new Internet connection very easy. All you have to do is input into the wizard some connection information that is supplied by your ISP. You'll have to supply the ICW with:

- A telephone number that you can use to access the Internet
- A username and password
- Your e-mail address (make sure it's in the form myname@domain.com)
- The names of the incoming and outgoing mail servers
- Your e-mail POP account name and password
- The name of your ISP's news server
- The name of an LDAP (Internet Address Book), if your ISP provides one

Using this information, all you need to do is click Start | Programs | Internet Explorer | Connection Wizard. The wizard then prompts you for your information at each screen.

However, there are occasions when you may want to go around the ICW and create your connection manually with Dial-Up Networking. For example, you may want to create a connection to a local Internet Service Provider. To create a connection with Dial-Up Networking:

1. Double-click My Computer.

2. Double-click Dial-Up Networking.

3. Double-click Make New Connection.

4. You can assign a name to your connection here and choose which modem (if you have more than one) to use. Click Next.

5. Enter the area code and phone number of the service you wish to dial. Click Next.

6. Click Finish.

You can create a shortcut to your dial-up connection on your desktop by going into the Dial-Up Networking folder and right-clicking and dragging the icon to your desktop. A context menu pops up with three choices: Copy Here, Move Here, Create Shortcut Here. Click Create Shortcut Here.

You're finished creating the connection; now it's time to log on. Double-click your shortcut, or the connection in the Dial-Up Networking folder. Fill in the username and password and click Connect. When the connection is established, an icon will appear in your System Tray (next to your clock). You can now start your Web browser or e-mail program.

If you're connecting to the Internet over your company's LAN, it's likely it'll be via a proxy server.

Proxy Server

Proxy Server is an application that runs on your company's firewall server, which is connected to the Internet. The firewall provides a secure connection between your company's network and the Internet.

Proxy Server allows everyone in the company access to the Internet. This way, every computer in the company does not require a modem and phone line.

Proxy Server also can control what parts of the Internet you have access to. If your administrator is tired of everyone clogging up the network by downloading the latest swimsuit issue cover, he can instruct the Proxy not to allow that particular address to be accessed.

exam
ⓦatch

Internet Explorer works only with proxy servers that are compliant with the CERN proxy server standard.

In this way, Proxy Server protects the network, yet makes it easy for an entire company to access it. Proxy Server also speeds up Internet access by *caching* pages that are frequently requested. Caching means that frequently accessed Web pages are stored on your hard disk. To set up your Web browser to use Proxy Server, you will need the address of your proxy server. Your network administrator can supply you with this information.

Configure Your Computer to Use a Proxy Server

1. Obtain the proxy server address from your system administrator.

2. On the View menu in the browser, click Internet Options.

3. Click the Connection tab.

4. In the Proxy Server area, check the Access The Internet Using A Proxy Server box. (See Figure 9-3.)

5. In the Address box, type the appropriate proxy server address and port. The Advanced tab lets you select other proxies for other services such as FTP and Gopher. Or you can elect to have the same proxy for all Web services. You can also enter the exceptions—Web sites that Web surfers will not be allowed to visit. These exceptions are local; that is, they only apply to the computer they are set up on. In

FIGURE 9-3

Internet Explorer
Connection configuration

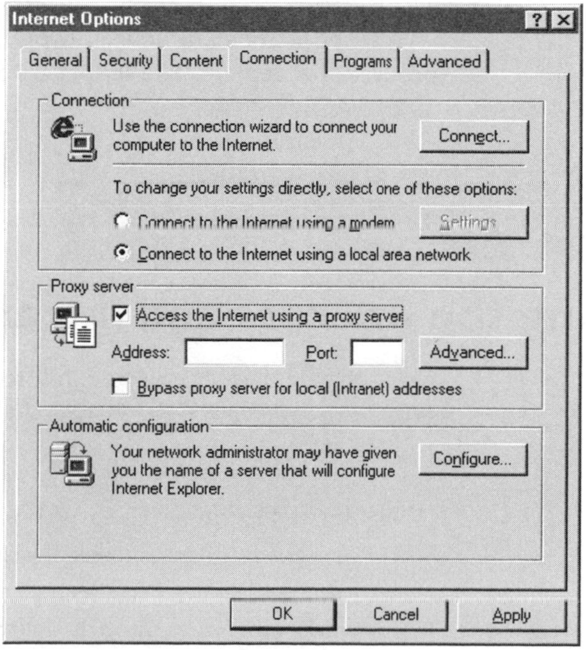

order to set up global exceptions that keep all the browsers on your network from accessing particular Web sites, you need to set up exceptions through Proxy Server directly.

Then next time you connect to the Internet, it will be over your company's network through a proxy server.

Internet Explorer 4 can also configure itself to use Proxy Server automatically. This would be a good idea for large companies, because the proxy settings would be centralized in one file.

EXERCISE 9-3

Automatically Configure Internet Explorer to Use a Proxy Server on a Corporate System

1. On the View menu in the browser, click Internet Options.

2. Click the Connection tab.

3. In the Automatic Configuration area, click Configure.

4. In the URL box, type the address or file supplied by your system administrator to automatically configure Internet Explorer.

5. If you want to apply the configuration settings now, click Refresh.

A script provided by your network administrator automatically sets your proxy server settings. The scripts are actually text files with an extension of .JS or .PAC.

CERTIFICATION OBJECTIVE 9.02

Browsing the Internet and Intranets

Many changes have been made to Internet Explorer 4 to make your surfing experience easier and more manageable. Among the features included in Internet Explorer 4:

- **Active Desktop** Use a Web page for wallpaper, hover over an icon to select it, or single-click an icon or folder to open or run it. You can also display "live" Web pages (Web pages with hyperlinks that work) on your desktop as wallpaper.

- **The Address Bar** Browse the Web from Windows Explorer, My Computer, and even Control Panel just by typing a URL into the address bar and pressing ENTER. An address bar is now built into all windows.

- **Security Zones** You can protect your computer from harmful files and programs by assigning different levels of security to different sites.

- **Explorer Bars** Internet Explorer 4 has four of them: Favorites, History, Search, and Channels. When you select one of them, your screen is split in half. The right pane contains the current Web page you are viewing and the left pane holds either your list of favorites, a history list of visited sites, a search engine page, or a list of Channels.

- **Full Screen viewing** This feature maximizes your viewing area while putting a small, specialized toolbar at the top of the screen.

- **Subscriptions/Channels** When you subscribe to a page, Internet Explorer 4 automatically retrieves update copies of the page when you are online, and allows you to view it offline. The content is updated regularly by the provider.

- **Outlook Express** This is an Internet e-mail client and newsgroup reader. Outlook Express has a three-paned view that allows you to preview messages without even opening them up.

- **NetMeeting** This feature allows people to share video, audio, files, and applications (even if the other party does not have the application installed) across an intranet or over the Internet.

- **FrontPage Express** This feature is a Web page creation tool. It even includes templates to simplify page creation.

- **Multi-Language support** If a Web site offers content in another language, you can add that language to Internet Explorer 4. You can add multiple languages and prioritize them so that content is provided in the language with the highest priority.

- **Personal Web Server (PWS)** This feature allows a Win98 machine to host a Web site on a peer-to-peer network, or a network that has no internal Web server.

For you Netscape users, installing Windows 98 can migrate your settings into Internet Explorer 4. Once Windows 98 is installed, separate user settings will apply to each browser. The proxy settings and custom bookmarks are imported. The security settings and the option to match Navigator's toolbar to Explorer's are used only if they are not the default settings. The e-mail settings are imported into Outlook Express.

To start Internet Explorer 4, double-click the icon on your desktop, or single-click the icon on the Quick Launch toolbar. Once your connection to the Internet has been established, you are taken to a start page, or home page. A home page is a default page that is opened up first, every time you start Internet Explorer 4. For example, if you would like to see the day's headlines every time you connect to the Internet, you can set your home page to CNN. (See Figure 9-4.)

It is from your home page that you start all Web navigation, either by clicking a hyperlink, or by typing a **URL** into the address bar and pressing ENTER. URL stands for Uniform Resource Locator. A URL is the "address" of a page or document that is located on the Internet. An example of a URL

FIGURE 9-4

CNN, my home page

would be http://www.cnn.com. Since all Web pages begin with Http://
Internet Explorer 4 makes that assumption for you, so you don't have to
key the whole address in.

*With the Address bar, you can also search for Web sites just by typing
find, go, or ?, followed by a word that you're searching for.*

Instead of pointing Internet Explorer 4 to a particular home page, you
can also put Web pages on your Desktop. This is part of Windows 98's
Active Desktop. Let's say you have set your home page to E-Investor.com
to watch stock prices flash across a stock ticker. But if you wanted to do
another task (edit a Word document, for example), you would have to
constantly switch between the two windows, or have the desktop split
between the windows. With Active Desktop, the stock ticker can be placed
onto your desktop and the stock prices will scroll across your desktop, but
behind your shortcuts, so you can use the desktop with a stock ticker
embedded in it. This way you can have your Web content brought to
you, instead of you going out to the Web. (See Figure 9-5.)

FIGURE 9-5

An example of the Active
Desktop with an ESPN
Web component
embedded into the
desktop

EXERCISE 9-4

Setting Up the Active Desktop to Display a Web Component

1. Right-click an empty part of the desktop.

2. Click Active Desktop.

3. Click View As Web Page.

4. Now repeat steps 1 through 3 and click Customize My Desktop.

5. Make sure View My Active Desktop As Web Page is checked.

6. Click New.

7. Click Yes. This is where you can add Web pages to your desktop. The Web site for Internet Explorer 4 contains a section called Gallery, in which Microsoft has Active components ready for you to plug into your desktop. (See Figure 9-6.)

8. Browse through the different items available. To add an item to your desktop, click the Add To Active Desktop button on the item's page in the gallery.

FIGURE 9-6

The Gallery of Active Web components at Microsoft's Web site

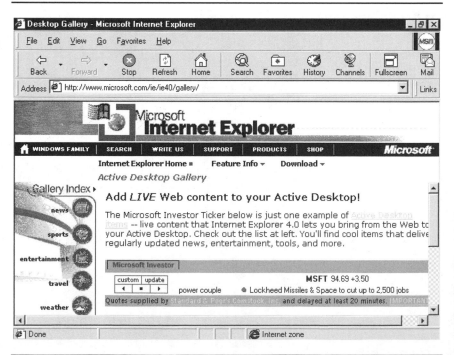

Or you can insert your own Web pages:

9. Repeat steps 5 through 7.

10. Click No.

11. Enter a URL or browse to the Web page you want embedded in your Desktop.

The Active Desktop is only one component of the personalized information delivery system that Internet Explorer 4 provides. In configuring the Active Desktop, you'll notice a channel bar already in the list of available components. (The channel bar is in the right-hand side of Figure 9-5.) This is a feature of Active Channels. With Active Channels, content is sent to your computer at intervals determined by the content provider. The content is stored on your hard disk, thus allowing you to view it offline. For example, let's say you want to read the latest small business articles from Fortune Magazine every day. You can set up a subscription to automatically download the page to your hard disk while you're online. Or Active Channels can dial the Internet by itself, so you can view the page offline. If the page content has changed, a little red gleam shows next to the site. You can also instruct it to download several layers of the Web site, so that as you navigate through the Web site, you don't have to retrieve any of the other pages from the Internet; they are all cached on your hard disk.

Another useful feature is browsing the Web from the address bar in any window. We can access the Internet from Windows Explorer simply by typing a URL into the address bar. For example, if we want to jump to Yahoo!, the search engine, we just type **www.yahoo.com** in the address bar. The right pane acts as the browser, displaying the Web page, while the left pane, toward the bottom of the tree, shows a node for Internet Explorer, and Yahoo! below that. Remember that you can type in the address bar of any folder—Printers or Control Panel, for example.

When typing addresses into the toolbar, Internet Explorer 4.0 uses Microsoft's IntelliSense technology to prevent you from typing the same Web addresses repeatedly. You can type in a partial address and Internet

Explorer 4 attempts to complete it with the addresses of sites you've visited. To use AutoComplete, try the following:

- Type a portion of an address, and then press the UP ARROW and DOWN ARROW keys to cycle through a list of possible matches. When you find the one you want, press ENTER to view the page.

- Type the domain of an address, such as **weather**, and then press CTRL-ENTER. Internet Explorer automatically wraps "http://www....com" around what you typed.

- If Internet Explorer 4 can't find a site with that domain, Internet Explorer 4 rotates through the various extensions until it is successful. For example, if you typed the .COM extension and that site could not be found, Internet Explorer 4 looks for the domain with the .EDU extension, then the .ORG extension, and so on.

- If you need to edit an address, you can move between different parts of the address by using CTRL-LEFT ARROW and CTRL-RIGHT ARROW.

Internet Explorer 4's toolbar has additional functions to help you navigate the Web. (See Table 9-3.)

TABLE 9-3

Internet Explorer Toolbar Buttons

Button	Function
Back	Brings up the last page visited
Forward	Brings up the next page
Stop	Stops loading the current page
Refresh	Reloads the current page
Home	Returns you to your home page
Search	Opens the search bar, where you can keep your list of search results in view while you browse the Web pages on the list
Favorites	Brings up the favorites bar
History	Brings up the history bar
Channels	Brings up the channel bar

Button	Function
Fullscreen	Reduces the toolbar and address bar to maximize the screen for viewing Web pages
Mail	Starts Outlook Express for e-mail and newsgroups
Print	Prints the current page
Edit	Displays the source code for the Web page in HTML

While browsing the Web, you may find that you need to navigate backward or forward from your current page. You can use the Back and Forward arrow buttons to navigate a page in either direction. You can also click the small Down arrow next to either button, which contains a history list of the last couple of pages you visited, and select a page from this list. Right-clicking the Back and Forward button will also bring up the history list.

When you get tired of waiting for a Web page that is taking way too long to load, you can click the Stop button. You can then click Refresh to begin downloading the page again. Sometimes the Stop and Refresh of a Web page is necessary when the Web gets bogged down with too much "traffic."

If you have navigated to a page you would like to revisit often, you can add the page to your Favorites list. This way you can navigate back to the Web page simply by clicking the link stored in your Favorites list. To add a page to your Favorites list:

1. Go to the page you want to add to your collection of favorite pages.

2. On the Favorites menu, click Add To Favorites.

3. Type a new name for the page if you want to.

4. Choose whether you want to be notified when there are changes, or you want the information downloaded to your computer automatically, or choose to be notified in e-mail when a site has been updated.

To keep track of your favorite pages, you can organize them into folders. Click the Create In button in the Add To Favorites dialog box.
To view pages you have added to your Favorites list:

1. Click the Favorites button.

2. The screen splits into two, with the left pane showing your Favorites list.

3. Click a favorite. That Web page will be displayed in the right pane.

4. Click the Favorites button again, and the Favorites pane is hidden.

To organize your favorites, left-click an item and drag it to its new location. If you use the Favorites menu, as opposed to the Favorites button, you can also select Organize Favorites, which allows you to move, rename, delete, and create folders. (See Figure 9-7.)

To search for an item on the Web, click the Search button. This opens the search pane. In the left pane, you will get access to a variety of search engines on one search page. The right pane displays Web pages. This allows you to view your search results at the same time you view the Web page. If you right-click in the Search frame, a context menu appears that allows you to move backward and forward between search pages by clicking the Back and Forward commands on the menu.

FIGURE 9-7

The dialog for organizing your Favorites

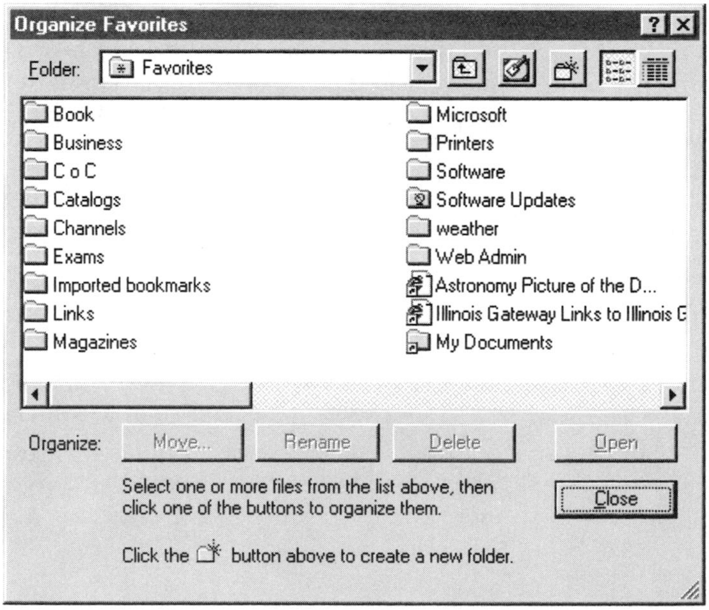

The Fullscreen button uses your entire desktop to display a Web page while using a small toolbar at the top of the screen. Clicking the Fullscreen button turns the feature on and off.

Clicking the Mail button starts Microsoft's e-mail and newsreader application, Outlook Express. Outlook Express replaces the Internet Mail application in older versions of Internet Explorer. When you click the button, you are presented with five choices: Read Mail, New Messages, Send Link, Send Page, and Read News. Outlook Express can send the current page in your browser to another person. If the recipient's e-mail program does not accept messages in HTML, you can select Send Link, which will send a person a hyperlink to the page you are viewing.

The Read News option connects Outlook Express to USENET newsgroups. Newsgroups are link bulletin boards where people can post messages and others can post replies. Depending on the news server you use, you can access over 30,000 different newsgroups. When you configure Outlook Express, you have to give it the name of your ISP's news server in order for you to browse newsgroups.

Printing in Internet Explorer 4 has also been enhanced. Now when you print a Web page, you have the choice of being able to print the page as it appears on your screen, to print only selected parts of it, or to print a certain frame. You can also specify that you want to include additional information in the headers and footers, such as the window title, page address, date, time, and page numbers.

The Edit button displays the source code for the Web page. You can then save this file and create your own Web pages from it.

Configuring Internet Explorer

There are many options that allow you to tailor Internet Explorer 4 to your own tastes. For example, you may want to change your home page from CNN to the Weather Channel; or you may want to enable the Content Advisor to protect younger surfers from unsuitable content on the Web. (Refer to Figure 9-3.)

EXERCISE 9-5

Changing Internet Explorer 4's Settings

1. Start Internet Explorer 4 via the desktop or Quick Launch toolbar.
2. Click View.
3. Click Internet Options at the bottom of the menu.
4. From the Options dialog box, click the tab of the appropriate option. (see Table 9-4.)
5. When you have made your changes, click OK.

Because security is a great concern on the Web, we'll take a closer look at setting up security and using the Content Advisor in Internet Explorer 4.

exam
ⓦatch

Internet Explorer is configured by clicking View, then clicking Internet Options.

TABLE 9-4	Tab	Options
Internet Explorer Configuring Options	General	Change your home page, set the amount of disk space that is used by temporary and history files, change Colors, Fonts, Languages and Accessibility of Web pages.
	Security	Assign Web pages to one of four security zones (see next section).
	Content	Use Ratings to control the content that can be viewed in Internet Explorer 4, use Certificates to identify yourself, create a Personal Profile that automatically fills out forms, and use the Wallet to store electronic payment information.
	Connection	Use the Connection Wizard to create an Internet connection, select whether you're connecting with a modem or via LAN, and choose options to configure access to the Internet using a proxy server.
	Programs	Choose default program to use for e-mail, news, and Internet calls; you can also select which program you use for your calendar and contact list.
	Advanced	Choose various options relating to Accessibility, Browsing, Multimedia, Security, Cookies, Java, Printing, Searching, Toolbar, HTTP settings.

Security

You can find out which zone you're in by using Internet Explorer 4 which has support for many emerging security standards. It allows you to control user authentication, protect your computer from potentially damaging files and applications via Authenticode Technology, and provides a means of positively identifying yourself. It also allows you to assign Web sites to zones of security. Looking at the status bar in the lower right-hand corner of the browser screen, Internet Explorer 4 checks the security settings for a particular zone every time you open or download content from the Web. (See Figure 9-8.)

Different levels of security that can be assigned to Web sites

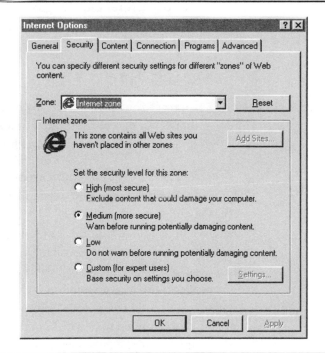

There are four different security zones with which you can assign one of three (Low, Medium, High) corresponding security settings in Internet Explorer 4. The following zones are shown with their default settings:

■ **Local Intranet zone (Medium)**   This zone contains any addresses that don't require a proxy server. The addresses included in this zone are defined by the system administrator in the IEAK. The default security level for the Local Intranet zone is Medium.

■ **Trusted Sites zone (Low)**   This zone contains sites you trust—sites that you believe you can download or run files from without worrying about damage to your computer or data. You can assign sites to this zone. The default security level for the Trusted Sites zone is Low.

■ **Restricted Sites zone (High)**   This zone contains sites you don't trust—that is, sites that you're not sure whether you can download or run files from without damage to your computer or data. You can assign sites to this zone. The default security level for the Restricted Sites zone is High.

■ **Internet zone (Medium)**   By default, this zone contains anything that is not on your computer or an intranet, or assigned to any other zone. The default security level for the Internet zone is Medium.

There is also a Custom Security zone. The Custom zone is for advanced users and administrators who would like more control over security options. The Custom zone allows you to selectively control how ActiveX, scripts, and Java plug-ins are handled. For example, when you download a new ActiveX control, you can choose to be prompted to download it, enable it to automatically download, or disable any downloading of ActiveX controls.

Another thing to keep in mind is that you cannot assign a folder or a drive on your local computer to a security zone. The files stored on your machine are assumed to be safe in order to prevent an interruption or prompting when you open or run them.

Assigning a Web Site to a Security Zone

1. On the View menu in the browser, click Internet Options.

2. Click the Security tab.

3. Select a zone in the Zone list pull-down.

4. Click Add Sites.

5. Type the address (URL) for the Web site, and then click Add.

The tremendous growth of the Internet has given us the ability to access a huge amount of information. However, that information may not always be suitable for every viewer. For example, we may not want to expose children to Web sites with violent or sexually oriented content. To provide this kind of protection, Internet Explorer 4 has Content Advisor (see Figure 9-9).

FIGURE 9-9

Properties for enabling the Content Advisor and setting up Certificates, a Personal Profile, and the Microsoft Wallet

exam
Ⓦatch

Once you have enabled Content Advisor, only content whose levels meet or exceed your settings will be displayed.

Content Advisor allows you to:

■ Control access to Content Advisor settings. You turn Content Advisor on, and view the settings, by setting up a password. You will need this password to change any Content Advisor settings, so you might want to write down your password for future reference.

■ View and adjust the ratings settings to reflect what you think is appropriate content in each of four areas: language, nudity, sex, and violence.

■ Adjust what types of content other people can view with or without your permission. You can override content settings on a case-by-case basis.

■ View and change the ratings systems and bureaus you use.

Once Content Advisor has been activated, sites have to be rated in order for someone to have access to them. If you go to a page whose ratings are below what you had set, a dialog box will appear informing you that you will not be able to view this site. However, this setting can be overridden with the correct password.

EXERCISE 9-7

Controlling Access to Internet Content

1. In Control Panel, double-click the Internet icon.
2. Click the Content tab.
3. In the Content Advisor area, click Enable.
4. If a supervisor password has not already been set up for your computer, you will be prompted to create one.
5. If one has been set up, you will be prompted to type it.

6. If this is the first time you have enabled Ratings, click a category in the list, and then adjust the slider to set the limits you want to use.

7. Repeat this process for each category you want to limit.

The Content tab also has a section for Certificates, which allows you to verify that a piece of software (Java applets or ActiveX controls, for example) that has been digitally signed comes from the author of the software. Before any code is downloaded, Internet Explorer 4 can check the status of a publisher's certificate to see if the Certificate has been revoked. Certificates are also timed-out, so that hackers do not have enough time to crack the Certificate's code.

There are other means of protecting various aspects of your privacy. One way is to use Secure Sockets Layer (SSL) and Personal Communications Technology (PCT). These services provide a secure channel over which you can conduct personal or business communications. The Personal Profile Assistant fills out information forms from Web sites with the information you have supplied, so that you do not have to repeatedly type in your name and address. The information is kept private and secure, so that others cannot view it without your permission.

Finally, there is a section for Microsoft Wallet. This is a secure method of storing vital information such as credit card numbers for making electronic payments over the Internet. You are also given the option to store this information on removable media, such as disks or smart cards.

CERTIFICATION OBJECTIVE 9.03

Sharing Resources on the Internet and Intranets

Information can be shared with others via the Internet or an intranet. Microsoft has included two tools to make creating, publishing, and sharing your Web pages easier.

- Web Publishing Wizard
- Personal Web Server

Web Publishing Wizard

To publish documents to the Internet or an intranet, Microsoft has included the Web Publishing Wizard. This allows you to post documents to your Web server quickly.

Using the Web Publishing Wizard

1. Click Start | Programs | Internet | Web Publishing Wizard | Next.
2. Type the name of a file or folder to be published to the Web site. Click Next.
3. Type a descriptive name for the Web server you are publishing to. Click Next.
4. Type in the URL or IP address of the Web site you are accessing, as well as the local directory on your computer that corresponds to the Web site. Click Next.
5. Enter your username and password to access your Web site. Click OK.
6. Connect to the Internet.
7. Select the method you connect to the Internet with: Dial-Up or LAN. Click Next.
8. Click Finish.

Once the pages are posted, you can start up your Web browser, type in the address of the Web site the new documents are posted to, and they should appear in your browser's window.

Personal Web Server 4.0

Personal Web Server is an application that comes with Windows 98 to serve up your Web pages. It's a great way to share information within your company, or for developing, testing and staging Web applications before they are posted to your Web site on the Internet. There is a variety of things that can be done on an intranet. You can post announcements, construct work schedules, or share documents for a project. Personal Web Server also works on Windows NT Workstation. Personal Web Server has been enhanced and now has the following new features.

- New user interface
- Site traffic monitoring
- Home Page Wizard
- Guest book and drop box options
- New programmability

Personal Web Manager is a utility that makes managing server operations easy. You can create virtual directories, log site traffic, and browse directories. You can display site traffic statistics in real time. (For example: requests per day, requests per hour, visitors per day, and visitors per hour.)

You can create and edit your own home page easily. With the Home Page Wizard, you don't have to know any HTML or scripting. All you have to do is answer a few simple questions and your home page is automatically created.

Make your site Interactive! There are two new features that add interactivity to your site automatically: The guest book and the drop box. You can select these options when you are creating your home page, or you can add them later. Visitors can sign the guest book and view comments left by others. With the drop box, visitors can leave private messages that only you can read.

Active Server Pages support has been added, as has expanded functionality in the File System component, and transaction processing for Web applications.

When installing Personal Web Server, you have three options: Minimum, Typical, Custom.

EXERCISE 9-9

Installing the Personal Web Server

1. Click Start | Settings | Control Panel.
2. Double-click Add/Remove Programs.

3. Click the Windows Setup tab at the top.

4. In the Components window, scroll down and select Internet Tools.

5. Click Details.

6. Check Personal Web Server.

7. Click OK.

Or you can put the Windows 98 CD-ROM into your CD-ROM drive. Click Start and then Run. Type *x:***\ADD-ONS\pws\setup.exe** (where *x* is the letter of your CD-ROM drive). Once installed, your home page is located in C:\INETPUB\WWWROOT\DEFAULT.ASP. You can edit this page to personalize it any way you want.

As for administration, Personal Web Server makes it easy! Open the Personal Web Manager (shown in Figure 9-10) and select the Advanced button. The Advanced menu allows you to share folders by creating virtual

FIGURE 9-10

The Personal Web Server main screen

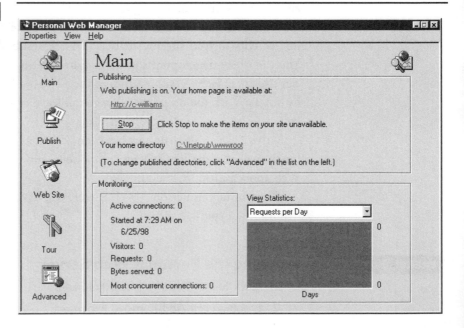

directories so that you can type in a Web address in your browser and the Web page in that folder appears in your Web browser.

To manage Personal Web Server, in the System Tray, double-click the Personal Web Server icon. Another method would be to right-click the Personal Web Server icon in the System Tray and click Properties.

Permissions for Web folders are set through the Sharing tab. When Personal Web Server is installed, a new tab is installed on the Sharing form, Web Sharing. From here you can share a folder, or not share it. If you choose to share a folder, you can set up multiple aliases for it. For example, if Personal Web Server is running on a machine called Sky, and there is a folder called Constellations, with a subfolder called Stars, you could create an alias for Stars called Stars. When somebody tries to view that folder in their Web browsers, all they need to type is http://Sky/stars.

Personal Web Server does not include all of the tools that come with Internet Information Server (IIS) on Windows NT Server, because it is designed to support small networks, or even peer-to-peer networks, with a small volume of hits on the Web server. Tools that come exclusively with IIS include Microsoft Site Server, Microsoft Certificate Server and Microsoft Index Server.

Once you have installed PWS, you should create a home page. Click the Publish button and it will automatically start the Home Page Wizard. The wizard will walk you through the steps of putting up your home page. Once you have customized your home page, go back to the Personal Web Manager. Click Web Site. You are now given the options of:

- Editing your home page
- Viewing your guest book
- Opening your drop box

To check your site statistics, go back to the Main page. The bottom half of the page is dedicated to monitoring your Web site. If you want to create a new alias or share, use the Advanced button.

FROM THE CLASSROOM

Web Sharing and File Sharing

Windows 98 includes support for Microsoft Personal Web Server (PWS) 4.0. PWS is a desktop Web server. If you are connected to an intranet, or a corporate network, you can share documents with your coworkers from your own computer. You can also use PWS to develop and publish a prototype of a Web site. Prototyping gives you the ability to test your Web site before you upload it to an Internet Service Provider.

With PWS installed, you now have two options for sharing files. To see these options, make sure the File and Printer Sharing service for Microsoft networks is installed by starting the Network Control Panel application and looking for the service.

If you have the service installed, you will be able to right-click any directory and select Sharing from the menu. Make sure you are looking at the Sharing tab of the Sharing dialog box. Initially, the Not Shared option will be selected. Select the Shared As button and set the appropriate options for the share name and security. When you click OK, you will have created a Microsoft Networking share.

Microsoft Networking shares work well as long as everyone you want to share files with is on a Microsoft network. That's not always the case. You may want to share files with other users on the Internet, or with users on other operating systems. With PWS installed, you can turn your Windows 98 computer into a Web server, and give access to your files to other users through their Web browsers.

To share a directory through the PWS, right-click on the directory and select Sharing from the menu. In the Sharing dialog box, select the Web Sharing tab. Click the Share This Folder option. In the Edit Alias dialog box, enter an alias name and the appropriate access permissions. When you click OK, the system will create a virtual directory off the root of your Web server. In other words, if I shared out a directory called DATA, and my system's DNS name was system.company.com, then anyone could access that directory through their Web browser with http:\\system.company.com\data. The user would be presented with a list of files in that directory that he could then click to download.

There's one trick to setting up Web Sharing. You must remember to select the option to enable directory browsing on PWS. This is done through the Personal Web Manager. The quickest way to get into the manager is to click the icon on the System Tray in the bottom right corner of your Start bar.

Web Sharing is a powerful feature of Windows 98 and the Personal Web Server. Be careful when setting this up. You might accidentally share out sensitive information. Remember that when you set this up, anyone on the Internet can access information in that directory.

—*By Robert Aschermann, MCT, MCSE*

Communicating on the Internet and Intranets

There are a couple of ways to communicate with others over the Internet or your company intranet. The first way is to send e-mail using Outlook Express. We touched briefly on Outlook Express earlier in this chapter under the section Browsing the Internet and Intranets.

The next method is to use an application called NetMeeting. NetMeeting allows you to share audio, video, and files over the Internet. Because these functions are based on industry standards, the people you communicate with do not have to have Microsoft products.

The final way to communicate is using Microsoft Chat 2.0. This used to be called Comic Chat, and used a comic strip format to display chat messages. You can still use Comic Chat, although the preferred chat is regular, Microsoft Chat 2.0.

There are two basic ways to start all of these applications. The Mail button in Internet Explorer 4 starts Outlook Express. You can also click Go from the menu, which gives you access to all of the programs. (See Table 9-5.)

NetMeeting needs to be configured the first time it is run.

TABLE 9-5		
Using the Go Menu	**To Open**	**Click This**
	Outlook Express Mail or your default e-mail program.	Mail
	Outlook Express News or your default newsreader program.	News
	Address Book or your default contact program.	Address Book
	NetMeeting or your default Internet call program.	Internet Call

Configuring NetMeeting

1. Start NetMeeting.

2. The NetMeeting Wizard appears. Click Next.

3. Check Log On to a Directory Server when NetMeeting Starts. Select a server from the pull-down list. Click Next.

4. On the next screen, enter your personal information. Click Next.

5. Choose a category where your personal information will appear. You can select Personal Use, Business Use, or Adults-Only Use. Click Next.

6. Select the speed you're connecting at. Click Next.

7. The wizard tunes up your settings. Click Next.

8. With the next screen, you confirm the audio devices installed in your computer. Click Next.

9. The next screen sets the audio volume. Speak into you microphone to have the program adjust the volume levels. Click Record. When finished, click Next.

10. Click Finish.

When NetMeeting is opened, you have a window with a navigation bar running vertically on the left with four icons: Directory, SpeedDial, Current Call, History. See Figure 9-11 for an illustration of this window.

- **Directory** provides you with a list of everyone logged on to that particular server.

- **SpeedDial** is almost like a Favorites list. You can call people just by clicking them in your SpeedDial list. Whenever you connect with a person using the Microsoft Internet Locator Service (ILS) they are automatically listed in your SpeedDial.

- **Current Call** is where you conduct your conferencing activities.

- **History** is a log of incoming calls along with your response (accepted, ignored, or rejected).

FIGURE 9-11

Directory screen of
NetMeeting

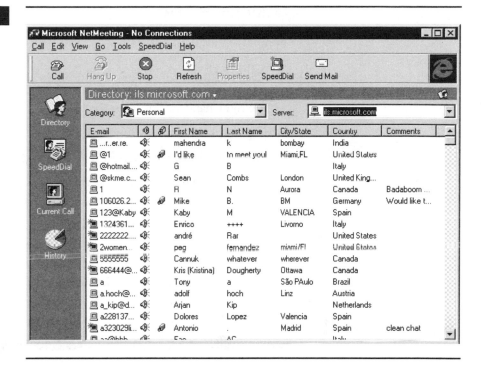

NetMeeting supports Multipoint Data Conferencing. Or in English, you can share information with two or more people. NetMeeting has a Whiteboard that allows all participants to draw, type, or create graphical information. The Whiteboard includes a Remote Pointer so that you can point out specific objects to the other participants.

You can also share an application. This is a big advantage, because only the person who is sharing the application has to have it installed on her computer, although that person can allow anyone else to control it. The Clipboard can also be shared, allowing anyone else to cut, copy and paste. This means that various participants can cut and copy from local documents on their own machines to a document being shared, or they can cut from the document and paste it locally. Files can also be transferred to a single conference participant, or to all. The transfer works in the background, so that everyone can continue working.

To chat with someone:

1. Connect to the Internet. Let the Directory list refresh itself.

2. A list of all users on this server will appear. (You can change which server you're connected to by using the pull-down titled Server on the right-hand side of the screen.)

3. Highlight the person you want to talk to.

4. Press the Call button. Confirm the information and click Call.

5. A list of everyone participating in your call is listed in the main window. To start a Chat session, click the Chat button. The Chat window opens.

6. The pull-down at the bottom of the Chat window determines who receives the call—everyone listed, or an individual person. A private chat with another person is known as a whisper.

FIGURE 9-12

Chat dialog box

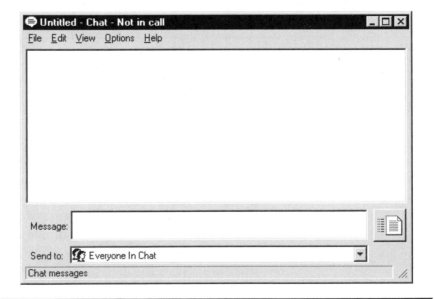

7. In the Message box, type your message and click the Send button next to the Message box.

8. To end the chat, click the Hang Up button.

You can tune your audio settings at any time simply by clicking the Tools menu, clicking Options, clicking the Audio tab, and then clicking Tuning Wizard.

To start a Chat session, a Whiteboard session, or a file transfer, use the NetMeeting toolbar and select Tools. Click the action you wish to perform. Whiteboard sessions can be saved for use in later sessions.

EXERCISE 9-11

Communicating with the NetMeeting Conferencing Software

1. Click Start | Programs | NetMeeting.

2. The NetMeeting Wizard appears. Click Next.

3. Check Log On to a Directory Server when NetMeeting Starts. Select a server from the pull-down. Click Next.

4. On the next screen, enter your personal information. Click Next.

5. Choose a category where your personal information will appear. You can select Personal Use, Business Use, or Adults-Only Use. Click Next.

6. Select the speed you're connecting at. Click Next.

7. The Wizard tunes up your settings. Click Next.

8. With the next screen you confirm the audio devices installed in your computer. Click Next.

9. The next screen sets the audio volume. Speak into your microphone to have the program adjust the volume levels. Click Record. When finished, click Next.

10. Click Finish.

11. Click the Directory button.

12. Click Call. Click Log On To Server to update the list of people logged onto the server.

13. Find a person you want to conference with and click Call.

Here are a few problem-solving scenarios concerning the topics covered in this chapter. You might encounter similar problems on the exam or in your work.

QUESTIONS AND ANSWERS

I want to use Windows 98 on our corporate intranet...	Make sure the TCP/IP protocol is installed, and find out if IP addresses are assigned through a DHCP server, or Windows 98's own Private IP Addressing scheme.
I would like to distribute a custom version of Internet Explorer 4.0 companywide...	Use the Internet Explorer Administrator's Kit (IEAK).
I want to get onto the Internet, but I don't know how...	Windows 98 automatically installs the setup for five commercial online services that also provider Internet access. Or you can use the Internet Connection Wizard, which will let you choose an Internet Service Provider from a preferred list.
I want to video-conference over the Internet...	Install NetMeeting as well as a video camera.
I want to host a Web site of my own...	Install Personal Web Server.
How can I design my Web site and post the pages?	Design your site with FrontPage Express and then publish it with the Web Publishing Wizard.
How do I prevent someone from viewing questionable or objectionable material on the Web?	Enable the Content Advisor by opening Control Panel, double-clicking the Internet icon, and clicking the Content tab. In the Content Advisor area, click Enable.

CERTIFICATION SUMMARY

The Internet and intranets run on the TCP/IP protocol. Windows 98 can be configured to run TCP/IP using DHCP, Private IP Addressing, or Static addressing. If access to the Internet is through a proxy, it can be configured manually or automatically.

The IEAK allows you to customize Internet Explorer 4. There are new Explorer bars to help you make the most of Web surfing: Search, Favorites, History, and Channels. When you type a URL into an address bar, the auto-complete feature saves you time by not requiring the entire address to be typed in if you have already been there. Internet Explorer 4 will also search automatically for a site if it cannot find it with the suffix you typed in.

Security has been enhanced to protect your computer from potentially damaging files and applications, including Java and ActiveX components. The content of a Web site can also be screened for inappropriate material such as nudity or violence. You can create global settings for Web sites by assigning them to security zones. You also have control over your personal information with the Profile Assistant.

If your company does not have an intranet, Windows 98 can fill the gap with Personal Web Server. With this feature, you can easily manage a Web site, log site statistics, and create multiple virtual directories. The Web Publishing Wizard helps you post Web pages to your intranet or to the Internet. The Home Page Wizard will help you create a Web page that you can post.

Communicating with others on the Internet, or on an intranet, has never been easier. Internet Explorer 4 comes with three tools to make communications a snap. You can send e-mail and browse newsgroups with Outlook Express; share audio, video, and files with NetMeeting; and you can chat with another person, or a group, using Microsoft Chat.

✓ TWO-MINUTE DRILL

❏ The biggest change from Windows 95 to Windows 98 is the integration of the Web browser with the Windows operating system.

❏ The distinction between the Internet and an intranet is simply that, on an intranet, you run the many Internet protocols over your own internal network.

❏ All Windows 98 needs to connect to an intranet, the Internet, or both is to have the TCP/IP protocol installed on it with the correct configuration.

❏ Remember that TCP/IP is loaded by default only if it is a new install and there is a network card installed in the machine.

❏ When Windows 98 is installed, DHCP is enabled by default.

❏ If a DHCP Server is not available to assign IP addresses, Windows 98 machines can use Automatic Private IP Addressing to assign IP addresses.

❏ Be familiar with the IEAK. Create custom setup files, set a default home page and proxy server, and you can choose which components get installed.

❏ If you don't have access to the Web via a LAN, you need to use the computer's modem and Dial-Up Networking.

❏ You can use the Internet Connection Wizard (ICW) to connect to your ISP or you can let the ICW download a list of ISPs that you can choose from.

❏ Proxy Server is an application that runs on your company's firewall server, which is connected to the Internet. The firewall provides a secure connection between your company's network and the Internet.

❏ Internet Explorer works only with proxy servers that are compliant with the CERN proxy server standard.

❏ Among the features included in Internet Explorer 4:
  ❏ Active Desktop
  ❏ The Address Bar

- ❑ Security Zones
- ❑ Explorer Bars
- ❑ Full Screen viewing
- ❑ Subscriptions/Channels
- ❑ Outlook Express
- ❑ NetMeeting
- ❑ FrontPage Express
- ❑ Multi-Language support
- ❑ Personal Web Server (PWS)

❑ With the address bar, you can also search for Web sites just by typing **find**, **go**, or **?**, followed by a word that you're searching for.

❑ There are many options that allow you to tailor Internet Explorer 4 to your own tastes.

❑ Internet Explorer is configured by clicking View, then clicking Internet Options.

❑ Internet Explorer 4 has support for many emerging security standards. It allows you to control user authentication, protect your computer from potentially damaging files and applications via Authenticode Technology, provides a means of positively identifying yourself, and allows you to assign Web sites to zones of security.

❑ There are four different security zones with which you can assign one of three (Low, Medium, High) corresponding security settings in Internet Explorer 4.

- ❑ Local Intranet zone (Medium)
- ❑ Trusted Sites zone (Low)
- ❑ Restricted Sites zone (High)
- ❑ Internet zone (Medium)

❑ Once you have enabled Content Advisor, only content whose levels meet or exceed your settings will be displayed.

❑ Microsoft has included two tools to make creating, publishing, and sharing your Web pages easier.

❑ Web Publishing Wizard

❑ Personal Web Server

❑ Web Publishing Wizard allows you to post documents to your Web server quickly.

❑ Personal Web Server is an application that comes with Windows 98 to serve up your Web pages.

❑ Personal Web Server has been enhanced and now has the following new features.

  ❑ New user interface

  ❑ Site traffic monitoring

  ❑ Home Page Wizard

  ❑ Guest book and drop box options

  ❑ New programmability

❑ There are a couple ways to communicate with others over the Internet or your company intranet.

  ❑ send e-mail using Outlook Express

  ❑ use NetMeeting to share audio, video, and files

  ❑ use Microsoft Chat 2.0

SELF TEST

The following questions will help you measure your understanding of the material presented in this chapter. Read all the choices carefully, as there may be more than one correct answer. Choose all correct answers for each question.

1. What does TCP/IP stand for?

   A. Trans Continental Protocol/Immediate Program

   B. Transmission Control Protocol/Internet Protocol

   C. Transmission Control Program/Internet Protocol

   D. Transmission Continued Passively/Intranet Program

2. You are installing Windows 98 on several machines. Machines A and C have Windows 95 installed. Machines B and D have DOS installed. Machines A and D have network cards. Which machines will have TCP/IP installed by default?

   A. A and C

   B. B and D

   C. None

   D. B

3. What does DHCP stand for?

   A. Device Helps Control Proxy

   B. Develop High Contrast Protocol

   C. Dynamic Home Control Page

   D. Dynamic Host Configuration Protocol

4. You are installing Internet Explorer 4 on a peer-to-peer TCP/IP network. What are your options for an IP addressing scheme?

   A. Automatic Private IP Addressing or Static addressing

   B. DHCP

   C. Automatic Private IP Addressing

   D. Static or DHCP

   E. None of the above

5. You need to customize 150 copies of Internet Explorer 4 for distribution. What is the quickest way to do this?

   A. Use the command SETUP /C

   B. Configure one copy of Internet Explorer, and then copy the files from one machine to another

   C. Can't be done

   D. Use Internet Explorer Administrator's Kit

6. What is one function of a proxy server?

   A. It screens junk e-mail

   B. It can control what Web sites you can view

   C. It alerts you to Cookies being saved on your hard disk

   D. All of the above

   E. None of the above

7. Your network administrator gave you a URL to automatically set up Internet Explorer 4 to work with a proxy server. Where do you go to do this?

A. File | Properties

B. Tools | Proxy

C. View | Internet Options

D. Edit | Configure

8. Which is not a new Explorer bar included in Internet Explorer 4?

A. History

B. Security

C. Favorites

D. Search

9. You want to search for "Monitors" on the Web and you decide to search directly from your address bar. What is the correct syntax?

A. Search:monitors

B. ? monitors

C. monitors find

D. lookup monitors

10. What keyboard combination automatically wraps "http://www……com" around a word? (For example, "weather" becomes www.weather.com.)

A. CTRL-ENTER

B. ALT-ENTER

C. SHIFT-ENTER

D. ALT-CTRL

11. How many different security zones are there?

A. 3

B. 5

C. 2

D. 4

12. You are going to create a share that can be assigned an alias with Personal Web Server. How do you create a Web share?

A. Right-click the folder, select Sharing, select Web Sharing

B. Right-click the folder, select Sharing

C. Right-click the folder, select Properties, select Sharing

D. Right-click the folder, select Aliases

13. You are going to use NetMeeting for a conference call. The party you are about to contact has to use which of the following programs in order for you to talk with them?

A. NetMeeting 1.0 or higher

B. Netscape Communicator

C. NetMeeting or Netscape Communicator

D. It doesn't matter

14. What is a whisper?

A. What somebody says when he wants you to speak softer

B. A private chat between two people

C. A button on the NetMeeting toolbar

D. A way to adjust your audio to be more quiet

10

Dial-Up Networking in Windows 98

Microsoft Windows 98 provides a rather elaborate but flexible implementation of Dial-Up Networking. Its functionality begins with the simple modem-based link, and extends to encompassing Virtual Private Networking, Infrared, and Direct Cable Connections. Microsoft places a great deal of emphasis on this piece of networking, as it is the key to Internet connectivity for many users, and an essential piece of telecommuting for many others.

CERTIFICATION OBJECTIVE 10.01

Dial-Up Networking

The role Dial-Up Networking plays in connectivity is to extend an existing network via modem link over a phone line. The link achieved allows the user to participate on the remote network as if he were actually there. The benefits to the telecommuter and Internet user are great; users are allowed access to the remote network from nearly anywhere. The current modem speeds of up to 56 Kbps provide an adequate link for e-mail and small transfers, but are rather inadequate for any sort of manipulation of large files. Higher-speed links are on the horizon that will use DSL (Digital Subscriber Line) technology, as well as the new Cable Modems. This will be discussed later in this chapter under the section titled Virtual Private Network (VPN).

History of Dial-Up Networking

The concept of dial-up is not a new one. The original dial-up connections were by dumb terminals via 110 bps connections. Fortunately, time allowed technology to grow. In the days of the 300 – 9600 bps modems, the dial-ups were made into Bulletin Board Systems (BBS) and other text-based services. Reflecting the limitations of the DOS world, one program at a time could be downloaded, and the user was required to perform two or three steps just to start the data transfer.

When speeds achieved 14400 bps, the use of dial-up networking in the better-known sense began. The purpose changed dramatically from providing a set of text-based services into a link providing an extension of the remote network. Initially many proprietary implementations were used, including products from Novell, Shiva, and Microsoft.

There were two standards used in the UNIX world, SLIP (Serial Line Interface Protocol) and PPP (Point-to-Point Protocol). PPP ended up becoming the de facto standard for both UNIX and PC dial-up communications. PPP was first present in Windows 95 and Windows NT 3.5.

Installation

The following exercise will allow you to install Dial-Up Networking, if you haven't already done so. If it is installed, you may want to remove it and reinstall it again to help solidify your understanding of the installation process.

| EXERCISE 10-1 |

Installing Dial-Up Networking

1. Make sure all applications are closed before you start installing Dial-Up Networking.

2. Open Start | Settings | Control Panel.

3. Click Add/Remove Programs.

4. You now see a window that has three selection tabs. Choose the tab labeled Windows Setup.

5. Click the Details button. From the selection of components, check the box next to Dial-Up Networking, as illustrated in Figure 10-1.

FIGURE 10-1

Installing Dial-Up
Networking

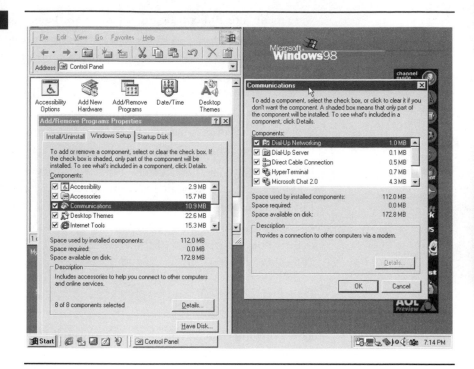

Configuration

After installing Dial-Up Networking, additional configuration can be performed via different interfaces.

- **Modems**   configured in Control Panel
- **Networks**   configured in Control Panel
- **Dial-Up Networking**   configured in My Computer

Virtually all items concerning Dial-Up Networking can be configured via these interfaces. The options at times can be similar, but the items to which these attributes apply vary greatly. The following sections will demonstrate the various configuration options and the effects each setting will have on the Dial-Up Networking configuration.

Control Panel | Modems

The Modem Properties configuration page allows for the control of various hardware settings, both of the modem itself and the communications (COM) port that it uses. The modem's port speed generally should be set to the highest level at which it will continue to operate. All modems 33.6 Kbps and above will easily handle 115200 bps. This setting is dependent upon the type of serial port in use. The internal modems contain their own serial port implementation, whereas external modems rely on an existing serial port.

The reason that we'd want to set the port speed to the maximum capable speed is that it increases the total throughput of data through the port. The port's capability to handle data rapidly is even more important during the transmission of compressible data, such as a text file, because the modem will attempt to compress this data during the send. The receiving modem will decompress the data and send the uncompressed data across the port from the receiving modem to the receiving PC. More information concerning modem compression standards can be obtained by searching for "v.42" and "standard" and "compression" on the Internet.

exam
ⓌatchWatch

Older serial (COM) ports are sometimes based on the 8250 UART, or serial port chip. The UART is the chip within the computer that provides the interface between the computer and the modem. This UART is very unreliable at port speeds above 9600 bps. The 16550 UART, or a variation thereof, is the port of choice, because it successfully handles 115200 bps by adding a FIFO (First In, First Out) buffer to enhance the port's stability at high speeds.

Note that in Figure 10-2 the key functions include not only the Modems Properties, but also Dialing Properties and Diagnostics.

Dialing Properties

In order to provide Windows 98 the capability to correctly dial the phone number when establishing a dial-up session, Microsoft provides the Dialing Properties sheet. The user's local dial-up settings are configured on this

FIGURE 10-2

Configuring the modem

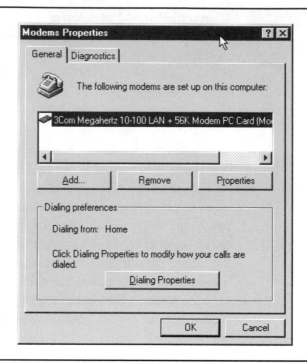

sheet. Settings such as disabling call waiting, setting any prefixes used for dialing (for example, dialing 9) can easily be configured. The greatest feature for the travelling laptop user is the ability to create multiple dial-up profiles for different locations, cities, or even countries. Figure 10-3 shows the Dialing Properties configuration page. The Dialing Properties screen can be reached by opening the Modems icon in Control Panel. Click the Dialing Properties button to change these settings.

Windows 98 adds a new feature within the Dialing Properties called Area Code Rules. This feature allows you to specify dialing within an area code on a prefix-by-prefix basis, if needed. This would be quite handy if you lived in Lincoln, NE and were calling Omaha, NE. Since both are in the 402 area code, the prefix would be the only property to differentiate between the two locations within that area code.

FIGURE 10-3

FIGURE 10-3

Dialing Properties

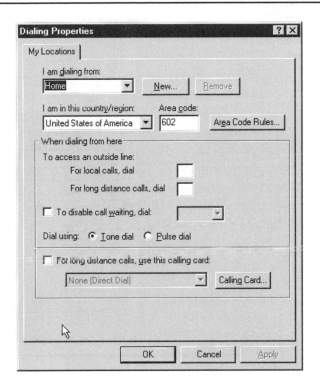

Control Panel | Networks

Since the Dial-Up Networking components comply with the Windows 98 networking architecture, many pieces can be configured from the Networks section of the Control Panel. The protocols bound to the Dial-Up Adapter, specifically TCP/IP, should not be modified at this screen. These settings are modified on each Dial-Up entry. This will be explained in greater detail later in this chapter.

The Network page is shown in Figure 10-4. The Configuration tab is what concerns us here. The Identification tab and Access Control tab pertain only to connections to Microsoft or Novell Networks, which are discussed extensively elsewhere in this book.

If you select the Dial-Up Adapter and click Properties, the page shown in Figure 10-5 appears. The Driver Type tab does not offer any configuration

FIGURE 10-4

The Configuration tab of
the Network applet

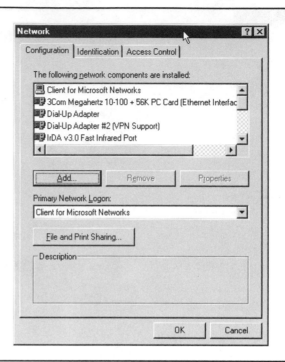

with this adapter. The Bindings tab lists the installed network protocols,
with checked boxes indicating the use of the protocol with this adapter.

exam

Watch

***The only available network protocols for any Dial-Up Adapter,
including the VPN adapter, are TCP/IP, IPX, and NetBEUI. Other
protocols are listed, but will not work.***

The Advanced configuration tab is shown in Figure 10-6. The four
settings control performance over the dial-up connection. The IP Packet
Size setting is new with Windows 98 and will affect performance when
changed, if the connection is configured for TCP/IP. Since the option is
new, no data is currently available as to its impact on a given connection,
but it is believed that the changes are similar to the many programs on the
Internet that modify the MaxMTU size. The MaxMTU is the size specified
for the Maximum Transmission Unit. The jury is still out on what the

FIGURE 10-5

Protocol bindings

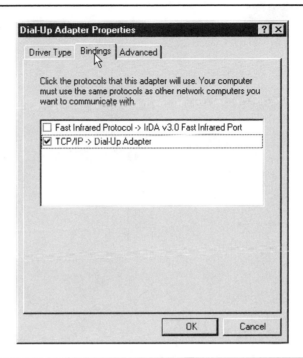

correct setting should be, so the default of Automatic is probably best for the IP Packet Size.

If you enable the Record a Log File option, general information will be recorded to a log file each time you connect and disconnect from a dial-up connection via Dial-Up Networking.

IPX Header Compression is an option to help increase performance over the dial-up link. It works by compressing the packet header information, which is at the beginning of each transmitted packet. Performance gains with this option are modest, due to the already small size of a packet's header information.

The Enable Point to Point IP option is used for general dial-up connections, such as to an NT RAS server or Internet Provider. The option causes the connection between your machine and the remote machine not to act in the typical IP network context of a subnet, but rather a directly

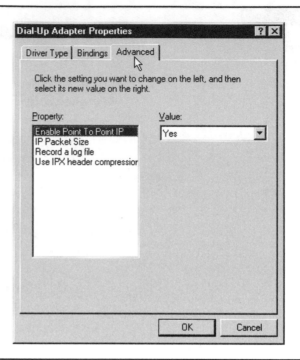

bonded connection. If it is disabled, routing may not work, which would render the connection useless.

It is not recommended that you change the TCP/IP settings bound to the Dial-Up Adapter at the Networks screen. The reason is that, if the user dials a number of different services, the global settings changed here may not be correct. The primary attributes that should not be configured here are:

- **Default Gateway** Designates the next hop from your machine. This is used for routing purposes.

- **DNS Addresses** Can be used to specify remote servers' addresses to be used for Domain Name Service resolution. The common Internet names, such as http://www.microsoft.com, are resolved via DNS servers to their IP addresses.

- **WINS Addresses** Is used to manually designate servers to be used for the Windows Intranet Naming Service, which resolves a common name to an IP address. WINS is used by programs that require the NetBIOS protocol. An example of this type of naming would be the Computer Name field that appears underneath the Identification tab in Network.

- **IP Address** Setting the IP address manually is sometimes necessary. If the IP address is automatically assigned when you log on, that automatic address will override any data inserted here. However, if an address is used that is not correct, the connection will not function correctly.

Note Figure 10-7. Microsoft provides a rather lengthy warning stating that the settings changed here will override those specified in the properties of the Dial-Up entry.

My Computer | Dial-Up Networking

The majority of the dial-up settings can be modified within the Dial-Up Networking folder in My Computer. The same screen can be reached by selecting Start | Programs | Accessories | Communications | Dial-Up Networking. The settings for a dial-up entry will be detailed in this section. Figure 10-8 shows the General configuration tab of a dial-up entry. The properties for a dial-up entry can be opened by right-clicking the icon and selecting Properties, or by highlighting the item and selecting the File | Properties.

FIGURE 10-7

Warning not to change
TCP/IP settings

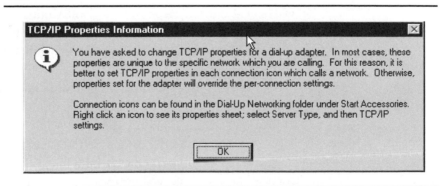

FIGURE 10-8

Editing the properties of
a dial-up entry

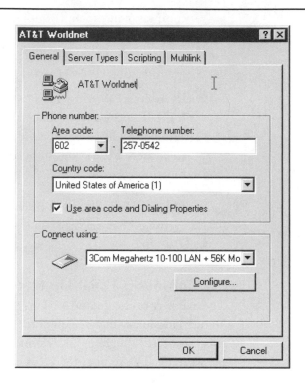

This page allows you to specify the phone number used for dial-up, and
the device to be used to make the connection. When you select Use Area
Code and Dialing Properties, the rules set by you in Control Panel |
Modems | Dialing Properties will be followed. Otherwise, the number
will be dialed exactly as shown. Note the Configure button underneath the
selected modem. If you click this button, the same page appears that would
appear in Control Panel | Modems if you highlighted the modem and
clicked Properties.

The Server Types tab has changed a bit in Windows 98. The greatest
differences can be noted in the Advanced Options section with the addition
of Require Data Encryption and Record A Log File For This Connection.
Figure 10-9 illustrates the current Server Types tab.

Recording a log file could be helpful in monitoring the use of a given
connection, as only general information is logged. This information

FIGURE 10-9

Server Types tab

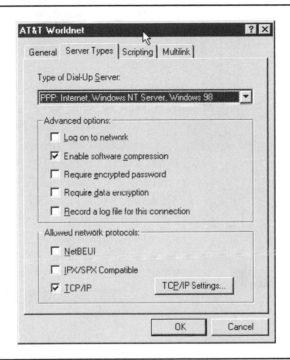

includes the connect time, date, duration, and bytes transferred. Information pertaining to activity while connected is not logged.

Data Encryption is currently not supported outside of the Windows 98 environment. Windows NT 4.0 does not currently support this feature, but Windows NT 5.0 will. Also, the benefit to Data Encryption is fully realized in the VPN scenario described in the Virtual Private Network (VPN) section of this chapter.

The option of using an encrypted password is available if it is a requirement to logging on to the remote host. The encryption referred to is proprietary to Microsoft and cannot be used with other systems.

When dialing into a Windows NT domain, selecting Log On To Network is helpful, as it will enable the full domain functionality, such as logon scripts, to work properly.

The Allowed Network Protocols section has not changed from Windows 95, and the only protocol with configuration beyond simply checking the box to enable the binding is TCP/IP.

As stated earlier, configuring TCP/IP for Dial-Up Networking is best done on an entry-by-entry basis. The settings shown in Figure 10-10 are identical to those contained in Windows 95. Generally, the use of Server Assigned IP Address and Specify Name Server Addresses works quite well. There are instances where these will need to be statically entered, but most of the time the settings can be left with their defaults. This philosophy also applies to the check box labeled Use Default Gateway on Remote Network.

IP Header Compression allows for a small gain in speed, due to the fact that information within the packet is compressed before it is sent over the slow modem link. The speed gain is nominal, but it is worth the benefit to

FIGURE 10-10

TCP/IP Settings

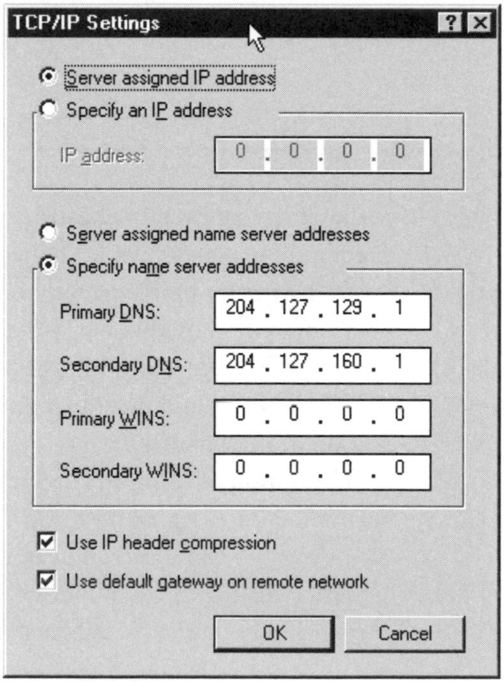

keep this enabled unless problems arise or you are instructed to disable this setting.

The Scripting tab, shown in Figure 10-11, provides the ability to add a Dial-Up Networking script to the configuration. The script controls how Dial-Up Networking will log on to the remote server. No script is usually needed, but there are exceptions to this rule. The exceptions should be limited to older ISPs and UNIX servers, especially when SLIP is used. When a script is selected, you do have the option to run the script in a step-by-step fashion for troubleshooting purposes. Also, if you wish to watch the script as it executes, remember to uncheck the Start Terminal Screen Minimized option. Several tools exist on the Internet for creating scripts to assist the logon process. A good place to look, not only for

FIGURE 10-11

The Scripting tab

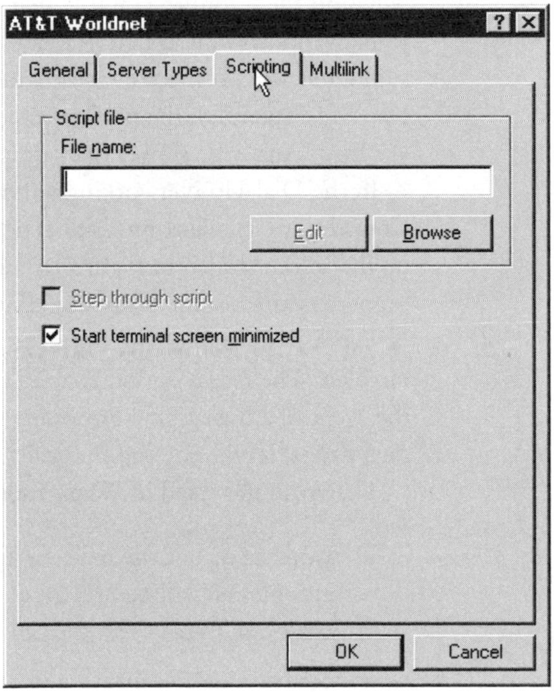

scripting tools, but general tools relating to Dial-Up Networking, would be http://www.tucows.com.

The Multilink configuration tab allows for the configuration of a multimodem connection to another server. This is commonly used with ISDN, but can be used with normal modems. There are a few requirements for this type of connection.

- More than one modem
- One phone line per modem
- The server to which you are dialing must support Multilink PPP
- All modems need to be the same speed

Windows 98 will connect with the first modem configured, and go through the list until all are connected. As it adds connected modems, it will bind them into the bundle that has been defined. This differs slightly from Windows NT in that NT dials all modems in the bundle simultaneously. If modem speeds are not the same (a 33.6 Kbps and a 14.4 Kbps, for example), the performance of the link will suffer greatly and will at times actually be slower than simply having one modem.

In the Dial-Up Networking window, there is a pull-down menu labeled Connections. By clicking Connections and selecting Settings, you will bring up the screen shown in Figure 10-12. These General Dial-Up Networking properties affect some of the functions of the dialing process of Dial-Up Networking. The most useful is the redial function, which is by default disabled. The redial option enables the computer to retry a connection in the event of a busy signal or no dial tone. If the connection is obtained, but then drops, it will not automatically redial.

The attributes listed in When Establishing a Dial-Up Connection control:

- whether or not the modem lights, which appear as two networked computers, will be present after the connection is made (Show An Icon On Taskbar After Connected)
- confirming user information prior to dialing (Prompt For Information Before Dialing)

- displaying a window stating that the connection was successful
  (Show A Confirmation Dialog After Connected)

The option of Save Password when connecting allows the password to be saved to that particular dial-up entry, and linked to the user currently logged on. This is a convenience in many instances when the password is either difficult to type or hard to remember. If a new user logs on, the password will appear blank so that security is not compromised.

The section concerning using Dial-Up Networking to establish a network connection indicates that when the option is selected, the computer will prompt the user to confirm a dial-up connection in order to complete the network request. If no prompting is requested, the computer will not automatically dial out, nor will it prompt the user to confirm such an action.

FIGURE 10-12

Connection settings

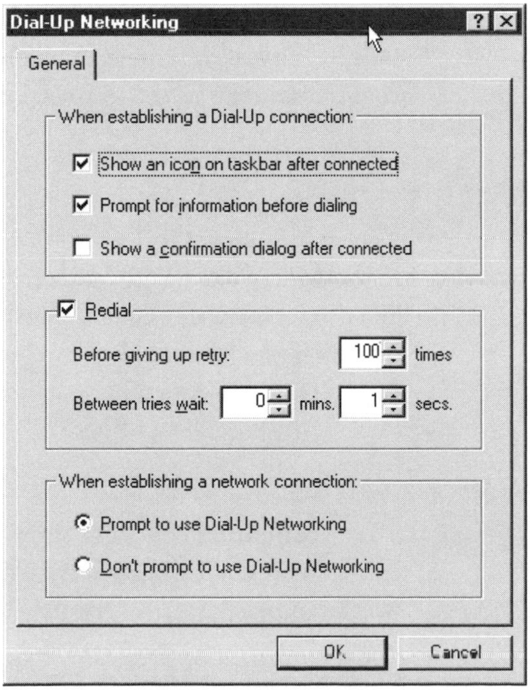

Virtual Private Network (VPN)

The Internet has in the past few years provided many new products and solutions. Virtual Private Networking is a great example of leveraging the Internet to create a temporary WAN. VPN works very well for those who are travelling and need inexpensive access to the company network. By dialing first into an Internet provider, a connection to the Internet is established. The second phase involves dialing over the Internet with the VPN Adapter. A few pieces of data are required for this to take place.

- IP Address or DNS name for VPN Server or PPTP (Point-to-Point Tunneling Protocol) Server
- Valid Internet Connection (AOL will not work, due to its proprietary nature and the firewalling that it performs)

The following sections will detail the installation and configuration of the VPN Dial-Up entry. Keep in mind that the technology is very new and making sure that all software revisions are current is essential to the proper functionality of the connection. The function of VPN is to create a connection over another connection. This is also called tunneling.

Installation

Though not shown in Figure 10-1, Virtual Private Networking is also listed in the Add/Remove Software section of Control Panel. It is underneath Windows Programs | Communications. For the purposes of our discussion of VPN in this chapter, it will be assumed that your connection to the Internet is currently valid.

Configuration

The configuration of a VPN entry is very similar to that of a regular dial-up entry. A new dial-up entry is created from the Dial-Up Networking window, which can be reached by opening My Computer and then opening Dial-Up

Networking. In Figure 10-13, note that instead of a modem, we select the Microsoft VPN Adapter as our device. The key difference is the use of an IP address in place of a phone number. Most other functions are identical to a standard dial-up configuration.

The next screen would normally prompt the phone number of the remote server. Since we are not dialing a phone number, but an IP address, we enter it as shown in Figure 10-14.

Since the VPN adapter is potentially sending sensitive data over the Internet, the encryption of this data is desirable. The VPN technology is quite new, so even though the option for encryption is available, the remote server may not provide support for encryption.

exam
ⓦatch

Remember that the Internet connection must be present in order for the VPN connection to be established. Even though your connection to the Internet is based on TCP/IP, you can create a tunnel with NetBEUI, TCP/IP, or IPX/SPX.

FIGURE 10-13

Selecting the VPN Adapter

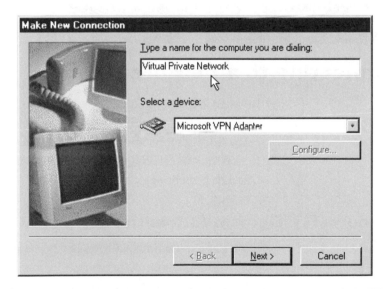

FIGURE 10-14

Specifying the remote IP
address

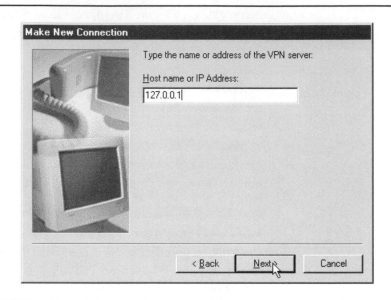

Connecting to a Remote Server

In order to initiate a connection to a remote server, a dial-up entry must
exist, as has been described earlier in this chapter. The logon name,
password, and phone number must also be valid. The troubleshooting
section later in this chapter will detail potential problems when establishing
Dial-Up Networking connections.

Windows NT Domain Authentication

If the remote site is a Windows NT domain, it is important to follow a few
guidelines to ensure full network functionality upon establishing
connectivity. Full connectivity includes the following:

- Domain Authentication as specified in the Control Panel | Networks
  | Client for Microsoft Networks | Properties

- Execution of logon scripts (where applicable)
- Appearance in the Domain Browse List

Many problems arise when users select Client for Microsoft Networks as the primary network logon when they do not have the domain controller available (in other words, they attempt to log on to a domain controller prior to establishing connectivity). A better solution is to use the Windows Logon as the primary logon and, when prompted with a domain logon, select Cancel when first powering on the machine. After the connection is made during dial-up and the Log On To Network is checked on the Server Types tab, the domain logon will pop up again. Verify the information and click OK. True domain authentication will take place.

When the logon process described is not adhered to, proper domain authentication will fail to take place when connected via dial-up networking. When these steps are followed, the logon script will run while dialed in, domain authentication will take place, and the user will be able to browse the network.

Successfully logging on to the domain via dial-up has been one of the greatest headaches of the network administrator. Understanding how the pieces fit together is essential not only to passing the exam, but also to providing a stable and productive networking environment.

CERTIFICATION OBJECTIVE 10.03

Hosting a Remote Client

Windows 98 includes the capability of acting as a dial-up server. In Windows 95 the functionality was available only with the Plus! pack. The two versions operate in a nearly identical fashion, but the Windows 98 version has a slightly more refined interface. There are a few limitations in the Dial-Up Server provided with Windows 98. Some of the Dial-Up Server's attributes include:

- TCP/IP can be used as a protocol, but it will not be routed outside of the server machine. This is a true point-to-point connection.

- IPX/SPX can be used, but it is not routed outside of the server machine.

- NetBEUI is bridged to the remote network, but keep in mind that NetBEUI is not a routable protocol. This means that anything beyond the segment local to the server machine is inaccessible.

- The fastest protocol for point-to-point communications is NetBEUI. This is because of its lack of routing information and greater data content per packet.

- A password is set on the server machine for dial-up. Domain authentication does not work here. This is essentially the dial-up equivalent of share-level security, so be careful not to set a blank password or an obvious password (for example, *password*).

Installation

As you may have noticed in Figure 10-1, the Dial-Up Server can be installed from the Control Panel | Add/Remove Programs | Windows Setup | Communications. Installation of the Dial-Up Server is very straightforward, as is its configuration.

Configuration

The Dial-Up Server component of Windows 98 is designed for casual use, and its configuration screens reflect that design philosophy. The two screens available to configure the Dial-Up Server are accessible from the Dial-Up Networking folder of My Computer. From the Dial-Up Networking folder, select Connections and Dial-Up Server, as shown in Figure 10-15.

The settings available are quite limited. By selecting Allow Caller Access you are enabling the feature. This will cause your computer to answer the phone line of the selected modem when a ring is detected. Also, the password can be set for the connection by checking the Change Password box.

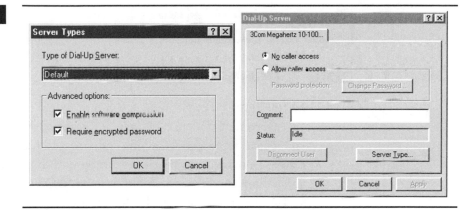

FIGURE 10-15

Dial-Up Server configuration screens

The Server Type button brings up the Server Types configuration window. The valid Server Types are:

- **Default**   Will attempt a PPP connection; but if not successful, it will fall back to the WFW/NT 3.1 connection type.

- **PPP**   This is the preferred connection type, as it is currently the most accepted connection type.

- **Windows for Workgroups and Windows NT 3.1**   This was Microsoft's proprietary RAS (Remote Access Service) dial-up protocol that premiered in 1993. It has been surpassed by the PPP connection, but is provided here for backward compatibility.

exam
⑩atch

Windows for Workgroups and NT 3.1 did not have PPP capabilities, and will not dial into a PPP server without third-party software. If the test question focuses around Windows for Workgroups or NT 3.1, keep this in mind. Windows 95 and Windows NT 3.5 and up do have PPP capabilities and are not limited by this compatibility issue.

CERTIFICATION OBJECTIVE 10.04

Direct Cable Connection

Microsoft provides the ability for two machines to connect to one another via either a null modem cable, which is a special serial cable with the transmit and receive wires reversed at one end, or a null parallel cable. The Direct Cable Connection is a much more robust, 32-bit version of the DOS application Interlink, which shipped with DOS 6.0-6.22.

The use of the Direct Cable Connection is generally looked on as a last resort. Infrared is faster. The floppy or zip drive is more convenient. Essentially, Direct Cable Connection is used to transfer data when a connection between two Windows 98 machines is needed and no other possibility exists, such as when all other connection types have failed.

The speed is somewhat limited via the serial implementation, but speeds of around 1 Mbps can theoretically be achieved by using the parallel solution, provided the parallel ports of each machine operate in what is called ECP or EPP mode. Even if the fast parallel port is not available, a regular parallel port is still faster than a serial port.

Microsoft provides an applet in the Accessories | Communications group to manage the connections. It is somewhat inhibited, to say the least, but when no alternatives are available (such as infrared), it functions quite well.

exam
ⓦatch

When using the Direct Cable Connection with a serial cable, be certain that the serial cable is of the null modem variety. A null modem cable is one with the transmit and receive wires swapped.

CERTIFICATION OBJECTIVE 10.05

Infrared Devices

With the influx of laptops in the computing world, the use of the infrared port has steadily increased. The infrared port allows a laptop user to print or exchange data with another compatible infrared device in a high-speed,

FROM THE CLASSROOM

Using Infrared Communications

Windows 98 includes support for infrared communications, using supported infrared devices such as the infrared ports built into many popular laptop computers. IR communications can be used for a variety of purposes. Most commonly, IR communications are used for wireless printing, but IR can also be used to transfer files, and control other IR-enabled devices.

To manage IR communications on your Windows 98 computer, you will use the Infrared Monitor. With Infrared Monitor, you can:

- Find out what infrared devices are within range of your computer

- Find out if your computer is currently communicating with an infrared device

- Control how Infrared Monitor reports status on the infrared activity it detects

- Decide what type of infrared activity to allow

Once infrared support has been installed and configured on a system, setting up infrared printing is easy. First, make sure your infrared printer is in range. Then, assign the printer to the infrared port. Finally, print as you would normally.

The one tricky part to using infrared is making sure that the device you are trying to send data to is in range. To determine whether a device is in range, follow the steps here:

1. Open the Infrared Monitor dialog box by clicking Start, pointing to Settings, clicking Control Panel, and double-clicking Infrared.

2. Click the Options tab.

3. Make sure Search For And Provide Status For Devices Within Range is selected, and that the time interval to search is a low value (such as three seconds).

4. Click Apply.

5. Click the Status tab.

6. Reposition the devices until Infrared Monitor confirms that the range is adequate.

—By Robert Aschermann, MCT, MCSE

wireless fashion. When the Infrared Port Adapter is in the Control Panel | Networks as an adapter, and the infrared protocol is bound to that adapter, communications can take place. The infrared port must be enabled on the laptop or desktop for this to take place.

When two infrared-enabled laptops are placed with their infrared ports facing one another at a distance of 3 – 6 feet (3 feet is the recommended distance), they will automatically establish connectivity. Once connectivity has been established, network drives shared on the other machine can be utilized. Connectivity can be terminated either by selecting for the infrared application to disconnect, or by moving one computer out of the other's range. The Infrared Monitor tool will monitor the active IR ports and notify you when another device is in range.

CERTIFICATION OBJECTIVE 10.06

Troubleshooting Dial-Up Networking

Here is a list of problems that commonly appear with Dial-Up Networking, along with their solutions.

QUESTIONS AND ANSWERS

Incompatible set of protocols…	Protocol not available at the server; or if it is TCP/IP, the server may not be able to obtain an address to give to the machine dialing in. When the dial-in server exhausts its pool of IP addresses, it cannot support additional TCP/IP-based connections. The error will not state that condition, but the Incompatible Set of Protocols error will appear.
Logged on all right, but don't have drive mappings…	User needs to hang up and reboot the machine. When he logs on, make sure he clicks Cancel on the Domain Logon screen. When he logs on via dial-up, the script should run to map his drives. This functionality also depends on the Logon to Network box being checked on the Server Types configuration page.
Invalid password…	Have user verify his logon name and password.

QUESTIONS AND ANSWERS

Doesn't dial successfully, or you hear a busy signal before it even finishes the dialing process...	User may need to dial 9 to get an outside line.
Modems try to negotiate, but never sync up...	Line noise or incompatible modems. With the new V.90 specification, this will be a common error until the bugs are worked out.
Modem connects, but never finishes verifying name and password...	The server being dialed may require a dial-up script on the local machine. Also, check the name and password for correctness. If a dial-up script is used, it may need to be verified as well.
Everything connects all right, but Web browsing or network browsing is very slow...	Name servers may not be correct. Verify the TCP/IP server settings on the dial-up entry being used.

CERTIFICATION SUMMARY

Microsoft Windows 98 provides a plethora of connectivity options with its Dial-Up Networking components. There are two Dial-Up Adapters listed in the Control Panel | Networks. One is for standard dial-up; the other is for VPN connectivity. The most common type of connection used is PPP, or Point-to-Point Protocol.

Virtual Private Networking operates over TCP/IP with the Point-to-Point Tunneling Protocol.

The most common protocol used for dial-up is TCP/IP. When modifying TCP/IP settings for dial-up, make sure that you do not modify the TCP/IP protocol bound to the Dial-Up Adapter, as this will override all changes you make to each dial-up session. When using TCP/IP, name servers (WINS and DNS) are essential for proper name resolution. If they are not present, a lack of connectivity will be the result. Name resolution is required for the task of resolving a common name, such as www.microsoft.com, to the appropriate IP address. Without name resolution, no communication using friendly names would be possible, and the resulting message would be Host Not Found.

The Dial-Up Server allows for a point-to-point dial-in connection. No connectivity is provided beyond the Windows 98 Dial-Up Server, with the exception of the NetBEUI protocol.

Direct Cable Connections and Infrared Connections are not very common, but understanding how to install and use them is beneficial when taking the MCSE exam.

TWO-MINUTE DRILL

- ❏ The role Dial-Up Networking plays in connectivity is to extend an existing network via modem link over a phone line.

- ❏ PPP ended up becoming the de facto standard for both UNIX and PC dial-up communications. PPP was first present in Windows 95 and Windows NT 3.5.

- ❏ Configuration of Dial-Up Networking can be performed via different interfaces.
    - ❏ **Modems** configured in Control Panel
    - ❏ **Networks** configured in Control Panel
    - ❏ **Dial-Up Networking** configured in My Computer

- ❏ Older serial (COM) ports are sometimes based on the 8250 UART, or serial port chip. The UART is the chip within the computer that provides the interface between the computer and the modem. This UART is very unreliable at port speeds above 9600 bps. The 16550 UART, or a variation thereof, is the port of choice, because it successfully handles 115200 bps by adding a FIFO (First In, First Out) buffer to enhance the port's stability at high speeds.

- ❏ The only available network protocols for any Dial-Up Adapter, including the VPN Adapter, are TCP/IP, IPX, and NetBEUI. Other protocols are listed, but will not work.

❑ Virtual Private Networking is a great example of leveraging the Internet to create a temporary WAN.

❑ Virtual Private Networking is also listed in the Add/Remove Software section of Control Panel. It is underneath Windows Programs | Communications.

❑ The configuration of a VPN entry is very similar to that of a regular dial-up entry.

❑ Remember that the Internet connection must be present in order for the VPN connection to be established. Even though your connection to the Internet is based on TCP/IP, you can create a tunnel with NetBEUI, TCP/IP, or IPX/SPX.

❑ In order to initiate a connection to a remote server, a dial-up entry must exist.

❑ Full connectivity includes the following:

   ❑ Domain Authentication as specified in the Control Panel | Networks | Client for Microsoft Networks | Properties

   ❑ Execution of logon scripts (where applicable)

   ❑ Appearance in the Domain Browse List

❑ Windows 98 includes the capability of acting as a dial-up server.

❑ The Dial-Up Server can be installed from the Control Panel | Add/Remove Programs | Windows Setup | Communications.

❑ The two screens available to configure the Dial-Up Server are accessible from the Dial-Up Networking folder of My Computer.

❑ Windows for Workgroups and NT 3.1 did not have PPP capabilities, and will not dial into a PPP server without third-party software. If the test question focuses around Windows for Workgroups or NT 3.1, keep this in mind. Windows 95 and Windows NT 3.5 and up do have PPP capabilities and are not limited by this compatibility issue.

❑ When using the Direct Cable Connection with a serial cable, be certain that the serial cable is of the null modem variety. A null modem cable is one with the transmit and receive wires swapped.

❏ The infrared port allows a laptop user to print or exchange data with another compatible infrared device in a high-speed, wireless fashion.

❏ There is a list of problems that commonly appear with Dial-Up Networking.

SELF TEST

The following questions will help you measure your understanding of the material presented in this chapter. Read all the choices carefully, as there may be more than one correct answer. Choose all correct answers for each question.

1. Dial-Up Networking is installed from:

    A. Control Panel | Add New Hardware | Modem

    B. It doesn't need to be installed, because it is part of the Windows networking

    C. Control Panel | Add/Remove Programs | Windows Setup | Communications

    D. Control Panel | Modems

2. Modems using a port speed higher than 9600 bps require the following UART chip:

    A. 15650

    B. 8250

    C. 5150

    D. 16550

3. The TCP/IP settings for Dial-Up Networking should be changed:

    A. In the Control Panel | Network.

    B. In My Computer | Dial-Up Networking. Select an entry, right-click, Properties.

    C. In the LMHOSTS file.

    D. In the MODEM.INF file.

4. Dial-up networking allows connectivity with all of the following protocols, with the exception of:

    A. NetBEUI

    B. IPX/SPX

    C. DLC

    D. TCP/IP

5. The Dial-Up Server provides which service to the remote client?

    A. Domain authentication

    B. TCP/IP connectivity to the Internet

    C. Point-to-point connectivity via TCP/IP

    D. The ability to log on to a Novell server after connected

6. Multilink connectivity is the ability to establish dial-up links with more than one modem. If the modems are not bundling, the cause could be:

    A. Multilink PPP not supported on the remote server

    B. The modems are not the same speed

    C. Line noise

    D. Multilink PPP requires the same modems to be at each end of the communications link

7. VPN allows for a connection to be made over the Internet. Which of the following protocols does the VPN adapter support?

    A. TCP/IP

B. IPX/SPX

C. NetBEUI

D. All of the above

8. The Direct Cable Connection supports which cable type?

A. Regular serial cable

B. Null modem serial cable

C. Ethernet

D. RG-58

9. What is the recommended distance between two infrared devices while communicating?

A. 12 inches

B. 2 feet

C. 3 feet

D. 6 feet

10. What is the default communications server type for a dial-up entry?

A. RAS

B. PPP

C. VPN

D. PPTP

MICROSOFT CERTIFIED SYSTEMS ENGINEER

11

Monitoring and Optimization

Anyone who works in an Information Systems department has probably heard the following statement many times from users: "My system is running slow. I need a new computer." If your business is like my business, you know there is no possibility of keeping up with the rapid changes in technology. Since you can't always go out and buy the newest technology, it is important to make sure the systems you are responsible for operate at peak efficiency.

In this chapter we will discuss factors that affect system performance, how to monitor system performance, as well as how to optimize virtual memory, enhance file system performance, and optimize Windows 98 networking.

Factors Affecting System Performance

There are several factors that can affect system performance. Some of the factors may be easier and faster for you to solve than others. For example, it should be faster for you to replace Real mode drivers with Protected mode drivers rather than add 32MB of physical memory to the system. System performance is enhanced immediately by replacing the 16-bit Real mode drivers with 32-bit Protected mode drivers.

Other factors that can affect system performance include the virtual memory settings, the performance of the file system, and network settings. We will examine these factors throughout the rest of the chapter.

Monitoring System Performance

How can you tell if system performance for your system is optimized? Should you just start modifying items in the hopes that system performance will increase? Well, I hope you answered a resounding NO to the second question! In order for you to increase the performance of your system you need to monitor the system to see what is causing it not to operate at its peak efficiency. Windows 98 includes two tools that help you to monitor your system, Net Watcher and System Monitor.

Net Watcher

If your system seems to be running more slowly than normal, and you have File and Printer Sharing enabled, you may want to use Net Watcher to look at the status of the system. Net Watcher allows you to monitor and manage connections to shared resources as well as to create, add, and delete shared resources. This is useful when you sense a slowdown to your system and you want to know if it is caused by someone who is connected to your computer, or by some other factor. Figure 11-1 shows the users connected to the system P400. What those users are doing can affect the reaction of your system to tasks you are trying to complete. Net Watcher is a tool that can be used on local or remote computers. To use it on a remote computer you must have remote administration enabled, as discussed in Chapter 5.

Net Watcher showing
the connections to the
computer named P400

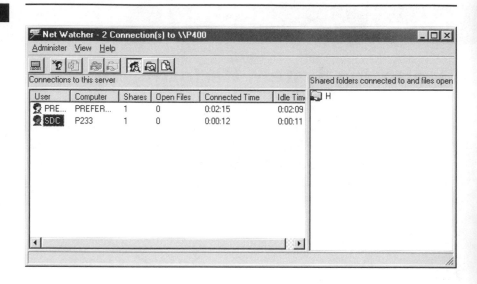

System Monitor

System Monitor is a tool you can use to help determine the cause of problems on your system by measuring the performance of hardware, software services, and applications. Imagine that you just changed your system configuration and you are wondering if what you did helped or hurt system performance. Using System Monitor prior to making the change and after making the change would give you the answer to that question.

System Monitor has several categories available to monitor, including File System, Memory Manager, and Kernel, to name just a few. Each category has several items available to monitor; for example, the Memory Manager category has 16 items available, including Page faults and Swapfile size. Figure 11-2 shows the System Monitor with several items from different categories displayed. System Monitor in Figure 11-2 shows the information using line charts. The information can also be displayed using bar charts and numeric charts. The choice is yours as to which display to use. The information is the same; just the method used to display it changes.

FIGURE 11-2

System Monitor showing
the statistics for a
computer system

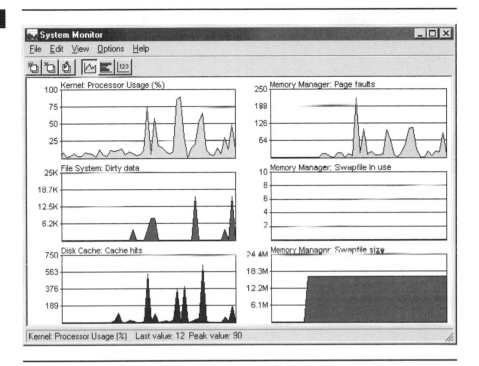

Exercise 11-1 gives you the chance to install System Monitor if it is not
already on your system. If it is already on your system, then proceed to
Exercise 11-2 to set up items to monitor on your system.

EXERCISE 11-1   ## Installing System Monitor

1. Click the Start button and select Settings | Control Panel.

2. Click the Add/Remove Programs icon.

3. Click the Windows Setup tab.

4. In the Components list, make sure Accessories is checked and
   highlighted, and click the Details button.

5. Place a check mark in the box to the left of System Monitor in the
   Components list, and click the OK button.

6. Click the OK button. System Monitor is installed.

Configuring System Monitor to Monitor Your System

1. Click the Start button and select Programs | Accessories | System Tools | System Monitor.

2. Choose Add Item from the Edit menu.

3. Highlight Memory Manager in the Category list and, while holding down the SHIFT key, select Swapfile In Use and Swapfile Size from the Item list so that they are both highlighted.

4. Click the OK button and both items are added to the System Monitor chart.

5. Choose Add Item from the Edit menu.

6. Highlight Kernel in the Category list and select Processor Usage (%) from the Item list so that it is highlighted.

7. Click the OK button and the item is added to the System Monitor chart.

8. Use the View menu and select the different views (Line Charts, Bar Charts, and Numeric Charts) to become familiar with the different types of views available to you.

9. Choose Exit from the File menu and close the System Monitor.

Table 11-1 shows some general guidelines and key settings for using System Monitor to troubleshoot performance problems.

TABLE 11-1   Using System Monitor to Troubleshoot Performance Problems

Category Item	Observation	Possible Cause
Memory Manager:Discards Memory Manager:Page Faults	Lots of activity on both items	The memory stress may be caused by a need for more physical memory in the system
Kernel:Processor Usage (%)	Processor usage high even when you are not using the system	Press the CTRL-ALT-DEL keys at the same time to look at the task list to try to determine which application may be causing the high processor usage

| TABLE 11-1 | | Using System Monitor to Troubleshoot Performance Problems (*continued*) |

Category Item	Observation	Possible Cause
Memory Manager:Page Faults	High amount of page faults are occurring when using an application	It is possible that the application has memory needs that are more than what the computer can provide
Memory Manager:Locked Memory Memory Manager:Allocated Memory	The computer is exceptionally slow and the locked memory value is a large section of the allocated memory value	Performance can be affected due to the inadequate quantity of free memory

CERTIFICATION OBJECTIVE 11.03

Optimizing Virtual Memory

The virtual memory file is used by Windows 98 to store information that is not currently needed in physical memory. To free up memory, Windows 98 swaps data from physical memory to the virtual memory file. When the information is needed, it moves the data back into physical memory. By extending the amount of memory available to Windows 98 (physical memory + virtual memory) you can run more applications than you could if only the physical memory was available to you.

The virtual memory file for Windows 98 is named WIN386.SWP and it is dynamic in nature. This means that it grows and shrinks as necessary, depending on what operations are happening with Windows 98 and also on the available space on the hard disk drive.

exam
ⓦatch

One of the best ways of optimizing virtual memory on Windows 98 is to make sure that the hard disk drive that is home to WIN386.SWP has plenty of free space available so that the virtual memory file can grow and shrink as necessary.

Windows 98 defaults to creating the virtual memory file on the C: drive. If your system has multiple hard disks, you can move the file to another drive. It is best to place the WIN386.SWP file on the fastest, least-used physical hard disk available. Placing the WIN386.SWP file on a drive that does not store the system files also prevents the swap file and operating system from competing for the disk reads and writes on the same disk. Figure 11-3 shows that the WIN386.SWP file has been moved to the G: drive, which has 395MB of space available for it to use.

Exercise 11-3 gives you the opportunity to change the location of the virtual memory file on your system. In order to perform this exercise you need to have at least two physical hard disks in your system.

EXERCISE 11-3

Changing the Location of the Virtual Memory File

1. Select the Start button and choose Settings | Control Panel.

2. Double-click the System icon.

FIGURE 11-3

The location of the WIN386.SWP file has been changed to the G: drive

3. Select the Performance tab.

4. Click the Virtual Memory button.

5. Click the radio button to the left of Let Me Specify My Own Virtual Memory Settings.

6. Select another physical hard disk from the Hard Disk drop-down list.

7. Click the OK button.

8. Click the Yes button to signify that you want to continue.

9. Click the Close button.

10. Click the Yes button to restart your system. When the system restarts, the WIN386.SWP file will be located and used from the drive you selected in step 6.

exam
ⓦatch

If you completely disable virtual memory, the system may not start properly; or if it does start, then performance may be hindered.

CERTIFICATION OBJECTIVE 11.04

File System Performance

There are many factors that can affect the performance of the file system in your system. Some of these items are hard disk drives, CD-ROM drives, and removable disk drives.

Hard Disk File System Performance

Windows 98 allows you to optimize file system and disk performance by choosing the profile that best meets the role that the computer is fulfilling. There are three different roles available for you to choose from, as shown in Table 11-2.

TABLE 11-2	Role	Purpose
Roles Available to a Windows 98 Computer	Desktop computer	This role signifies a computer that is either a standalone system or a network client that has the minimum amount of physical memory and does not use battery power.
	Mobile or docking system	This role signifies a computer that has limited physical memory and that runs on battery power. Since it uses battery power, this role flushes the disk cache regularly.
	Network server	This role signifies a computer that has ample physical memory and frequent disk activity, such as a file or print server, so the computer is optimized for a heavy quantity of disk access.

Five values are changed in the Registry depending on the role that is chosen for your file system. Table 11-3 shows the five values and their purposes.

TABLE 11-3	Value	Purpose
Values Changed in the Registry Based Upon the Profile Selected	PathCache	This value specifies the size of the cache that will be used to save the locations of the most recently used directory paths. The Desktop profile has a value of 32, the Mobile profile has a value of 16, and the Network server profile has a value of 64.
	NameCache	This value specifies the size of the cache that will be used to save the locations of the most recently used filenames. The Desktop profile stores 8KB of names, which is approximately 677 names. The Mobile profile stores 4KB of names, which is approximately 337 names. The Network server profile stores 16KB of names, which is approximately 2729 names.
	BufferTimeout BufferAgeTimeout VolumeIdleTimeout	Controls the time between when changes are placed in the buffer and when they are written to the hard disk drive.

The values for each profile type are located at the following Registry subkey: HKEY_LOCAL_MACHINE\SOFTWARE\MICROSOFT\ WINDOWS\CURRENTVERSION\FS TEMPLATES.

The settings for the profile type in use are located at the following Registry subkey: HKEY_LOCAL_MACHINE\SYSTEM\ CURRENTCONTROLSET\CONTROL\FILESYSTEM.

Figure 11-4 shows a system that is configured to be a Network server. That particular system is used as a file and print server for a network of 12 computers. But where did the settings get changed to make that system a Network server? Did I go and modify the Registry key, or is there an easier way? Exercise 11-4 will give you the opportunity to change the typical role of your machine.

Configuring the Typical Role of a Machine

1. Select the Start button and choose Settings | Control Panel.

2. Double-click the System icon.

3. Select the Performance tab.

File System Properties for a system configured as a network server

4. Click the File System button.

5. Choose Network server from the Typical Role Of This Computer drop-down list.

6. Click the OK button.

7. Click the Close button.

8. Click Yes to reboot your system so that the changes take effect.

If you do not want your system set to use the network server role, complete Exercise 11-4 again and in step 5 change to the role that was on your system prior to performing Exercise 11-4.

CD-ROM File System Performance

Not only can you optimize the performance of your hard disk file system, you can also optimize the performance of your CD-ROM file system if your system has a CD-ROM drive. The cache used by the CD-ROM is separate from the cache used by the hard disk, because the CD-ROM cache can be paged to the hard disk. Hard disk cache stays in physical memory. The amount of cache that is used for the CD-ROM cache is dependent on the speed of your CD-ROM drive. Table 11-4 shows the cache settings, depending on the CD-ROM speed of your drive.

You choose the speed of your CD-ROM drive from the Optimize Access Pattern For drop-down list located at the Performance | File System | CD-ROM tab of the Control Panel | System icon, as shown in Figure 11-5. The Supplemental Cache Size slider allocates more physical memory for caching data from the CD-ROM drive when it is slid to the right.

TABLE 11-4	CD-ROM Drive Speed	Size of the Cache
Cache Size Settings for Different Speed CD-ROM Drives	No read-ahead	1088KB
	Single-speed drive	1088KB
	Double-speed drive	1138KB
	Triple-speed drive	1188KB
	Quad-speed or higher	1238KB

FIGURE 11-5

File System Properties for a system configured with a Quad-speed or higher CD-ROM drive

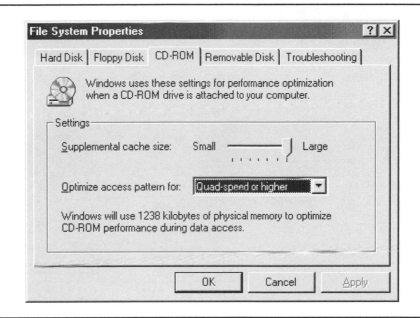

DVD File System Performance

Windows 98 includes support for DVD disk drives. DVD disk drives utilize the Universal Disk Format (UDF) as their file system. This type of file system uses the main file system cache so there are no settings that can be changed to enhance the performance of DVD disk drives.

Removable Disk Drive File System Performance

Windows 98 includes the capability to enhance the performance of different types of removable disk drives by enabling write-behind caching. Some examples of removable disk drives are the Syquest SparQ, the Iomega ZIP, and the Iomega JAZ.

Write-behind caching is enabled from the Performance I File System I Removable Disk tab of the Control Panel I System icon, as shown in Figure 11-6.

FIGURE 11-6

The Enable Write-Behind
Caching option for
removable disk drives

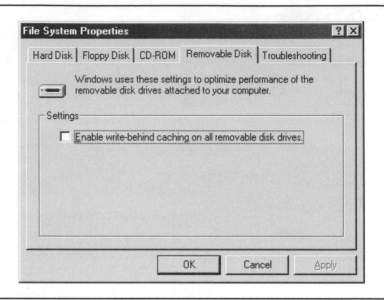

Now that you are familiar with different methods of enhancing file system performance within Windows 98, here is a quick reference for possible scenario questions, and the appropriate answer.

QUESTIONS AND ANSWERS

Lucille just received a new computer system with a 24x CD-ROM drive, and she wants it optimized for the best performance...	Change the Optimize Access Pattern For setting from the CD-ROM tab of File System Properties to Quad-speed or higher, to set the cache to 1238KB of physical memory.
Arvin's computer is on the company network and has 16MB of physical memory. He wants to make sure that the hard disk drive is optimized for his situation...	Select Desktop computer from Typical Role Of This Computer on the Hard Disk tab of File System Properties, to make sure that the PathCache and NameCache settings are appropriate for the minimal amount of memory in his system.
Neal has a Iomega JAZ drive hooked into his computer. He wants to optimize its performance under Windows 98...	Enable write-behind caching for all removable drives from the Removable Disk tab of File System Properties, to enhance the performance of the JAZ drive.

Disk Defragmenter

When you first start using your hard disk, the file system has no problem with keeping the files contiguous, as there is plenty of room for it to work with. However, after you have used your hard disk for a period of time, the file system will have to scatter the data blocks to wherever it can find room to fit them on the drive. This has the effect of slowing your system down. The Disk Defragmenter is a useful tool for optimizing your hard disk drive because it will take the noncontiguous data and place it back into a contiguous space.

The Windows 98 version of Disk Defragmenter has been enhanced to watch how you use applications and arrange the files in an order that can start them up faster based upon your pattern of usage. The method it uses to accomplish this is that Windows 98 creates a log file in the C:\WINDOWS\APPLOG folder for each application that you open. It then uses the log files to arrange the applications in the order they are accessed when the application starts. The Disk Defragmenter can be started by choosing it from the Programs | Accessories | System Tools menu. Figure 11-7 shows the Disk Defragmenter in action.

ScanDisk

ScanDisk is a utility included with Windows 98 that is used to perform analysis and repair on disk drives. Windows 98 includes an enhanced version of ScanDisk that can fix problems with FAT32 drives. ScanDisk works with both compressed and uncompressed drives. ScanDisk cannot be used on CD-ROM drives or network drives.

There are two versions of ScanDisk included with Windows 98, a Graphical User Interface (GUI) version and a MS-DOS-based version. If Windows 98 is shut down incorrectly, then the MS-DOS-based version will run automatically the next time Windows 98 is booted, so that it can check for errors on the drive(s).

ScanDisk can detect and fix several problems on your disk drives. These items include:

- Problems with FAT16 and FAT32

- The directory tree structure
- The file system structure to include cross-linked files and lost clusters
- Problems with long filenames
- Bad sectors on the physical surface of the disk drive
- The volume header, volume file structure, volume signatures, and compression structure on DriveSpace 3 and DoubleSpace drives (we will cover DriveSpace 3 more in the next section)

The two types of tests that ScanDisk can perform are the Standard test and the Thorough test. The Standard test checks files and folders for errors. The Thorough test not only checks files and folders for errors, but also scans the disk surface for errors. A Thorough scan takes a long time if you have an extremely large drive that it needs to scan. Figure 11-8 shows ScanDisk performing a Standard scan on a disk drive.

FIGURE 11-7

Disk Defragmenter running on drive H

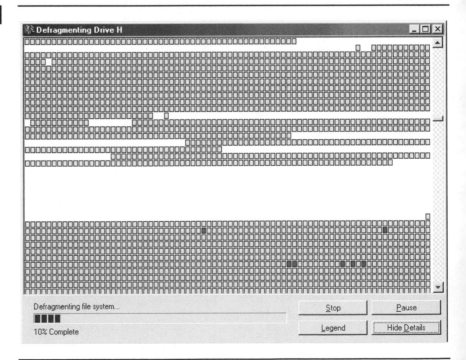

FIGURE 11-8

ScanDisk performing a
Standard test on drive H

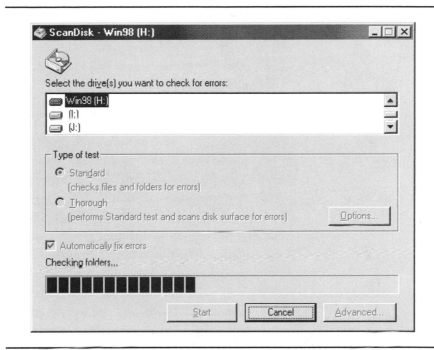

Now it is time for you to practice running the ScanDisk utility to check
for errors on your drive. Exercise 11-5 shows you how to run ScanDisk.

EXERCISE 11-5

Using ScanDisk to Check a Disk Drive for Errors

1. Select the Start button and choose Programs | Accessories | System
   Tools | ScanDisk.

2. Highlight the C: drive so that the ScanDisk will be performed on it.

3. Make sure that the radio button to the left of Standard is selected as
   the type of test to perform.

4. Place a check mark in the box to the left of Automatically Fix Errors.

5. Click the Start button to start ScanDisk. After ScanDisk completes,
   it will display a Results window.

6. Click the Close button after you are finished reviewing the results in
   the review window. Did your drive have any errors on it?

7. Click the Close button to close the ScanDisk utility.

DriveSpace 3

Windows 98 includes DriveSpace 3, which can be used to compress disk drives, as well as manage drives that have been compressed with DriveSpace 3 or DoubleSpace. The DriveSpace 3 that ships with Windows 98 can identify FAT32 drives, but it cannot compress a FAT32 drive.

DriveSpace 3 can be used to compress and uncompress data on several different types of media, including floppy disks, hard disks, and removable media. Using DriveSpace 3 to compress data or space on a drive can provide theoretically 50 – 100 percent more free space than before DriveSpace 3 was used. A compressed drive is not a real disk drive, but most applications think that it is a real drive. For example, a compressed drive exists on a hard disk drive as a compressed volume file (CVF). The CVF is located on an uncompressed drive that is named the CVF's host drive. The CVF is stored in the root folder of the host drive and has a name like DRVSPACE.000 or DRVSPACE.240. The suffix can range from 000 to 254. Do NOT delete this file, because if you do, you will lose all information that was in the compressed drive! Don't let the size of the CVF fool you. It may only be 250MB, but it may contain 500MB of compressed data. The data in the CVF file is accessed by a drive letter that DriveSpace 3 assigns it. This drive letter is different from the one assigned to the host drive. DriveSpace 3 can create a compressed drive up to 2GB in size.

If you want to install DriveSpace 3 on your system, you can find it located at Programs | Accessories | System Tools | DriveSpace. Figure 11-9 shows DriveSpace 3 right after it has been started. It shows a list of drives available on your system. Keep in mind that not all of the drives shown may be able to utilize DriveSpace 3, either because there is not enough room on the drive, or because it is a FAT32 drive.

Compression Agent

The Compression Agent is used in conjunction with DriveSpace 3 to maximize the compression of files. The Compression Agent will not function until after DriveSpace 3 has been utilized, as shown in Figure 11-10.

The Compression Agent lets you designate different compression methods for different files. The two methods of compression that the

FIGURE 11-9

DriveSpace 3 displaying
the available drives in a
computer system

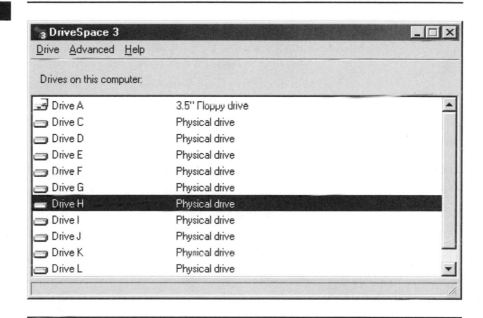

Compression Agent supports are HiPack and UltraPack. HiPack
compression uses the same encoding format as standard compression,
whereas UltraPack compression offers better compression than either
standard compression or the HiPack method. The drawback with UltraPack
compression is that the files compressed with it are slower to decompress
than the other methods.

FIGURE 11-10

Dialog box prompting
for DriveSpace 3 to be
run prior to using the
Compression Agent

There are three methods of running the Compression Agent: manually, with Scheduled Tasks, or by using the Maintenance Wizard. If you want to run the Compression Agent manually on your system, you can find it located at Programs | Accessories | System Tools | Compression Agent. We will discuss the Task Scheduler later in the chapter, and you will be able to see how to use it with the Compression Agent in that section. Figure 11-11 shows the Compression Agent right after it has been started.

Scheduled Tasks

As its name suggests, the Task Scheduler allows you to schedule tasks to be accomplished automatically. Programs can be scheduled using a variety of criteria such as time, date, or if the computer is idle. Windows 98 has several scheduled tasks automatically installed, as shown in Figure 11-12.

FIGURE 11-11

The Compression Agent dialog window

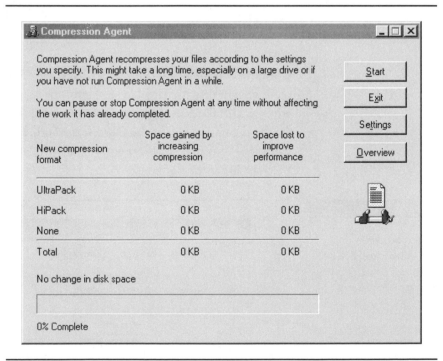

FIGURE 11-12

Default Scheduled Tasks
in Windows 98

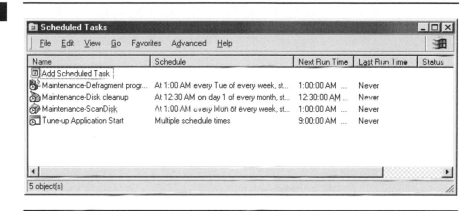

Scheduling a task is very easy. A wizard guides you through the process.
In the last section I mentioned that you could schedule the Compression
Agent to run automatically by using the Task Scheduler. Exercise 11-6 gives
you the opportunity to set up a scheduled task using the Compression Agent.

EXERCISE 11-6

Scheduling a Task Using the Task Scheduler

1. Select the Start button and select Programs | Accessories | System
Tools | Scheduled Tasks.

2. Click Add Scheduled Task in the Scheduled Tasks window. The
Scheduled Task Wizard starts.

3. Click the Next button.

4. Highlight Compression Agent from the scroll-down list.

5. Click the Next button.

6. Toggle the radio button to the left of Weekly.

7. Click the Next button.

8. Place 4:40 PM in the Start Time dialog box.

9. Place a check mark in the box to the left of Sunday.

10. Click the Next button.

11. Click the Finish button.

A new task appears in the Scheduled Tasks window, signifying the successful addition of the Compression Agent, as shown in Figure 11-13. If you want to delete the task, then highlight it and press the DEL key.

Drive Converter (FAT32)

A method of optimizing the amount of hard disk space being utilized by Windows 98 is to convert a FAT16 drive to FAT32 using the Drive Converter (FAT32) utility. FAT32 provides several enhancements over FAT16.

■   FAT32 supports drive sizes up to 2 terabytes in size.

■   FAT32 uses smaller clusters, so it uses hard disk space more efficiently. For example, it uses 4KB clusters for drives up to 8GB in size, whereas FAT16 uses 32KB clusters for 2GB drives.

■   FAT32 has the capability of using the backup copy of the File Allocation Table instead of the default copy.

■   FAT32's smaller cluster sizes allow applications to load up to 50 percent faster.

It is easy to convert a FAT16 drive to FAT32. The conversion utility can be found at Programs | Accessories | System Tools | Drive Converter (FAT32). Once you start the utility you need to pick a drive to convert, as

---

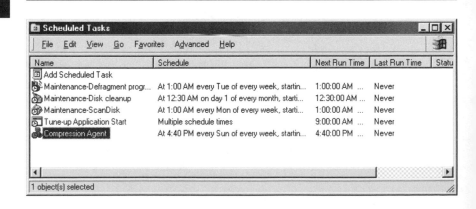

shown in Figure 11-14. Notice that the utility is smart enough to determine which drives have already been converted to FAT32.

After the Drive Converter has finished converting a hard disk from FAT16 to FAT32, the Disk Defragmenter utility will run. Let it finish uninterrupted. If you don't, then the drive will be slower and less efficient than prior to converting the drive to FAT32.

exam
ⓦatch

The Drive Converter Wizard is a one-way converter. It converts from FAT16 to FAT32 but it cannot convert a drive from FAT32 back to FAT16. Windows 98 does not include any utility to perform a conversion from FAT32 to FAT16.

System Configuration Utility

The System Configuration Utility included in Windows 98 can be used to modify the system configuration so that you can resolve problems and optimize your system startup. It provides a GUI to the Windows 98 startup files, as shown in Figure 11-15.

FIGURE 11-14

Picking a drive to convert to FAT32

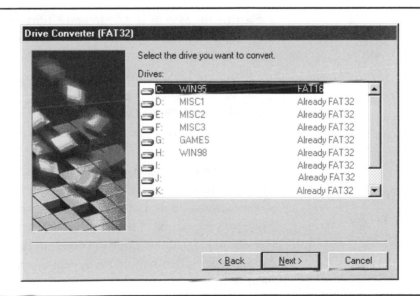

FIGURE 11-15

The General tab of the System Configuration utility

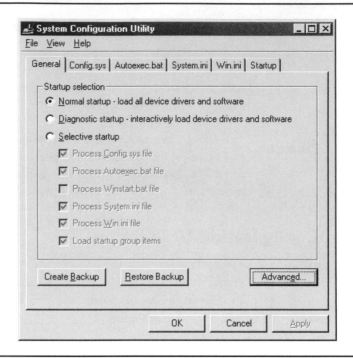

Starting the System Configuration Utility isn't as easy as other utilities that we have used in this chapter. You have probably noticed that we have used several tools from the System Tools submenu, but is the System Configuration Utility listed there? As you see, it is not listed on the System Tools submenu, but we can get to it from another tool listed there. First you need to select Programs | Accessories | System Tools | System Information. After System Information starts, you choose System Configuration Utility from the Tools menu.

The System Configuration utility consists of six tabs, of which four are for startup files such as AUTOEXEC.BAT and SYSTEM.INI. The General tab has a provision for backing up the system files, and the Startup tab allows you the capability of changing items that start when your system is booting. My system has nothing in the Startup group, but Figure 11-16 shows the items that start on my system during bootup. You may be able to optimize your system by preventing some of these items from starting. Just

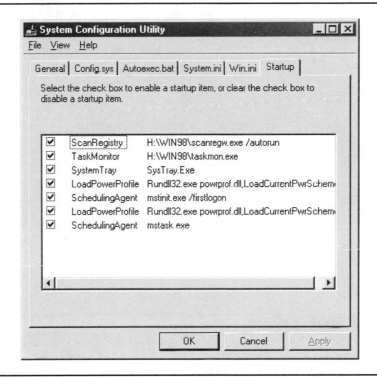

FIGURE 11-16

The Startup tab of the
System Configuration
utility

be careful, as you may cause other problems on your system. For example, if
you use Scheduled Tasks, it isn't wise to stop the SchedulingAgent. You
may speed up your booting of the system by a few seconds, but none of
your scheduled tasks will complete.

Windows Update

Windows Update is a Web-based utility that helps to make sure that your
Windows 98 configuration is current. It is a one-stop shop for maintaining
your system with the newest device drivers and system software.

Windows Update scans your system and compares its findings to the
versions of files located on the master server at the Microsoft Windows
Update Web site. Windows Update notifies you of the updates that are
applicable to your system. Any drivers that are installed by Windows

Update are listed on the Install/Uninstall tab of the Add/Remove Programs applet in Control Panel.

Windows Update is an ActiveX control, so it requires a browser that supports ActiveX controls. It can be started by choosing the shortcut from the Start menu. The shortcut will open your default browser and dial-up networking to establish a connection to the Windows Update Web site. As long as your default browser supports ActiveX controls you should have no problem connecting to the site. You may be prompted to install an updated version of the ActiveX control so be sure to do that. After connecting to the Web site, select Product Updates from the left frame and see what updates are available for your system. There are several categories of product updates that may appear: critical updates, recommended updates, and device drivers. Figure 11-17 shows two recommended updates that are selected to be installed using Windows Update.

FIGURE 11-17

Retrieving two recommended updates using the Windows Update utility

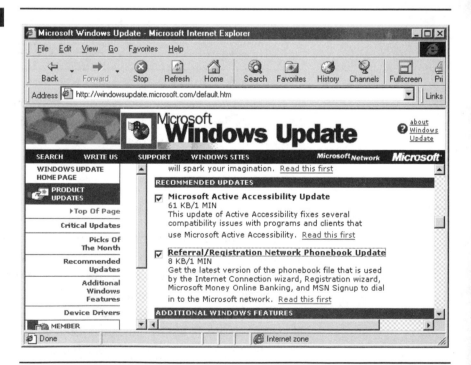

Signature Verification Tool

The Signature Verification Tool is used to decide whether or not a file has been signed by Microsoft with a digital signature. If the file is signed, it signifies that the file has not been altered since the digital signature was applied to it. The Signature Verification tool can be used to:

- Search for signed files in an exact location
- Search for unsigned files in an exact location
- View the certificates of signed files

Figure 11-18 shows the certificate for a signed file verifying that the file has not been tampered with.

Perform Exercise 11-7 to verify certificates on signed files on your system.

FIGURE 11-18

The Details tab of
Certificate Properties
showing the certificate
is valid

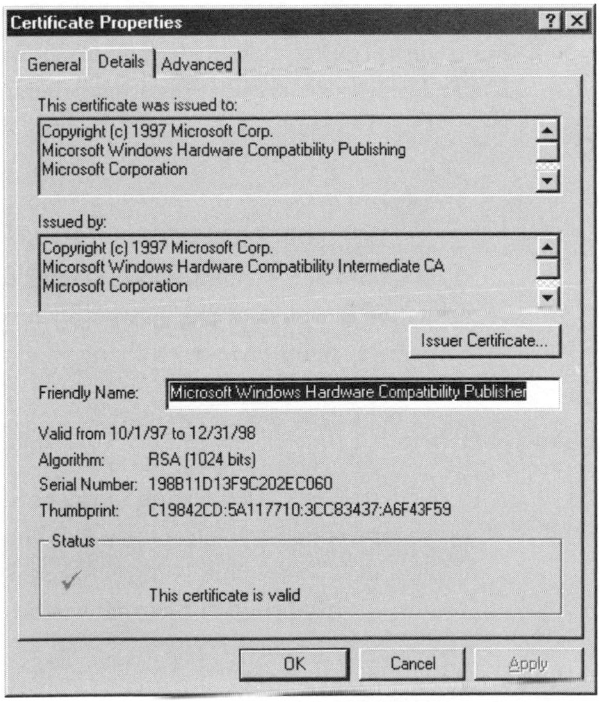

EXERCISE 11-7

Using the Signature Verification Tool

1. Select the Start button and choose Programs | Accessories | System Tools | System Information.

2. Select Signature Verification Tool from the Tools menu.

3. Select Signed Files from the Look For drop-down list.

4. Select the drive that is home to your WINDOWS folder from the Look In drop-down list.

5. Click the Find Now button.

6. Scroll down the list and highlight WSOCK32.DLL.

7. Click the Details button. Information will be displayed showing whether the file has been altered after it was signed.

Maintenance Wizard

The Maintenance Wizard can be used to enhance the speed of your applications, check your hard disk for errors, and free up space on your hard disk. You're probably wondering how it performs these miracles, aren't you? The wizard actually uses other programs to accomplish these feats, such as Disk Defragmenter, ScanDisk, and Disk Cleanup. It creates a scheduled task using the Task Scheduler, based upon input you provide as shown in Figure 11-19.

The Maintenance Wizard is started by selecting Programs | Accessories | System Tools | Maintenance Wizard from the Start menu. When it is first started it will prompt you with a window asking whether you want to perform maintenance, or change the maintenance settings or schedule.

Disk Cleanup

I referred to Disk Cleanup in the previous section on the Maintenance Wizard. The Disk Cleanup Wizard helps to free up disk space on your hard disk. It searches your drive and lists temporary files, cache files, and unnecessary program files that can be safely deleted. Disk Cleanup is started

FIGURE 11-19

Tasks configured to be
performed using the
Maintenance Wizard

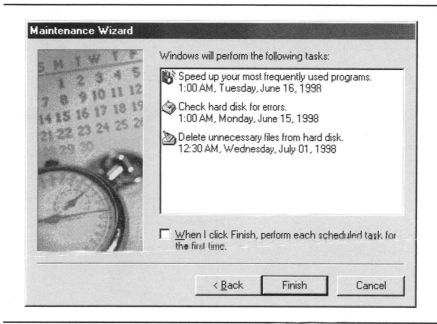

by selecting Programs | Accessories | System Tools | Disk Cleanup from the
Start menu. After it is started it will prompt you for the drive to clean up.
Once it has scanned the selected drive, it will report the space that can be
saved, as shown in Figure 11-20.

Selecting the More Options tab of Disk Cleanup gives you the
opportunity to remove Windows components and/or installed programs
to free up even more disk space. Placing a check mark in the box on the
Settings tab will make Disk Cleanup automatically run when the drive runs
low on disk space.

System File Checker

Another tool that helps you to make sure that your system is running
optimally is the System File Checker. Just as its name implies, this tool
checks system files to make sure that they are not corrupt by verifying their

FIGURE 11-20

Disk Cleanup displaying
the amount of disk space
to be gained

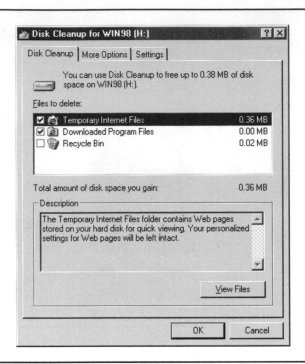

integrity. If the System File Checker encounters a corrupt file, it notifies
you and offers to restore it with a valid copy of the file. It can also scan for
missing or changed files. Other things that the System File Checker can
accomplish: customizing search criteria based on file extension, creating a
new verification file, and choosing a different verification data file.

Figure 11-21 shows the System File Checker after it has first been
started. Notice that you can scan for altered files or extract one file from the
installation disk. Exercise 11-8 gives you the chance to run the System File
Checker on your system to make sure that no files are corrupt.

FROM THE CLASSROOM

Freeing Disk Space

Microsoft provides a number of ways for you to free up disk space on your hard disk. Listed next are some of the common approaches, and a way to automate them.

- Convert to FAT32 using Drive Converter
- Compress using DriveSpace 3
- Delete files using Disk Cleanup
- Correct errors using ScanDisk

Drive Converter (FAT32) converts your drives from the standard File Allocation Table (FAT) to FAT32. FAT32 is a very efficient system for storing files on large disk drives (over 512MB). Converting to FAT32 may create some free disk space. When I converted a 1.3GB hard disk to FAT32, I recovered almost 400MB of storage space. Even if your results aren't that dramatic, they will certainly be noticeable.

DriveSpace 3 can be used to compress both hard and floppy disks. Compression greatly increases the storage space for files. However, you cannot compress drives that use FAT32. You will also sacrifice a little bit of CPU performance, because data must be compressed and uncompressed on its way to and from the hard disk. Compression may not be a good solution for 486-class machines.

Disk Cleanup helps you free up space on your hard disk by removing unneeded files. Disk Cleanup searches your drive, then lists temporary files, Internet cache files, and unnecessary program files that you can safely delete. I'm still a little uncomfortable with my computer deciding what it needs and what it doesn't, but I will admit that as far as I know, my system hasn't deleted anything I really needed. If it has, it hasn't admitted it.

One last thing you should do periodically is run ScanDisk to detect any errors, like lost clusters, that may be taking up valuable disk space. ScanDisk will detect and correct many problems with your file systems.

Once you are familiar with how these utilities work, you should consider automating them with the Maintenance Wizard. The Maintenance Wizard helps you get the best performance from your system. You can run Maintenance Wizard to make your programs run faster, check your hard disk for problems, and free hard disk space. For example, by leaving your computer on overnight, you can schedule these utilities to run at a specified time each night, once a week, or another interval of your choice. By scheduling these utilities to run on a regular basis, you can be sure that your computer is performing at its best.

—*By Robert Aschermann, MCT, MCSE*

FIGURE 11-21

The System File Checker
ready to scan for altered
files

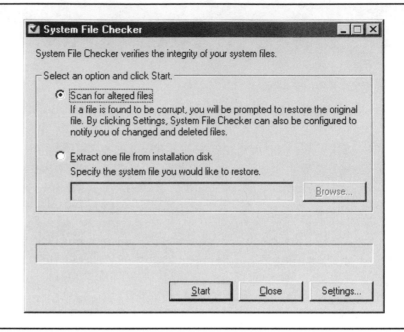

EXERCISE 11-8

Using the System File Checker

1. Select the Start button and choose Programs | Accessories | System Tools | System Information.

2. Select System File Checker from the Tools menu.

3. Make sure that the radio button to the left of Scan For Altered Files is selected.

4. Click the Start button. Be sure to watch for any dialog box that may prompt you for action.

The System File Checker scans your system using a file named DEFAULT.SFC. The DEFAULT.SFC file is copied from the Windows 98 media when the operating system is installed. DEFAULT.SFC contains Cyclical Redundancy Check (CRC), date, time, version, and size information for each of the system files.

Registry Checker

The last tool that we are going to discuss in this chapter is the Registry Checker. The Registry Checker is used to find and resolve problems with the Registry, and to back up the Registry regularly.

The Registry Checker automatically runs every time your computer is started. It checks for inconsistent structures, and if it does not find any, it will perform a compressed backup of the Registry. The Registry Checker will make one backup per day, and maintain the last five compressed backups. The name of the backup file created is RB*xxx*.CAB. The *xxx* in the filename is a unique number assigned when the file is generated.

The Registry Checker actually consists of two executable files, SCANREG.EXE and SCANREGW.EXE. Both ScanReg and ScanRegW use settings from the SCANREG.INI file. Figure 11-22 shows the default SCANREG.INI file.

FIGURE 11-22

Setting in the default
SCANREG.INI file

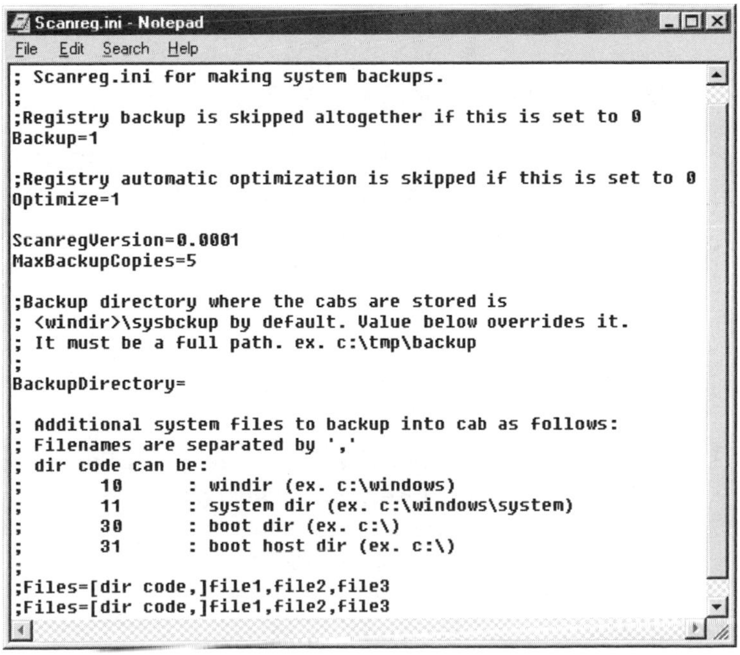

```
Scanreg.ini - Notepad
File  Edit  Search  Help

; Scanreg.ini for making system backups.

;Registry backup is skipped altogether if this is set to 0
Backup=1

;Registry automatic optimization is skipped if this is set to 0
Optimize=1

ScanregVersion=0.0001
MaxBackupCopies=5

;Backup directory where the cabs are stored is
; <windir>\sysbckup by default. Value below overrides it.
; It must be a full path. ex. c:\tmp\backup
;
BackupDirectory=

; Additional system files to backup into cab as follows:
; Filenames are separated by ','
; dir code can be:
;      10      : windir (ex. c:\windows)
;      11      : system dir (ex. c:\windows\system)
;      30      : boot dir (ex. c:\)
;      31      : boot host dir (ex. c:\)
;
;Files=[dir code,]file1,file2,file3
;Files=[dir code,]file1,file2,file3
```

ScanReg

ScanReg is an MS-DOS-based program. It is run if ScanRegW encounters a problem with the Registry. ScanRegW prompts you to restart the computer and that invokes ScanReg to be run. ScanReg will restore the Registry from a good backup, or it will repair the current Registry if no good backups are available. It also can be used to optimize the Registry if ScanRegW detects the need for optimization. ScanReg will optimize the Registry during the next system startup.

ScanRegW

ScanRegW is a Windows-based program. ScanRegW scans the Registry for problems and determines if it needs to be optimized. If it encounters no corruption, it will back up the following system files:

- USER.DAT
- SYSTEM.DAT
- WIN.INI
- SYSTEM.INI

The scan is performed automatically during each system startup, but it can be invoked manually if you want to force a scan and backup of the four files mentioned. It is started manually by choosing Registry Checker from the Tools menu of System Information. ScanRegW backs up the Registry and other system files to the C:\WINDOWS\SYSBCKUP folder in a compressed .CAB file. To differentiate between ScanRegW and ScanReg, take a look at Table 11-5. It compares the two programs that make up the Registry Checker.

exam
Ⓦatch

Remember that to restore an earlier version of the Registry you must use ScanReg, not ScanRegW.

TABLE 11-5	Item	ScanRegW	ScanReg
	Operating System	Windows	MS-DOS
Comparing the Differences Between ScanRegW and ScanReg	Mode	Protected mode	Real mode
	Scans Registry	Yes	Yes
	Fixes Registry	No	Yes
	Backs up the Registry	Yes	Yes
	Runs in Safe Mode	Yes	No
	Compresses the Backup	Yes	No
	Automatically Runs	Yes, each time the computer is started	Yes, if a Registry problem is detected by ScanRegW
	Restores the Registry	No	Yes

Optimizing Windows 98 Networking

Windows 98 automatically optimizes several system parameters in regards to network performance. For example, it changes network time-out values to fit varying local area network (LAN) topologies.

Normally it is not necessary to manually optimize any settings to enhance network performance, but there are steps that you can take to make sure that your Windows 98 system is operating as efficiently on the network as is possible. Some of the items to optimize are:

■ Make sure that you use a 32-bit Protected mode network client. A Protected mode network client can take advantage of caching and other automatic tuning features controlled by Windows 98.

■ Only use the protocols necessary to function on the network. Unnecessary protocols create additional system overhead, which consumes additional memory and slows down network connections.

■ Remove Dial-Up Networking if you do not have a modem installed in your system.

■ Use the network adapter drivers provided with Windows 98, as well as a new 32-bit network adapter. Using a new 32-bit network adapter can really improve network performance over an older 16-bit network adapter card.

CERTIFICATION SUMMARY

Two methods of monitoring the performance of your system are to use Net Watcher and System Monitor. If your system is on a network and is running more slowly than normal, Net Watcher can tell you if it is the network causing it to be slow. If you use the System Monitor prior to making changes to your system, it is useful in seeing if the changes you made enhance performance or are detrimental.

Windows 98 uses a combination of physical memory and virtual memory. The virtual memory file is dynamic, so it grows and shrinks as necessary. Performance in Windows 98 can be enhanced by moving the virtual memory file to the fastest, least-used hard disk drive in your system.

File system performance can be modified for several hardware items in your system. Items that can be modified include hard disk drives, CD-ROM drives, and removable drives such as Syquest SparQ and Iomega JAZ.

Windows 98 includes several utilities to optimize the performance of your system. Some of these utilities are the Disk Defragmenter, ScanDisk, Task Scheduler, Drive Converter (FAT32), Maintenance Wizard, and Disk Cleanup.

 # TWO-MINUTE DRILL

❑ There are several factors that can affect system performance.

❑ Some factors that can affect system performance include the virtual memory settings, the performance of the file system, and network settings.

❑ In order for you to increase the performance of your system you need to monitor the system to see what is causing it not to operate at its peak efficiency. Windows 98 includes two tools that help you to monitor your system, Net Watcher and System Monitor.

❑ Net Watcher allows you to monitor and manage connections to shared resources as well as to create, add, and delete shared resources.

❑ System Monitor is a tool you can use to help determine the cause of problems on your system by measuring the performance of hardware, software services, and applications.

❑ System Monitor has several categories available to monitor, including File System, Memory Manager, and Kernel.

❑ The virtual memory file is used by Windows 98 to store information that is not currently needed in physical memory.

❑ The virtual memory file for Windows 98 is named WIN386.SWP and it is dynamic in nature.

❑ One of the best ways of optimizing virtual memory on Windows 98 is to make sure that the hard disk drive that is home to WIN386.SWP has plenty of free space available so that the virtual memory file can grow and shrink as necessary.

❑ If you completely disable virtual memory, the system may not start properly; or if it does start, then performance may be hindered.

❑ Some factors that can affect the performance of the file system in your system are hard disk drives, CD-ROM drives, and removable disk drives.

❑ Windows 98 allows you to optimize file system and disk performance by choosing the profile that best meets the role that the computer is fulfilling. The three profiles are:

   ❑ Desktop computer

   ❑ Mobile or docking system

   ❑ Network server

❑ The values for each profile type are located at the following Registry subkey: HKEY_LOCAL_MACHINE\SOFTWARE\ MICROSOFT\WINDOWS\CURRENTVERSION\FS TEMPLATES.

❑ The settings for the profile type in use are located at the following Registry subkey: HKEY_LOCAL_MACHINE\SYSTEM\ CURRENTCONTROLSET\CONTROL\FILESYSTEM.

❑ You can also optimize the performance of your CD-ROM file system if your system has a CD-ROM drive. The amount of cache that is used for the CD-ROM cache is dependent on the speed of your CD-ROM drive.

❑ Windows 98 includes support for DVD disk drives. DVD disk drives utilize the Universal Disk Format (UDF) as their file system.

❑ Windows 98 includes the capability to enhance the performance of different types of removable disk drives by enabling write-behind caching.

❑ The Disk Defragmenter is a useful tool for optimizing your hard disk drive because it will take the noncontiguous data and place it back into a contiguous space.

❑ ScanDisk is a utility included with Windows 98 that is used to perform analysis and repair on disk drives.

❑ Windows 98 includes DriveSpace 3, which can be used to compress disk drives, as well as manage drives that have been compressed with DriveSpace 3 or DoubleSpace.

❑ The Task Scheduler allows you to schedule tasks to be accomplished automatically.

❑ A method of optimizing the amount of hard disk space being utilized by Windows 98 is to convert a FAT16 drive to FAT32 using the Drive Converter (FAT32) utility.

❑ The Drive Converter Wizard is a one-way converter. It converts from FAT16 to FAT32 but it cannot convert a drive from FAT32 back to FAT16. Windows 98 does not include any utility to perform a conversion from FAT32 to FAT16.

❑ The System Configuration Utility included in Windows 98 can be used to modify the system configuration so that you can resolve problems and optimize your system startup.

❑ Windows Update is a Web-based utility that helps to make sure that your Windows 98 configuration is current.

❑ The Signature Verification Tool is used to decide whether or not a file has been signed by Microsoft with a digital signature.

❑ The Maintenance Wizard can be used to enhance the speed of your applications, check your hard disk for errors, and free up space on your hard disk.

❑ The Disk Cleanup Wizard helps to free up disk space on your hard disk.

❑ The System File Checker checks system files to make sure that they are not corrupt by verifying their integrity.

❑ The Registry Checker is used to find and resolve problems with the Registry, and to back up the Registry regularly.

❑ Remember that to restore an earlier version of the Registry you must use ScanReg, not ScanRegW.

❑ Windows 98 automatically optimizes several system parameters in regards to network performance.

SELF TEST

The following questions will help you measure your understanding of the material presented in this chapter. Read all the choices carefully, as there may be more than one correct answer. Choose all correct answers for each question.

1. What tool is available to make sure that the most current system files are on your system?

   A. ScanRegW

   B. Maintenance Wizard

   C. Windows Update

   D. System Monitor

2. Your system is acting funny and you think that there may be some missing files in the C:\WINDOWS folder. What tool can you use to verify that no system files are missing?

   A. System Configuration Utility

   B. System Verification Utility

   C. System File Checker

   D. Registry Checker

3. What executable file(s) make up the Registry Checker?

   A. RegScanW

   B. RegScan

   C. ScanRegW

   D. ScanReg

4. What role should a Windows 98 computer be configured for, if it runs on a battery?

   A. Desktop computer

   B. Mobile or docking station

   C. Network server

   D. It doesn't matter

5. You notice lots of activity while using System Monitor to watch Memory Manager:Discards and Memory Manager:Page Faults. What can be causing all the activity?

   A. There is not enough virtual memory in the system

   B. There is not enough physical memory in the system

   C. There is not enough Level 10 cache in the system

   D. The memory is not fast enough for the system

6. What is the name of the file Windows 98 uses for virtual memory?

   A. WIN386.SWP

   B. PAGEFILE.SYS

   C. SWAPPER.DAT

   D. 386SPART.PAR

7. What tool is used to check the physical surface of your hard disk?

   A. Disk Defragmenter

   B. System Monitor

   C. System Verification Utility

   D. ScanDisk

8. What file(s) does Disk Cleanup remove from your system?

   A. Temporary Internet files

   B. Downloaded program files

   C. Duplicate system files

   D. Files in the Recycle Bin

9. What file runs automatically each time Windows 98 starts?

   A. System Monitor

   B. System File Checker

   C. Windows Update

   D. ScanRegW

10. How many backups of the Registry does the Registry Checker keep by default?

    A. 3

    B. 4

    C. 5

    D. 6

11. What type of component is Windows Update?

    A. Java

    B. VBscript

    C. JavaScript

    D. ActiveX

12. What tool lets you know if a file has been altered since it was signed?

    A. Signature Verification Tool

    B. Signature Configuration Tool

    C. Signature File Checker

    D. Signature Monitor

13. What tool can be used to modify system startup?

    A. System Verification Utility

    B. System File Checker

    C. System Configuration Utility

    D. System Monitor

14. Which of these files are backed up by the Registry Checker?

    A. SYSTEM.INI

    B. USER.DAT

    C. WIN.INI

    D. SYSTEM.DAT

15. What extension is on the compressed file created by the Registry Checker?

    A. .REG

    B. .CMP

    C. .RAC

    D. .CAB

MICROSOFT CERTIFIED SYSTEMS ENGINEER

12

Troubleshooting Windows 98

CERTIFICATION OBJECTIVES

Microsoft has the ability to change a situation when there is a problem. They can go into the operating system or application, change the code, and voilà!—no problem. When the rest of us have a problem, we have to use the resources available. That's what troubleshooting is: using knowledge and tools to diagnose and solve a problem.

It is not by accident that the troubleshooting items are always the last ones listed in the Microsoft Certification objectives for any given test. Indeed, the troubleshooting objective will test everything you have learned to this point, and will show up on the exam in numerous scenario questions. It is almost as if Microsoft is saying, "Now that you have learned the material, do you know how to apply it?" In this chapter, you will prepare for the Troubleshooting Windows 98 objective. We will start by diagnosing installation failures, then look at resource access problems, and finish by looking at what to do when Registry files are corrupt.

CERTIFICATION OBJECTIVE 12.01

Installation Failures

There are actually two types of installation failures. There are the kinds where it seems everything goes wrong. The machine will not boot off the hard disk—it seems the computer has been turned into a paperweight. The computer will not load DOS, it will not load Windows, and it seems to be dead. On these occasions, it is helpful to have a bootable floppy disk. Fortunately, these occurrences are rare, as the Windows 98 setup routine works very well. In the other type of installation failure, the computer is able to boot up into Windows 98, but devices are not properly configured. Perhaps there are some resource conflicts and some drivers do not load, but at least the machine will load Windows. The good news here is that Windows 98 has some great tools for resolving these situations. Let us look at the log files created by Windows 98 installation to assist in our troubleshooting efforts.

Setup Logs

The Windows 98 Setup program creates two log files during the hardware detection process (SETUPLOG.TXT, and DETLOG.TXT), and other log files (NETLOG.TXT and BOOTLOG.TXT) as Windows 98 starts up the first time. The following sections look at these files in detail

SETUPLOG.TXT

SETUPLOG.TXT is a text file that contains setup information used by Windows 98 during installation. As Windows 98 installs, entries are recorded in this text file for each step in sequence. This file shows error conditions encountered during the process. The Windows 98 Setup program uses it in case of setup failure, and you can use it to troubleshoot errors during the installation process as well. As you can see in Figure 12-1, SETUPLOG.TXT is a large file, and must be loaded into WordPad to be

SETUPLOG.TXT provides great troubleshooting information in the event of an installation crash

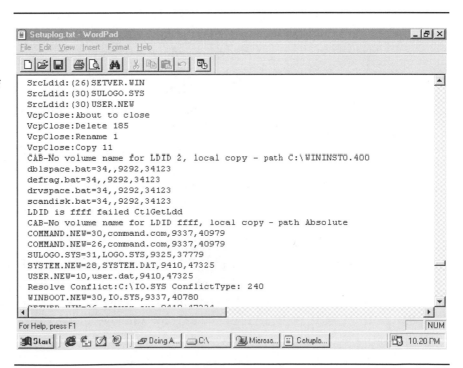

viewed. It does provide vital information for determining the cause of a failed installation of Windows 98.

The Windows 98 Setup program uses the entries in SETUPLOG.TXT to ensure that Setup does not bomb twice on the same problem. When you restart Windows 98 Setup after a failure, Setup reviews the file to see which process started, but did not complete successfully. These processes are skipped, and the next process in sequence is run. Setup also uses DETLOG.TXT and DETCRASH.LOG to skip any hardware detection modules that failed.

DETLOG.TXT

DETLOG.TXT is also a text file. This file contains a record of all devices found during the hardware detection phase of installation. All the parameters are identified and recorded for each device detected during this phase.

If the hardware detection phase causes the computer to freeze or lock up, a binary file named DETCRASH.LOG is created. While DETLOG.TXT is an ASCII file that you can read, the Windows 98 Setup program reads the binary information in DETCRASH.LOG to determine what steps successfully completed. DETCRASH.LOG is not a file you would be able to read using a text editor such as Notepad.

DETLOG.TXT is stored as a hidden file on the computer's root directory. As you can see in Figure 12-2, information is added to this file in the same order as the hardware detection phase. If you need to find out what caused Windows 98 Setup to fail or lock up, look at the entries at the bottom of this file before running Setup again. The information contained in this file can save you hours of frustration and tedium wrestling with some off-brand unsupported device.

DETCRASH.LOG

DETCRASH.LOG is a binary file that is only of use during the hardware detection phase of Windows 98 Setup. It is used to track the progress of hardware detection in case a device caused Setup to crash. You cannot read this file; it is used only by Windows. If you needed to do any

FIGURE 12-2

DETLOG.TXT provides troubleshooting information on the detection of devices during installation

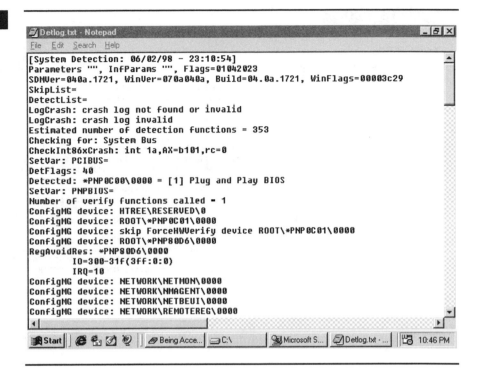

```
Detlog.txt - Notepad                                                    _ 8 x
File   Edit   Search   Help
[System Detection: 06/02/98 - 23:10:54]
Parameters "", InfParams "", Flags=01042023
SDMVer=040a.1721, WinVer=070a040a, Build=04.0a.1721, WinFlags=00003c29
SkipList=
DetectList=
LogCrash: crash log not found or invalid
LogCrash: crash log invalid
Estimated number of detection functions = 353
Checking for: System Bus
CheckInt86xCrash: int 1a,AX=b101,rc=0
SetVar: PCIBUS=
DetFlags: 40
Detected: *PNP0C00\0000 = [1] Plug and Play BIOS
SetVar: PNPBIOS=
Number of verify functions called = 1
ConfigMG device: HTREE\RESERVED\0
ConfigMG device: ROOT\*PNP0C01\0000
ConfigMG device: skip ForceHWVerify device ROOT\*PNP0C01\0000
ConfigMG device: ROOT\*PNP80D6\0000
RegAvoidRes: *PNP80D6\0000
        IO=300-31f(3ff:0:0)
        IRQ=10
ConfigMG device: NETWORK\NETMON\0000
ConfigMG device: NETWORK\NMAGENT\0000
ConfigMG device: NETWORK\NETBEUI\0000
ConfigMG device: NETWORK\REMOTEREG\0000
```

Start | 🎮 🎮 🎮 🎮 | Being Acce... | C:\ | Microsoft S... | Detlog.txt - ... | 10:46 PM

troubleshooting of hardware detection, you would use DETLOG.TXT, not DETCRASH.LOG. Do not get these two files confused.

NETLOG.TXT

NETLOG.TXT is another text file that lists all the network components detected during installation. There are four distinct steps to the network detection phase. These steps can be compared to the four class types of network configuration: network clients, network protocols, network adapters, and network services (such as file and print sharing).

This file is a non-hidden file stored in the root directory of the computer. Information is written to this file in the same order as the network detection phase. If you are troubleshooting networking problems resulting from the Windows 98 Setup program, then look at the entries in this file. As shown in Figure 12-3, NETLOG.TXT provides information as to how Windows

FIGURE 12-3

Troubleshooting
networking problems
often leads you to
NETLOG.TXT

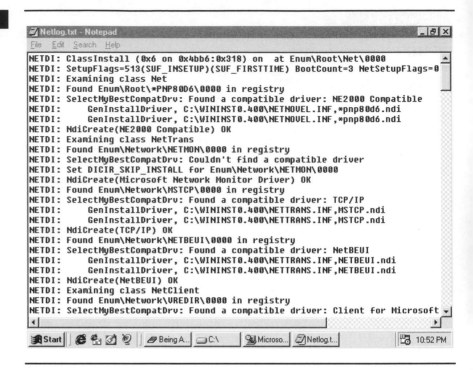

98 detected your network interface card. This can often provides clues for troubleshooting a particularly vexatious network adapter.

BOOTLOG.TXT

BOOTLOG.TXT is a text file that contains a record of the current startup process when starting Windows 98. When Windows 98 starts for the first time, this file is automatically created. This file records the Windows 98 components and drivers as they are loaded and initialized, and records the status of each step.

The information in BOOTLOG.TXT is written in sequence during startup. If an error occurs, you might need to examine it closely to determine what failed. An easy way to do this is to load BOOTLOG.TXT into Notepad and do a search for the word "fail." This way, you can quickly identify the culprit. As shown in Figure 12-4, the status of each driver is recorded in BOOTLOG.TXT.

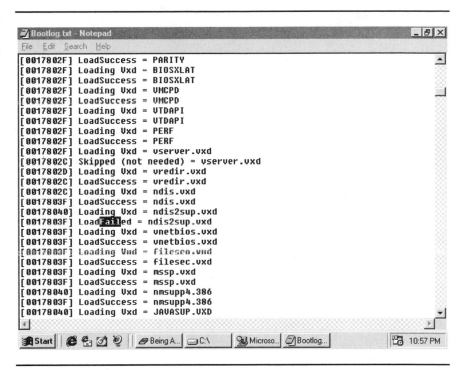

FIGURE 12-4

BOOTLOG.TXT provides aids in troubleshooting by quickly telling you which drivers are loading

This file is stored as a hidden file in the root directory of your computer. Information is added to the file during the Windows 98 startup process. If you are troubleshooting a Windows 98 failure or lockup, examine the entries within this file before restarting the computer.

Using the System Information Utility

Once you get Windows 98 to boot into graphical mode, then the troubleshooting scenario changes just a little. You are no longer forced to wade through numerous text files. Windows 98 has some very nice utilities to use to assist in troubleshooting installation. One of these new tools is the System Information Utility. The System Information Utility is located in the System Tools group under Accessories. As shown in Figure 12-5, the main screen of the System Information Utility provides a good overview of high-level information about your computer. Information such as version

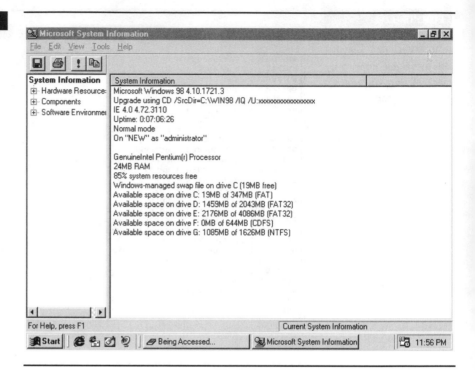

FIGURE 12-5

The System Information Utility provides both overview and detailed information for your PC

numbers, files system, and system resources are often instrumental in solving installation problems. You can also print out reports from the System Information Utility by selecting Print from the File menu. However, you need to be aware that the report is quite large and can easily go to nearly 100 pages. For historical purposes, you can also save your current configuration information to a .NFO file. (By default it will be placed in your Windows directory.) There is also a History button you can select that will display changed information from each category.

If you are having a problem with device detection from Windows 98 Setup, you will want to look at the Conflicts/Sharing section under Hardware Resources in the System Information Utility. If your system has Legacy Devices, or a limited number of resources, then it is quite possible that there are IRQ conflicts or sharing problems. As shown in Figure 12-6,

FIGURE 12-6

Conflicting hardware
devices are quickly
identified using the System
Information Utility

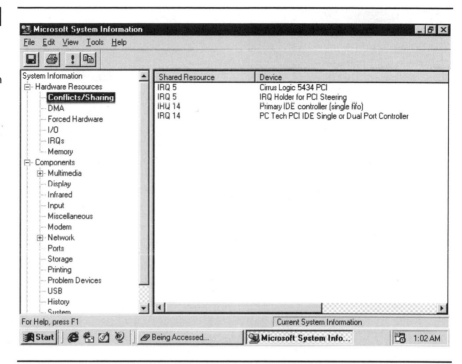

this view can quickly point out conflicting hardware resources that would
prevent the initialization of the devices.

Under the Components section, the Problem Devices lists items that
were detected but not initialized, because they are disabled manually or are
in conflict. The Advanced view details Registry entries, driver version, and
resource information. If your installation of Windows 98 is an upgrade,
then it is possible that Setup overwrote a needed driver and therefore the
device failed to initialize.

The Startup Programs section can provide illumination on an installation
failure, particularly in an upgrade situation. Armed with this information,
you can then go to the System Configuration Utility (discussed later in the
section on Boot Process Failures) and safely remove the offending program.
As you can see in Figure 12-7, this utility even tells you where in the
Registry or configuration file the program is loading from.

The System Information
Utility tells you where
startup programs are
loading from

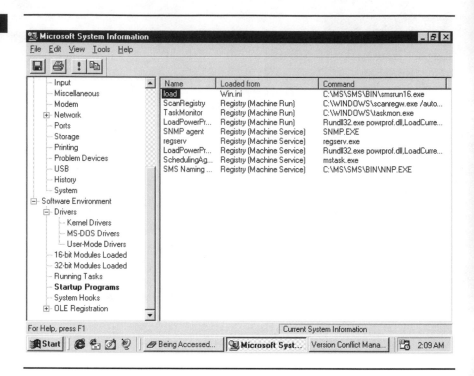

Using the Version Conflict Manager

The last item in troubleshooting installation failures is to look at the
Version Conflict Manager. This utility applies specifically to the upgrade
scenario in which a more current file was overwritten during the installation
of Windows 98. During installation, Windows 98 Setup makes backup
copies of files before overwriting them. Later, if your computer does not
start up properly, you can access the Version Conflict Manager from the
Tools menu in the System Information Utility to see what files were
replaced during installation. As you can see in Figure 12-8, the replaced files
are listed by version number. You then have the option of selecting a file
from the list and choosing Restore Selected Files. This is a very easy tool to
use, but it must be employed with discretion, as it does not tell you if things
will be made worse by replacing the installation files with your originals.

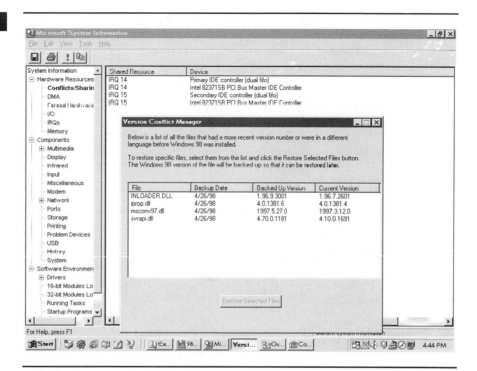

FIGURE 12-8

The Version Conflict
Manager makes it
easy to replace files
that were overwritten
during installation

CERTIFICATION OBJECTIVE 12.02

Boot Process Failures

Boot process failures are one of the more annoying problems facing users of
Windows 98, as these problems can manifest themselves in a variety of
ways. Certain drivers may fail to load, or Startup and Shutdown may seem
to take forever, or just hang indefinitely. Of course, a computer that winds
up in SafeMode is always a very real possibility as well. Therefore, what do
you do if one of these situations happens to you? Well, Windows 98 has
some improved tools for dealing with boot process failures. The System
Configuration Utility allows you to configure safely the startup and

shutdown functions of Windows 98 in an easily controlled environment. In the next section we will look at the various ways this tool can be utilized to assist us in troubleshooting Boot Process Failures in Windows 98.

System Configuration Utility

The System Configuration Utility is launched from the Tools menu of the System Information Utility, and it consists of a mere six tabs and a couple of menu items. However, within this little utility are the tools that can make you a hero to your users or clients. The General tab, shown in Figure 12-9, allows you to configure the startup routine for your computer. While it is still

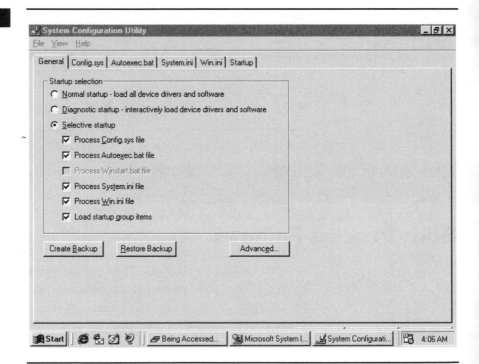

possible to press the F9 key while Windows 98 is starting, it is much more difficult to do than it was in Windows 95, because the "Starting Windows" notice is gone. You would have to watch the screen very closely to discern the exact moment to press the F9 key. Additionally, the System Configuration Utility provides a greater degree of control over the startup process than was previously available.

In the Diagnostic Startup routine, you are asked whether you want to process each of the startup files, such as CONFIG.SYS, AUTOEXEC.BAT, SYSTEM.INI, and WIN.INI. This allows you to isolate an errant driver and to duplicate the boot process problem. The Diagnostic Startup routine also gives you the option to create a new BOOTLOG.TXT (the old one will be saved as BOOTLOG.PRV). (For information on using BOOTLOG.TXT, refer to the section on Setup Logs earlier in this chapter.)

If your troubleshooting scenario has led you to suspect a particular Startup file (or the Startup group items), then you can speed the boot process along by choosing the Selective Startup button, and selecting the files to process or exclude, as appropriate to your situation. This is also an effective method for quickly testing out various startup configurations based upon selections you can make from the other tabs in the System Configuration Utility. For instance, if you need to make a change to your AUTOEXEC.BAT file, you simply select the AUTOEXEC.BAT tab, choose the line you wish to modify, and press the Edit button, as shown in Figure 12-10. If you want to boot up and not read the line at all, then you clear the check in the box, and that line will not be parsed. If you make a mistake editing one of the Startup files, all you have to do is click the Cancel button and answer No when you are prompted to save changes. As an additional precaution, you can select Create Backup from the General tab, and the System Configuration Utility will create an additional backup set of your startup files.

If you feel the problem lies with your Startup programs, then you can easily manage all your Startup programs from one place with the Startup

FIGURE 12-10

Startup files can be directly edited using the System Configuration Utility

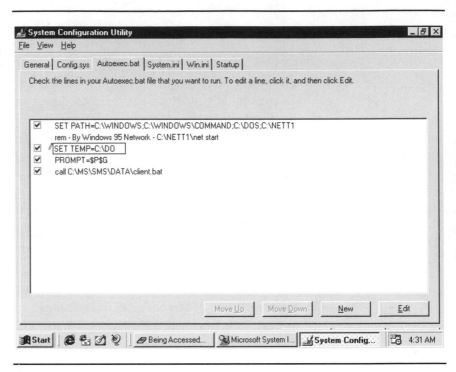

tab. This makes it very easy to remove a program and determine the effect it has on the boot process. If you need to add the program back into the Startup grouping, put the check mark back in the box. This is a lot easier than having to manually edit an assortment of text files, as was common in earlier versions of Windows.

Additional boot process control can be obtained by using the Advanced features from the General tab, shown in Figure 12-11. These features will degrade Windows 98 performance, but they are useful for troubleshooting boot problems. For instance, if a PC is hanging on shutdown, you might want to disable the Fast Shutdown feature of Windows 98, as some computers could have trouble with this feature. If you suspect a memory problem, then you might want to limit the amount of available memory by selecting that particular box, and then choosing how much memory to use. Each of the other Advanced Troubleshooting Settings can be selectively employed to assist in diagnosing problems when they arise.

FIGURE 12-11

By using the Advanced
Troubleshooting Settings,
you can customize the
behavior of your machine
as you diagnose boot
process problems

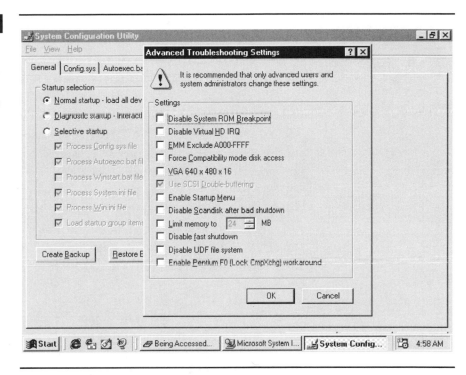

CERTIFICATION OBJECTIVE 12.03

Connectivity Problems

Nearly all of the new features of Windows 98 depend upon some kind of
connectivity. The days of the standalone PC are pretty much gone; if a
computer isn't connected to a LAN, it's almost certainly connected to the
Internet. With the widespread dependency of networks, the quick
resolution of connectivity problems is crucial.

Due to the number of people using the Internet, the protocol of choice
these days is TCP/IP. Fortunately, it is easier to troubleshoot TCP/IP issues
than it once was, due in part to the Windows 98 utility WINIPCFG.
WINIPCFG, which existed in Windows 95, has not changed much in the
current version of Windows. As explained in the next section, WINIPCFG
provides essential information in a compact format.

WINIPCFG

Typing **WINIPCFG** from the Start | Run box, launches WINIPCFG. However, since it is such a useful tool, it is a good idea to place a shortcut to it on the desktop. As seen in the default view in Figure 12-12, WINIPCFG will quickly let you view important troubleshooting information such as IP address, and Subnet mask. If a DHCP server assigns the IP address, then the first item to check is whether an IP address has been granted to the computer. If the IP address box has 0.0.0.0 listed as the IP address, then you have not obtained an address, and as a result the computer will not be able to communicate with any other machine by using TCP/IP.

Let us now look at the different information that can be obtained through WINIPCFG.EXE. The following list explains the settings and how to use them. Refer to Figure 12-12 to see where the information appears in the box.

- The drop-down box at the top of the screen lists the adapters configured in the machine. It might be an Ethernet adapter, or a modem with an IP address bound to it. A modem will be listed as simply a PPP Adapter.

- The Adapter Address for the Ethernet card is a string of unique hexadecimal numbers hard coded by the manufacturer. This number must be unique on the network for proper communication to take

---

FIGURE 12-12

WINIPCFG indicates at a glance whether IP communication will be possible

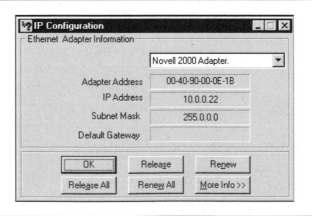

place. You will sometimes see the Adapter Address referred to as simply the Ethernet address, or the MAC (Media Access Control) address. If the adapter is a modem, then a bogus number displays in this box, because a modem does not have such a number assigned to it.

■ The IP Address is a set of four decimal-separated values bound to the previous adapter to enable communication between machines using this protocol. This number is either manually assigned to the machine when the TCP/IP is configured, or dynamically allocated when the computer is connected to the network.

■ The Subnet Mask is assigned when TCP/IP is configured. A subnet mask tells the computer whether the address of another machine is on the same network, or if it is on a remote network. Every machine using TCP/IP must have a subnet mask assigned to it.

■ When the subnet mask indicates a particular destination is on a remote network, then the Default Gateway is used in order to gain access to a remote network.

By pressing the More Info button in WINIPCFG, you gain information about lease TTL (Time To Live), DHCP servers, and other information, as shown in Figure 12-13. Please refer to the figure as we discuss the use of these items.

■ The Host Name (seen at the top of the IP Configuration box in Figure 12-13) is the name that identifies your computer on the network. It is configured under Network Properties in Control Panel, and must be unique to avoid conflict on the network.

■ The DNS Servers (second block from top) identifies the server that provides name resolution for your machine. This server keeps a list of IP addresses and domain names for the network. For instance, a DNS Server allows you to send message traffic to microsoft.com, instead of having to type in the IP address for it. If you are able to connect to a machine by typing in the IP address, but not by typing in the domain name, then you have a name resolution problem.

FIGURE 12-13

By pressing the More
Info button on WINIPCFG,
you gain access to
additional features

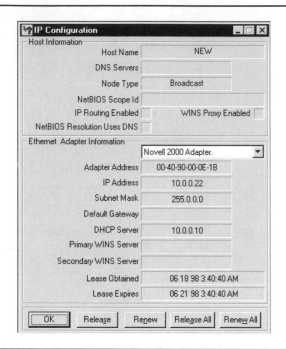

- In a routed Windows NT environment, WINS provides name resolution similar to the DNS server listed previously. It maintains a database of computer names and maps them to IP addresses. In Figure 12-13, the two WINS Server blocks list the IP addresses of the Primary and Secondary WINS Server. If you are able to connect to a machine by typing in the IP address, but not by typing in the machine name, then you might take a look at your WINS Server settings.

- If the IP address is dynamically allocated from a DHCP server, then lease information is displayed in the two boxes near the bottom of the WINIPCFG box. When the server grants you an IP address for your machine, it also sets an expiration time for the address. This allows computers to share a limited number of IP addresses. When one computer leaves the network, the address is still reserved for it until it either is released by the computer, or expires due to age. It must be renewed before the address lease expires or else the PC will drop off the network. If you are having sporadic connectivity using TCP/IP, it might be due to the settings for lease expiration. The lease duration can be adjusted on the server, depending on your particular situation.

■ The Release, Renew, Release All, and Renew All buttons are helpful in troubleshooting IP address leasing problems. You can release the address, reboot the machine, and see if it picks up the address again. In addition, you can attempt to renew the address and see if you are able to obtain a renewal of your lease.

Net Watcher

One of the more underrated utilities in Windows 98 (and Windows 95) is Net Watcher. While Net Watcher will allow you to remotely administer a Windows 98 server, it is also a very useful troubleshooting tool for connectivity issues. In Figure 12-14 we can immediately see who is

---

FIGURE 12-14

Net Watcher enables you to see at a glance what resources are shared, and who is connected to them

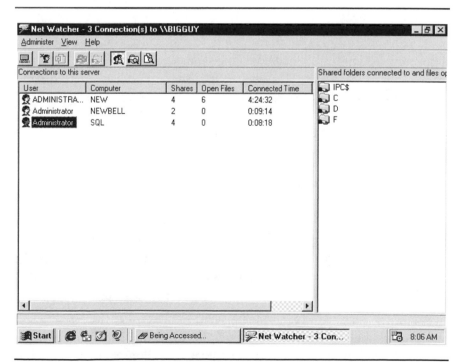

connected to a particular machine. Therefore, if one machine is able to connect, but another computer cannot connect, you can begin looking at the configuration of the machine that is having trouble (after you have verified rights and permissions on the server machine).

CERTIFICATION OBJECTIVE 12.04

Printing Problems

Printer problems can be frustrating, mainly because a problem isn't noticed until you need to print something, and that something is usually important and time sensitive! Fortunately, most of the time, these problems are ones that other professionals have experienced. I say this is fortunate, because that means the solution has been documented, which allows you to benefit from others' experience.

Problems with specific printers are documented in the PRINTERS.TXT file on the Windows 98 compact disc. This file provides information about troubleshooting issues associated with the latest printers and Windows 98.

Usually, though, printer problems aren't specific to a model or make of printer. They are issues that occur with all printers. Windows 98 provides a Print Troubleshooter that aids with such common issues, and it should be your first stop in resolving a print problem. The Print Troubleshooter is shown in Figure 12-15.

The Print Troubleshooter is an excellent resource, and is as easy to use as any help feature in Windows 98. The following exercise takes you through running the Print Troubleshooter.

EXERCISE 12-1

Using Print Troubleshooter for Help to Solve Printing Problems

1. From the Start menu, click Help. When Windows 98 Online Help opens, select the Index tab.

2. Type **troubleshooting**, and watch as the list of topics scrolls to the Troubleshooting section. You'll notice there are a number of

subtopics to troubleshooting. Scroll down until you see the Printers subtopic, and select it.

3. Click the Display button.

4. In the right panel, you will see a hypertext link to start the Print Troubleshooter. Click the hyperlink to start the Print Troubleshooter.

5. Answer the questions that deal with your problem, and follow the instructions to solve that problem.

Sometimes the problem isn't with the printer but with the protocol. This is the case when network-connected printers are involved, such as those manufactured by Hewlett-Packard. HP network-connected printers use the DLC protocol. If this protocol isn't installed on your Windows 98 machine, you will be unable to print.

Print Troubleshooter is used to resolve common print problems

A common question on Microsoft exams involves printing to HP network-connected printers. If you are unable to print to such a printer, always consider that the DLC protocol isn't installed.

Other problems occur when users wish to share a printer connected to their machine with others on the network. Usually the cause for such problems is that something isn't installed or configured properly.

If you want to use File and Printer Sharing for Microsoft Networks, you must have Client for Microsoft Networks installed as well. In addition to this, you can't have File and Printer Sharing for NetWare Networks running on the same machine. Only one of the two can be installed at one time on one machine.

Similarly, if File and Printer Sharing for NetWare Networks is going to be used, you must also have Client for NetWare Networks installed. You cannot use the client software supplied by Novell. Also, you cannot have File and Printer Sharing for Microsoft Networks running on the same machine.

CERTIFICATION OBJECTIVE 12.05

File System Problems

No matter how advanced a file system you have, problems will always arise. Hard disks age, and areas of that hard disk can go bad. Sometimes a file can have an invalid date (like 20 years in the future or past), causing programs or backups to work improperly. These are just a few of the problems that ScanDisk deals with.

ScanDisk

While the frontline of defense against file system problems is regular backups, the frontline of maintaining and troubleshooting file systems is ScanDisk. ScanDisk allows you to check disks for both logical and physical errors. Depending on how it's configured, the tests it performs range from basic to advanced. Not only will it check the disk surface for physical errors, (such as those that occur when sections of the hard disk are damaged), but it will check files for invalid dates and times, invalid filenames, cross-linked files, and lost file fragments. When experiencing file system problems, ScanDisk should always be used.

Two areas of file system problems that people get confused are cross-linked files and lost file fragments. In the file systems that Windows 98 supports, files are stored in blocks that are called clusters. When you save a file to a directory, the location of the first cluster is stored in that directory. Each cluster not only contains data, but also points to the location of the next cluster. This continues until the end of the file. Unfortunately, sometimes a cluster is corrupted and points to a cluster of another file. The clusters that are lost in this process are referred to in ScanDisk as "lost file fragments," while the clusters pointed to in the other file are called "cross-linked." Figure 12-16 illustrates the two concepts.

As with most problems ScanDisk helps to resolve, you can configure how ScanDisk deals with cross-linking. After starting ScanDisk, you can click the Advanced button to display the screen shown in Figure 12-17. From this screen, you are offered three methods of dealing with cross-linked files, and two methods of dealing with lost file fragments.

Cross-linked files can be deleted (removing the data from use), ignored (leaving the problem as it is), or copied. When copies are made, both files are provided with a copy of the cross-linked clusters. While obviously one file will be using the wrong data, the other file is at least able to use its proper data. Copying is the only solution that doesn't corrupt both files

How cross-linking occurs

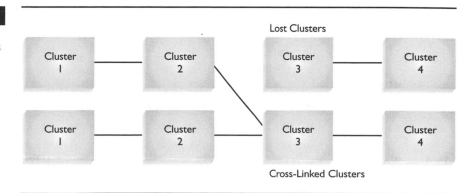

FIGURE 12-17

ScanDisk's Advanced Options allows you to set how ScanDisk deals with certain problems

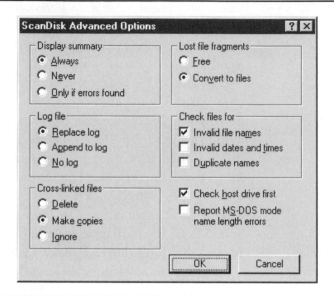

When cross-linked files are deleted, both files lose the data. When it is ignored, the file that isn't supposed to be using those clusters can write to them, thereby corrupting data used by the proper file. While none of the solutions is entirely palatable, ScanDisk gives you the ability to salvage a good chunk of your data.

That solves one-half of the problem, but what about the orphaned clusters that aren't being used by any of the files? That's where the Lost File Fragments options come in. You can convert the orphaned clusters to files, which gives you the chance to salvage this lost data. Your other option is to "free" the lost clusters, which translates to deleting them and freeing up the lost hard disk space.

In addition to these physical problems, users can experience bad sectors on their hard disk. When ScanDisk finds a bad sector, it moves the data contained there to a new location and marks that sector as bad. No data is written to this sector in the future. In addition to repairing hard disks that are in use, you should always use ScanDisk to check new hard disks that are installed. In doing so, you are making sure that you're not writing good data to bad sectors. A good method of troubleshooting is shooting down a problem before it occurs!

Unfortunately, some older programs require certain files to be stored in a specific location. If ScanDisk were to move certain system or hidden files, such programs may not work correctly. To this end, you can set ScanDisk not to move such files. When you click the Options button on ScanDisk's main screen, the Surface Scan Options screen appears. Here you can check or uncheck the box labeled Do Not Repair Bad Sectors In Hidden And System Files. Checking the box will disable such moves, while unchecking it allows ScanDisk to repair the problem.

CERTIFICATION OBJECTIVE 12.06

Resource Access Problems

If you can't access resources through Windows 98, you definitely have problems (the largest of which is the temper of the user you're dealing with). While a user will generally think it's his fault if an application screws up, the network administrator catches all the blame when the user can't access resources on the network. Even the most mild-mannered user will turn into a bloodthirsty, sarcastic monster when this happens. I know, because I turned into one when I was taking my TCP/IP exam. Half-way through it, the exam program bombed because it couldn't access a shared hard disk! Can anyone say "rewrite"?

Fortunately, you don't have to worry about dealing with the issues of irate users on the Microsoft exam. What you do have to know is how to fix, and what causes, resource access problems. Whether it's a test question or the real world, the key is to maintain a cool, calm, analytical mind.

Problems with networks consisting of NetWare and Microsoft machines can be interesting, to say the least. There may be times when you can't even access the NetWare network from Windows 98. When this happens, make sure that Client for NetWare Networks is installed on Windows 98. In addition to this, you should verify that IPX/SPX-Compatible Protocol is installed. This protocol is also referred to as NWLink in NT installations, and is Microsoft's implementation of NetWare's IPX/SPX protocol. Since IPX/SPX is the protocol of choice on NetWare networks, it usually runs on NetWare networks. This means that, unless otherwise specified on the Microsoft exam, you should assume that you need the IPX/SPX-Compatible Protocol to communicate with the NetWare network. Verifying that this protocol and Client for NetWare Networks are installed can be done through the following exercise.

| EXERCISE 12-2 |

Verifying That Components Required to Connect to NetWare Networks Are Installed

1. In Control Panel, double-click the Network icon. Click the Configuration tab.

2. In the list of installed components, see that Client for NetWare Networks and IPX/SPX-Compatible Protocol appear. If both appear, click OK and end the exercise. If Client for NetWare Networks is missing (or both the Client for NetWare Networks and IPX/SPX is missing), follow steps 3-5. If only IPX/SPX is missing, proceed to steps 6-8.

3. If Client for NetWare Networks doesn't appear, click the Add button to bring up the Select Network Component Type dialog box.

4. Select Client from the list and click the Add button. The Select Network Client dialog box will appear.

5. Choose Microsoft from the list of manufacturers, and then choose Client for NetWare Networks from the list of network clients. After clicking OK, both the client and the IPX/SPX-Compatible Protocol appear on the list of installed network components. If this protocol wasn't loaded previously, Windows 98 automatically installs it.

6. If IPX/SPX doesn't appear, click Add to bring up the Select Network Component Type dialog box.

7. Choose Protocol from the list, and click the Add button to bring up the Select Network Protocol dialog box.

8. Choose Microsoft from the list of manufacturers, and then choose IPX/SPX-Compatible Protocol from the list of network protocols. Click OK. The protocol will install and bind itself to the network adapter.

Another problem with accessing resources on NetWare networks concerns incorrect frame types. If you are using an incorrect frame type with the IPX/SPX-Compatible Protocol, you may not be able to see the NetWare servers. This can easily be remedied by changing the Frame Type setting (in Advanced Properties for IPX/SPX-Compatible Protocol in the Network applet of Control Panel) from its default Auto setting to the frame type that your NetWare network is using.

exam
ⓦatch

A common question on Microsoft exams is one dealing with incorrect frame types. If one computer is unable to see NetWare servers, and other computers aren't having a problem, always consider that an incorrect frame type is being used.

Whether you're dealing with Microsoft or NetWare networks, there are certain things that should be checked. One of these is making certain that the bindings are correct for the protocol and network adapter. This is done through the Configuration tab of the Network applet in Control Panel. After selecting your network adapter from the list, just click the Properties button. After the Properties dialog box appears, click the Bindings tab. The protocol your network uses should appear in the list with a check mark beside it. If it does not, click the check box to bind the protocol, or install the protocol.

Another problem common to accessing resources on a network is the computer belonging to the wrong workgroup. By choosing the Identification tab of the Network applet in Control Panel, you can check and (if necessary) change the workgroup you belong to. From this same tab, you can change the computer name (also known as the NetBIOS name) if there was a conflict of two computers on the network having the same name.

CERTIFICATION OBJECTIVE 12.07

Hardware Device and Device Driver Problems

"My, what a lovely, expensive paperweight you have on your desk." This is the last thing anyone wants to hear, but if your computer can't access its hardware, an expensive paperweight is exactly what you have! Problems with hardware devices and device drivers are a real issue with computing, and because of that, Microsoft has included such questions on the exam.

Windows 98 includes some tools that make dealing with this issue less painful. They include the Automatic Skip Driver Agent, System Information Tool, and the Add New Hardware Wizard. Together, they simplify troubleshooting hardware device and device drivers.

Automatic Skip Driver (ASD) Agent

Automatic Skip Driver (ASD) Agent detects operations and device drivers that fail at startup. When a problem exists with your hardware, the device driver for it can fail to load. If such a failure occurs, ASD records the failure to C:\ASD.LOG. After two failed attempts to load, it turns off the device driver so that Windows 98 can start without any problems. By using ASD, you can identify which devices failed when Windows 98 starts, and which failures are preventing Windows 98 itself from starting.

ASD also allows you to view which device drivers fail, and provides recommendations for solving the problem. These features are available whenever a device fails. If you do not have a failure, ASD will display a message box that states, "There are no current ASD critical operation failures on this machine." After you exit the message box, ASD shuts down.

EXERCISE 12-3

Resolving Device Driver Failures with ASD

1. Run ASD by either launching it from the Tools menu of System Information, or by clicking Start | Run and typing ASD.EXE.

2. Select the operation that failed from the Hardware Troubleshooting Agent dialog box.

3. Click Details.

4. Read the recommendation that appears in the Enumerating A Device Details dialog box.

Microsoft System Information Utility

As was mentioned earlier in this chapter, the System Information Utility is useful for discovering problems with hardware devices. Aside from launching other troubleshooting tools, System Information collects information about your computer and displays it under associated topics. By using this tool, you can investigate whether certain devices aren't working because they're trying to use the same system resources.

The information displayed by this tool is for reference only. In other words, if your modem isn't working, you can view in System Information that it and another device are using the same IRQ. You can't change the modem's IRQ from within the System Information Utility. To change the resource conflicts among devices, you would have to use another utility, such as Device Manager.

Add New Hardware Wizard

Occasionally, device drivers and information may be corrupted to the point that Windows 98 will "lose" the device, or require it to be reinstalled. In some cases, this may prove to be the easiest, most effective way of resolving hardware device and device driver problems. The Add New Hardware Wizard is available from the Control Panel, and provides an easy, user-friendly way of installing (or reinstalling) hardware devices.

Legacy devices (what Microsoft calls non-Plug and Play) can be installed or reinstalled very easily. By clicking the Add New Hardware Wizard in Control Panel, the wizard will attempt to detect the device. If the wizard finds a device, it will ask you if the device it found is the correct one. If you choose No, or if no device is found, then you can choose the device from a list of hardware devices. You are also given the option of installing the drivers provided with the Windows 98 CD, or using an installation disk that came with the hardware.

If a device is Plug and Play, and needs to be reinstalled, Windows 98 will automatically detect the hardware when it is restarted. It will then go through the process of installing the drivers for the device. This is the recommended method of reinstalling Plug and Play devices. If Windows 98 doesn't detect the device, this means that there is a problem with the hardware, the device isn't actually Plug and Play, the device isn't physically installed in your computer correctly, or (oops!) the device isn't installed at all. This final possibility may seem like a strange one until you remember that corporate theft is rampant. It's also possible that a well-intentioned person removed the device from the computer.

CERTIFICATION OBJECTIVE 12.08

Registry Troubleshooting

The Registry is a huge database of almost all the information on your computer. While it's one database, it is actually two files: SYSTEM.DAT and USER.DAT. As with any file, corruption can occur, and when that happens all heck can break lose! If you imagine the Registry as the brains of Windows 98, corrupt Registry files would equate to brain damage.

Because of the importance of the Registry, Windows 98 includes the Registry Checker. On startup, the Registry Checker examines the Registry for problems. If there aren't any, it creates one backup of the Registry per day, which contains the USER.DAT, SYSTEM.DAT and both the SYSTEM.INI and WIN.INI. Up to five compressed backups are maintained at any given time.

The Registry Checker consists of SCANREG.EXE and SCANREGW.EXE. As its name implies, ScanRegW is the Windows version of the Registry Checker, while ScanReg is a DOS version that can be run from the DOS prompt. Though two separate programs, they both make up the Registry Checker.

Although the Registry is examined and backed up at each startup, you can use Registry Checker to analyze (and optionally back up) the Registry anytime you feel there might be a problem.

EXERCISE 12-4

Checking for Corrupt Files and Backing Up the Registry with Registry Checker

1. From the Start menu, click Run and type **ScanRegW**.

2. A message box will appear stating that Registry Checker is scanning the Registry.

3. Registry Checker will display a message box informing you of the scan's results. If no problems are found, you are given the option to back up the Registry. To do so, click the Yes button.

Most of the time, Registry Checker works behind the scenes. When you start Windows, Registry Checker detects whether there is a problem with the Registry. If a problem is found, it will automatically restore one of the good backups, or (if a backup isn't available for some reason) it will attempt to fix the Registry. If the Registry files are so corrupt that Windows 98 can't start, IO.SYS will detect it, and bump you to the DOS prompt. A warning will be displayed on the screen, advising you to run the DOS version of Registry Checker, called ScanReg.

EXERCISE 12-5

Restoring the Registry with Registry Checker

1. From the DOS prompt type **SCANREG /RESTORE**.

2. Wait as ScanReg checks the current Registry.

3. A list of existing backups will appear on the screen. Select the most recent backup that you know is good, and click Restore.

4. Click Restart to reboot the computer.

It is important to note that you cannot restore the Registry with Registry Checker from within Windows 98. Attempting to do so will merely start the Windows version of Registry Checker, which will examine the Registry and offer you the chance to back it up. You must be at the actual DOS prompt, not the command prompt that's available from Start | Programs | MS-DOS Prompt.

FROM THE CLASSROOM

Registry Checker and Windows Update

Windows 98 includes quite a few new utilities to help you keep a computer functioning properly and to help you recover a system in the event it crashes. Two of these new utilities are the Registry Checker and the Windows Update utility.

The Registry Checker is a system maintenance program that finds and fixes Registry problems. Each time you start your computer, Registry Checker automatically scans the Registry for inconsistent data structures. Registry Checker backs up the Registry each day. If the Registry Checker finds a serious problem in the Registry, it will restore the Registry from a backup copy. Registry Checker maintains up to five compressed backups of the Registry. If the current Registry successfully starts Windows 98, then the current Registry is saved as a backup.

If you are familiar with Windows NT, you might recognize that this process is similar to the use of the LastKnownGood option in the Windows NT boot process. If you make a change to the Registry that prevents the system from booting, you have the option of returning to an earlier version of the Registry. If the Registry Checker can't find a backup of a Registry that has failed, the Registry Checker will attempt to fix the Registry.

Setup runs Registry Checker automatically each time you upgrade your computer's operating system. When you install Windows 98, the Registry Checker will fix most of the inconsistencies that might exist in your Registry, even those that you weren't aware of. This greatly improves your chances of successfully installing Windows 98 on the first attempt.

Windows Update is Microsoft's new Web-based resource site. The purpose of the site is to automate driver and system file updates and to provide up-to-date technical support. Windows Update can review device drivers and system software on your computer, compare those findings with a master database on the Web, and then recommend and install updates specific to your computer. You can also revert to a previous device driver or system file using the Uninstall option. Being able to go back to a previous version of a driver is one of the nicest features of Windows Update. I've been caught a number of times installing updates that made things worse instead of better.

The Windows Update icon is located prominently on the Start menu. Windows Update is the beginning of a new generation of Microsoft Technical Support. You'll no longer need to call Microsoft, or search endlessly for

FROM THE CLASSROOM

the latest version of a driver or patch. All you have to do is connect to the site, let the utility scan your configuration, and provide you with a list of updates. You also have the ability to register your copy of Windows 98 and your system resources on the site. This should

expedite a support call with a Microsoft Support Technician, because the technician will have all of your system information available when you call.

—By Robert Aschermann, MCT, MCSE

QUESTIONS AND ANSWERS

My network uses DHCP, and I think a computer is being issued the wrong IP address. I need to see what IP address has been issued to a computer.	Use WINIPCFG to view information on what has been issued to you by the DHCP server. Using this tool, you can view the IP address, subnet mask, default gateway, and other information on what has been issued by the DHCP server.
I want to see what errors occurred during the setup process of Windows 98.	View the SETUPLOG.TXT file with any text editor (such as EDIT.EXE). This file is used by Windows 98 during installation, and contains information on all errors that occurred during setup.
A user is complaining that she can't connect to my Windows 98 computer.	Use Net Watcher. This will allow you to view connections to your machine, and view the configuration of the remote computer.
I haven't shut off my computer in a long time, and want to make a backup of my Registry.	Run ScanRegW and have it back up the Registry when prompted.
I want to back up all of my system startup files.	Use the System Configuration Utility to backup your AUTOEXEC.BAT, CONFIG.SYS, WIN.INI, and SYSTEM.INI.
I want to see if any hardware devices are having any conflicts with IRQs.	Use System Information Utility. Under Hardware Resources, select Conflicts/Sharing and wait for the utility to inspect your system. Any conflicts in IRQs will appear in a list on the right of the screen.

CERTIFICATION SUMMARY

Like a mechanic needs to know the tools required to complete a job, a good part of troubleshooting is knowing the tools Microsoft has made available to you. Even though Windows 98 is a much more stable, "trouble-free" system than its predecessors, problems will crop up that you'll need to troubleshoot.

When installation failures occur, using the text files created by Windows 98 can help you narrow down problems with your system. These files consist of SETUPLOG.TXT, DETLOG.TXT, NETLOG.TXT, and BOOTLOG.TXT. In addition to these there is DETCRASH.LOG, which is the binary file that Windows 98's setup program uses to determine what steps it has completed.

Aside from these text files, there are numerous programs to aid you with troubleshooting when installation is complete. Version Conflict Manager allows you to view files (such as drivers) that are replaced during an upgrade, and—if you're experiencing problems with the newer version—allows you to restore previous versions. System Information Utility is a reference source for information about your entire system. Startup problems can often be resolved with the System Configuration Utility. If connectivity is a problem, WINIPCFG allows you to view TCP/IP-related information about your system, while Net Watcher lets you view configurations and connections of other computers. Together, these programs are interactive resources that make troubleshooting less of a headache.

In this chapter, we also covered issues with printing, accessing resources, and programs that repair malfunctions with your system. Automatic Skip Driver not only checks what operations and device drivers failed to start, but provides information on how to fix the problem. If you suspect disk problems, Microsoft provides ScanDisk. If you need to reinstall—or check the installation of—hardware, the Add New Hardware Wizard will step you through the installation process, and help you to determine if the device isn't physically installed properly.

Finally, it is important to remember how vital the Registry is to Windows 98. The Registry Checker scans the Registry, and allows you to back up and restore the Registry files when corruption occurs. Most of the work it does is behind the scenes, but it allows you the control to back up, restore, scan, and fix the Registry when you suspect a problem.

TWO-MINUTE DRILL

- ❏ SETUPLOG.TXT is a text file that contains setup information used by Windows 98 during installation. It contains information on errors that occurred during the setup process.
- ❏ DETLOG.TXT is a text file that contains a record of all devices found during the hardware detection phase of installation.
- ❏ DETCRASH.LOG is a binary file that is used by Windows 98's Setup program to determine what steps have been completed successfully.
- ❏ NETLOG.TXT is a text file that lists all the network components detected during installation.
- ❏ BOOTLOG.TXT is a text file that contains a record of the components and drivers that were loaded and initialized when Windows 98 started. When Windows 98 starts for the first time, this file is automatically created.
- ❏ System Information Utility is a program that collects information about your system, and displays it in a hierarchical menu. It is useful for determining hardware conflicts and troubleshooting your configuration. In addition, it displays historical data about your system, and can be used to launch numerous troubleshooting tools.
- ❏ Version Conflict Manager is used to view which files were replaced during an installation. It also backs up replaced files, and allows you to restore the original files.
- ❏ System Configuration Utility provides a graphical interface to edit your AUTOEXEC.BAT, CONFIG.SYS, WIN.INI, and SYSTEM.INI files. In addition, it allows you to control how Windows 98 starts, and which programs are started with Windows 98.
- ❏ WINIPCFG is a Windows utility that allows you to view TCP/IP configurations and parameters. With it, you can view information that enables you to interact with other users on TCP/IP networks.
- ❏ Net Watcher is another connectivity tool that allows for remote administration of a computer. With it, you can view which machines are connected to your computer. Net Watcher enables an administrator to view the configurations of machines that aren't connecting properly.
- ❏ Print Troubleshooter allows for an easy, step-by-step method of resolving printer problems. To print to an HP network-connected

printer, you must have DLC installed. For computers on the network to print to a printer connected to your Windows 98 machine, you must have Client for Microsoft Networks and File and Printer Sharing for Microsoft Networks, or Client for NetWare Networks and File and Printer Sharing for NetWare Networks running on your machine.

❏ A common question on Microsoft exams involves printing to HP network-connected printers. If you are unable to print to such a printer, always consider that the DLC protocol isn't installed.

❏ ScanDisk is a tool that checks a disk's surface for physical errors. It also checks files for invalid dates and times, invalid filenames, cross-linked files, and lost file fragments.

❏ Common resource access problems with NetWare servers involve such things as failure to install Client for NetWare Networks or IPX/SPX-Compatible Protocol, or having the incorrect frame type set. Other common problems involve the network adapter, such as improper bindings to protocols.

❏ A common question on Microsoft exams is one dealing with incorrect frame types. If one computer is unable to see NetWare servers, and other computers aren't having a problem, always consider that an incorrect frame type is being used.

❏ Automatic Skip Driver (ASD) Agent detects operations and device drivers that fail at startup. This utility provides recommendations on how to fix the problem when such a failure occurs.

❏ The Add New Hardware Wizard allows you to reinstall hardware. If you are unable to install the hardware effectively with this program, Windows 98 can determine whether the device is damaged, improperly installed in the computer, or missing.

❏ The Registry Checker is used to detect corrupt files in the Registry, and is made up of two programs: ScanRegW (the Windows version) and ScanReg (the DOS version). It creates a backup of the Registry each time Windows 98 is started. If an error occurs, the Registry Checker will attempt either to restore the Registry from one of five existing backups, or to fix the problem if no backup exists. If the Registry is too corrupted to allow Windows 98 to start, you can restore the Registry with the DOS version of the Registry Checker.

SELF TEST

The following questions will help you measure your understanding of the material presented in this chapter. Read all the choices carefully, as there may be more than one correct answer. Choose all correct answers for each question.

1. Which of the following tools detects operations and device drivers that fail at startup?

   A. Automatic Skip Driver Agent

   B. Version Conflict Manager

   C. System Configuration Utility

   D. ScanDisk

2. You suspect problems with your hard disk. Which tool will check your hard disk, and mark damaged areas so that they won't be used in the future?

   A. Automatic Skip Driver Agent

   B. Version Conflict Manager

   C. System Configuration Utility

   D. ScanDisk

3. You are using Windows 98 that has IPX/SPX-Compatible Protocol and Client for NetWare Networks installed. You attempt connecting to the NetWare network. Other Windows 98 machines are able to see the NetWare servers, but you find that you cannot. What is the cause of this problem?

   A. Incorrect subnet mask

   B. Incorrect frame type

   C. Incorrect default gateway

   D. Invalid IP address

4. You are attempting to print to a Hewlett-Packard laser printer that is connected to the network. You find that you are unable to print. Why?

   A. IPX/SPX isn't installed

   B. TCP/IP isn't installed

   C. DLC isn't installed

   D. LCD isn't installed

5. You have started your computer, and wind up at the DOS prompt. A message appears on the screen telling you to use a program to restore the Registry. What will you type to restore the corrupted Registry?

   A. REGSCAN /RESTORE

   B. SCANREG /RESTORE

   C. SCANREGW /RESTORE

   D. SCANREG

6. A user wants to share his printer with both the NetWare and Microsoft users of the network. Which of the following must the user install for this to work? Choose all that apply.

   A. Client for Microsoft Networks

   B. Client for NetWare Networks

   C. File and Printer Sharing for Microsoft Networks

   D. File and Printer Sharing for NetWare Networks

   E. It can't be done

7. You suspect that two devices are using the same IRQ. Which of the following utilities will you use to confirm your suspicions?

   A. System Configuration Utility

   B. System Information Utility

   C. Automatic Skip Driver

   D. WINIPCFG

8. You want to edit your startup files and manage how Windows 98 starts. Which utility will you use?

   A. System Configuration Utility

   B. System Information Utility

   C. System Startup Utility

   D. WinConfig

9. You have just installed Windows 98 on a computer. You want to see a listing of all hardware devices that Windows 98 found during installation. Which of the following text files will provide this information?

   A. SETUPLOG.TXT

   B. NETLOG.TXT

   C. DETLOG.TXT

   D. BOOTLOG.TXT

10. You are experiencing connectivity problems. Which of the following tools will you use to view and release your lease? Choose all that apply.

    A. WINIPCFG

    B. System Information Utility

    C. System Configuration Utility

    D. Net Watcher

A

Self Test
Answers

Chapter I Answers

1. Which of the following is not a feature of Windows 98?

   A. Support for Digital Video/Virtual Disk

   B. Support for the IEEE 1394 specification, a.k.a. FireWire

   C. Support for NTFS file system

   D. Support for Accelerated Graphics Ports

   C. Windows 98 does not support NTFS file system.

2. FAT32 is a feature of Windows 98 that can:

   A. Be read by Windows NT 4.0 in a dual boot partition

   B. Efficiently use space on the hard disk due to the smaller cluster size

   C. Boot an OS/2 PC

   D. Be installed on a drive that is 32 times smaller in size than a typical FAT hard disk

   B. FAT32 can use larger hard disks than FAT, and with a smaller cluster size it uses that space more efficiently.

3. In order to use two monitors to increase desktop space, how must the hardware be configured?

   A. A laptop with a monitor plugged into the Video port

   B. Two monitors plugged into the same AGP port

   C. Two monitors plugged into an AGP port and a legacy standard 16-color VGA port

   D. Two monitors plugged into two separate PCI video adapter cards

   D. Multiple monitor support requires two PCI video adapters and two monitors, each plugged into its own adapter card.

4. If Windows 98 is installed on a PC with a Universal Serial Bus, and a new USB device is added to that PC, what is the process for installing the new USB device?

   A. Simply plug in the device to the USB and power, and install the drivers.

   B. Windows 98 must be powered down, the device plugged into power and into the USB. Then, when Windows 98 is powered on again, install the drivers.

   C. First, install the drivers and power Windows 98 down. Then plug in the device into the USB and the power. Then power up Windows 98 and the drivers will select the correct settings.

   D. It can't be done. Windows 98 does not support USB devices.

   A. Universal Serial Bus devices are hot-swappable—simply plug in and go.

5. PhysInc is a group of medical doctors networked via frame relay. They have all decided to upgrade their systems to be identical to the other doctors' systems, in order to share and reduce their administration costs. There will be no data stored on local hard disks; all critical and secure files are stored on NetWare file servers. Some doctors have requested AGP hardware in order to implement

faster video-conferencing. Some doctors want Windows NT 4.0 and others have asked about Windows 98. Which is the better client operating system?

A. Windows NT 4.0, since there are critical secure files

B. Windows 98, since it supports frame relay directly

C. Windows NT 4.0, since it supports AGP hardware

D. Windows 98, since it supports AGP hardware
   D. Windows 98, since the doctors will use AGP hardware for video-conferencing and Windows NT 4.0 does not support it.

6. MovieFun is a family-owned company that runs theaters across the entire state of Arizona. Each theater has a workstation that dials into the main office to update the SQL database with the day's receipts. The theater is concerned about the security of the files on the workstations in the remote theaters, since there was an incident in which one receipts file had been changed by an as-yet-unknown hacker in order to embezzle funds. MovieFun is upgrading all its workstations in order to prevent further hacker attacks. Which is the better client, Windows 98 or Windows NT 4.0?

A. Windows 98, since MovieFun will probably use DVD

B. Windows NT 4.0, since MovieFun uses a SQL database

C. Windows 98, since MovieFun uses a SQL database

D. Windows NT 4.0, since MovieFun must secure their receipts files on local hard disks
   D. Windows NT 4.0 is the best choice for securing the receipts files.

7. Gary is a new administrator with the task of upgrading all his dual-boot PCs from OS/2 and DOS to OS/2 and Windows 98 on the same partition. In the past, all files were shared between both DOS and OS/2 without a problem. Hard disks are getting crowded, and Gary wants to know if he can convert all the Windows 98 systems to FAT32 to conserve space.

A. Yes, converting the drives to FAT32 will conserve space

B. No, even though conversion will save space, OS/2 will not work

C. No, space will be wasted since OS/2 uses FAT32 differently than Windows 98

D. Yes, FAT is the same thing as FAT32 and OS/2 supports FAT
   B. OS/2 will not work because it shares a partition with Windows 98. The conversion would change that partition to FAT32 which OS/2 does not support.

8. Ron wants to share a file with other NetWare users on his NetWare network. What must he do if he is running Windows 98?

A. Nothing, all files are shared automatically with NetWare

B. He must install the service for file and printer sharing on Microsoft networks, since Windows 98 is a Microsoft product

C. He must install the service for file and printer sharing on NetWare networks, in addition to the Client for NetWare Networks, the appropriate adapter, and IPX/SPX protocol, and then configure user-level access control, and finally must create the shares and grant access to them

D. Ron cannot share files with NetWare users in Windows 98

C. The process for sharing files with NetWare users includes the installation of the Client for NetWare Networks, the adapter, the IPX/SPX-compatible protocol, and the service for file and printer sharing on a NetWare network. User-level access control must be configured to point to the NetWare server, in order to grant access to NetWare users when creating the shares.

9. Which of the following security strategies can edit the local Registry of a Windows 98 PC?

A. System Policy Editor

B. User Profiles

C. File and Printer Sharing

D. User-level or share-level access control

A. The System Policy Editor can open and edit a local Registry.

10. When accessing a Windows NT domain, where does the domain name get placed in the Control Panel?

A. In the Network icon of the Control Panel in the properties of the Protocol, and in the Workgroup space on the Identification tab of the same Network icon

B. In the Network icon of the Control Panel in the properties of the Adapter, and in the Name space on the Identification tab of the same Network icon

C. In the Network icon of the Control Panel in the properties of the Client, and in the Workgroup space on the Identification tab of the same Network icon

D. In the Network icon of the Control Panel in the properties of the Service, and in the Name space on the Identification tab of the same Network icon

C. The two places where an NT domain name should be placed are in the Workgroup space on the Identification tab on the Network icon, and in the properties of the Client for Microsoft Networks.

Chapter 2 Answers

1. Which of the following are the types of setup presented in Windows 98?

    A. Standard, Laptop, Minimum, Complete

    B. Standard, Portable, Minimum, Custom

    C. Typical, Portable, Compact, Custom

    D. Default, Laptop, Compact, Custom
    C. The four types of setup are Typical, Portable, Compact, and Custom.

2. Which type of setup will install the Games components?

    A. Typical

    B. Portable

    C. Compact

    D. None of the above
    D. None of the setup types will install Games components by default. They must be specified by the installer.

3. What does the switch /IE do?

    A. Ignores the creation of the emergency disk

    B. Ignores extended memory check

    C. Ignores crosslinked files

    D. Skips the License Agreement screen
    A. When SETUP.EXE is used with /IE, it will ignore the step for creating the emergency diskette.

4. What does the HCL do?

    A. It helps in troubleshooting hardware problems

    B. It is used in preparation for deploying Windows 98

    C. It lists hardware compatible with Windows 98

    D. All of the above
    D. The HCL is the Hardware Compatibility List. It is used in determining whether hardware is compatible with Windows 98. The HCL can be used during the preparation for deployment and when troubleshooting setup problems.

5. What program(s) can be used to create MSBATCH.INF files?

    A. EDIT

    B. Notepad

    C. Batch 98 or any text editor

    D. Wordpad
    C. Batch 98 or any text editor can be used to create MSBATCH.INF files.

6. What is the minimum processor that Windows 98 will support?

    A. Pentium II 300 Mhz

    B. 486DX2 66 Mhz

    C. 286

    D. 386DX 33 Mhz
    B. The minimum processor that Windows 98 supports is a 486DX2 66 Mhz.

7. Which icon in the Control Panel would an installer use to change a graphics card's properties?

   A. Add New Hardware icon

   B. Add/Remove Programs icon

   C. PC Card icon

   D. System icon
   D. Hardware properties can be edited from the System icon in the Control Panel.

8. If an installer wants to add WebTV support after Windows 98 is installed, what does he do?

   A. He uses the EXTRACT utility to obtain the WebTV drivers, and copies them to the Windows\System directory.

   B. He obtains the WebTV software and runs SETUP from the Start | Run command dialog box.

   C. He uses the Add/Remove Programs icon and selects WebTV components from the Windows Setup tab.

   D. He cannot do this. Windows 98 does not support WebTV.
   C. The installer can use the Add/Remove Programs icon to add the optional Windows 98 components for WebTV support.

9. If a setting has to be changed in the Registry, how does the installer make the change?

   A. He uses SYSEDIT

   B. He uses REGEDIT

   C. He uses System Information

   D. He opens the SYSTEM.DAT and USER.DAT files in Wordpad
   B. REGEDIT is the Windows 98 Registry Editor. This is the utility to use when making changes to the Registry.

10. How can a user change his settings to use an HTML page as wallpaper?

    A. He cannot do this, since Windows 98 doesn't support this feature

    B. He must edit the Folder Options from within Explorer

    C. He can change to an HTML page using the Internet Explorer settings

    D. He must click Start | Settings | Active Desktop and check View As Web Page. Then he must select an HTML page using the Control Panel Display icon.
    D. To use an HTML page as wallpaper, the Desktop must be set to be viewed as a Web page using Start | Settings | Active Desktop | View As Web Page. Then the HTML page can be chosen from the Control Panel Display icon.

Chapter 3 Answers

1. What are two advantages of using FAT32?

   A. Use of only SCSI disks and faster performance

   B. Supports larger hard disks and faster performance

   C. Supports larger hard disks and more efficient use of large hard disks

   D. Use of only SCSI disks and more efficient use of large hard drives
   C. Supports larger hard disks and more efficient use of large disks. FAT32 supports drives up to 2 terabytes in size, and can use smaller allocation units on larger hard disks (4KB allocation units on drives up to 8GB in size).

2. Which one of the following would prevent you from using DriveSpace?

   A. FAT

   B. FAT32

   C. A small hard disk

   D. A large hard disk
   B. FAT32. DriveSpace is not compatible with FAT32. You cannot compress a FAT32 drive.

3. You are having trouble reading a data file from your hard drive. Which tool would be most helpful in fixing this problem?

   A. Disk Defragmenter

   B. DriveSpace

   C. System File Checker

   D. ScanDisk
   D. ScanDisk. Problems reading a small number of files usually have to do with errors on the drive. ScanDisk is designed to fix this sort of error. Disk Defragmenter would make your drive more efficient, DriveSpace would make it bigger, and System File Checker is only for problems with system files.

4. What does Enable Large Disk Support do?

   A. Makes Windows 98 SCSI drive compatible

   B. Allows you to format a drive using FAT32

   C. Allows you to format a drive using FAT

   D. Enables Iomega ZIP drives under Windows 98
   B. Allows you to format a drive using FAT32. When FDISK asks whether to enable large disk support, answering Yes will result in all drives created during that FDISK session formatting FAT32. If you answer No, they will all be FAT.

5. After converting a FAT drive to FAT32, how can you convert back to FAT?

   A. You cannot convert back

   B. Run Disk Converter with the /U option

   C. Right-click the drive and select Undo

D. Download the FAT32 to FAT conversion utility from Microsoft's Web site

A. You cannot convert back. Microsoft's conversion to FAT32 is a one-way process. In order to go back to FAT, you must delete the partition and redefine it with large disk support enabled, then format it.

6. How can you control what commands Windows 98 runs during the boot process?

A. Press F5

B. Press F8 and select Safe Mode

C. You cannot control the boot process

D. Press F8 and select Step-by-Step

D. Press F8 and select Step-by-Step. When you press F8 you are presented with a menu of boot options. Step-by-Step lets you allow or disallow commands to run as the system boots.

7. What utility would you use to make your applications open faster?

A. Disk Defragmenter

B. ScanDisk

C. FDISK

D. Automatic Skip Driver utility

A. Disk Defragmenter. This utility rearranges files so that they occupy contiguous space on the drive. So when the application opens, it can read its code sequentially, rather than from random spots all over the disk.

8. What utility would you use to automatically find and delete files that are wasting disk space?

A. ScanDisk

B. Disk Defragmenter

C. Disk Cleanup

D. FDISK

C. Disk Cleanup. This utility looks for files that are left behind after programs are removed. It also looks for temporary files that are no longer needed. Once found, it deletes these files, providing you with more disk space.

9. How would you update your Windows 98 system?

A. ScanDisk

B. Automatic Skip Driver

C. Registry Checker

D. Windows 98 Update

D. Windows 98 Update. This "program" is actually a link to a special Microsoft Web site that will analyze your system, and allow you to pick any available updates and have them automatically installed.

10. You suspect your Registry is corrupt. How would you fix this problem?

A. ScanDisk

B. Registry Checker

C. Windows 98 Update

D. REGEDIT

C. Registry Checker. This utility automatically scans the Registry for errors and corruption. If it encounters problems, it allows you to reload a good copy of the Registry. If there are no problems, it backs up the Registry in case of future problems.

11. Where can you find nearly all of Windows 98 tools for maintaining your system?

    A. Start | Settings

    B. Start | Programs | Accessories | System Tools

    C. C:\WINDOWS\SYSTEM TOOLS

    D. http:\\www.microsoft.com\ systemtools.htm
    B. Start | Programs | Accessories | System Tools. This menu contains nearly every Windows 98 utility, including ScanDisk, Disk Cleanup, Disk Defragmenter, Drive Converter, Windows Tune-Up, and more.

12. What does the Automatic Skip Driver do?

    A. Skips drivers that are not necessary on your computer

    B. Skips Windows 98 drivers to use a manufacturer driver

    C. Detects any drivers that are failing to load and allows you to disable them

    D. Skips unnecessary system prompts
    C. Detects any drivers that are failing to load and allows you to disable them. If a driver fails to load, the system will detect it. Running Automatic Skip Driver will show you a list of these failing drivers and allow you to skip them the next time you boot up. Useful for troubleshooting hardware problems.

13. What is the largest drive size supported with FAT32?

    A. 2GB

    B. 2TB

    C. 8GB

    D. 512MB
    B. 2TB. FAT32 supports single drives as large as 2 terabytes. FAT32 is most efficient on drives as large as 8GB, but drives must be at least 512MB in order to gain efficiency.

14. What system utility is useful for finding out more details about a computer?

    A. Registry Checker

    B. REGEDIT

    C. ScanDisk

    D. Microsoft System Information
    D. Microsoft System Information. This utility provides detailed information about the computer, its hardware and its software.

15. What provides an easy-to-use interface for making copies of system and user data files?

    A. Backup Wizard

    B. Registry Checker

    C. Drive Converter

    D. Automatic Skip Driver
    A. Backup Wizard. When the Windows 98 backup utility is started, you can choose to create a new backup session using the Backup Wizard. The wizard guides you through each step to back up the system and data files, then lets you save the session for later use.

Chapter 4 Answers

1. John buys a new computer and a new printer that are both Plug and Play. He connects the printer and turns the computer on, but the printer is not automatically installed. What could be the problem?

   A. The printer is out of ink

   B. The computer's hard disk is full

   C. There is no such thing as a Plug and Play printer

   D. His printer cable is not IEEE 1284 compliant

      D. The printer cable is not IEEE 1284 compliant. IEEE 1284 is the standard for Plug and Play. The computer and printer use bi-directional communication to obtain information about each other.

2. Your computer supports ECP, your printer cable is IEEE 1284 compliant, and your printer is Plug and Play. You would like to take advantage of the enhanced performance that the ECP provides. How do you know if the computer's ECP has been enabled?

   A. Call your computer's manufacturer.

   B. Check the Details tab of the printer's Properties window.

   C. Check the Ports (COM and LPT) in Device Manager.

   D. Print a test page. The port details are on the test page.

      C. Check the Ports (COM and LPT) in Device Manager. If the ECP has been enabled, Device Manager will label the LPT port as an ECP LPT port.

3. You have just installed a new printer. How can you make sure that the printer is properly installed and that everything works correctly?

   A. Pull the printer cable to see if it comes loose

   B. Knock on the printer

   C. Call Bill Gates and ask him

   D. Print a test page

      D. Print a test page. When you have installed a new printer, the Add Printer Wizard gives you the option to print a test page right away. If the test page does not print properly, you can bring up the Print Troubleshooter. You can print a test page at any time by going to the Properties of a printer. On the General tab is the button to print a test page.

4. You have two Epson 800 printers in your organization. One is color and one is black and white. What can you do to help your coworkers distinguish between the two?

   A. Rename each printer with a name that corresponds to its ink type.

   B. Nothing. Printers can't be renamed.

   C. Install a different printer driver.

D. Make one printer the default printer.
A. Rename each printer. In the Printers folder, you can right-click a printer and click Rename to give the printer any name you want that can help users identify each printer.

5. You want to use drag-and-drop printing. What should you do first?

   A. Enable drag-and-drop printing

   B. Disable EMF spooling

   C. Install the proper printer driver

   D. Make the printer the default printer
   C. Install the proper printer driver. If the driver is not properly installed, nothing will print.

6. Which of the following cannot be accomplished in Print Manager?

   A. Check the status of a print job

   B. Rename a print job

   C. Cancel a print job

   D. Pause a print job
   B. Rename a print job. Print Manager does not allow you to rename a print job.

7. You have accidentally sent a document to the printer. You open Print Manager to delete the document, and you see several other documents waiting in the queue. How do you remove the one document you accidentally printed from Print Manager?

   A. Highlight the print job, click Document and then click Purge

   B. You can't remove just one document; all documents have to be removed

   C. Highlight the print job, click Document, and then click Cancel

   D. Highlight the document, click File, and then click Delete
   C. Highlight the print job, click Document, and then click Cancel. If you wanted to delete all the documents from Print Manager you could click Printer and then Purge Print Documents.

8. You have several documents waiting to be printed in Print Manager. You would like to place a print job ahead of the document that is currently printing. From inside Print Manager, how do you do this?

   A. You can't put a print job ahead of one that is currently printing

   B. Click and drag the waiting document ahead of the printing document

   C. Click Printer, then Print Now

   D. Click Document, then Print Now
   A. You can't put a print job ahead of one that is currently printing. Once a document is printing from the printer, its order in Print Manager cannot be changed.

9. You can print a document even though there is no printer connected to your computer. What is this feature called?

   A. Deferred printing

   B. Print Pausing

   C. Offline printing

D. None of the above
A, C. Offline or Deferred printing. Offline and Deferred printing are the same thing. This process saves the print job to your hard disk so that it can be printed at a later time, when you are connected to a printer.

10. What does ICM stand for?

A. Interprocess Control Manager

B. Integrated Color Management

C. Image Color Matching

D. Image Color Management
C. Image Color Matching. This was developed by Kodak and conforms to the InterColor 3.0 specification.

11. How many minidrivers does Windows 98 have?

A. Two: EMF and RAW

B. It depends on how many printers you have installed

C. One: the universal minidriver

D. It depends on whether or not your printer is PostScript
B. It depends on how many printers you have installed. Each printer has a minidriver that sits between the universal driver and each printer.

12. When you print a document on your laser printer, it takes some time before control of the application is returned to you. How could you speed up the return of control?

A. Buy an IEEE 1284-compliant cable

B. There is no way to speed up return of control

C. From Print Properties, click Details, click Spool Settings, click Start Printing After First Page Is Spooled

D. From Print Properties, click Details, click Spool Settings, click Start Printing After Last Page Is Spooled
D. You should click Start Printing After Last Page Is Spooled. This requires more disk space and increases total print time, but the application is freed up more quickly, because as soon as the EMF file is spooled, control is returned to you.

13. Your printer is printing slowly. You suspect that older spool files have not been deleted. Where is the spool file?

A. *<systemroot>*\SYSTEM\SPOOL

B. *<systemroot>*\SYSTEM\

C. *<systemroot>*\SYSTEM\PRINTERS\ SPOOL

D. *<systemroot>*\SPOOL\PRINTERS
D. *<systemroot>*\SPOOL\PRINTERS. The print spool file is stored there and has an extension of SPL. Any files spooled using EMF will take the form of EMF*xxxxx*.TMP.

14. You are printing a file that is not using EMF spooling. When does the application release control back to you?

A. When the EMF spooling is done

B. As soon as you click OK on the Print dialog box

C. When the RAW file has been sent to the printer

D. After you quit the application
C. When the RAW file has been sent to the printer. As soon as Print Manager releases the application, the application returns control back to you.

15. What Windows component generates an EMF file during the print process?

A. The Kernel

B. The GDI

C. Print Manager

D. Print Spooler
B. The GDI. The Graphical Device Interface generates the EMF, which is then passed on to the print subsystem, which is then sent to the printer.

16. A PostScript file will not print correctly on a PostScript printer. You disable EMF spooling, but the file still doesn't print correctly. Why not?

A. EMF spooling can't be disabled

B. EMF has nothing to do with printing

C. For PostScript printing, Windows 98 does not generate an EMF file

D. EMF spooling is only available on Windows 3.1
C. Windows 98 does not generate an EMF file for PostScript printing. Instead PostScript generates its own description file and does not need EMF.

17. Why would you want to remove a printer driver for an existing printer?

A. Never. You should never remove a printer driver.

B. The printer needs to be taken in for repairs.

C. To install a new toner or inkjet cartridge.

D. To troubleshoot a printing problem.
D. To troubleshoot a printing problem. If you are having problems with your printer, you can delete the printer driver and reinstall it.

18. You are running out of disk space as you try to print from Windows 98. What is the best solution to fix this problem?

A. Delete temporary files and archive older files to make more room

B. Turn the printer off and then on again

C. Enable the ECP port

D. Reinstall the printer driver
A. Delete temporary files and archive older files to make more room. This will create more room for a spool file to be written to your hard disk, and ensure a successful print job.

Chapter 5 Answers

1. Which of these are viable solutions for deploying an installation script to upgrade a Windows 95 workstation to Windows 98?

    A. Microsoft Deployment Manager

    B. Microsoft Systems Management Server

    C. Attaching a batch file to an e-mail message

    D. Modifying the logon script
        B, C, D. Microsoft Systems Management Server, an e-mail message, and modification of a logon script are all possibilities for deploying an installation script. There is no such thing as Microsoft Deployment Manager.

2. Which of the following statements are true?

    A. USB can support up to seven devices with single channel, and up to 14 devices with dual channel

    B. With the high speeds supported by USB, it is an ideal choice for videodisc players and external storage

    C. Both FireWire and USB support both isochronous and asynchronous as their transfer protocols

    D. USB is Plug and Play, but FireWire must be configured manually
        C. Both modes of data delivery are supported by both external bus standards. Isochronous connections

have guaranteed delivery, and asynchronous data can only be transferred whenever there is no isochronous traffic on the bus.

3. Which feature of Microsoft's Personal Web Server is no longer supported in version 4.0?

    A. Active Server Pages

    B. FTP Server

    C. RAD—Remote Deployment Support

    D. Drag-and-drop capabilities
        B. FTP Server capabilities are no longer supported in version 4.0.

4. Which of the following would be a valid reason for implementing ATM across your network?

    A. Not quite as fast as 10baseT, but much easier to implement and manage

    B. Uses Time-Division for allocating bandwidth

    C. Integrates seamlessly with standard TCP/IP LANs

    D. Use of Label Multiplexing
        D. Label Multiplexing allows ATM to allocate bandwidth to traffic requests that need it, rather than allotting it at fixed intervals.

5. PPTP in a Virtual Private Network supports which of the following protocols?

    A. TCP/IP

    B. IPX/SPX

    C. NetBEUI

D. All of the above
   D. All of the protocols listed can be encapsulated and tunneled within a PPTP connection.

6. Which two statements here are correct?

   A. Share-level access assigns a password to each resource

   B. User-level access assigns a password to each resource

   C. Share-level access requires each user or group to be granted individual rights

   D. User-level access requires each user or group to be granted individual rights
      A, D. Share-level access allows you to assign different passwords to each resource, while user-level access requires you to grant and revoke rights on an individual or group basis.

7. Which of the following utilities are included with Windows 98 for remote access management?

   A. System Policy Editor

   B. Microsoft Remote Console

   C. Registry Editor

   D. System Monitor
      A, C, D. System Policy Editor, Registry Editor, and System Monitor are all included, as well as another utility, named Net Watcher. There is no utility named Microsoft Remote Console.

8. Which of the following protocols are routable?

   A. TCP/IP

   B. IPX/SPX

   C. NetBEUI

   D. All of the above
      A, B. Both TCP/IP and IPX/SPX are routable, but NetBEUI can only be bridged.

9. Which classification of address is 127.72.101.80?

   A. Class A

   B. Class B

   C. Class C

   D. None of the above
      D. The network address of 127.*x.x.x* is reserved for loopback functions.

10. Which of the following statements about the filtering performed by routers and bridges are true?

   A. Routers use network addresses, and bridges use MAC addresses

   B. Routers use MAC addresses, and bridges use DNS resolution

   C. Routers use DNS resolution, and bridges use MAC addresses

   D. Routers use MAC addresses, and bridges use network addresses
      A. Routers examine the network address of the protocol, whereas bridges look at the MAC address for the destination NIC.

Chapter 6 Answers

1. Fred did not install and configure all networking options during Windows 98 Setup. How can he configure networking support after installing Windows 98?

    A. By using the System option in Control Panel

    B. By using the Network option in Control Panel

    C. By restarting Windows; all networking options will be configured automatically

    D. By using the Add New Hardware option in Control Panel
    B. He should use the Network option in Control Panel. The System option is used to check drivers and settings for hardware. Restarting windows will not automatically set up networking options.

2. Carol is adding Windows 98 computers to her existing network. She wants to protect shared network resources on the computers running Windows 98 with individually assigned passwords. Which of the following types of security would be appropriate?

    A. Pass-through security

    B. System security

    C. User-level security

    D. Share-level security
    D. Share-level security would be appropriate. With share-level, users assign passwords to their shared resources. User-level leverages an existing security, as with Windows NT. Pass-through is the process of using Windows NT security.

3. What is a TCP/IP subnet mask?

    A. Another name for the IP address

    B. The address of the DHCP server for the subnetwork

    C. A value that allows a computer to distinguish the network number from the host ID

    D. The network number
    C. A subnet mask is a value that allows a computer to distinguish the network number from the host ID. This allows a computer to determine if another computer is local or remote. The address for the DHCP server is not needed in TCP/IP settings, and the network number is a portion of the IP address.

4. Crystal did not install TCP/IP when she installed Windows 98. How can she install TCP/IP now?

    A. By using the Add New Hardware Wizard

    B. By using the Network option in Control Panel

    C. By using the Modems option in Control Panel

    D. By using the Mail and Fax option in Control Panel

B. By using the Network option in Control Panel. She needs to use the Add button in the Network dialog box.

5. You cannot use TCP/IP to establish a connection. One of your friends suggested you use the TCP/IP diagnostic utilities to isolate network hardware problems. Which utility should you use if you want to check the route to a remote computer?

   A. PING.EXE

   B. NBTSTAT.EXE

   C. NETSTAT.EXE

   D. TRACERT.EXE
   D. Only TRACERT.EXE enables you to check the route to a remote computer.

6. You want to use the PING command to check the TCP/IP configuration. However, you cannot use the command successfully. What are some of the possible causes of this problem?

   A. The IRQ setting is invalid

   B. The IP address of the default gateway is invalid

   C. The local computer's IP address does not appear correctly in the TCP/IP Properties dialog box

   D. The IP address of the remote host is invalid
   B, C. If PING doesn't work successfully, check that the local computer's IP address is valid, and that the address of the default gateway and remote host is correct.

7. Robyn wants to share her printer with other users. What should she do?

   A. Use the Add New Hardware option in Control Panel

   B. Edit the Sharing tab on the printer's property sheet

   C. Drag the Printer icon to her desktop

   D. Use the Add Printer Wizard
   B. Before Robyn can share the printer, File and Print sharing must be enabled using the Sharing tab on the printer's Properties.

8. Your Windows 98 computer is protected with user-level security. Which of the following access rights can be assigned to the folders on your computer?

   A. Read Only

   B. Custom

   C. Full

   D. Execute
   A, B, C. These are three of the fields in the Add Users dialog box when you are creating a share.

9. IP addresses are assigned by a DHCP server. You are curious to see what IP address and other IP information was assigned to your computer. How would you do this?

   A. Open a DOS prompt and type **IPINFO**

   B. Open a DOS prompt and type **WINIPCFG**

C. Use the START/RUN command and type **IPCONFIG /all**

D. Select TCP/IP Properties from the Network dialog box
B. WINIPCFG is the utility used to see the IP settings of a Windows 9*x* computer. IPCONFIG is used for Windows NT machines. The TCP/IP Properties can be used when the IP address has been entered manually.

10. Which of the following statements are NOT true of deferred printing in Windows 98?

A. When deferred printing is enabled, the printer will be dimmed in the Printers folder

B. When deferred printing is enabled on a network, print jobs are stored in the print queue, and will be printed when the computer is reconnected to the network

C. Deferred print jobs are stored on the local computers

D. Deferred printing only works with print jobs generated by Win32-based applications
D. Deferred printing works with Win16-based, Win32-based, and MS-DOS-based applications.

Chapter 7 Answers

1. What are the three clients that Windows 98 supports natively?

A. VLM

B. NetBIOS

C. NETX

D. Microsoft Client for NetWare Networks
A, C, D. Windows 98 supports the Novell NETX and VLM clients, as well as the 32-bit Microsoft Client for NetWare Networks.

2. What client can be used with the Client for Microsoft Networks?

A. VLM

B. NetBIOS

C. NETX

D. Microsoft Client for NetWare Networks
D. The Microsoft Client for NetWare Networks is a 32-bit client, as is the Client for Microsoft Networks. Only 32-bit clients can be used with other 32-bit clients.

3. Roger has a Windows NT server, a NetWare 4.11 server, and a NetWare 2.15 server on his network. He is upgrading all his OS/2 PCs to Windows 98. What protocols must he install?

A. TCP/IP and IPX/SPX

B. IPX/SPX-Compatible Protocol

C. TCP/IP, and NETX or VLM

D. NetBIOS and NCP
B. IPX/SPX-Compatible Protocol must be installed for NetWare connectivity, but Windows NT servers also support this protocol. The 32-bit clients must also be installed.

4. What needs to be configured if the administrator wants all the Windows 98 PCs to log on to a particular NetWare 3.12 server?

   A. Preferred Server

   B. IPX/SPX-Compatible Protocol

   C. Service for NetWare Directory Services

   D. Frame Type
   A. The Preferred Server directs which server is logged onto by default.

5. In a large enterprise Ethernet network with over 50 NetWare servers of various versions, Georgette is installing Windows 98 using a batch method. The business unit that she is creating the batch for uses only NetWare 4.1 servers. What options should Georgette specify in the batch file?

   A. Source Routing should be Yes

   B. Frame Type should be Ethernet 802.3

   C. File and Printer Sharing for NetWare Networks should be installed

   D. Service for NetWare Directory Services should be installed
   D. The Service for NetWare Directory Services should be installed to access NetWare 4.1 servers.

6. Alice installed a new printer on the queue HPQ on her NetWare 4.1 server, NWS312 in the NDS tree NDSTREE. What does she need to type in the Add Printer Wizard dialog box when prompted to specify the printer or queue name?

   A. \\NDSTREE\NWS312\HPQ

   B. .CN=HPQ.O=NDSTREE

   C. NWS312:\HPQ

   D. \\NWS312\HPQ
   D. The \\NWS312\HPQ is the correct UNC format.

7. Julie is visiting from Houston and is borrowing a PC in the New York branch office. All the Windows 98 PCs in New York have been set with the default context, .OU=NY.O=MAGE. Julie's ID JULIEM is in the HOU organizational unit. What must she type in for the username when logging on?

   A. JULIEM

   B. .O=MAGE.CN=JULIEM

   C. .CN=JULIEM.OU=HOU.O=MAGE

   D. HOU
   C. The correct fully distinguished name must be typed in, and it is .CN=JULIEM.OU=HOU.O=MAGE

8. Kelly installed the Service for File and Printer Sharing for NetWare Networks on her Windows 98 PC, but other users can't "see" any resources in their Network Neighborhood icons. What went wrong?

   A. Kelly installed the wrong service

   B. Kelly did not share out any resources yet

   C. Kelly does not have IPX/SPX-Compatible Protocol installed

D. Kelly did not set up a Preferred Server
B. To share resources, the service must be installed, and then the resources must be shared out to the users.

9. Frank is a new administrator for a NetWare network with 50 Windows 98 PCs. On his second day, he received numerous phone calls, pages, and voice messages complaining that no one could log on. Everyone was able to log on the day before. What should Frank check first?

   A. That the server is up and running
   B. The protocol properties
   C. The client properties
   D. The service properties
   A. When multiple users cannot log on, the first thing to check is whether the server is available.

10. Greg has a NetWare 3.11 network consisting of seven servers. He is gradually upgrading them all to NetWare 4.11. His pilot NetWare 4.11 server went online, but soon afterward, users found that they couldn't log on to the network if they rebooted. Users who didn't reboot were able to continue working. What should Greg check first?

   A. That the NetWare 3.11 servers are up and running
   B. The Frame Type settings
   C. The Preferred Server settings
   D. The default Context settings

B. The default frame type for NetWare 3.11 is Ethernet 802.3. The default frame type for NetWare 4.11 is Ethernet 802.2. When rebooting, the PC detects the 802.2 frame type first, and cannot locate the NetWare 3.11 servers.

Chapter 8 Answers

1. How can you prevent a user from using the MS-DOS prompt?

   A. Implement a roaming user profile for the user
   B. Restrict it from the default user with the System Policy Editor
   C. Implement user profiles
   D. Restrict it from the user with the System Policy Editor
   D. Restrict the MS-DOS prompt from the user by adding her to the CONFIG.POL file. If you restrict it from the default user, then others will not be able to use the MS-DOS prompt—not just the user you are trying to prevent from using it.

2. What file is the template used by the System Policy Editor?

   A. The .AMD file
   B. The .PLO file
   C. The .ADM file
   D. The .POL file
   C. The .ADM file is the template used by the System Policy Editor. Windows

98 ships with the ADMIN.ADM template file.

3. You want to implement a mandatory user profile for a troublesome user. What file do you need to place in his home directory on the Windows NT server?

    A. USER.NAM

    B. USER.MAN

    C. USER.DA0

    D. USER.DAT
    B. To implement a mandatory user profile for a user, you need to place the USER.MAN file in the user's home directory.

4. You encounter a Windows 98 computer in your IS department, on which System Policy Editor is open, with the Local User and Local Computer icons displayed. What can you determine about the state of the System Policy Editor?

    A. The System Policy Editor has opened the Registry of the Windows 98 computer

    B. The System Policy Editor has opened the .POL file of the Windows 98 computer

    C. The System Policy Editor has closed the Registry of the Windows 98 computer

    D. The System Policy Editor has closed the .POL file of the Windows 98 computer
    A. If the Local User and Local Computer icons are visible, it means that the System Policy Editor has opened the Registry of the Windows 98 computer. If this were a new policy, then there would be default computer and user icons.

5. In what order are group priorities downloaded to a Windows 98 computer?

    A. From highest priority to lowest priority

    B. From lowest priority to highest priority

    C. The highest priority is processed first

    D. The lowest priority is processed last
    B. Group priorities are downloaded to a Windows 98 computer starting with the lowest priority and working up to the highest priority. This is why it is very important to make sure that you have the groups arranged in the correct order for your network.

6. Where are user profiles stored for a standalone Windows 98 computer?

    A. In the NETLOGON folder

    B. In the SYS:PUBLIC directory

    C. In the USER PROFILES folder

    D. In the PROFILES folder
    D. User profiles are stored in the PROFILES folder on Windows 98 computers. Normally this is C:\WINDOWS\PROFILES.

7. How are profiles enabled on a Windows 98 computer?

A. From the Profiles applet in Control Panel

B. From the Users applet in Control Panel

C. From the System applet in Control Panel

D. From the Passwords applet in Control Panel
B, D. Profiles are enabled by using either the Users applet or the Passwords applet located in the Control Panel. If the Passwords applet is used, then the User Profiles tab needs to be selected.

8. What state does a grayed-out box signify for a function in the System Policy Editor?

A. Selected

B. Cleared

C. Dimmed

D. Complete
C. A grayed-out box signifies that the function is dimmed, and that the policy will not change the existing condition for the function, regardless of whether it is selected or cleared.

9. What type of file includes the statement CLASS MACHINE?

A. A .POL file

B. A .MAN file

C. A .DAT file

D. An .ADM file
D. ADM can include the CLASS MACHINE statement as well as CATEGORY, POLICY, PART, END CATEGORY, END POLICY, and END PART statements.

10. Several Windows 98 computers on your network don't seem to be implementing group policies correctly. What can cause this to happen?

A. The GROUPPOL.EXE file is not installed on the Windows 98 computers

B. The GROUPPOL.EXE file is not installed on the network servers

C. The GROUPPOL.DLL file is not installed on the Windows 98 computers

D. The GROUPPOL.DLL file is not installed on the network servers
C. If group policies are not working for several Windows 98 computers on your network, then they do not have the GROUPPOL.DLL file installed. Group policies can be installed using the Windows Setup tab on the Add/Remove Programs applet in Control Panel.

11. System policies are not being implemented for any of the users on your Windows NT network. What can be causing this problem?

A. The ADMIN.ADM file is not located in the SYS:PUBLIC directory

B. The CONFIG.POL file is not located in the SYS:PUBLIC directory

C. The ADMIN.ADM file is not located in the NETLOGON folder

D. The CONFIG.POL file is not located
in the NETLOGON folder
D. If system policies do not function
for all of the users on your Windows
NT network, make sure that the
CONFIG.POL is located in the
NETLOGON folder for all domain
controllers that validate user logons.

12. How is a string value displayed in an
.ADM file?

A. ??

B. !!

C. ?

D. !
B. String values are displayed using !!
in an .ADM file.

13. You have enabled roaming user profiles
for the Windows 98 computers on your
network. What must you ensure to keep
the roaming profiles working correctly?

A. That the clocks for all computers on
the network are synchronized

B. That the directories for all computers
on the network are the same size

C. That the amount of RAM is the same
for all computers on the network

D. That the computers on the network all
have sound cards
A. To make sure that roaming profiles
work correctly on your network, you
need to synchronize the clocks for all
computers so that time is accurate.
Accuracy is important because
Windows 98 keeps two copies of the

USER.DAT file when roaming user
profiles are used. One copy stays on
the local machine, and one exists on
the server. The two USER.DAT files
are compared, and the copy with the
newer time is the one that is used.

14. Marissa has not had any problems using
her roaming profile until today, when she
could not use it correctly on a machine on
the second floor. What could have caused
her problem?

A. Windows 98 is installed in the
WINDO98 folder on that system

B. Windows 98 is installed on the D:
drive on that system

C. She is not set up to use a roaming
profile

D. She did not log on to the Banyan
VINES server correctly
A, B. If Windows 98 is installed in a
different directory, or a different hard
disk, than the one where the roaming
profile was set up, then it will not
function correctly.

15. What must the system policy file be
named if you plan on using it on a
Windows NT or Novell NetWare
network?

A. CONFG.POL

B. ADMIN.POL

C. CONFIG.POL

D. ADMN.POL
C. The file must be named
CONFIG.POL if you plan on using it

on either a Windows NT or a Novell NetWare network.

Chapter 9 Answers

1. What does TCP/IP stand for?

   A. Trans Continental Protocol/Immediate Program

   B. Transmission Control Protocol/Internet Protocol

   C. Transmission Control Program/Internet Protocol

   D. Transmission Continued Passively/Intranet Program
   B. Transmission Control Protocol/Internet Protocol.

2. You are installing Windows 98 on several machines. Machines A and C have Windows 95 installed. Machines B and D have DOS installed. Machines A and D have network cards. Which machines will have TCP/IP installed by default?

   A. A and C

   B. B and D

   C. None

   D. B
   D. Machine B. Windows 98 only installs TCP/IP if it is not an upgrade, which Windows 95 would be. The machine also has to have a network card installed.

3. What does DHCP stand for?

   A. Device Helps Control Proxy

   B. Develop High Contrast Protocol

   C. Dynamic Home Control Page

   D. Dynamic Host Configuration Protocol
   D. Dynamic Host Configuration Protocol.

4. You are installing Internet Explorer 4 on a peer-to-peer TCP/IP network. What are your options for an IP addressing scheme?

   A. Automatic Private IP Addressing or Static addressing

   B. DHCP

   C. Automatic Private IP Addressing

   D. Static or DHCP

   E. None of the above
   A. Windows 98 cannot be a DHCP server, so you could use either Automatic Private IP Addressing or Static addressing.

5. You need to customize 150 copies of Internet Explorer 4 for distribution. What is the quickest way to do this?

   A. Use the command SETUP /C

   B. Configure one copy of Internet Explorer, and then copy the files from one machine to another

   C. Can't be done

   D. Use Internet Explorer Administrator's Kit
   D. You can customize many features with the IEAK. In this case, you can create a single install file to distribute to everyone.

6. What is one function of a proxy server?

   A. It screens junk e-mail

   B. It can control what Web sites you
   can view

   C. It alerts you to Cookies being saved on
   your hard disk

   D. All of the above

   E. None of the above
   B. Proxy servers can block out certain
   Web sites from being accessed.

7. Your network administrator gave you a
   URL to automatically set up Internet
   Explorer 4 to work with a proxy server.
   Where do you go to do this?

   A. File | Properties

   B. Tools | Proxy

   C. View | Internet Options

   D. Edit | Configure
   C. The Connection tab for
   configuring a proxy server is under
   View | Internet Options.

8. Which is not a new Explorer bar included
   in Internet Explorer 4?

   A. History

   B. Security

   C. Favorites

   D. Search
   B. Security. There is no such thing as
   a Security bar. Although Windows 98
   does have security zones, they must be
   set from Internet Explorer View |
   Internet Options | Security.

9. You want to search for "Monitors" on the
   Web and you decide to search directly
   from your address bar. What is the correct
   syntax?

   A. Search:monitors

   B. ? monitors

   C. monitors find

   D. lookup monitors
   B. The only acceptable syntax is
   "find," "go," or "?," followed by your
   query.

10. What keyboard combination
    automatically wraps
    "http://www......com" around a word?
    (For example, "weather" becomes
    www.weather.com.)

    A. CTRL-ENTER

    B. ALT-ENTER

    C. SHIFT-ENTER

    D. ALT-CTRL
    A. CTRL-ENTER wraps
    http://www.....com around a word
    to create a URL.

11. How many different security zones
    are there?

    A. 3

    B. 5

    C. 2

    D. 4
    D. There are 4 security zones: Local
    Intranet, Trusted Site, Restricted,
    Internet.

12. You are going to create a share that can be assigned an alias with Personal Web Server. How do you create a Web share?

    A. Right-click the folder, select Sharing, select Web Sharing

    B. Right-click the folder, select Sharing

    C. Right-click the folder, select Properties, select Sharing

    D. Right-click the folder, select Aliases
    A. Right-click the folder, select Sharing, select Web Sharing. You can also create the alias for this directory from this screen.

13. You are going to use NetMeeting for a conference call. The party you are about to contact has to use which of the following programs in order for you to talk with them?

    A. NetMeeting 1.0 or higher

    B. Netscape Communicator

    C. NetMeeting or Netscape Communicator

    D. It doesn't matter
    D. NetMeeting is based on industry standards; it doesn't matter which program they use.

14. What is a whisper?

    A. What somebody says when he wants you to speak softer

    B. A private chat between two people

    C. A button on the NetMeeting toolbar

    D. A way to adjust your audio to be more quiet
    B. A private chat between two people.

Chapter 10 Answers

1. Dial-Up Networking is installed from:

    A. Control Panel | Add New Hardware | Modem

    B. It doesn't need to be installed, because it is part of the Windows networking

    C. Control Panel | Add/Remove Programs | Windows Setup | Communications

    D. Control Panel | Modems
    C. It is installed with the default setup of Windows 98, but it is not necessary to have it installed to run Windows networking. The installation can be found in the Control Panel | Add/Remove Programs | Windows Setup | Communications.

2. Modems using a port speed higher than 9600 bps require the following UART chip:

    A. 15650

    B. 8250

    C. 5150

    D. 16550
    D. The 16550 provides the stability needed to operate a modem or other serial device above 9600 bps. Earlier UARTs, such as the 8250, were not able to exceed 9600 bps.

3. The TCP/IP settings for Dial-Up Networking should be changed:

    A. In the Control Panel | Network.

    B. In My Computer | Dial-Up Networking. Select an entry, right-click, Properties.

    C. In the LMHOSTS file.

    D. In the MODEM.INF file.
    B. In My Computer | Dial-Up Networking. Select an entry, right-click, Properties. Changing the settings in the Control Panel can result in severe problems with your dial-up entries. The results will depend on the difference between the settings made in the Control Panel and those made with each dial-up entry.

4. Dial-up networking allows connectivity with all of the following protocols, with the exception of :

    A. NetBEUI

    B. IPX/SPX

    C. DLC

    D. TCP/IP
    C. DLC cannot be used with dial-up networking, as it is not supported via dial-up by the server or the client.

5. The Dial-Up Server provides which service to the remote client?

    A. Domain authentication

    B. TCP/IP connectivity to the Internet

    C. Point-to-point connectivity via TCP/IP

    D. The ability to log on to a Novell server after connected
    C. Point-to-point connectivity via TCP/IP. All others are not supported. IPX and TCP/IP are not routed beyond the Windows 98 Dial-Up Server.

6. Multilink connectivity is the ability to establish dial-up links with more than one modem. If the modems are not bundling, the cause could be:

    A. Multilink PPP not supported on the remote server

    B. The modems are not the same speed

    C. Line noise

    D. Multilink PPP requires the same modems to be at each end of the communications link
    A. If the modems connect, but bundling the lines is unsuccessful, the problem is the remote server. If the line drops quite often, or connects at a very low rate, line noise could be an issue, but it would not affect the bundling process. If the modems are not connecting at the same speed, or are not the same type at each end, that is inconsequential. The difference in link speeds would not cause it to fail to connect, but it would make a drastic difference in link performance.

7. VPN allows for a connection to be made over the Internet. Which of the following protocols does the VPN adapter support?

   A. TCP/IP

   B. IPX/SPX

   C. NetBEUI

   D. All of the above
      D. All the protocols listed can be bound to the VPN adapter.

8. The Direct Cable Connection supports which cable type?

   A. Regular serial cable

   B. Null modem serial cable

   C. Ethernet

   D. RG-58
      B. Null modem serial cable. The parallel crossover cable is also supported by the Direct Cable Connection program.

9. What is the recommended distance between two infrared devices while communicating?

   A. 12 inches

   B. 2 feet

   C. 3 feet

   D. 6 feet
      C. 3 feet is the recommended distance between two IR devices.

10. What is the default communications server type for a dial-up entry?

    A. RAS

    B. PPP

    C. VPN

    D. PPTP
       B. PPP (Point-to-Point Protocol) is the default communications type.

Chapter 11 Answers

1. What tool is available to make sure that the most current system files are on your system?

   A. ScanRegW

   B. Maintenance Wizard

   C. Windows Update

   D. System Monitor
      C. The Windows Update tool connects you to the Microsoft Windows Update Web site and compares the files on your system with those on the master server.

2. Your system is acting funny and you think that there may be some missing files in the C:\WINDOWS folder. What tool can you use to verify that no system files are missing?

   A. System Configuration Utility

   B. System Verification Utility

   C. System File Checker

   D. Registry Checker
      C. The System File Checker checks for missing and corrupt system files. It also checks for files that have been altered since the last time it was run.

3. What executable file(s) make up the Registry Checker?

   A. RegScanW

   B. RegScan

   C. ScanRegW

   D. ScanReg
   C, D. The two executable files that make up the Registry Checker are ScanRegW and ScanReg. ScanRegW is the Windows-based portion and ScanReg is the MS-DOS-based portion.

4. What role should a Windows 98 computer be configured for, if it runs on a battery?

   A. Desktop computer

   B. Mobile or docking station

   C. Network server

   D. It doesn't matter
   B. The computer should be set for mobile or docking station if it runs from a battery. Setting it for this role flushes the disk cache regularly. This way, if the battery dies no data should be lost.

5. You notice lots of activity while using System Monitor to watch Memory Manager:Discards and Memory Manager:Page Faults. What can be causing all the activity?

   A. There is not enough virtual memory in the system

   B. There is not enough physical memory in the system

   C. There is not enough Level 10 cache in the system

   D. The memory is not fast enough for the system
   B. Lots of activity on those two items of the Memory Manager indicate that there is not enough physical memory in the system.

6. What is the name of the file Windows 98 uses for virtual memory?

   A. WIN386.SWP

   B. PAGEFILE.SYS

   C. SWAPPER.DAT

   D. 386SPART.PAR
   A. Windows 98 uses the file named WIN386.SWP for virtual memory. WIN386.SWP is a dynamic file that grows and shrinks as needed.

7. What tool is used to check the physical surface of your hard disk?

   A. Disk Defragmenter

   B. System Monitor

   C. System Verification Utility

   D. ScanDisk
   D. ScanDisk can check the physical surface of your hard disk for bad sectors, as well as for errors with your files and folders.

8. What file(s) does Disk Cleanup remove from your system?

   A. Temporary Internet files

   B. Downloaded program files

   C. Duplicate system files

D. Files in the Recycle Bin

A, B, D. Disk Cleanup removes temporary Internet files, downloaded program files, and files in the Recycle Bin. Disk Cleanup can be configured to remove Windows components and/or installed programs to free up even more disk space.

9. What file runs automatically each time Windows 98 starts?

   A. System Monitor

   B. System File Checker

   C. Windows Update

   D. ScanRegW

   D. ScanRegW runs each and every time Windows 98 starts. If it does not detect any corruption to the Registry, it automatically creates a compressed backup of the Registry.

10. How many backups of the Registry does the Registry Checker keep by default?

    A. 3

    B. 4

    C. 5

    D. 6

    C. The Registry Checker keeps a maximum of 5 backups by default. This can be changed by modifying the MaxBackupCopies= setting in the SCANREG.INI file.

11. What type of component is Windows Update?

    A. Java

    B. VBscript

    C. JavaScript

    D. ActiveX

    D. Windows Update is an ActiveX component, so you need to use a browser that supports ActiveX in order to use it.

12. What tool lets you know if a file has been altered since it was signed?

    A. Signature Verification Tool

    B. Signature Configuration Tool

    C. Signature File Checker

    D. Signature Monitor

    A. The Signature Verification Tool lets you check a file to make sure that it has not been altered since it was signed. If the file is signed, then it signifies that the file has not been altered since the digital signature was applied to it.

13. What tool can be used to modify system startup?

    A. System Verification Utility

    B. System File Checker

    C. System Configuration Utility

    D. System Monitor

    C. The System Configuration Utility can be used to modify system startup. You may want to modify the startup of your system to see if you can optimize the speed of your startup. The System Configuration Utility shows items that aren't seen in the Startup group.

14. Which of these files are backed up by the Registry Checker?

    A. SYSTEM.INI

    B. USER.DAT

    C. WIN.INI

    D. SYSTEM.DAT
    A, B, C, D. The Registry Checker backs up the SYSTEM.INI, USER.DAT, WIN.INI, and SYSTEM.DAT files in a compressed file.

15. What extension is on the compressed file created by the Registry Checker?

    A. .REG

    B. .CMP

    C. .RAC

    D. .CAB
    D. The extension on compressed files created by the Registry Checker is .CAB.

Chapter 12 Answers

1. Which of the following tools detects operations and device drivers that fail at startup?

    A. Automatic Skip Driver Agent

    B. Version Conflict Manager

    C. System Configuration Utility

    D. ScanDisk
    A. Automatic Skip Driver Agent detects device drivers and operations that fail during Windows 98 startup.

2. You suspect problems with your hard disk. Which tool will check your hard disk, and mark damaged areas so that they won't be used in the future?

    A. Automatic Skip Driver Agent

    B. Version Conflict Manager

    C. System Configuration Utility

    D. ScanDisk
    D. ScanDisk will scan disks for bad (damaged) sectors, move the data to a valid location, and mark the bad sector so that it won't be used in the future.

3. You are using Windows 98 that has IPX/SPX-compatible protocol and Client for NetWare Networks installed. You attempt connecting to the NetWare network. Other Windows 98 machines are able to see the NetWare servers, but you find that you cannot. What is the cause of this problem?

    A. Incorrect subnet mask

    B. Incorrect frame type

    C. Incorrect default gateway

    D. Invalid IP address
    B. When other computers can see NetWare servers, but yours cannot, always consider that an incorrect frame type is being used. The other choices offered here involve TCP/IP and not IPX/SPX. Even if it is not mentioned in the exam question, assume that the NetWare network is

using IPX/SPX. It is the default protocol of NetWare networks.

4. You are attempting to print to a Hewlett-Packard laser printer that is connected to the network. You find that you are unable to print. Why?

A. IPX/SPX isn't installed

B. TCP/IP isn't installed

C. DLC isn't installed

D. LCD isn't installed
   C. DLC is a protocol used to communicate with mainframes and Hewlett-Packard network-connected printers. When experiencing a problem with printing to an HP network printer, always consider that DLC isn't installed on Windows 98.

5. You have started your computer, and wind up at the DOS prompt. A message appears on the screen telling you to use a program to restore the Registry. What will you type to restore the corrupted Registry?

A. REGSCAN /RESTORE

B. SCANREG /RESTORE

C. SCANREGW /RESTORE

D. SCANREG
   B. To restore the Registry, you must type **SCANREG /RESTORE**. This will start the DOS version of Registry Checker, and enable you to choose a backup of the Registry to restore.

6. A user wants to share his printer with both the NetWare and Microsoft users of the network. Which of the following must the user install for this to work? (Choose all that apply.)

A. Client for Microsoft Networks

B. Client for NetWare Networks

C. File and Printer Sharing for Microsoft Networks

D. File and Printer Sharing for NetWare Networks

E. It can't be done
   E. It can't be done. To use File and Printer Sharing for Microsoft Networks, you cannot have File and Printer Sharing for NetWare Networks running on the same machine. Likewise, to use File and Printer Sharing for NetWare Networks, you can't be running File and Printer Sharing for Microsoft Networks.

7. You suspect that two devices are using the same IRQ. Which of the following utilities will you use to confirm your suspicions?

A. System Configuration Utility

B. System Information Utility

C. Automatic Skip Driver

D. WINIPCFG
   B. The System Information Utility allows you to view information on your system, and view such things as IRQ settings. By viewing this information, you can see if two devices are both attempting to use the same

system resources (such as the same IRQ).

8. You want to edit your startup files and manage how Windows 98 starts. Which utility will you use?

A. System Configuration Utility

B. System Information Utility

C. System Startup Utility

D. WinConfig
A. The System Configuration Utility is the only utility listed that allows you to edit startup files and manage how Windows 98 will start.

9. You have just installed Windows 98 on a computer. You want to see a listing of all hardware devices that Windows 98 found during installation. Which of the following text files will provide this information?

A. SETUPLOG.TXT

B. NETLOG.TXT

C. DETLOG.TXT

D. BOOTLOG.TXT
C. DETLOG.TXT contains a record of all devices found during the hardware detection phase of installation. None of the other files contain this information.

10. You are experiencing connectivity problems. Which of the following tools will you use to view and release your lease? (Choose all that apply.)

A. WINIPCFG

B. System Information Utility

C. System Configuration Utility

D. Net Watcher
A. WINIPCFG is the only program that provides the TCP/IP information used by your computer, and allows you to release and renew the lease on your IP address.

B

About the CD

CD-ROM Instructions

his CD-ROM contains a full Web site accessible to you via your Web browser. Browse to or double-click **Index (Click.htm)** at the root of the CD-ROM and you will find instructions for navigating the Web site and for installing the various software components.

Electronic Book

An electronic version of the entire book is in HTML format.

Interactive Self-Study Module

An electronic self-study test bank is linked to the electronic book to help you instantly review key exam topics that may still be unclear. This module contains review questions, the same questions that appear at the end of each chapter. If you answer a multiple choice question correctly by clicking on the right answer, you will automatically link to the next question. If you answer incorrectly, you can click the "Click here for further review" button to get more information.

Installing Sample Exams

You should install the sample exams directly from Windows Explorer by opening the Demo Exams folder on the CD-ROM.

The demo exam, its subdirectory, and the file required to run the installation, are listed here:

Product	Installation File
Microhard MCSE Quest	../Demo Exams/MCSEQuest/qustdemo.exe
Transcender CERT	../Demo Exams/Transcender/setup.exe

Product	Installation File
VFX MCP Endeavor	../Demo Exams/VFX Endeavor/setup.exe
Self-Test Software PEP	../Demo Exams/Self-Test Software/pep.exe

As of the printing of this book, the Microhard MCSE Quest, Transcender CERT, and Self-Test Software PEP exams are current through Windows 95. Check the following sites for updated demos:

- www.microhard.com
- www.transcender.com
- www.stsware.com
- www.vfxtech.com

Once they are installed, you should run the programs via the "Start Programs" task bar on your desktop.

MICROSOFT CERTIFIED SYSTEMS ENGINEER

C

About the Web Site

Access Global Knowledge Network

A s you know by now, Global Knowledge Network is the largest independent IT training company in the world. Just by purchasing this book, you have also secured a free subscription to the Access Global Web site and its many resources. You can find it at:

http://access.globalknowledge.com

You can log in directly at the Access Global site. You will be e-mailed a new, secure password immediately upon registering.

What You'll Find There. . .

You will find a lot of information at the Global Knowledge site, most of which can be broken down into three categories:

Skills Gap Analysis

Global Knowledge offers several ways for you to analyze your networking skills and discover where they may be lacking. Using Global Knowledge Network's trademarked Competence Key Tool, you can do a skills gap analysis and get recommendations for where you may need to do some more studying. (Sorry, it just may not end with this book!)

Networking

You'll also gain valuable access to another asset: people. At the Access Global site, you'll find threaded discussions as well as live discussions. Talk to other MCSE candidates, get advice from folks who have already taken exams, and get access to instructors and MCTs.

Product Offerings

Of course, Global Knowledge also offers its products here—and you may find some valuable items for purchase: CBTs, books, courses. Browse freely and see if there's something that could help you.

D

What's New in the Windows 98 Exam

Thore are a number of changes from the Windows 95 to the Windows 98 exam. This is mainly due to new technologies being added to the operating system. Like any kid with new toys, Microsoft wants to show them off, and has added these topics to the Windows 98 exam. Understanding these innovations is vital to passing the Microsoft exam.

While little that appeared on the Windows 95 exam is missing from the Windows 98, there are a number of additions. This is because Microsoft has added numerous programs to the operating system. Not only does the system itself run better, the tools and features allow you to get what you want out of the system more easily. Each of the tools and features is listed in this chapter by the category it will appear under on the exam.

Perhaps one of the most striking changes from the 95 to the 98 exam is the emphasis on Novell NetWare. Almost every section of the exam requires you to deal not only with Microsoft networks, but a mixed Microsoft/NetWare environment. While NetWare questions appeared on the older exam, they are more numerous on the Windows 98 version.

Planning

Windows 98 offers a choice between the old File Allocation Table (FAT) that we've used for years, and FAT32. FAT32 is a more efficient file system than its predecessor, and superior when dealing with large disk drives (which Microsoft calculates at being over 512MB).

There are two important things to remember when dealing with FAT32. One is that Windows NT 4.0 (and earlier) cannot read them. Therefore, when faced with a question that has a dual boot system of Windows 98 and NT 4.0, remember that NT won't be able to read the FAT32 disk. If there is only one hard disk on the computer, this also means that NT won't even be able to boot!

The second consideration with FAT32 is DriveSpace3, which is a disk compression utility that comes with Windows 98. If you're thinking of using FAT32 and then gaining additional space with DriveSpace3, think again. FAT32 drives can't be compressed with such programs.

Another area that's stressed on the Windows 98 exam deals with share-level access control versus user-level access control. Questions on this topic will deal with both Microsoft and Microsoft/Novell networks. Access control is set on the Access Control tab of the Network applet in Control Panel. For more information, refer to the appropriate chapter in this book.

Installation and Configuration

The installation and configuration section of the exam has undergone some major changes, due to new technology support and components that have been added to Windows 98.

Windows 98 Server Components

Microsoft Personal Web Server 4.0 allows for publishing web pages on a small intranet. You can develop and publish a web page written in HTML, and share documents with other members of your company from your own computer. Another use for Personal Web Server is testing Web pages before putting them on the Internet. While not as powerful as Internet Information Server, it is nevertheless a useful tool.

Dial-Up Networking Server allows remote computers to connect to yours via modem. It is set up by starting Dial-Up Networking, clicking the Connections menu, and then clicking Dial-Up Server. If you choose Allow Caller Access, Windows 98 will answer when your phone rings, and enable remote users to access files on your computer.

Installing and Configuring Network Components

This section deals with getting your computer to "play nice" on the network. Client for Microsoft Networks and Client for NetWare Networks allow you to interact on Microsoft and Novell networks, respectively. While these clients allow you to use their file and printer sharing capabilities, there are times when you want to allow others to access the files and printer attached to your machine. For that purpose there is File and Printer Sharing for Microsoft Networks, and File and Printer Sharing for NetWare

Networks. If you're connecting to a NetWare 4.x network, you'll need Service for NetWare Directory Services (NDS), which allows you to connect to NDS printer and file resources. All of these clients and services are installed through the Network applet in Control Panel.

Virtual Private Network (VPN) is a sweet innovation to Windows 98 that allows you to connect to your network through the Internet. The heart of VPN is Point to Point Tunneling Protocol (PPTP), which allows you to send your data securely over the Internet. Using VPN and PPTP, you're able to interact with your company's LAN securely, while saving the long distance fees associated with other forms of remote computing.

When you view resources on the network, where does that information come from? The answer is the Browse Master. This is a computer on the network that contains a list of resources available on the network. Further information on the Browse Master and Backup Browsers can be found in Chapter 5.

Network Protocols

Microsoft Infrared 3.0 allows Windows 98 to transfer data with Fast Infrared Devices speeds of up to 4 Mbps. For more information on this topic, refer to Chapter 5.

Install and Configure Hardware Devices

There have been a number of new advances in computer technology since Windows 95, and a few older ones that are just making an appearance in Windows 98. This component of the exam is where you will see most of the questions on these advances.

The Universal Serial Bus (USB) has actually been around for a few years, but has had little support. It allows you to plug hardware (scanners and printers, for example) into your computer, and have them work immediately, without the need to reboot. In addition to this, power is supplied through the connection cable, meaning that you don't need power cords with USB devices.

Multiple Display Support allows you to run up to nine monitors through Windows 98. In doing so, you can view different documents on different monitors, and drag and drop between them.

FireWire is actually an Apple term for the IEEE 1394 bus, and offers many of the capabilities that Universal Serial Bus does. The difference is that it's designed for applications that use huge amounts of data, such as those that work with digital video. Because graphics contain large amounts of information, this computer bus was developed to rapidly transfer the information.

IrDA stands for the Infrared Data Association and, as you might suspect, deals with infrared wireless transmission. This support comes in the form of Microsoft Infrared version 3.0. For more information on this technology, refer to Chapter 5 of this book.

Multilink allows you to increase your bandwidth when connecting to such things as the Internet or other dial-up PPP connections. Multilink allows two ISDN devices, or two modems with two phone lines to combine their bandwidth and act as a single link.

Microsoft's Power Management enables your computer to conserve power by shutting down monitors and hard disks. Not only is this a great feature for laptops, it also allows you to cut your energy bills by conserving power on your desktop computer.

Configuring and Managing Resource Access

If your computer were unable to access resources, it would be little more than a giant bookend! The new questions on this topic that appear on the Microsoft exam deal with enabling large disk support, converting your hard disk to FAT32, and backing up and restoring the Registry.

Backing Up and Restoring the Registry

While backing up and restoring data has always been a topic on Microsoft exams, a new twist has been added with the backing up and restoring of the Registry. There are several methods of performing this task, and each is covered in this book. For more information, turn to Chapter 3 and

Appendix E. Since the Registry is basically the brains of Windows 98, the importance of understanding this information can't be stressed enough.

Managing Hard Disks

It is important to remember that if you are partitioning a large hard disk, you need to enable Large Disk Support (LDS). This is done through the FDISK program. When you partition a large disk that can be formatted with FAT32, FDISK will ask you if you want to enable LDS.

FAT32 theoretically supports drives as large as 2TB. In the real world, drives this size don't exist yet, but it still makes the point that FAT32 can handle large hard disks. Not only can it handle them, it handles them much more efficiently than its 16-bit predecessor.

Converting to FAT32 is done with the Drive Converter (FAT32) application found under System Tools in the Start menu. The process takes several hours, but it is well worth it if you don't dual boot with NT. For more information on this topic, refer to Chapter 3.

Integration and Interoperability

The new kid on the block for Integration and Interoperability on the Windows 98 exam is Proxy Server. Proxy Server is a program that runs on a server connected to the Internet. It provides security and allows you to censor what your users can access, and whether users are able to access the Internet from their workstations. This is a particular issue when users on a network are tying up the bandwidth by downloading graphics or playing graphic-intensive games over the Internet. For more information on this topic, refer to Chapter 9.

Monitoring and Optimization

How big is big enough? The answer, when it comes to space on a hard disk, is that it's never big enough! You can never have enough free space. That's the thinking behind DriveSpace3 and Compression Agent. You'll find them both on your Windows 98 machine, and on the Microsoft exam.

Compressing data by using DriveSpace3 is easy and relatively fast. Those who have used previous versions of DriveSpace (and the old DoubleSpace) will find this version a marked improvement. DriveSpace3 compresses data on your hard disk, increasing the amount of space available.

In addition to this, there is Compression Agent, which allows you to optimize your disk compression. You can set that certain files are to be uncompressed (increasing performance), or that certain files have greater compression if they haven't been used for a particular amount of time. Compression Agent balances performance with compression, allowing you to set levels of compression to your needs.

Every so often, Microsoft releases improved versions and bug fixes of Windows components. Previously, you had to connect to their BBS, scour their Web site, or do other legwork to find and set up the fixes. While that option is still available to you, Windows 98 now offers the Windows Update. By clicking this on your Start menu, you will connect with Internet Explorer 4.0 to an area of their Web site that can check your system and inform you if you need an update of any kind. Windows Update will even install it on the system for you!

The Signature Verification Tool checks files to see if they are really from Microsoft. If a buddy sends you a file stating that it's a Microsoft update, you can use the Signature Verification Tool to verify that it's really from Microsoft. It's an added measure of security that can save you from enormous problems, like viruses.

Remembering to use ScanDisk, DEFRAG, and Compression Agent, and to perform other optimization tasks can be a pain. Now you don't need to keep track of these maintenance tasks. Automating tasks by using Maintenance Wizard is a simple procedure that takes a few minutes, and will perform all these tasks for you. You can set when these events occur, so that your computer isn't bogged down with maintenance tasks during the times you are using it.

Scheduling tasks by using Task Scheduler (or Scheduled Tasks, as the program is actually called at the time of this writing), allows you to set tasks to run at a specific time. With the Scheduled Tasks Wizard, you can easily configure such things as anti-virus programs (and other programs) to run as often as you like.

System File Checker allows you to check for corrupt files in Windows 98, and restore them. It also allows you to extract files from installation disks. You can also have System File Checker back up the existing files before restoring the original files.

Troubleshooting

No matter how good an operating system is, problems arise. This is where troubleshooting comes in. Windows 98 provides a number of tools to help you in this endeavor, and newcomers that will appear on the exam include System Configuration Utility, Registry Checker, Version Conflict Manager and the System Information Utility. Each of these will aid you immensely in finding and correcting errors on your system. For more information on troubleshooting with each of these tools, refer to Chapter 12 of this book.

Diagnose and Resolve Installation Failures

Installation failures can be interesting to figure out at times. Two new features of Windows 98 that you can expect to see on the exam are Version Conflict Manager and the Microsoft System Information Utility, which deal with resolving file and driver version conflicts.

In Windows 95, before a file was replaced with an older version by a setup program, you would be given a message box asking if you wanted to replace the file. It was sort of an all-or-nothing approach. The Version Conflict Manager is a new feature to Windows 98 that extends from that old Windows 95 feature. The Version Conflict Manager handles version conflicts by keeping the current file, and storing the older one in the WINDOWS\VCM directory. This backup can be restored with the Version Conflict Manager, if any problems arise with your upgrade.

The Microsoft System Information Utility collects configuration information, and displays it under four categories: System Information, Hardware Resources, Components, and Software Environment. By looking through these topics, you can acquire specific information about the system that will enable you to fix problems.

The System Information Utility also allows you to launch other applications for optimizing, analyzing, and troubleshooting your system. Each of the applications listed in Table D-1 is accessible from the Tools menu of System Information.

Tool	Description
Windows Report Tool	This tool takes a snapshot of your operating system (computer settings, and selected system and application files). The information is used by Microsoft to fix problems that you report.
Update Wizard Uninstall	This tool uninstalls previously installed Windows updates.
System File Checker	Checks that system files aren't corrupted, and enables you to extract files from compressed files.
Signature Verification Tool	Checks files for a digital signature, to verify that they are from Microsoft.
Registry Checker	Checks Registry for errors, and enables you to back up and restore the Registry.
Automatic Skip Driver Agent	If Windows 98 stops responding on a startup, this tool will identify the failure. It will then mark the file that caused the problem, so it is bypassed on future startups.
Dr. Watson	This tool will generate a snapshot of your system that can then be submitted to support technicians.
System Configuration Utility	Allows you to edit the AUTOEXEC.BAT, CONFIG.SYS, WIN.INI, and SYSTEM.INI files, and to modify how Windows 98 starts.
ScanDisk	Checks your hard disk for errors.
Version Conflict Manager	Keeps a backup of previous versions of files that have been upgraded. You are able to restore the previous version if problems arise.

Diagnose and Resolve Boot Process Failures

Before System Configuration Utility, the only way to edit configuration files was with a text editor, or by running SYSEDIT.EXE from the command line (or Start | Run). System Configuration Utility allows users to edit the AUTOEXEC.BAT, CONFIG.SYS, SYSTEM.INI, WIN.INI, and control how Windows 98 starts up. Tabs on this utility allow you to set which programs load during startup, and how the system starts.

Diagnose and Resolve Hardware Device and Device Driver Problems

Every so often, the Registry screws up. Corrupt Registry files can be a nightmare, and could result in reinstalling Windows. Windows 98 offers two programs that together make up the Registry Checker. They are ScanReg and ScanRegW.

Registry Checker creates a compressed backup of the Registry each time the computer is started. Previous backups are retained, so that up to five backups of the Registry will exist on your system. It also checks the existing Registry for errors when Windows 98 starts. If it finds a problem, it will do one of two things:

- Automatically restore a previous working version of the Registry
- If a previous backup cannot be found, it will attempt fixing the problem

ScanRegW is the Windows version of this program, while ScanReg can be run from the DOS prompt. When you type **ScanReg/Restore** from the DOS prompt, you'll be given a list of available Registry backups, which you can then restore.

In addition to the troubleshooting chapter (Chapter 12), further information on the Registry Checker is available in Chapter 3 and Appendix E of this book.

E

The Registry

I f there is one component of Windows 95 and Windows 98 that consistently confuses, frustrates, and intimidates people, it is the Registry. When Microsoft released Windows 95, the Registry seemed to appear with little more information than "There it is. Don't touch it." It is a philosophy that remains evident in most documentation.

The unfortunate part of this philosophy is that occasionally you have to manipulate the Registry. At the very least, you should understand what it is, why it is, and what it does. Beyond knowing this, you should know how the Registry structure is set up, and when to manipulate the data it contains.

This appendix has something for everyone. If you're new to Windows or upgrading from 3.*x*, you'll find a step-by-step introduction to the Registry. If you're an experienced and knowledgeable user, you'll be happy to learn that there haven't been significant changes since Windows 95, but there have been improvements: The code that handles the Registry is faster, the Registry automatically detects and fixes certain problems, and new tools have emerged.

No matter what your experience level, you're in for a treat—the Registry explained in a way that's not akin to stereo instructions mixed with brain surgery!

Overview of the Registry

Simply put, the Registry is a huge database of all the configuration information about your computer. It contains information on such things as the configuration of Windows 98, the PC hardware, Win32-based applications, and user preferences. When you change the wallpaper on your desktop, or install a Plug and Play device, the information dealing with these changes to the computer is stored in the Registry. Windows 98 refers to this information as needed. To use the wallpaper example, when Win98 loads, it checks the Registry to see what wallpaper you're using, and puts it on the screen. This is why you don't have to reset the wallpaper each time you start Windows 98.

INIs on the Way Out

Older incarnations of Windows (3.1 and older) used text files for the purpose that the Registry now fulfills, and to a large degree the Registry replaces these files. These files were mostly initialization files (with the INI extension). Not only did they clutter the WINDOWS directory, but also, as any programmer will tell you, programs are slower reading text files than database files.

Although entries in the Registry are faster and more manageable than INI files, Windows 98 still supports them. This is because some applications, such as older 16-bit Windows programs and setup programs, use INI files. In addition to this, other text files like the AUTOEXEC.BAT and CONFIG.SYS files also exist for compatibility with these programs (and to allow users to change some default system settings, like setting the PATH environment variable). Because newer Win32 applications are able to store initialization information in the Registry, the support for INI files is a backward compatibility issue.

Unfortunately, the INI origin of the Registry has resulted in a problem that happens occasionally in the real world, and often in Microsoft exams. With a little editing with a text editor, such files were similar enough to swap from one computer to another. If a problem occurred on your computer, you could always get a copy of an INI or SYS file from your buddy, and plunk it on your system. This is not the case with the Registry.

The information contained in the Registry is specific to the computer running Windows 98. The Registry's SYSTEM.DAT file contains information on starting and running applications, on the hardware attached to the computer, and more. Because it's a representation of your entire system, which is different from other computers, you can't take a SYSTEM.DAT from one computer and put it on another. If you did, the information from the other computer wouldn't match yours, and Windows 98 would not start! It is important to remember this both in the real world, and for your Microsoft exam.

The Registry: It's Not Just One File!

The Registry is referred to as a single entity, but in reality it is two or three separate files. These files are the USER.DAT and SYSTEM.DAT. If system policies are used, there is also the POLICY.POL file. These different files, containing different kinds of information, together make up the Registry.

As touched on earlier, SYSTEM.DAT is the file that contains settings that are specific to the computer you are using. It contains the hardware profiles, configuration information, and settings for applications and Plug and Play devices. It is individual to the computer it resides on, and is found as a hidden file in the Windows directory.

While SYSTEM.DAT contains system-specific settings, USER.DAT contains user-specific settings. This file contains your Desktop and Start menu settings, logon names, and other information that deals with the user (or users) of that computer. Like SYSTEM.DAT, it resides in the Windows directory as a hidden file. Unlike its counterpart, this Registry file doesn't have to remain there. Depending on how you've configured Windows 98, it can be found in one of two other places: your network's server, or the PROFILES directory of your local machine.

If you've configured your system to have user profiles (see Chapter 8 for more information on implementing them), then you will have a different USER.DAT for each user that has a profile. In \WINDOWS\PROFILES there will be a subdirectory for every user that has a profile. These subdirectories have the same name as the user it is for. For example, if your user name is mcross, there will be a subdirectory called \WINDOWS\PROFILES\MCROSS, and mcross's USER.DAT will be stored in it.

If you are using Windows 98 on a network, you can also store the USER.DAT on your central server. When you wish to implement roaming profiles, this has an added benefit, as a user's USER.DAT is stored on the server, and then copied to the local hard disk after logging on. Users are then able to maintain their desktop settings no matter which computer they log on to.

The final component of the Registry is the only one that is optional. The POLICY.POL file is the only one not required for Windows 98 to function. POLICY.POL is the file that contains system policies, which override any settings contained in the other two files. System policies are created and edited with the System Policy Editor, and can set restrictions on what the user (or the computer itself) can do on the local machine and network. Be careful with the System Policy Editor. Due to the number of restrictions you can implement, it is very possible to restrict yourself right out of a computer! You might, for example, need to edit the Registry and not be able to, because you've implemented a system policy that disables Registry editing tools. Though not a mandatory part of the Registry, the System Policy Editor is nevertheless a powerful component.

Tools for the Registry

While we promised that we wouldn't make managing the Registry sound like brain surgery, maybe that is the best analogy. The Registry is essentially the brain of Windows 98, and it is quite possible to incapacitate Windows by doing something wrong in the Registry. The only way to access Windows 98 after such an event would be to restore the Registry from an existing backup.

This is by no means meant to scare you off all attempts to change the system. It's your computer, and Microsoft expects that you will want (and need) to make it your own individual system. The safest tools for changing the Registry are contained in the Control Panel. Here you can change display settings, add hardware and software to your system, and much more. The applets in the Control Panel are meant for every level of experience. In addition to this, there are several other safe methods of manipulating the Registry.

- **Open With**   When right-clicking a file (in Windows Explorer or My Computer), you can select Open With to change registered file types.

- **File Types**   This tool, found in Folder Options on the Start menu, is also accessible from other areas. Just click the File Types tab. This will allow you to view and modify registered file types.

- **Property Sheets**   Win32 applications are able to store settings in the Registry. By modifying options on their property sheets, you're able to alter these settings.

However, sometimes the safest method isn't enough. As you develop your knowledge, there is a more advanced tool to aid you in your endeavors.

The most advanced Registry tool you'll come across in Windows 98 is the Registry Editor. As we mentioned, it is quite possible to edit the Registry so that you can't access Windows 98. It is for this reason that the Registry Editor doesn't appear anywhere in the Start and Programs menu. You must start this program by opening the Start menu, clicking Run, and typing **Regedit**. The Registry Editor will start, and you'll see the screen shown in Figure E-1.

FIGURE E-1

The Registry as seen through Registry Editor

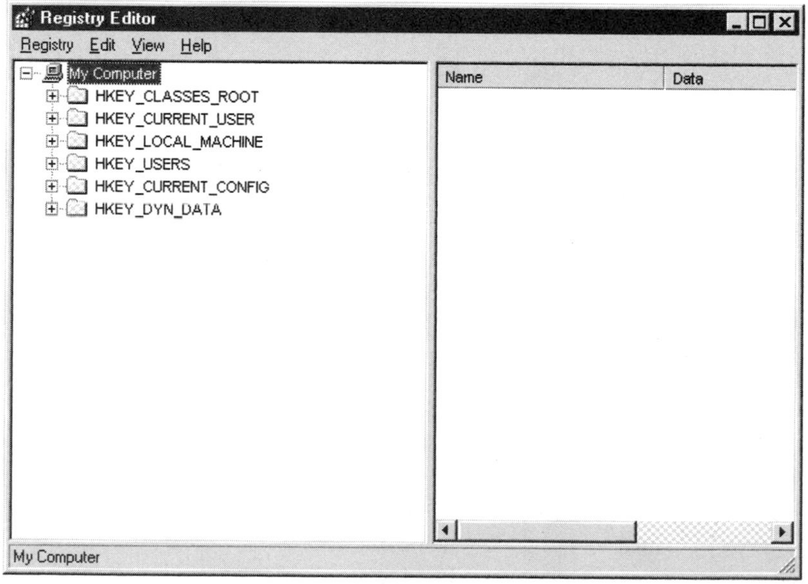

The screen shows the Registry with its hierarchical structure, much the same way that folders and subfolders are shown in Windows Explorer. The items displayed here are called keys. By double-clicking one of them (or clicking the ı symbol beside the key), you can expand it to show additional subkeys. You can continue down the hierarchy until entries that contain various types of data are displayed.

The Registry menu has a number of items that allow you to import and export sections of the Registry, or the entire Registry itself. As an example, let's say that you were going to make changes to an entry, but wanted to cover yourself (just in case the result wasn't what you were expecting). You would select the subkey or entry you were going to change, then click Export Registry File from the Registry menu. The exported settings are saved as a REG file. If you wanted to restore these settings to their previous state, you would click Import Registry File from the Registry menu, select your saved REG file, and click OK. These features allow for easy backups and restores of the Registry.

In addition, the Registry menu allows you to connect to a remote computer's Registry. By doing so, a network administrator is able to manage another computer's Registry without ever leaving his own computer.

New to Windows 98

The features in Registry Editor are not the only way of backing up and restoring the Registry. Windows 98 also comes with the Registry Checker. When Windows 98 starts, the Registry Checker scans the Registry for problems. If no problems are found, it creates one backup of the Registry per day. This backup contains both the USER.DAT and SYSTEM.DAT files, as well as the SYSTEM.INI and WIN.INI. Due to the importance of the Registry, five compressed backups are maintained!

The Registry Checker is actually two programs in one: SCANREG.EXE and SCANREGW.EXE. The reason there are two programs is because ScanRegW is the Windows version of the program, and ScanReg is the DOS version. The reason for having two programs becomes obvious when you look at what happens when a problem with the Registry occurs.

As we mentioned, the Registry Checker creates a backup each time you restart your computer. If you're like me, and leave your computer on for incredible lengths of time, you can run Registry Checker and create a backup by typing **ScanRegW** from the command line (or Start | Run). Registry Checker will analyze the Registry, tell you if a backup was created today, and give you the option of creating a backup.

In either case, a compressed file named RB*xxx*.CAB (where *xxx* is a unique number) is created in the \WINDOWS\SYSBCKUP directory. There can be up to five backups, and the oldest file is always replaced by the newest.

If a problem is found the next time you start your computer (or run ScanRegW from Start | Run), Registry Checker will attempt to fix the problem. If for some reason a backup can't be found (which is rare), Registry Checker will attempt to fix the Registry. If a backup is found, Registry Checker will automatically restore the Registry from a good backup.

Occasionally though, the worst happens. Your Registry can be so damaged that Windows 98 can't even start. The IO.SYS will detect it, and a DOS menu will appear. This warning will tell you that the Registry is corrupt, and will instruct you to run ScanReg from the DOS prompt. Being a wise person, you'll follow this advise and type: **SCANREG/RESTORE** from the prompt. This will give you a list of backups that you can use to restore the Registry, and get you back in business.

Understanding the Keys

The Registry database is organized in a hierarchical fashion. At the topmost level of this hierarchy are six root keys, whose names begin with the word HKEY. This signifies that the key is a unique identifier called a handle. In fact, the term HKEY stands for "Key Handler." The six root keys are as follows:

- HKEY_CLASSES_ROOT
- HKEY_CURRENT_USER

- HKEY_LOCAL_MACHINE
- HKEY_USERS
- HKEY_CURRENT_CONFIG
- HKEY_DYN_DATA

Just as directories can contain subdirectories, keys can contain subkeys. A subkey is a key contained within one of the root keys. In addition to this, a key (or subkey) can contain values, which contain data. This is similar to a file being contained within a directory or subdirectory.

The data contained in values can be of different types. It can be text, binary or DWORD. Table E-1 explains each of these data types.

If you're unfamiliar with the Registry, you'll probably want to review these terms a bit. A key to answering exam questions that deal with Registry structure is knowing the terms. Understand what is contained in each of the root keys. When you're comfortable with these terms, move on to the next step of looking at what these keys, values, and data do.

HKEY_CLASSES_ROOT

This section of the Registry is actually a pointer to another part of the Registry, and is used to describe certain software settings. The HKEY_CLASSES_ROOT points to the HKEY_LOCAL_MACHINE\ SOFTWARE\CLASSES. If you look in one, you'll find the same information as the other.

This key is used to display OLE and association mappings so that drag-and-drop functions will work under Windows 98. Other items

TABLE E-1	Data Type	Description
The Three Data Types	Text	This is a string of characters that can be alphanumeric. The entry can be of varying length.
	Binary	A hexadecimal number of varying length.
	DWORD	DWORD is an abbreviation of "double word value." It is a single 32-bit value, and appears as an 8-digit hexadecimal number.

displayed here are the core aspects of the user interface, and OLE links such as shortcuts that appear on your desktop.

HKEY_CURRENT_USER

As is the case with several of the root keys, the HKEY_CURRENT_USER is a pointer to another part of the Registry. In this case, it points to a subkey of the HKEY_USERS key.

As its name suggests, information on the user currently using the system is displayed under this key. Subkeys for each user who logs on to the system are created under the HKEY_USERS key. When you log on to Windows 98, HKEY_CURRENT_USER points to the subkey for your account under HKEY_USERS. In doing so, all of the default settings for applications you use (your desktop configuration, for example) are accessed.

HKEY_LOCAL_MACHINE

This key contains all the hardware-specific information about your system. Information on installed hardware and software settings is stored here. This information is constant to every user who logs on to the system.

HKEY_USERS

This root key contains all the information on all the users who use the Windows 98 machine. Your desktop settings, default settings for applications, and more, are stored under this key. Subkeys are created for each account on the system under this key. When you log on to the system, the HKEY_CURRENT_USER points to the subkey created for your account.

HKEY_CURRENT_CONFIG

This root key is a pointer to the HKEY_LOCAL_MACHINE\CONFIG subkey. It contains information on the current hardware profile being used, and handles Plug and Play. If you were using a laptop, you might have two separate hardware profiles: one for regular use, and one for when you're docked to the network. In such cases, this key would point to the subkey that reflects the current configuration of hardware attached to the computer.

HKEY_DYN_DATA

When you make changes in Device Manager, you're actually viewing information contained under this key. It contains dynamic data—data stored in RAM. Any changes to the system, as devices are added or removed, are reflected automatically under this key.

Glossary

Access Control Entries (ACE)   Specify auditing and access permissions to a given object, for a specific user or group of users.

Access Control List (ACL)   Checked by each resource's file and print servers before they allow a user to access a file or use a printer. If the user, or a group to which the user belongs, is not listed in the ACL, the user is not allowed to use the resource.

Access Mask   Required by every ACE, the Access Mask tells the ACE which attributes are available for a particular object type. The ACE can then grant permissions based on that mask. For example, a file can set Read, Write, Execute, Delete, Take ownership, and Change permissions, because an Access Mask defines these attributes.

access methods   The rules governing the use of the physical network by various devices.

account lockout   Can be set to lock out an account after a certain number of unsuccessful logon attempts. (Three bad attempts is a common choice.) This prevents hackers from breaking into your account.

account policies   Set from the User Manager to change how passwords are used. This is where you can set the account lockout policy to help prevent your system from being hacked into.

Active Desktop   Windows 98 feature that creates content that is periodically updated on the World Wide Web, and then updated on the PC behind the scenes.

active partition   The partition that the operating system will boot from; it is often called the boot partition.

Active Server   Uses the functions of the Windows NT Server Internet Information Server (IIS) to provide access to Exchange from a Web browser. Using a Web browser, an authorized user can access any public folder, mailbox, or schedule, irrespective of the operating system on the client.

administrator account   The account used to manage the workstation's user accounts, policies, and resources. This account cannot be locked out or disabled.

AGLP   Acronym to help you remember that Accounts are added to Global groups, which are added to Local groups, which are assigned Permissions.

AppleTalk   The protocol designed for communicating with Macintosh computers.

Application Layer   (1) OSI layer that provides a consistent way for an application to save files to the network file server, or to print to a network printer. (2) TCP/IP layer that is the highest layer in the TCP/IP model. It is used by applications to access services across a TCP/IP network. Examples of applications that operate at this layer are a Web browser, file transfer protocol (FTP), and a remote logon program.

ARP (Address Resolution Protocol)   Used to determine a host's MAC address from its IP address. This utility is also used to view and make changes to IP address-to-MAC address translation tables. (See also **MAC**.)

ARPANET (Advanced Research Project Agency Network)
Funded as a research project by the Department of Defense, the Internet was first known as the ARPANET.

asymmetric multiprocessing (ASMP)   Uses one processor for the operating system functions, and any other processors for user threads.

ATM (Asynchronous Transfer Mode)   A cell-switching protocol. ATM uses cell switching, which is marked by its small, fixed-length cells.

Attached Resource Computer Network (ArcNet)   A networking standard that was very common, but has lost popularity due to its limited transmission speeds.

backup browser   Helps the master browser by giving its browse list to clients who request it.

Backup Domain Controllers (BDC)   After a domain has been created, the entire account database is basically mirrored on each BDC, and the PDC keeps the information updated within five minutes by default. (See also **PDC.**)

baseband transmission   Technique used to transmit encoded signals over cable using digital signaling. (See also **broadband transmission.**)

baseline   A snapshot of your system that is established by the Performance Monitor under normal operating conditions and used as a yardstick to measure future abnormalities.

big endian processors   Processors like the Apple Macintosh that expect the first, or most significant, byte to appear first. (See also **little endian processors.**)

binary representation   A 32-bit address broken down into four groups of binary digits.

bindery-style logon   Requires a user to attach or log on to a server before gaining access to services on the server.

binding   The linking of network components on different levels to enable communication between those components. For example, binding links protocols to network adapters.

bit order   Computers can start at either end of a binary number when transmitting it across a network. This is known as bit order.

Blue Screen of Death   Text mode STOP messages that identify hardware and software problems that have occurred while running Windows NT Server.

boot partition   See active partition.

BOOT.INI file   Created by Windows NT when it is first installed, this file is where you can configure the many ways your system behaves when Windows NT is booted.

bottleneck   (1) Indicates that a component within your system has limitations that impede the system as a whole from operating at its maximum potential. (2) The resource that consumes the most time while a task is executing.

bound applications   Applications that are designed to run under either OS/2 or MS-DOS.

bridges   Used to connect similar LAN segments. Bridges look at the destination and source address of a network packet, and decide whether to pass that packet on to the LAN segment. A bridge can be used to filter out traffic for a local subnet and prevent it from being passed on to an unnecessary LAN segment.

broadband transmission   Techniques used to transmit encoded signals over cable using analog signaling. (See also **baseband transmission**.)

broadcast storm   Occurs when there are so many broadcast packets on the network that the capacity of the network bandwidth approaches or reaches saturation.

broadcast   Data packets sent without a specific destination address, intended for all the computers it can reach.

browser election   An attempt to find the most robust computer to be the master browser.

browser   (1) Web application that uses HTTP to access URLs, and to download and display Web pages (documents that are usually written in HTML). (2) Computer used to locate resources on the network.

browsing   A process that allows computers on a network to find each other.

bulk encryption key   See **secret key cryptography**.

bus topology   When the computers in your network are all connected in a row along a single cable or segment. (See also **star topology** and **ring topology**.)

byte order   Larger binary numbers consist of two or more bytes. Just as a computer can start reading at either end of a single binary number, it can also start reading at either end of a group of bytes. This is known as byte order.

cable modem   A device that uses a cable system (such as cable TV) to connect to an ISP.

Cache   See disk caching.

callback security   Security feature implemented within RAS. When a user is configured to use callback, and dials in to a RAS server, the server disconnects the session, and then calls the client back at a preset telephone number or at a number provided during the initial call.

carrier service   Provides the transmission media. Carrier services are traditionally telephone companies.

carrier signal   An analog signal whose characteristics—the frequency, the amplitude, and/or the phase—have been modulated to represent data.

CDFS   Read Only CD-ROM file system. On a CDFS volume, the files are burned into the volume or marked Read Only.

Character-Based Setup   The first part of a Windows NT Server installation. During this phase Windows NT Server performs an in-depth examination of your system.

checksum   A form of error checking that simply counts the number of bits sent and sends this count along. On the receiving end, the bits are once again counted and compared with the original count. If the two counts match, it is assumed the data was received correctly.

Class A IP address   Assigned to networks with a very large number of hosts. A Class A IP address has a 0 in the Most Significant Bit location of the first octet. The network ID is the first octet. Class A addresses range from 0.1.0.0 to 126.0.0.0.

Class B IP address   Assigned to medium-sized networks. A Class B IP address has a 1 0 in the two Most Significant Bit locations of the first octet. The network ID is the first and second octet. Class B addresses range from 128.0.0.0 to 191.255.0.0.

Class C IP address   Usually assigned to small local area networks (LANs). A Class C IP address has a 1 1 0 in the three Most Significant Bit locations of the first octet. The network ID is comprised of the first three octets. Class C addresses range from 192.0.1.0 to 223.255.255.0.

Class D IP address   Used for multicasting to a number of different hosts. Data is passed to one, two, three, or more users on a network. Only those hosts registered for the multicast address will receive the data. A Class D IP address has a 1 1 1 0 in the four Most Significant Bit locations of the first octet. Class D addresses range from 224.0.0.0 to 239.255.255.255.

Class E IP address   An experimental address block that is reserved for future use. A Class E IP address has a 1 1 1 1 0 in the five Most Significant Bit locations of the first octet. Class E addresses range from 240.0.0.0 to 247.255.255.255.

client   (1) The workstation accessing the resources in a client/server model. (See also **client/server model**.) (2) The software that enables communications for various network services. (3) A computer that accesses resources on servers via the network.

client/server messaging   One program on one computer communicating with another program (usually on another computer).

client/server model   Model in which data is requested by the client from the server. The server fulfills this request and sends the data to the client. The client does any processing that it wishes on the data and sends the modified data back to the server.

coaxial (or coax) cable   One of the three types of physical media that can be used at the OSI Physical Layer. (See also **twisted-pair cable** and **fiber-optic cable.**) A coaxial has one strand (a solid-core wire) that runs down the middle of the cable. Around that strand is insulation. There are two different types of commonly used Ethernet coaxial cables: thickwire and thinwire.

Complex Instruction Set Computing (CISC)   Computers with processors that require large sets of processor instructions. Such processors (including Intel 80xxx processors and most other processors on the market) use expanded instruction sets that require several execution cycles to complete. (See also **Reduced Instruction Set Computing (RISC.)**)

container object   A container object can contain other objects and can inherit permissions from its parent container. (See also **noncontainer object** and **object.**)

cryptography   See **public key cryptography**, **secret key cryptography**, and **symmetric cryptography.**

CSNW (Client Services for NetWare)   One of the two installable network components, CSNW is the client redirector (which allows Microsoft workstations to interact with NetWare networks), and NWLink is the IPX/SPX-compatible network transport protocol. (See also **NWLink.**)

cyclical redundancy check (CRC)   Form of error checking that involves running a byte or group of bytes through a mathematical algorithm to produce a single bit or byte to represent the data (a CRC). The CRC value is transmitted with the data. When the data reaches its destination, the receiver runs it through the same mathematical algorithm. The results are compared with the original CRC, and if they match, the receiving computer assumes that data is correct. If they do not match, the receiver must discard the data and try again.

data bus   Connects the network interface card (NIC) to the processor. The data bus provides power, control information, and data to the card.

Data Link Control (DLC) protocol   A method for communication and connectivity with IBM Mainframes, as well as Hewlett-Packard's network-attached printers.

Data Link Layer   OSI layer that handles many issues for communicating on a simple network.

DCE (Data Circuit-terminating Equipment)   The communications hardware.

demand paging   The process of swapping information from disk or memory in 4K pages, as needed. This process requires the use of the NT paging file, which is an actual file on your hard disk reserved for this use.

device drivers   Small programs called upon when the system needs to communicate with the various hardware components in the system.

Device Manager   Manages devices within Windows 98. New devices can either be automatically detected and installed (if they are Plug and Play), or manually added (if they are non-Plug and Play).

device sharing   Prevents inbound calls from going to anything but the specified device. Device sharing is particularly useful in the small home office where there is usually only one phone line, but multiple phone-enabled devices such as phones, fax machines, or modems.

DHCP (Dynamic Host Configuration Protocol)   A dependable, flexible alternative to manual TCP/IP configuration that provides PCs with automatic configuration of the three necessary TCP/IP parameters: IP address, subnet mask, and default gateway.

Dial-Up Networking (DUN)   Dialing-out service that is set up when RAS is installed as a service. DUN allows you to connect to any dial-up server using the Point to Point Protocol (PPP) as a transport mechanism, allowing for TCP/IP, NetBEUI or IPX/SPX network access over your analog modem, ISDN, or X.25 Pad devices.

Dial-Up Networking Server   Allows Windows 98 to host a single dial-up network connection. Any client with support for PPP can dial in using IP, IPX, or NetBEUI as the connection protocol. Windows 98 can then act as a server sharing its files and printers, just as it does on a LAN, or it can act as a gateway for an IPX or NetBEUI network.

Digital Voltage Meter (DVM)   Used to test the continuity of a connection cable to see if there are any shorts in it.

Directory Replication   A Windows NT service that makes an exact copy of a folder and places it on another server.

Directory Service   One of the four core components of Exchange Server. The Directory Service contains addresses, public folders, mailboxes, distribution lists, and site configuration.

directory synchronization   (1) The Windows NT process of synchronizing the BDCs with the PDC on a periodic basis. (2) In the Microsoft Exchange Server, directory synchronization is the exchange of addresses between a Microsoft Exchange Organization and a foreign mail system, such as Microsoft Mail and cc:Mail.

discovery   Process that occurs when a non-domain controller computer starts up and looks across the network for a domain controller in its domain and in all trusted domains.

discretionary access   Access control when the person who created the file or folder is the owner and is responsible for securing those files and folders.

Disk Administrator   A program that creates and manages partitions.

Disk Cache Manager   Manages disk caching by reducing the amount of I/O traffic to the hard disk. It does this by storing frequently used data in physical memory rather than having to read it each time from the hard disk.

disk caching   Storing frequently used data in physical memory rather than having to read it each time from the hard disk.

disk duplexing   Exactly like mirroring except that it uses two disk controller cards—one card for each drive in the mirror. This provides redundancy in case one of the controllers fails. (See also **disk mirroring**.)

disk mirroring   Used by RAID 1 to duplicate information to another hard disk.

distributed applications   Applications that split processing between computers on your network, such as a client/server application, in which processing is divided between the client computer and a more powerful server computer. Normally, the part that runs on the client computer is called the front end, and the part that runs on the server computer is called the back end.

DMA (Direct Memory Access)   A process whereby some devices can directly access memory on the system without the intervention of the CPU.

DNS zone file   Contains one host name, one IP address, and a record type.

domain   A group of computers containing domain controllers that share account information and have one centralized accounts database. (Not to be confused with Internet domains, such as microsoft.com.)

Domain model   A model in which a Windows NT Server acts as a domain controller. The domain controller authenticates users into the domain before they can access resources that are a part of the domain.

Domain Name System (DNS)   A protocol and system for mapping IP addresses to user-friendly names. It resolves host names to IP addresses, and vice versa (with reverse lookups).

dotted-decimal representation   Consists of four 8-bit fields written in base 10, with dots (periods) separating the fields. Each 8-bit field is represented by a number ranging from 0 to 255.

driver   A small application that the operating system calls when it needs the device to perform a function.

DriveSpace   A Windows 98 disk drive compression software package. With DriveSpace, you can take all or part of a hard disk, and create a new compressed drive. All data stored on the compressed drive is automatically compressed, giving you more free space.

DTE (Data Terminal Equipment)   The generic term for both the PC and for the remote access server.

Dynamic Host Configuration Protocol (DHCP)   Assigns TCP/IP configuration parameters to networked clients.

dynamic routing   Protocols that advertise the routes they are familiar with and pass on the metrics, number of other routers, or hops required to get from their host to another network, either directly or indirectly through another router.

election datagram   A packet that includes that system's election criteria. All browsers receive the datagram. If a browser has better election criteria than it receives, it sends out its own election datagram and enters an election in progress.

Emergency Repair Disk (ERD)   Disk that can repair missing Windows NT files and restore the Registry to include disk configuration and security information.

encapsulation   The process of encoding data for transmitting it across the network.

encrypted authentication   Methods for secure network transmission that include the simple Password Authentication Protocol (PAP), which permits clear-text passwords, and the Shiva Password Authentication Protocol (SPAP), used by Windows NT workstations when connecting to a Shiva LAN Rover.

end-to-end communication   Communication on networks that are concerned only with the two ends of the conversation dealing with each other directly (for example, a telephone call).

environment subsystems   Provide support for the various application types that can be run, such as POSIX, Win32, and OS/2. They mimic the original environment the application expects to see.

error checking   Used when sending data across a network to ensure that the data received is identical to the data that was sent originally. (See the three error checking methods: **parity bit**, **checksum**, and **cyclical redundancy check (CRC)**.)

Ethernet   A networking technology defined by the Institute of Electrical and Electronic Engineers (IEEE) as IEEE standard 802.3. This Physical Layer technology is the most popular Data Link Layer protocol because of its speed, low cost, and worldwide acceptance.

ETRN   An ESMTP command used to signal a server to transfer queued mail.

Executive Services   Windows NT Executive Services (also called System Services) acts as an interface between the Kernel and the environmental subsystems. It is comprised of the following components: Object Manager, Security Reference Monitor, Process Manager, Local Procedure Call Facility, Virtual Memory Manager, and I/O Manager.

export server   The computer that provides the directories to be replicated. These directories are kept in the export directory located by default at %systemroot%SYSTEM32\REPL\EXPORT.

Extended Capabilities Port (ECP)   Windows 98 port that provides high-speed printing and support for ECP-compliant devices.

FAT (File Allocation Table) file system   The FAT file system is predominantly used for operating systems such as Windows 3.x and Windows 95. To support backward compatibility, Windows NT fully supports the FAT file system. This is also because of FAT's universal acceptance and accessibility through other operating systems.

FAT32   The Windows 98 32-bit upgrade to the FAT file system that originally came from DOS. The benefits of FAT32 include optimal use of disk space and larger partition sizes than the maximum 2GB size allowed by FAT.
Note: Windows 98 supports only FAT and FAT32 file systems, and Windows NT does not support FAT32.

fault tolerance   The ability of a computer to ensure that data and resources remain functional in the event of emergency.

FDDI (Fiber Distributed Data Interface)   A high-speed token-passing network architecture that is much faster and more fault tolerant, and can cover more distance, than token ring. This technology uses fiber optic cabling to reach speeds of 100 Mbps. FDDI is an alternative to standard Ethernet implementations, often used as a high-speed backbone to connecting LANs.

fiber-optic cables   One of three types of physical media that can be used at the Physical Layer to carry digital data signals in the form of modulated pulses of light. An optical fiber consists of an extremely thin cylinder of glass, called the core, surrounded by a concentric layer of glass, known as the cladding. There are two fibers per cable—one to transmit and one to receive. (See also **coaxial cable** and **twisted-pair cable**.)

FIFO (First In, First Out)   The first data in the buffer will be the first out when the buffer becomes full.

File Transfer Protocol (FTP)   Protocol used to transfer files from one computer to another on a TCP/IP network (such as the Internet).

firewall   Software that prevents unauthorized traffic between two networks by examining the IP packets that travel on both networks. Firewalls look at the IP address and type of access the packet requires (such as FTP or HTTP) and then determines if that type of traffic is allowed.

FireWire   In Windows 98, an external connection standard geared more toward higher-speed devices than USB is. Capable of supporting videodisc players and external storage boxes, it is a very promising addition to future computers. (See also **USB**.)

four-octet address   The 32-bit IP address is broken into four octets that can be represented in binary (11010100 00001111 10000100 01110101) or decimal (212.15.132.117) format.

fragmentation   (1) Fragmentation occurs when there is unused space within contiguous pages. (2) The process in which networks chop or fragment large pieces of data into more manageable units before transmission. When data is fragmented, it is important to ensure that all the pieces make it to the other end in the right sequence. If they are not in order, it is sometimes possible to resequence the data into the right order.

frame relay   A packet-switched protocol.

full-duplex dialogs   Used by OSI Session Layer to let data flow in both directions simultaneously.

full synchronization   In a full synchronization, the PDC sends a copy of the entire user accounts database to a BDC.

fully qualified domain name (FQDN)   FQDN is a full Internet site name. It identifies the type of service by preceding the domain name with a service name. (For example, support.microsoft.com.)

gateway   A device or service that translates communication protocols. Gateways enable two dissimilar systems that have similar functions to communicate with each other.

global groups   Created on domain controllers and used to assign local permissions to domain users.

Gopher   An arcane Internet service that can be used as an index to look for information on the Internet, or on your own company's Intranet.

Graphical Mode   The second part of a Windows NT Server installation. When the graphical mode starts, Setup is running under the Windows NT Server operating system.

Graphical Device Interface (GDI)   Graphics engine that controls the display of graphics on the monitor and printers. It is responsible for communication between applications and the graphics devices.

group accounts   Accounts used for grouping together users who perform the same function or require access to the same resources. If it were not for group accounts, you would have to grant access to resources on a per-user basis.

groupware   Any software that enhances a group's ability to collaborate in the performance of a task.

guest account   Used for limited access for remote users or users from other domains. Disabled by default, the guest account provides low-level access to the computer for users that do not have a user account of their own.

half-duplex dialogs   Used by OSI Session Layer to allow data to flow in two directions, but only one direction at a time. With half-duplex dialogs, replies and acknowledgments are possible.

Hardware Abstraction Layer (HAL)   The layer between the operating system and the hardware located in the computer. Separates the Kernel from the hardware to provide an intermediary layer, so that the Windows NT Kernel does not have to perform communication with the hardware. HAL is what makes NT portable to other architectures.

Hardware Compatibility List (HCL)   A compilation of computer systems and hardware that have been tested for compatibility with a given operating system.

hardware profile   An alternate configuration you can select from a startup to specify various options. Laptop users employ one hardware profile for the docked configuration, and another for the undocked, or travel configuration.

heterogeneous   A mixed network operating environment involving different operating systems like NT, UNIX, and Novell.

home directory   An option for an account in a domain that can give the user an accessible place to store files from anywhere in the domain.

host ID   The portion of the 32-bit address that identifies any device that has an IP address on your network.

HOSTS file   Contains mappings of remote host names to IP addresses.

Hotfix   When an error occurs because of a bad sector, the file system moves the data that was located in this sector (if possible) to another sector, and labels the original sector as bad. Hotfixes are transparent to the user. A feature of NTFS and SCSI hardware, but not the FAT file system.

HTTP (HyperText Transfer Protocol)   The protocol that you use to connect to the Internet to view Web pages.

hub   A device that connects networked devices to each other.

I/O Manager   Windows NT utility responsible for all input and output for the operating system.

IDE (Integrated Drive Electronics)   One of two common interface types you will encounter in a tape drive. IDE is mainly used in the slower and lower-capacity QIC-style tape drives, while SCSI is used in the high-capacity, high-performance DAT and DLT drives. (See also **SCSI**.)

IEEE (Institute of Electrical and Electronic Engineers)   A large and respected professional organization that is also active in defining standards.

impersonation   Technique for a server process to access objects that it doesn't have permissions to. If the client process has proper access permissions, the server process impersonates the client process in order to access the object.

import computer   Systems that receive the replicated files and directories from the export server. The directories are kept in an import directory located by default at %systemroot%SYSTEM32\REPL\IMPORT.

Information Store One of the four core components of Exchange Server. The Information Store consists of two databases, the public Information Store (PUB.EDB) and the private Information Store (PRIV.EDB). This is where all electronic messages are stored.

inherited permission Permission inherited from the parent folder when a file or folder has been copied.

Integrated Services Digital Network (ISDN) Connections that take place over digital lines and provide faster and more reliable connectivity. The primary benefit of ISDN is its speed and reliability. ISDN is commonly found in two speeds: 64 Kbps and 128 Kbps.

Internet Control Message Protocol (ICMP) Allows systems on a TCP/IP network to share status and error information. Two of the most common uses of ICMP messages are PING and TRACERT.

Internet Engineering Task Force (IETF) Group responsible for the operation, management, and evolution of the Internet. The steering committee of the IETF is known as the Internet Engineering Steering Group (IESG).

Internet Explorer See Microsoft Internet Explorer.

Internet Information Server (IIS) Provides FTP, Gopher, and Web services in Windows NT.

Internet layer TCP/IP layer that is responsible for handling the communication from one computer to another computer. It accepts a request to send data from the Transport layer. The Internet layer consists of two protocols, the Internet Protocol (IP) and the Internet Control Message Protocol (ICMP).

Internet Mail Service (IMS)   The Internet Mail Service enables users on Microsoft Exchange Server to send messages to, and receive messages from, users on the Internet.

Internet Network Information Center (InterNIC)   The central authority responsible for issuing all network IDs that will be used on the Internet. InterNIC operates under contract from the National Science Foundation (NSF).

Internet News Service   Allows an Exchange Organization to participate in USENET newsgroups.

Internet Protocol (IP)   Provides packet delivery for all other protocols within the TCP/IP suite.

internetworks   Repeaters, bridges, and routers are devices used to link individual LANs together to form larger internetworks. (See also **repeaters**, **bridges**, and **routers**.)

interoperability   Characteristic of a system like NT that not only integrates with other network operating systems, but also provides tools to facilitate a smooth migration.

interprocess communications (IPC)   Methods of communication between one program and another. Depending on the IPC method being used, this communication can even be across a network. IPC is often used in the client/server environment as a means of communication between the server and the client across the network.

intersite communication   Communication that uses messaging connectors to connect two sites together. Messaging connectors include the simple-to-implement Site Connector, the complex but extensible X.400 Connector, the Dynamic RAS Connector, and the Internet Mail Service.

intrasite communication   Communication that takes place among servers in the same Exchange Server site. Intrasite server communication uses Remote Procedure Calls. RPCs can be used over several protocols, including IPX/SPX, TCP/IP, and NetBEUI.

IP address   Uniquely identifies a computer on the network. It is 32 bits long, with four octets separated by dots. This number is then converted to binary and used as a unique identifier.

IPCONFIG   A command-line utility that displays current TCP/IP configuration information for each NIC in a Windows NT system.

IPX/SPX (Internetwork Packet Exchange/Sequenced Packet Exchange)   Protocol that is primarily used by Novell NetWare networks, but which can be used by other networks (such as Microsoft networks) as a routable protocol or to connect to Novell networks.

IRQ (interrupt request line)   Used by the device to interrupt the processor and request service.

Jetpack   Windows NT Server utility that can be used to compact a WINS or DHCP database.

Kernel   (Also called Microkernel.) Refers to the core of code in an operating system. This is the most important part of the operating system and is responsible for all functions on the system, such as creating, managing, and scheduling threads.

Kernel Mode   Also called Privileged Mode, the Kernel Mode has direct access to the hardware. Some components of NT that used to run as User Mode components now run as Kernel Mode components. These are the Window Manager, GDI, and graphics device drivers.

Key Management Server   An integrated component within Exchange Server. It is used to provide advanced security to an Exchange Server organization. The Key Management Server uses public key cryptography and secret key cryptography. (See also **public key cryptography** and **secret key cryptography**.)

LastKnownGood   The configuration that was saved to a special control set in the Registry after the last successful logon to Windows NT.

least significant bit   When a computer starts reading at the last digit of a binary number, it is using the least significant digit. When a computer starts with the first digit, it is using the most significant digit. (See also **most significant bit**.)

licensing   A method that legally permits a client computer to connect to a server. A license must be purchased from Microsoft for each computer on a network, or each connection to a server. Windows NT Server allows two licensing modes: Per Server and Per Seat. Per Server licensing means that you have purchased a number of licenses for each concurrent connection that is made to a particular server. The licensing only applies to that server. Per Seat licensing means that you have purchased a license for each computer on your network, so that they can access multiple servers through that license.

little endian processors   Processors such as IBM-compatible PCs contain little endian processors, which expect the last, or least significant byte of data to appear first. (See also **big endian processors**.)

LMHOSTS file   A special text file that helps map NetBIOS names to IP addresses.

local area network (LAN)   A collection of computers connected in a geographically close network.

local groups   Groups that access resources on a single domain.

Local Procedure Call Facility   Responsible for passing information between processes.

Local Security Authority   The heart of the Windows NT security subsystem. It creates security access tokens, authenticates users, and manages the local security policy.

logon scripts   Used to start applications or set environment variables for a computer at startup.

long filename capability   Frees you from the restrictive 8.3 naming scheme that was a part of previous versions of Windows. With longer file names, you can adopt a more intuitive naming scheme.

MAC (Media Access Control)   A networked computer's unique address for its network interface card (NIC). Data is transported over networks in packets that always contain the source and destination MAC addresses. A bridge reads this information off the packets it receives to fill its routing table.

mailboxes   Your mail is held in a mailbox until you retrieve it. In most cases, when you retrieve it, the mail is then removed from your mailbox to make room for other messages. These mailboxes are stored on a mail server within directories or databases.

mail client   Software application that retrieves the messages from the mailbox, and then in most cases, deletes them from the mailbox. In addition, most mail clients allow you to send outgoing e-mail, and have some type of message decoding built in. Some popular mail clients include Microsoft Outlook, Eudora, and Pegasus.

mail routing   Mail transfer from one location to another.

Management Information Base (MIB)   Defines management objects for a network device.

mandatory logon   Windows NT uses mandatory logon to force everyone to log on before it grants access to the system.

Master Domain Model   All user accounts are located in a single domain called the master domain. Resources, like printers and files, are shared in other domains called resource domains. This model allows for central administration.

Mbps   Megabits per second.

Member Server   Any Windows NT Server computer in a domain that is not acting as a domain controller.

memory   Physical memory (which is the actual RAM) and virtual memory (which is hard disk space acting as though it is additional RAM).

Message Transfer Agent (MTA)   One of the four core components of the Exchange Server. The MTA is responsible for delivering messages between Exchange servers by means such as Exchange Site Connectors, other X.400 MTAs, Microsoft Mail Connectors, and the Lotus Notes Connector.

Microsoft Backup   Microsoft utility for backing up and restoring files from your hard disk to both removable and non-removable disks or tapes.

Microsoft Batch 98   The program created by Microsoft to help create the files required for Windows 98 automated setup. Microsoft Batch 98 is included in the Windows 98 Resource Kit.

Microsoft Distributed File System (DFS)   Windows 98's way of simplifying the task of sharing and finding resources for users.

Microsoft Exchange Server   A powerful messaging, communication, and collaboration server. The Exchange Server architecture is component based. There have always been four core components: System Attendant, Directory Services, Message Transfer Agent, and the Information Store.

Microsoft Infrared   In Windows 98, a wireless transmission used for network connectivity and for printing to infrared-ready printers. Infrared devices can now be used in Windows 98 just like devices that are normally connected directly with a cable.

Microsoft Internet Explorer   A Web browser that Windows 98 has integrated into the desktop.

Microsoft Outlook   A leading messaging client. The client for Exchange Server 5.5.

Microsoft Personal Web Server (PWS)   A Web server that runs on the Windows 98 platform. PWS can be used on a small intranet to share documents and information, or it can be used for testing and development of production Web sites. PWS supports Active Server Pages as well as drag-and-drop publishing capabilities.

Microsoft Proxy Server   Proxy Server allows a single connection to the Internet to be shared by many users, allowing outbound FTP and Web access (and other supported TCP/IP ports). Proxy Server accomplishes this by making requests for Internet resources on behalf of your users so that only a single TCP/IP address appears to be initiating Internet access.

Microsoft System Information utility (MSI)   Provides easy Read Only access to detailed information regarding the Windows 98 operating system, computer hardware, and even third-party software.

MIME attachments   A type of Internet message. MIME messages are made up of headers and bodies. MIME is the preferred way to send and receive messages, because a MIME message's content is categorized by a richer set of type.

mirroring   Duplicating information to another hard disk. If one hard drive fails, the other hard drive is immediately available with the very same information.

mode   Determines how a process accesses the hardware. (See also **User Mode** and **Kernel Mode**.)

modem (modulator/demodulator)   A form of data communication equipment that can transfer data between a network and an access line.

modularity   Feature of each layer in the TCP/IP protocol stack, which means that it communicates with only the layer above or below it. Modularity also refers to hardware and software design. When a program is modular, it has been broken down into modules (small units) that each provide a certain service or task. These modules can then be installed or removed, depending on the software's requirements. Windows NT and Windows 98 are modular operating systems.

most significant bit   When a computer starts reading with the first digit of a binary number, it is using the most significant digit. When a computer starts reading with the last digit, it is using the least significant digit. (See also **least significant bit**.)

MS-DOS subsystem   The most important subsystem in Windows NT for compatibility. The DOS environment is called the virtual DOS machine (VDM).

multi-homed system   When a computer is configured with more than one IP address, it is referred to as a multi-homed system.

Multilink Channel Aggregation Feature of Windows 98 that multiplies the total bandwidth between the remote PC and the host by combining two or more modem or ISDN lines. The only issue with using this technology is that there must be a separate telephone or ISDN line for each modem or ISDN device that is used.

Multi-Modem Adapters with NT Server (Multilink) Combines two or more physical links, most commonly analog modems, into a logical bundle, which acts as a single connection to increase the available bandwidth/speed of your link.

Multiple Display Windows 98 feature that works by creating a virtual desktop, with each monitor being customized to view a certain portion of it.

Multiple Master Domain model Managed much like the master domain model, except it can handle more users. The multiple master domain is actually two or more master domain models joined by a two-way trust.

multiprocessing Capability of the system to increase processing power by adding more processors. (See the two categories of multiprocessing: **asymmetric** and **symmetric**.)

multitasking The capability to run several applications at once using one processor. There are two kinds of multitasking: *Preemptive* multitasking gives the operating system the ability to take control of the processor without the consent of the application. This is the most common type of multitasking in Windows NT. *Cooperative* multitasking, or non-preemptive multitasking, requires an application to check the queue for other waiting applications and relinquish control to those applications.

multithreading The capability of an application to start two or more threads of execution, which can then be concurrently processed.

multivendor gateways   Provide a translation method between one type of mailbox server to another type of mail client. The gateway allows clients such as Microsoft Outlook to read data from hosts that are not the same as Outlook.

NBTSTAT   This utility is for relating protocol statistics; current active NBT connections describe NetBIOS over TCP/IP.

NetBEUI (NetBIOS Extended User Interface)   A small, efficient protocol that evolved over ten years ago when computer networks were much smaller than today, and did not require routers to connect to different networks. NetBEUI protocol is best suited for local area networks that do not connect to the Internet. It is not routable.

NetBIOS (Network Basic Input/Output System)   An interface that software can use and is commonly called an application programming interface (API).

NETSTAT   This utility is for relating protocol statistics and current active connections utilizing TCP/IP.

NetWare Directory Services (NDS)   In Windows 98, a database that catalogs all NetWare resources, including the user IDs, printers, servers, volumes, and any other network resources.

network   Any type of interactive information-carrying system.

Network Client Administrator   Tool that gives administrators the ability to customize the way they install networking clients.

Network Dynamic Data Exchange (NetDDE)   Allows two applications to communicate, with a link always maintained.

network interface card (NIC)   Also called an adapter card or interface card, it is installed in a computer to allow it to communicate with other computers over a network. A NIC changes the parallel signals inside the computer into serial signals that go over the network cable.

Network Interface Layer   The lowest level in the TCP/IP model. It accepts the datagram from the Internet layer and transmits it over the network.

Network Layer   OSI layer that manages addressing and delivering packets on a complex internetwork such as the Internet. Internetworks are joined by devices known as routers, which utilize routing tables and routing algorithms to determine how to send data from one network to another.

Network Monitor   A tool that "sniffs out" packets on the network and helps diagnose any problems concerning protocols. It is a very helpful tool when you are trying to diagnose network traffic, Windows Internet Name Service (WINS), Domain Name System (DNS), or name resolution issues on your network.

Network Neighborhood   An application available from the Windows 95, 98, and NT desktops that allows you to view computers in a workgroup or domain, and access the resources they are sharing. In Windows 98, Network Neighborhood allows a user to browse the resources available on the NetWare network.

Network Operating System (NOS)   Manages and controls other file systems, other printers connected to workstations, or input or output to network devices.

New Technology File System (NTFS)   A secure file system developed for Windows NT. NTFS is transaction oriented, allows permissions to be assigned to both files and directories, and has the capability to compress files. It can only be read by NT operating systems, and therefore cannot be used on computers with single hard disks that dual boot with other operating systems.

newsfeeds   See the two kinds of newsfeeds: **push feed** and **pull feed**.

NFS (Network File System)   A protocol for file sharing that allows a user to use network disks as if they were connected to the local machine.

noncontainer object   A noncontainer object doesn't contain other objects. (See also **container object** and **object**.)

non-MIME   A type of Internet message usually encoded as BINHEX or UUENCODE. These are both older standards used to send binary images over the Internet. They still are the method of choice with Internet POP clients such as Eudora and most Macintosh mail readers.

NSLOOKUP   Used to examine information from DNS servers.

NTHQ   A Windows NT utility that identifies what hardware is installed in your computer, including PCI, EISA, ISA, and MCA devices.

NWLink   Microsoft's implementation of Novell's IPX/SPX protocol suite. NWLink is a routable transport protocol for Microsoft networks, and for connecting to NetWare networks through CSNW or GSNW. (See also **CSNW**.)

object   In Windows NT, just about everything is an object. A file is an object and so is a window. NT controls access to objects. (See also the two classes of objects: **container object** and **noncontainer object**.)

Object Manager   Responsible for the creation and use of objects. This includes naming, managing, and security for objects. Objects are everywhere in Windows NT, and have a type, various attributes, and a set of operations. They can be physical devices (such as a COM port), or they can be abstract (such as a thread).

open protocol standards   Non-proprietary. For example, because TCP/IP is not tied to an operating system, any vendor developing a new operating system with a network component can reference the RFCs to build a TCP/IP component.

Open Systems Interconnect (OSI) model   The most common network model used in PC networks. Consists of seven layers: Application, Presentation, Session, Transport, Network, Data Link, and Physical.

OS/2 subsystem   The most limited of the subsystems provided with Windows NT. There is less and less need to create a fully functional OS/2 subsystem, because support for the OS/2 environment has dwindled.

Outlook Web Access client   A Web browser that supports JavaScript and frames accessing an IIS server with the proper Active Server Pages loaded.

packet   Small, manageable pieces of data that are transmitted over the network. The packet must include a header section, a data section, and in most cases, a cyclic redundancy check (CRC) section (also called a trailer).

page   The size of the smallest portion of memory that can be managed, which is 4KB.

paging file   System used by Windows NT to move an unused portion of memory to the hard disk, and to retrieve the data when it is needed. This also can be called demand paging. The paging file is actually a file called PAGEFILE.SYS, and is located in the root directory of the drive you specify in the Virtual Memory dialog box.

parity bit   A basic method of checking for errors with transmitted data. Before sending data, the number of individual bits that make up the data are counted. If there are an even number of bits, a parity bit is set to one and added to the end of the data so that the total of the bits being sent is odd. If there are an odd number of bits, the parity bit is set to zero and added to the end. The receiving computer adds up the bits received, and if there are an even number of bits, the computer assumes that an error has occurred. The parity method is not foolproof, since if an even number of bits is corrupted, they will offset each other in the total.

partial synchronization   The automatic, timed replication to all domain BDCs of only those directory database changes that have occurred since the last synchronization.

partition   A logical division of a physical disk. After partitioning the hard disk, you need to decide which partition will be the system partition and which will be the active partition. (See also **active partition** and **system partition**.)

pass-through authentication   Occurs when you choose a domain to log on to from your Windows NT computer, but your computer doesn't have an account in that domain.

Peer to Peer networking   In a peer-to-peer network there are no dedicated servers. There are no hierarchical differences between the workstations in the network.

Peer Resource Sharing   In Windows 98, the ability to simulate a server by sharing its files, drives, and printers across a network.

Peer Web Services   A scaled-down version of the Internet Information Server (IIS) that allows you to publish Web pages on your company's intranet.

Performance Monitor   A Windows NT tool that tracks the usage of resources by the system components and applications.

performance tuning   The art of taking your existing configuration and maximizing its performance to achieve the optimal outcome.

phonebook entry   Stores the information required to connect to a remote network. Entries are stored as individual dial-up connections in a phonebook file.

Physical Layer   Bottom OSI layer that is only concerned with moving bits of data on and off the network medium. The Physical Layer does not define what that medium is, but it must define how to access it.

PING (Packet InterNet Groper)   Utility for verifying IP-level connectivity.

Point-to-Point Protocol (PPP)   A serial protocol used for sending information over a dial-up connection. This protocol allows sending of IP packets, supports compression, allows IP address negotiation, and is the successor to the older SLIP protocol.

Point-to-Point Protocol Multilink Protocol (PPP-MP)   Protocol used to enable multiple ISDN devices or multiple modems using separate phone lines to aggregate their bandwidth. By using two or more devices for a single dial-up link, the bandwidth of the devices is combined, thereby increasing your total bandwidth.

Point-to-Point Transmission (PPT)   Many computer networks use point-to-point transmission methods, where there may be one to dozens of points between the source and the destination of a message. (E-mail is a good example of this.) Each point is only concerned with transferring data to the next point downstream.

Point-to-Point Tunneling Protocol (PPTP)   An Internet standard allowing multiple protocols, such as NetBEUI and IPX, to be encapsulated within IP datagrams and transmitted over public backbones such as the Internet.

POP(3)   The most common standard for e-mail, POP(3) defines how mail can be transferred from the mailbox server and then read by the mail client.

portability   The capability of a system such as Windows NT to be ported to other architectures, such as DEC Alpha, MIPS, and Motorola's PowerPC.

POSIX (Portable Operating System Interface)   A standard developed by the Institute of Electrical and Electronic Engineers (IEEE) for file naming and identification based on UNIX. In order to be POSIX-compliant, the software must fulfill certain requirements, such as case-sensitive filenames, hard links (which can be compared to Windows NT shortcuts, in which many entries can point to the same file), and additional time stamping. POSIX is supported by Windows NT.

preferred master browser   When browser elections are held, these computers have an edge on winning the election to become the master browser.

Presentation Layer   OSI layer that ensures that data sent by the Application Layer and received by the Session Layer is in a standard format. If it is not, the Presentation Layer converts the data.

Primary Domain Controller (PDC)   The central server in a Microsoft network, which contains the master copy of computer, security, and user accounts databases. All changes to these databases are made through the PDC.

print device   The actual hardware that prints the document. The three basic types of print devices are raster, PostScript, and plotter.

print driver   The software that allows an application to communicate with printing devices. Print drivers are composed of three files, which act together as a printing unit: printer graphics driver, printer interface driver, and characterization data file.

print job   Source code consisting of both data and commands for print processing. All print jobs are classified into data types. The data type tells the spooler what modifications need to be made to the print job so it can print correctly on the printing device.

print monitor   Controls access to the printing device, monitors the status of the device, and communicates with the spooler, which relays this information via the user interface. Controls the data going to a printer port by opening, closing, configuring, writing, reading, and releasing the port.

print processor   Completes the rendering process. (See also **rendering**.)

print router   Routes the print job from the spooler to the appropriate print processor.

print spooler   A service that intercepts print jobs to the printer, and redirects them to disk or memory until the printer is ready for them.

printer   See **printing software**.

printer pooling   An efficient way to streamline the printing process. It sends print jobs to a pool of printing devices, in which only one printing device actually prints the document.

printing software   Considered the printer. A printer is software that manages a specific printing device (or devices, in case of printer pooling). The printer determines how the print job gets to the printing device—via parallel port, serial port, or the network.

process   Every running application.

Process Manager   Responsible for process and thread objects, including deleting, creating, and managing these objects. A process is a program, or a part of a program, that has an address space, contains objects, and spawns threads that need to be processed.

program   The application you are using, such as Microsoft Word or Excel.

protocols   Languages used by computers. In order for two computers to talk to each other they must speak the same language (use the same protocol).

protocol stacks   Protocols are grouped together to form protocol stacks, which are capable of doing everything from receiving data from an application, to putting the data onto the network cable.

Proxy Server   A local server between the client workstation and the Internet itself. A proxy server provides security, remedies the need for each workstation to have a direct connection to the Internet, and allows several computers to use a single Internet connection.

public folders   Used by the Exchange Server to facilitate collaborative workflow processes.

public key cryptography   Public key cryptography consists of a public key and a private key. The public key is given freely to anyone who needs it, and the private key is kept secret by the keys' owner and is stored in the user's security file.

Public Switched Telephone Network (PSTN)   The technical name for the medium you use every day to make phone calls and send faxes. The Remote Access Service allows for connections across several media. The most common of these is PSTN.

Public Wireless Networks   Public data networks operated by third parties that receive a monthly fee from users in exchange for providing wireless data service.

pull feed   A newsfeed that occurs when the local host initiates the communication to start the replication of messages.

pull partner   A WINS Server that pulls in replications of database entries from its partner by requesting and then accepting the replications.

push feed   A newsfeed that occurs when the service provider configures its servers to send news messages to your server.

push partner   A WINS server that sends update notification messages to its partner when its WINS database has changed.

RAID (Redundant Array of Inexpensive Disks)   Provides system redundancy and can also improve system performance.

Reduced Instruction Set Computing (RISC)   Processors such as DEC Alpha, MIPS, CISC, and PowerPC are all based on the RISC design, which allows for fast, efficient processing of a small number of instructions.

Registry   (1) In Windows NT, a central repository that contains your system's hardware and software configuration. (2) In Windows 98, the Registry is a set of two files: SYSTEM.DAT and USER.DAT. SYSTEM.DAT contains hardware and global settings. The USER.DAT file contains user settings, and can also be located in each user profile directory.

Registry Editor   A Microsoft tool for searching the Registry. Both the new tool, REGEDT32.EXE, and the traditional Registry editor, REGEDIT.EXE, are included.

Remote Access Service (RAS)   Enables users to connect over a phone line to your network and access resources as if they were at a computer connected directly to the network.

Remote Procedure Call (RPC)   Used by programmers to create an application consisting of multiple procedures—some run on the local computer, and others run on remote computers over a network.

rendering   The process of translating print data into a form that a printing device can read.

repeaters   Connects network cables by regenerating signals so they can travel on additional cable lengths.

reservation   An IP address that is reserved for a specific DHCP client.

resource domains   A resource domain is a domain in the Master Domain model (and Multiple Master Domain model) that has control of its own resources. The master domain controls account information, while resource domains control resources, like printers and files, within their domain.

RFC (Request for Comments)   An invitation to develop standards, recommendations, or requirements for TCP/IP and the Internet. It is a method of asking for multiple solutions and choosing the best one.

ring topology   When the computers in a network form an electrical loop with their connecting cable. (See also **bus topology** and **star topology**.)

roaming profile   The roaming profile enables you to keep your user preferences in one location so that any changes you make to the profile are used on any computer that you log on to. Gives the user the same desktop environment on any workstation he logs on to.

roaming user   A user who logs on to the network at different times from different computers.

ROUTE   Command that can be used to add, modify, delete, and display route information for one or all interfaces. Used to configure network routing tables.

routers   Use the destination network address to see where a packet should go. (See also **routing**.)

routing   Process of forwarding a packet from one segment to another segment until it arrives at its final destination. A router makes decisions as to where to send network packets by looking at the network addresses of the packets it receives before passing them on.

routing table   Used by routers to determine whether data is destined for the local network.

RS-232C Null Modem Cable   Null modem cables, or LapLink cables, can be used to connect the RAS server serial port directly to the serial port of the client machine.

SAM (Security Access Manager)   A database that maintains all user, group, and workstation accounts in a secure database.

satellite   A communication satellite functions as an overhead wireless repeater station that provides a microwave communications link between two geographically remote sites.

scalability   Scalability is the capability to expand to meet future needs (in other words, to upgrade). It is a characteristic of both software and hardware.

SCSI (Small Computer Systems Interface)   One of the two common interface types you will encounter in tape drives, CD-ROMs, and hard disks. It is a high-speed, mass-storage connection standard. (See also **IDE (Integrated Drive Electronics)**).

secret key cryptography   Secret key encrypts and decrypts messages using a single secret key called a bulk encryption key in the Key Management Server. Two examples of secret key cryptography are DES and CAST. The Key Management Server supports CAST 40 and CAST 64. DES and CAST 64 are available only in North America.

security descriptors   Describe the security attributes for an object, and have the following parts: Owner security ID (identifies the owner of the object, which allows that person to change the permissions for the object); Group security ID (only used by the POSIX subsystem); Discretionary access control list (identifies the groups and users who are allowed and denied access).

Security ID (SID)   Used to uniquely identify each user, workstation, and server on the network.

Security Reference Monitor   Verifies that the user has permissions to access the requested object, and then performs that action.

server   A computer that provides shared resources to network users.

server alert   Used to send notification messages to users or computers. Server alerts are generated by the system, and relate to server and resource use. They warn about security and access problems, user session problems, printer problems, and server shutdown because of power loss, when the UPS service is available.

Server Manager   A utility not only for managing servers, but for managing workstations and the domain.

Session Layer   OSI layer that manages dialogs between computers. It does this by establishing, managing, and terminating communications between the two computers. (See the three types of dialogs that the Session Layer uses: **simplex dialogs**, **half-duplex dialogs**, and **full-duplex dialogs**.)

shared processing   When the processing for a task is not done on only the client, or only the server, but on a combination of both the client and server.

share-level security   Used to give other users access to your hard disk via the network. The four types of share permissions are No Access, Read, Change, and Full Control.

Simple Mail Transfer Protocol (SMTP)   Used to send and receive mail over the Internet.

Simple Network Management Protocol (SNMP)   (1) An Internet standard for monitoring and configuring network devices. An SNMP network is composed of management systems and agents. (2) Used for managing SNMP-compliant network devices such as hubs and routers.

simplex dialogs   Used by the OSI Session Layer to allow data to flow in only one direction. Since the dialog is one way, information can be sent, but not responded to, or even acknowledged.

single instance storage   Single instance storage means that a message is sent to more than one recipient on that server, and the message is stored only once on that server. The Exchange Server's Information Store uses single instance storage.

SLIP (Serial Line Interface Protocol)   An older protocol used to carry TCP/IP over low-speed serial lines.

SMTP Service Extensions (ESMTP)   A standard that permits the receiving host to tell the sending computer of the extensions it supports.

SNA (Systems Network Architecture)   A set of network protocols developed by IBM.

star bus topology   If you replace the computers in a bus topology with the hubs from star topology networks, you get a star bus topology.

star ring topology   Also called star wired ring. The smaller hubs are internally wired like a ring and connected to the main hub in a star topology.

star topology   In a star topology, all computers are directly cabled to a hub. (See also **bus topology** and **ring topology**.)

static routing   Configuration method used by early routers. It meant programming exactly which networks could be routed between which interfaces, especially if there were many network interfaces.

stripe sets without parity   Like volume sets, except they provide performance gains. They can combine 2 – 32 areas of free space as a single logical drive. However, the free space must be on different hard disks, and each hard disk must contain the same amount of free space that you want to use for the size of the stripe set.

striping data   RAID 5 uses a method of striping data across several hard disks, with parity information also included. This parity information is striped across the drives, rather than being stored on a single hard disk.

subnet mask   Used to hide part of the IP address in order to distinguish the network from the host on the network.

switch   A common solution to traffic problems, a switch calculates which devices are connected to each port.

symmetric cryptography   So named because both the sender and receiver use a single key.

symmetric multiprocessing (SMP)   The ability of threads to be processed simultaneously by any processor in the system.

System Attendant   One of the four core components of Exchange Server, the System Attendant performs several functions. When a new recipient is created in the directory, it generates an e-mail address for that user. It also builds the routing tables for the site where the server is a member. Other functions of the System Attendant on each server include maintaining message-tracking logs, and managing server and link monitors. The System Attendant also sets up advanced security for the clients. Finally, it reclaims space made available by deleted directory objects.

System File Checker (SFC)   Windows 98 tool for automatically checking that all system files are in order and that none is corrupt.

system partition It is interesting (and sometimes confusing) that the system partition is where the operating system boots from, and the active (boot) partition is where the system files are stored. (See also **active partition**.)

System Policy Editor Tool creating a policy that restricts users, groups, or computers on the local domain.

Task Manager Tool for observing and deleting processes; also provides a more granular level of detail when looking at processes and threads, including the option of removing or setting the priority of individual processes.

task A program that is currently running.

TCP/IP (Transmission Control Protocol/Internet Protocol) An industry standard suite of protocols designed for local and wide area networking. Widely used for Internet communication.

TechNet A searchable database of all of Microsoft's articles, and documentation on nearly all of their products.

Telephony Application Programming Interface (TAPI) Enables applications to use Windows NT 4.0 on PSTN-, ISDN-, PBX-, or IP-based networks, shielding the programmer from any need to code custom interfaces. TAPI speeds application development by simplifying what programmers have to know about individual phone switches, and reducing everything to a common set of APIs that work across a broad spectrum of manufacturers.

Telnet Used for terminal emulation for character-based communicating.

thrashing   Thrashing is what occurs when information is being swapped in and out of memory, to and from the paging file, at a tremendous rate. It's caused by a deficiency of RAM.

thread   The smallest unit of code in a process.

thunking   Process used by Windows NT to translate the calls from one subsystem to another.

Time Domain Reflectometer (TDR)   A device that sends an electronic pulse down the network cable. The pulse is reflected when it reaches a flaw or the end of the cable.

Token Ring   Networking standard second only to Ethernet in popularity. A Token Ring network has great reliability, but is costly compared to other network architectures.

topology   The physical layout of computers, cables, and other components on a network.

TRACERT   Utility commonly used to locate failures along a TCP/IP communications path by tracing the route from origin to destination. Each router interface encountered is echoed to the screen along with some statistical information about the path timing.

transceivers   Portion of the network interface that actually transmits and receives electrical signals across the transmission media. They are also the part of the interface that actually connects to the media.

Transport Layer   (1) OSI layer that ensures reliable delivery of data to its destination. The Transport Layer consists of two protocols, the Transmission Control Protocol (TCP) and the User Datagram Protocol (UDP). (2) TCP/IP layer that is located at layer three of the TCP/IP model. The main responsibility of the Transport Layer is to provide communication from one application to another application.

Trivial File Transfer Protocol (TFTP)   Similar to the file transfer protocol, but does not require user authentication.

trusted domain   A domain in which your workstation doesn't have an account. A user in one domain also can be authenticated to another domain by establishing trust relationships. There are two possible trust configurations, one-way trust and two-way trust. In a one-way trust, one domain trusts the users in the other domain to use its resources. A two-way trust is actually comprised of two one-way trusts. Each domain trusts the user accounts in the other domain.

twisted-pair cable   This type of network cabling is the most common Ethernet implementation used today. (See also **coaxial cable** and **fiber-optic cable**.)

UARTs (Universal Asynchronous Receiver/Transmitters)
The hardware pieces designed for the computer to send information to a serial device.

unattended backup   The backup program launches at a scheduled time, does the specified backup, then terminates.

UNC (Universal Naming Convention)   Each computer in the domain or workgroup is given a "friendly name," which Windows NT converts into the TCP/IP address, MAC address, or other identifiable means of routing the information. The syntax for the UNC name is \\computername\sharename. A full UNC consists of the server's name and the name of the share on the server that you wish to use. The names are then put together in the format of \\<Server Name>\<Share Name>\ to form a UNC.

UPS (Uninterruptible Power Supply)   A device connected through the serial port that keeps power running to a system in the event of an emergency, such as a blackout.

URL (Uniform Resource Locator)   To navigate the Web, Internet users have to know the address (URL) for a Web site.

USB (Universal Serial Bus)   In Windows 98, an external bus standard that allows devices to be added and automatically installed and configured without the need for user intervention or rebooting. USB allows up to 127 simultaneous connections, with connection speeds up to 12 Mbps. This slower speed makes USB suitable for devices such as keyboards, mice, and joysticks.

user account   Represents a user who accesses the resources on the domain. User accounts do not have to represent individuals; they can also be accounts for services, such as an SQL Server account.

User Environment Profile   Allows you to control the system environment according to which user is logged on.

User Manager   The administrative tool used to manage user accounts, groups, and policies. You can copy, rename, or delete user accounts with User Manager.

User Mode   Also called non-privileged processor mode, this is where most of Windows NT code is located. This is also where applications and the various subsystems arc run. User Mode is designed to prevent applications from bringing down the operating system.

user profile   Stores user preferences such as screen savers and last documents used, and environmental settings such as program groups and network connections. The user profile is the set of stored characteristics that set the default desktop configuration for each individual user account. (See also the two types of user profiles: **roaming** and **local**.)

user rights   Allow you to control which operations a user or group performs. Each right enables the user to perform specific operations on the computer.

VDM (Virtual DOS Machine)   A 32-bit application run in a separate memory space that is capable of being multitasked with other applications (thereby increasing performance). This subsystem will run DOS applications and it will also run Windows applications that require DOS.

verify operation   Used to compare files on the hard disk to files that have been backed up to tape.

Virtual File Allocation Table (VFAT)   With the Windows 95 operating system, enhancements were made to FAT, and the new version was called Virtual File Allocation Table (VFAT). VFAT enables the use of long filenames, while maintaining the 8.3 naming convention for older applications viewing the same file.

virtual memory   Created by Windows NT to simulate RAM on a computer when more memory is needed. It does this by using the computer's hard disk as needed.

Virtual Memory Manager (VMM)   Responsible for the use of virtual memory and the paging file in the system.

Virtual Private Networks (VPNs)   VPNs use PPTP or other protocols for secure connections to a remote network. By using PPTP or a similar tunneling protocol, you are able to tunnel through an Internet or LAN connection without compromising security.

volume sets   Used to combine different sized areas of free space as a single volume (drive letter) from any type of hard disk (IDE, SCSI, or ESDI). Volume sets don't provide any fault tolerance or performance gains. They are simply used to combine multiple areas of free space as one logical drive.

Wide Area Network (WAN)   Multiple local area networks (LANs) linked together over a broad physical distance.

Win32   The primary subsystem for NT, it is responsible for all user input and output. The Win32 subsystem is also responsible for receiving requests from the other environment subsystems.

Windows 98 Hardware Compatibility List   This list is updated with hardware components that have been tested and found to meet the Windows 98 requirements.

Windows Internet Name Service (WINS)   Microsoft's name server that resolves computer names to IP addresses.

Windows Scripting Host   Windows 98 shell that lets an administrator use more robust, language-independent commands in logon scripts through ActiveX scripting.

Windows Update   Windows 98 principal Internet-based troubleshooting tool that will automatically compare your system configuration to the most recent available from Microsoft and allow you to easily download and install any updates and fixes.

wireless bridge   Provides wireless connectivity of remote Ethernet networks, and is fully transparent to network protocol and applications.

wireless connectivity   Can be achieved through the use of existing cellular telephone links.

workgroup   An organizational unit that groups computers together if they don't already belong to a domain. Workgroups are typically used in small offices, where there are only a few computers, and which need only Peer to Peer networking. (See also **Peer to Peer networking**.)

X.25   A protocol that runs on a worldwide network of packet-forwarding nodes that deliver X.25 packets to their designated X.121 addresses. X.25 networks transmit data with a packet-switching protocol, bypassing noisy telephone lines.

INDEX

D

G

H

I

V

W

Z